BRITISH SOCIAL POLITICS

BRITISH SOCIAL POLITICS

MATERIALS ILLUSTRATING CONTEMPORARY
STATE ACTION FOR THE SOLUTION
OF SOCIAL PROBLEMS

BY

CARLTON HAYES

BOOKS FOR LIBRARIES PRESS
FREEPORT, NEW YORK

First Published 1913
Reprinted 1972

362.9
H 417 b

INTERNATIONAL STANDARD BOOK NUMBER:
0-8369-6722-4

LIBRARY OF CONGRESS CATALOG CARD NUMBER:
72-37885

PRINTED IN THE UNITED STATES OF AMERICA
BY
NEW WORLD BOOK MANUFACTURING CO., INC.
HALLANDALE, FLORIDA 33009

82-625

PREFACE

The following pages are an attempt to place at the command of college and university students some first-hand materials for the study of current political and social problems. From many volumes of parliamentary debates, reports, and statutes have been selected, in the first place, a few of the most important Acts which have been passed by the British Parliament since the Liberal Government came into power in 1905, dealing with a vast range of social problems and activities that the Industrial Revolution had brought face to face with a typical modern democracy; and secondly, extracts from the debates in the House of Commons and in the House of Lords with a view to illustrating different points of view which various classes, political parties, and prominent persons have entertained on these liberal and radical proposals.

To study the social problem in Great Britain should be a valuable introduction to the study of all the grave problems that confront every modern industrial state. To appreciate the efforts of contemporary statesmen in Great Britain to provide governmental solutions, partial at least, for these problems should be illuminating not only to the student of present-day affairs, but likewise to the historian who would sketch the development of society and social legislation or trace the marvellous growth of state activity in modern times. And possibly knowledge of these matters will not be confined to professional scholars ; the speeches of Mr. Asquith and Mr. Lloyd George and Mr. Churchill and many another have not an exclusively academic flavour or interest — they are making history.

An introductory chapter serves as an apology for the title and scope of this book. It makes no pretension to deal exhaustively or even adequately with any special event of the nineteenth century —

merely to point out a lane of approach to the study of contemporary British history and how such study may be profitably linked up with the great highway of general nineteenth-century history.

Many topics indirectly of social and political significance might have been included in the volume had space permitted. But, in general, land laws, Irish Home Rule, and Welsh Disestablishment have been inexorably crowded out by Employers' Liability, Labour Unions, Child Welfare, Old Age Pensions, Budget Reform, the decline of the House of Lords, and National Insurance. It is quite obvious, too, that the very nature of the subject-matter will militate against its permanence. Most of the enactments herein presented will no doubt be superseded, or, at least, amended in detail, in the near future, for finality is not a common attribute of governmental regulations, and the solution of one problem frequently acts to create another. It is hoped, however, that occasional new editions may keep the work near to date.

To several authorities I am under obligations. First of all should be mentioned the reporters of the great mass of parliamentary proceedings, who, quite as anonymous as the monastic chroniclers of the Middle Ages, have infinitely surpassed the monks in the wealth of information with which they have supplied us. Then I would express gratitude to the compilers of the "Annual Register" and to the writers on the *London Times* and the *Spectator*, from whose digests and reports I have drawn freely. And I would confess the stimulus which has been given this work by the perusal of the writings of such enthusiastic British Liberals as Mr. David Lloyd George, Mr. Winston Churchill, Mr. J. A. Hobson, and Mr. Percy Alden. To my colleague, Professor Charles A. Beard, I am indebted for the immediate suggestion of the work, as well as for a lively sympathy with its purpose and valuable criticism in its completion.

CARLTON HAYES

Columbia University

CONTENTS

CONTENTS

BRITISH SOCIAL POLITICS

INTRODUCTORY NOTE

I

Two historical factors have conspired to bring about in our own day a fundamental change in the convictions of many thoughtful persons as to the proper scope and functions of government. In the first place, the French Revolution not only abolished legal class privilege and defined civil " rights " uniform for all citizens, but it sounded the death knell of absolutism ; and its great dreams of individual liberty and social equality and political brotherhood provided a powerful stimulus, throughout the nineteenth century, to ever-recurring and increasingly successful movements throughout Europe for the extension of the suffrage and the removal of legal disabilities in society. In France, political democracy was gradually evolved through kaleidoscopic changes of Legitimate Monarchy, July Monarchy, Republic, Empire, and Republic. In England, a like process was painfully in evidence during Peterloo Massacres, and Chartist riots, and Reform agitations. In both countries, before the close of the century, the electorate had supposedly attained a democratic mastery over one great institution — the government.

Of greater importance to us than the more or less theoretical political principles proclaimed and exemplified by the French Revolution are the very practical problems created by that series of marvellous mechanical inventions and adaptations which has passed under the name of the Industrial Revolution. Within the last hundred years the whole social fabric has undergone a complete transformation, until it has brought forth present-day capitalism and the factory system and a wage-earning proletariat huddled in great towns ; and novel facts have presented themselves which could not be faced in the manner of the eighteenth century nor run away from as the *laissez-faire* economists of the last century would have done. So long as highly-developed industrial states — countries directly affected by the Industrial Revolution — pursued a frank policy of governmental non-intervention, the capitalist class seemed to grow wealthier and more powerful, while the mass of wage-earners appeared to grow relatively poorer and more degraded. Under such conditions, written constitutional guarantees of religious toleration and political equality did not suffice to render democracy real and vital. Soon after the French Revolution, Babœuf had declared :

> When I see the poor without the clothing and shoes which they themselves are engaged in making, and contemplate the small minority who do not work and yet want for nothing, I am convinced that government is still the old conspiracy of the few against the many, only it has taken a new form.

Gradually the working classes, whom the Industrial Revolution called into being, came to share Babœuf's opinion and to complain that they suffered from class privileges infinitely more oppressive than any of those against which the French revolutionists contended. They began to believe that political rights and written constitutions, of themselves, might be quite sterile, and to demand the employment of political agencies in order to secure equality of opportunity for all classes and the well-being of each and every citizen, worker as well as capitalist. It followed quite naturally from the interesting union of two revolutionary currents — the political and the industrial — that the people of each affected state thought of using their democratic representative mastery over government, in proportion to the extent to which they had achieved it, as a means through which to undertake industrial regulation and general social control. That has meant the socialisation of politics — government, in its widest significance, of the people and for the people.

" Social politics " thus becomes a convenient phrase to indicate, loosely perhaps, the present-day development of political democracy and its utilisation for social purposes. Social equality is its goal. Mr. Percy Alden, one of its distinguished advocates in the British Parliament, writes in a recently published volume [1]:

> Without claiming too much for the new programme which the Liberal party has put forward, this, at least, may be asserted with confidence, that it implies a desertion of the old individualist standard and the adoption of a new principle — a principle which the Unionists call socialistic. If it be true that a positive policy of social reconstruction savours of socialism, then, of course, this contention can be justified. The main point is that the function of the State in the mind of the Liberal and Radical of to-day is much wider in scope than seemed possible to our predecessors. The State avowedly claims the right to interfere with industrial liberty and to modify the old economic view of the disposal of private property. Liberalism recognises that it is no longer possible to accept the view that all men have an equal chance, and that there is nothing more to be done than merely to hold evenly the scales of government. As a matter of fact, the anomalies and the injustices of our present social system have compelled even our opponents to introduce ameliorative legislation. But the Liberal of to-day goes further. He asks that such economic changes shall be introduced as will make it possible for every man to possess a minimum of security and comfort. Property is no longer to have an undue claim; great wealth must be prepared to bear burdens in the interests of the whole community. Our social system must have an ethical basis.

At least since Bismarck prevailed upon the German Reichstag to enact measures to insure workingmen against sickness, accident, unemployment, and old age, the progressive governments of every civilised state have concerned themselves with a vast range of social legislation. The labour of a life-time would hardly suffice to study the various forms and activities of social politics in Australia and New Zealand, in the Scandinavian states and in Belgium, in France and in Germany, in Great Britain and in our own

[1] Democratic England, pp. 5–7.

American Union. Yet the subject is of such interest and immediate importance to every student of comtemporary history and politics — so portentous for the future — that its extent and complexity should not stagger us; there is but an increased need of a dispassionate and scientific review of the causes and results of social politics.

II

It would be difficult to find any country better adapted to an introductory study of social politics than England, where, in a nation of first-rate importance, the two requisite factors, to which reference has been made, have been very much in evidence throughout the nineteenth century. On the one hand, the revolutionary spirit of democracy, since the time of Burke and Pitt, has coursed through the veins of the old-time corporation government of the country and has remade the body politic, until now not a nation in the world can boast a more simple, direct, and truly representative form of political democracy than the United Kingdom. On the other hand, no country has been more, or worse, affected by the Industrial Revolution; no nation has had graver industrial problems to face. It was in Great Britain that the most important mechanical inventions were made; it was British manufacturers who had a start of at least a score of years over their continental rivals; and to those islands throughout the nineteenth century has clung that boasted preëminence in industry and in trade. And anyone who takes the trouble to peruse thousands of pages of parliamentary records and commission reports can begin to understand at what tremendous cost that industrial supremacy has been secured and upheld — a cost of veritable millions of human lives and of the physical and spiritual degradation of other millions.[1] The most serious social questions have confronted England's political democracy.

[1] Cf., in addition to the various Factory Commission and Poor Law Commission Reports, Charles Booth, Life and Labour of the People in London, and Seebohm Rowntree, Poverty: A Study of Town Life.

Nor would it be easy to find a country better fitted than England to illustrate the elements of opposition to such a social-ising tendency, for it must not be supposed that democracy has been evolved in the United Kingdom suddenly, or without a struggle, or that the entire English nation have at any time thor-oughly understood the social problem or been over-anxious to cope with it. The interested conservative classes have always had their many apologists, whether of the obscurantist type who seek to justify opposition to change by reference to the mysterious workings of a Divine Providence, or of the so-called scientific turn who aim to clothe existent inequality and injustice in the language of the economic schools. In fact, many clergymen and other ethical teachers, and political economists with their *laissez-faire* theories, and lawyers and judges with their juristic explanations of the Englishman's right to freedom of contract, all contributed support, directly or indirectly, throughout the greater part of the nineteenth century, to that compact conservatism which, in the name of law and order and security, or of sound economic doc-trine, or even of God, checked the growth of the social democracy and prevented the application of its remedies.[1]

The whole problem has been rendered especially difficult in the United Kingdom by reason of an established church and a landed aristocracy, both of which have been naturally bent upon the pres-ervation of the *status quo*. They have enjoyed the prestige which belongs to ruling classes, and not only have they declined to see advantage in a change which might molest their own abundant wealth and large estates, but they have succeeded in inculcating in many others a similar attitude of mind. The Return which Lord Derby asked for in 1872, as a result of a criticism by John Stuart Mill, incomplete and inaccurate as it was, showed certainly that in that day 2250 persons owned nearly half the enclosed land of England and Wales, 1700 owned nine tenths of Scotland, and

1 Cf. A. V. Dicey, Lectures on the Relation between Law and Public Opinion in England during the Nineteenth Century (1905).

1942 owned two thirds of Ireland. From the same Return we learn that 28 dukes held estates to the amount of nearly 4,000,000 acres, 33 marquises 1,500,000 acres, 194 earls 5,862,000 acres, and 270 viscounts and barons 3,785,000 acres. Since 1872, the number of landowners has considerably increased, but not to such an extent as materially to alter the fact that, over against an enormous land monopoly in the hands of the aristocracy, the vast majority of British subjects possess no right whatsoever to their native soil. Any such monopoly is bound to be inimical to political democracy and social equality, yet it is not without its defence by economists, jurists, and divines.

Of course, the landed aristocracy have by no means universally opposed social legislation. For several decades, jealous of the increasing wealth of manufacturers and merchants and traders whom the new industrial system immediately benefited, and envious of this newer aristocracy that was springing up about them, they contributed important support to the first discomfiture of the new capitalists. Such a man as Shaftesbury furnished a conspicuous example in his support of factory legislation. These noblemen were often zealous to attack the manufacturers, but were rigidly conservative in the defence of their own landed interests. In time, however, as the profits of their estates were invested more and more in commercial and industrial enterprises, the former friction tended to disappear, and the whole aristocracy, whether founded originally on land or on trade or on manufacturing, have, in our own time, discovered common interests in opposing labour legislation all along the line.

In the political institutions of the country these privileged classes have been deeply intrenched. For centuries the statutes have been promulgated under the form, " Be it enacted by the King's most Excellent Majesty, by and with the advice and consent of the Lords Spiritual and Temporal, and Commons, in this present Parliament assembled and by the authority of the same." Of course, the crown was practically deprived of its legislative powers by the " Glorious

Revolution " of 1688, and Queen Anne exercised the sovereign's veto right in 1707 for the last time. But the Lords Spiritual and Temporal — the House of Lords — remained long afterwards a powerful factor in legislation, or, more often, in staying legislation. At the beginning of the nineteenth century not only was this House an important governmental institution, of equal powers with the Commons, save in strictly fiscal affairs, but its members, by means of indirect influence or direct patronage, actually controlled a large number of seats in the other House, and although the passage of the Reform Bill of 1832 served partially to free the Commons from the Lords, nevertheless the Upper Chamber remained to our own day a conservative and usually successful opponent of democratic legislation. The House of Lords has been a curious survival, a historical anachronism, in the progress of British democracy.

Nor has the House of Commons achieved its present position without a very long struggle. Emancipated in part from the Anglican hierarchy and the higher nobility by the Reform Bill of 1832, and rendered more representative of the country than it had ever been before, it still remained far from democratic. Its restricted electorate and peculiar method of election tended quite naturally to limit its membership to the country gentry and to the newer industrial and commercial magnates; and the counsels of these classes customarily prevailed in Commons' debates. To tell the story of how the democratic spirit in the nation reacted upon the House, and how the reforms of 1867, of 1872, of 1884, and of 1885 were secured, would far exceed the space and purpose of this introductory note.[1] The movement was painfully slow; and it has been only of comparatively recent date that the House of Commons has become largely representative and able to assume seriously and interestedly the responsibilities of social politics. Even now, certain property qualifications prevent some half million of adult British male citizens, who are in particular need of remedial

---

[1] Cf. May, Constitutional History of England, edited by Francis Holland, 3 vols. (1912).

legislation, from exercising the suffrage, to say nothing of all the female citizens of the kingdom.

Without entering into a discussion of the matter, it may not be amiss at this point to suggest a possible further difficulty in the British polity — the two-party system. For many years every voting Englishman was identified, largely by reason of historical accident, with one of two parties — the Tory, or Conservative, and the Whig, or Liberal. The two-party system, whatever may be its advantages, has certain defects, as we in the United States know only too well, — a devotion to names rather than to principles, a traditional, almost hereditary, alignment of voters on important questions, and a loyalty to party often transcending loyalty to the nation at large, — and evidences of these defects are not lacking in English history. When one thinks of the party squabbles over protection and imperialism and Irish Home Rule, and of the time and energy spent in gaining some slight tactical advantage for a political party, he wonders whether the most successful operation of real democracy will not be through channels other than the two-party system. At all events, the group systems that prevail in Germany and in France, and that are now appearing in Great Britain, do not seem to be barren of achievement.

III[1]

That the old-line British parties promoted real progress along certain lines is indisputable. Thus, it was the Whigs, or Liberals, who sponsored the great Reform Bill of 1832 and a good deal of the subsequent reform legislation, such as the democratisation of

---

[1] The following brief outline of the development of the political parties in England should be supplemented by readings in May, Constitutional History of England, ed. by Francis Holland, 3 vols. (1912); Sir William R. Anson, Law and Custom of the English Constitution, 2 vols. (2d ed., 1896) ; H. Paul, A History of Modern England, 5 vols. (1904–1906) ; S. Walpole, History of England since 1815, 6 vols. (1890), and History of Twenty-five Years, 2 vols. (1904) ; A. Dicey, op. cit., and The Law of the Constitution (1885) ; A. L. Lowell, The Government of England, 2 vols. (1908) ; and J. A. R. Marriott, English Political Institutions (1910).

the towns and cities, the repeal of the corn laws and establishment of free trade, the abolition of slavery in the colonies, the reform of the poor law, and the mild beginning of factory legislation. But the Liberals, recruited chiefly from the townsfolk, the middle-class traders and manufacturers, and the dissenters and Non-Conformists, appeared far more anxious to rid their brethren of black slavery beyond the seas than to check the growth of white serfdom in their own factories at home. The free-trade agitation of Cobden and Bright was the extreme radical plank in the Liberal platform of those days; the party failed utterly to appreciate the aggravated distress of the working classes, or, if they did appreciate it, their self-interest or economic principles restrained them from applying remedies; and it was Liberals quite as much as Tories who ridiculed and suppressed the Chartist movement. In their repugnance to a wider democracy and to state action for the improvement of the general welfare, the Liberals of the mid-century held fast to the faith of their forefathers, the Burkes and the Pitts.

On the other hand, the Tory, or Conservative, party were taught novel and strange doctrines by that bizarre and paradoxical genius, Disraeli. While that remarkable leader never lost an opportunity, in novel-writing or in parliamentary debate, to keep alive the Tory tradition of exalting the prestige of the landed aristocracy and the Anglican Church, and of proclaiming them as the bulwarks of English liberty, he was moved by the same *Zeitgeist* which supplied political theories to a Napoleon III and to a Bismarck. Disraeli, like his great contemporaries on the continent, declared that something definite should be done for the poorer and working classes in the community and that they should be educated to a proper sense of what they owed to the crown, the lords, and the church; and in the meantime, a vigorous foreign and imperialistic policy would distract public attention from the graver domestic ills. It was Disraeli who both championed the Reform Act of 1867 and subordinated social legislation at home to the prosecution of a glorious diplomacy in India, in Afghanistan, in Egypt, in the Russo-Turkish

War. And if the Conservative party were by no means unanimous in endorsing the Reform Act, the rest of his policy they accepted quite readily, so that imperialism thenceforth became a Tory shibboleth, along with the preservation of the landed aristocracy and of the established church. There is no doubt of the sincerity and good intentions of the great mass of Conservatives who supported Disraeli's platform, but for some reason or other it would not stand continued wear. Perhaps in the long run the working classes came to the conclusion that foreign glory is not the most certain way of feeding hungry stomachs or clothing half-naked bodies.

When Gladstone returned to power, the Liberals managed to increase the electorate considerably by means of the Reform Bill of 1884, and to effect educational reforms and several other changes along the line of political democracy. And a few minor acts were passed to conciliate the working classes ; but the party leaders still adhered too closely to the *laissez-faire* preachments of the Manchester school to be able to shake themselves free, or even want to shake themselves free, from the strong grip of the manufacturing and commercial classes. Such an honest philanthropist as John Bright was blinded by prejudice to the advantages which the country at large might gain from better factory legislation, shorter hours, and higher wages, all of which he insisted upon treating as an interference with individual liberty. Then, too, party tactics and the Irish question played the same rôle in drawing the attention of the Liberals away from immediate social legislation as imperialism had in the case of the Conservatives. Of course, from the standpoint of the thoroughgoing democrat, the labours of the Gladstonian Liberals in behalf of Ireland deserved high praise : it was an attack upon privilege to disestablish the Anglican Church in that island and to seek to destroy the land monopoly ; to espouse Home Rule was in the interest of representative and responsible government. But only a beginning was made in dealing with the Irish problem, and its most obvious result in Great Britain was the disruption of the Liberal party, a considerable group of Liberal

Unionists following Mr. Joseph Chamberlain into the Conservative party, which had opposed the Irish reforms even more naturally than it had advocated imperialism.

A period of almost complete stagnation, so far as social legislation was concerned, followed the Unionist victory of 1895. The new government gladly turned to imperialism once more, but the conduct and final outcome of the Boer War were not such as to enhance their reputation. An important group of the Conservative party which gradually gathered about Mr. Joseph Chamberlain in his advocacy of a close federation of the self-governing colonies with the mother-country, urged with him, as a means to that end, and in order to promote the national welfare, a complete revolution in the fiscal arrangements of the state, involving the abandonment of free trade and the adoption of a frankly protective tariff, with special provisions for a system of preferential tariffs within the empire. The earnest opposition or quiet indifference of Lord Lansdowne, Mr. Balfour, and other influential Conservatives to protectionism, tended to create dissensions within the party ; and as long as the general financial policy of the government was uncertain, it was impossible to satisfy the business interests of the country or to provide any large surplus to utilise in radical social reforms. Mr. Chamberlain, certainly, preached social reform in season and out of season, and although he succeeded in pledging the Conservative party to deal with the problems of the aged and of the unemployed, the funds were never forthcoming to ensure effective legislation. Whether he grew tired of being as one crying in the wilderness or despaired of human nature or merely of his colleagues, it was Mr. Chamberlain who, after most enthusiastic and repeated declarations in behalf of old age pensions, finally stood aside with the somewhat cynical remark, " It is not in my department."

It is significant that the fall of the Unionist government in 1905 and the beginning of radical social legislation under Liberal auspices coincided with the appearance of the new Labour party. Since 1875, when they were finally legalised, the trade unions had been slowly increasing in influence and power and pressing for political redress of their grievances. This agitation, carried on outside the two great parties and aided by the propaganda of the Social Democrats and the educative campaign of the Fabian Society, was crystallised into the Labour party directly as a result of the celebrated legal decision known as the Taff Vale Railway Company *v.* the Amalgamated Society of Railway Servants, in which the court held that trade unions were corporations that were liable to costs and damages for the action of any of their agents whenever such action had caused loss to other persons. Representatives of trade unions and socialist societies were at once assembled in order to form what was called a Labour Representation Committee, and at the first annual conference, in February, 1901, over forty-one trade unions, with 353,000 members, together with seven trade councils, the Fabian Society, and the Independent Labour Party (a socialist organisation which Mr. Keir Hardie had founded in 1893), joined the committee. Thenceforth the movement spread rapidly. At the election of 1906, out of 50 Labour Representation candidates 29 were elected, as well as 11 members of Parliament in connexion with the miners' associations, which were not then affiliated. Fourteen other workmen were elected either as Independent Labour men or as Liberals, making a total of 54 who more or less represented labour. The most recent conference of the new party represented 1,450,648 trade unionists and the two socialist societies, the Independent Labour Party and the Fabian Society, while 155 trades councils and local labour parties were also affiliated, the reported total membership being 1,481,368.

Next in significance to the rise of the Labour party was the increasing radicalism of the Liberals. Undoubtedly the secession of the Unionists, to which reference was made above, while it temporarily weakened the Liberal party and drove them from office, nevertheless in the long run consolidated the Gladstonian Liberals and afforded them a broader social outlook than they had ever had before. Likewise the parallel growth of the Labour party, and the realisation that there was an important public work to be done, fired the altruistic spirit of many younger men, such as Masterman, Churchill, Lloyd George, and J. A. Hobson, who entered the Liberal party full of enthusiasm for humanity and for social reform. Another generation was to do a greater work than Gladstone's. By 1905, the ever-waning prestige of the Conservatives, the enthusiastic organising of the Labourites, and the optimism of the Liberals, all betokened a revolution in British politics. Up to that time both Conservatives and Liberals, acting on opportunist principles, had occasionally allowed collectivist measures, particularly for Ireland, to pass into law; both, more or less unwittingly, had enlarged the area of State interference and replaced older individualistic methods by public action and safeguards. For a number of years after 1905, the controlling majority set about purposely to adapt political democracy to social needs. The hour for major social politics had struck in the United Kingdom.

IV

In the parliamentary session of 1905 the Conservative government of Mr. Balfour presented three important proposals for social legislation: a Trade Unions and Trade Disputes Bill, an Unemployed Workmen Bill, and a Workmen's Compensation Bill. The first-mentioned, which, among other objects, was designed to legalise " peaceful picketing " in strikes, to free trade unions from the dangers involved in the law of conspiracy, and to protect the funds of the unions against the dangers opened up by the Taff Vale judgment, was so mutilated in committee discussion, — even ministers, particularly Sir Edward Carson, the solicitor-general, voting for every destructive amendment, — that in May at the instance of its promoters the bill was withdrawn. The collapse of this measure undoubtedly represented the mature judgment of the Tory majority, but it could hardly fail to stultify the ministry and to cause a considerable amount of irritation among the classes whose expectations had been raised. Nor was the fate of the other measures more advantageous to the government. The Unemployed Workmen Bill provided for setting up an organisation for the assistance of unemployed workmen — the establishment of a local body in each metropolitan borough and a central body for the whole area of London, whose duties would be to inquire into the cases of applicants for employment and to divide them into two classes : applicants honestly desirous of obtaining work but unable to do so from exceptional causes, and applicants who might be regarded as proper objects of ordinary Poor Law relief ; but most of the powers conferred by the measure were made discretionary rather than obligatory, and the bill was finally enacted with an amendment limiting its duration to three years. The Workmen's Compensation Bill, an extension of the principle of employer's liability to several classes of workmen not enumerated in the Act of 1897, was amended out of any semblance of its original form and at length failed completely.

Parliament was prorogued on August 11, 1905, the speech from the throne setting forth a very meagre record of successful legislation ; and the Conservative ministry, weakened by internal dissensions and stultified before the country, resigned on December 4. A few days later, Sir Henry Campbell-Bannerman, the Liberal leader, formed a cabinet which included Mr. Herbert Asquith as Chancellor of the Exchequer ; Sir Robert Reid as Lord Chancellor ; the Earl of Crewe as Lord President of the Council ; the Marquess of Ripon as Lord Privy Seal ; Mr. Gladstone, Home Secretary ; Sir Edward Grey, Foreign Secretary ; the Earl of Elgin, Colonial Secretary ; Mr. Haldane, War Secretary ; Mr. John Morley, Secretary for India ; Mr. James Bryce, Secretary for Ireland ; Mr. John Sinclair, Secretary for Scotland ; Lord Tweedmouth, First Lord of the Admiralty ; Mr. David Lloyd George, president of the Board of Trade ; Mr. John Burns, president of the Local Government Board ; Earl Carrington, president of the Board of Agriculture ; Mr. Augustine Birrell, president of the Board of Education ; and Mr. Sydney Buxton, Postmaster-General.

Preparations were already well under way for what proved to be the most exciting and startling general election since 1880, if not since 1832. As early as May 19, Sir Henry Campbell-Bannerman, in a speech before the Council of the National Liberal Federation at Newcastle-on-Tyne, had practically identified his position with that of the Labour members of Parliament. The Council unanimously passed a resolution declaring that immediate steps ought to be taken " to restore to workmen the right of effective combination of which they have been deprived by recent decisions of the courts." And the Liberal leader referred to the " deplorable spectacle " when the Trade Unions and Trade Disputes Bill had been so mauled and maimed in committee under the inspiration of the Conservatives, led by their own solicitor-general, that the Labour and Liberal members had been obliged to leave the room. He also expressed his sympathy with the movement for giving members of Parliament a modest stipend, and, speaking broadly, maintained that there was no material difference between Liberal ideas and the ideas of those directly representing labour in Parliament.

Two days earlier Mr. Joseph Chamberlain, from a different standpoint, had directed a Conservative appeal to the trade unionists and workingmen generally. The great need of the labouring classes, he said, was more employment; that was the object of trade unions, and it was his object. Tariff reform, and by that, of course, he meant protection, would provide more employment.

The Trade Union Congress which was held at Hanley in September was attended by some 450 delegates, representing about a million and a half organised workers. The report of the Parliamentary Committee took notice, among other matters, of the mutilation of the Trade Unions and Trade Disputes Bill and its subsequent withdrawal by its promoters, and of the failure of the Workmen's Compensation Bill, and in conclusion urged that the time was now ripe for great efforts on the part of trade unionists. They found capital, said the Parliamentary Committee, arrayed against the workers, organised as it ,had never been before, supported by the immense influence of an unjust state of law. The first and foremost need was for more Labour men to be sent to Parliament. The president of the congress, Mr. Sexton, in his opening address spoke contemptuously of the Unemployed Workmen Bill in the form in which it had ultimately become law, and avowed the opinion that the abolition of private monopoly in the land was the one way to solve the problem of unemployment. Among the resolutions passed were declarations in favour of municipal trading, municipal banking, and the nationalisation of mines, railways, and canals. A resolution deprecating any departure from the principles of free trade in the way either of protection, retaliation, or preference, was carried by a majority representing 1,253,000 against 23,000. An educational programme was approved, embracing gratuitous education at all stages, with maintenance scholarships so arranged that all young people whose usefulness would be enhanced by secondary or technical or university education should be able to enjoy it, and secular education in all state schools, — such schools to be administered by directly elected representatives of the people, but all additional cost involved in the proposed changes to be borne by the national exchequer, aided by the restoration and democratic administration of valuable misappropriated educational charities and endowments. In accordance with another important resolution adopted by the congress, the resources of the state were to be drawn upon exclusively for the establishment of a system of universal pensions of five shillings a week, to be enjoyed by all citizens on attaining the age of sixty.

In dislike of the Tories and hatred for the House of Lords, the Irish Nationalists were one with the Labourites. The United Irish League of Great Britain, in a manifesto published on January 1, 1906, reviewed and denounced the alleged results of the " twenty years of resolute government for Ireland " demanded by Lord Salisbury in 1886. During eighteen years of the interval, said the manifesto, the Conservatives had been in power, and there was administrative confusion, growing poverty, universal discontent, and a decrease of 700,000 in the population of Ireland. Irishmen in Great Britain were urged to aid to their utmost the discomfiture of the Unionist coalition. The interests of Catholic schools would be best protected by increasing the power and influence of the Irish party. Irish electors were advised to support the Labour candidate if one were standing; if there was no Labour candidate, they were to vote for Liberals, except Unionist Liberals supporting Lord Rosebery's policy. No reference was made to the great Unionist gifts to Ireland — Land Purchase and Irish Local Government — perhaps because the initiative had first come from the Liberal party.

A manifesto of the Social Democratic Federation, published on the same day, demanded State maintenance of children, the State organisation of unemployed labour, and old age pensions instead of "workhouse pauperisation." It strongly denounced protection.

The final results of the election of 1906 showed 378 Liberals, 53 Labourites, and 83 Nationalists, a total coalition of 514 supporting the ministry, against 131 Conservatives and 25 Liberal Unionists, a total of 156 in opposition. Of the Labour members, however, 29 were approved by the Labour Representation Committee and pledged to sit and act as an independent party; the other 24 were more or less identified with the Liberal party, making its total 402. Of the Nationalists, again, three or four, including Mr. William O'Brien, were independent of the regular Irish parliamentary party. Within the Opposition, according to the statement of the Duke of Devonshire, on March 6, 102 were tariff reformers in Mr. Chamberlain's sense, 36 followed Mr. Balfour's extremely mild programme of tariff revision, while 16 were returned as Unionist Free Fooders and 2 as independents. The Liberal and Labour majority over all other groups combined was 134, and the prediction that Sir Henry Campbell-Bannerman's government would be dependent on Nationalist votes was falsified.[1]

[1] Annual Register, 1906, p. 12.

The territorial distribution of parties also calls for some remark. The Unionist strongholds were in Birmingham and its neighbourhood, in the better-class residential districts of London and its suburbs, in Kent, and, of course, in Ulster, where the Protestant, Unionist "garrison" struggled successfully against the Nationalists. The universities, which still ranked as parliamentary constituencies, were uniformly Unionist. Labour members were numerous in Lancashire and Yorkshire, and came from most of the regions where the population was predominantly industrial. Wales did not return a single Unionist, and Scotland again became predominantly Liberal.

In 1906, at the opening of the new Parliament, with its immense majority in favour of liberal, radical, and progressive principles, Sir Henry Campbell-Bannerman declared that underlying every proposal of his government would be a policy of social reconstruction looking toward a greater equalisation of wealth, and the destruction of the oppressive monopolies of the land and of liquor. Mr. Asquith, who succeeded him in 1908 in the leadership of the Liberal party and in the premiership, stated that the injustice of the existing social system rendered a popular attack upon it inevitable. "Property," said he, "must be associated, in the mind of the masses of the people, with the ideas of reason and justice."

Notwithstanding the overwhelming popular majority of the Liberals in the House of Commons and the determination of their leaders to effect social legislation along radical lines, a hereditary Tory majority dominated the House of Lords, quite as overwhelming in numbers and quite as determined to thwart any attack upon the existing social order. The House of Lords resolutely came to the defence of all the interests and privileges represented by its members. The Lords wrecked Mr. Birrell's Education Bill because it appeared to clash with the rights of the Anglican Church. They vetoed the Licensing Bill because it penalised a trade which had given active and unremitting support to the Conservative party and was ably represented in the Upper

Chamber. Proposals for a general land valuation and for the abolition of plural voting were equally banned by the Lords as leading to "dangerous novelties" and to a disregard of vested interests. Finally, the Budget of Mr. Lloyd George, with its graduation of real estate duties and income tax, its distinction between earned and unearned income, and its licensing duties, roused all the forces of Conservatism to vigorous action; in the forefront were the Lords. "Old Age Pensions, Trade Boards, Labour Exchanges, Small Holdings, Housing and Town Planning, all these measures might have been overlooked, but the policy which places the control of industry in the hands of the people and provides equal opportunities for self-development, which asserts the claims of the State to a share of the unearned increment, is a policy which has aroused the fiercest opposition, finally culminating in the revolt of the Lords and an attempt to assert their supremacy. The famous Budget of Mr. Lloyd George discriminated between income that is earned and income that is unearned."[1] The test was to be not so much what wealth a man had as how he secured it. And this test was in essence revolutionary.

In following, therefore, the debates and statutes contained in this volume it is well to bear in mind not only the great, governing principles of the Liberal-Labourite coalition, but the theories and tactics that from time to time handicapped or obstructed them. The grave social problem has been complicated at every turn by a serious political and constitutional problem. And although the two general elections of 1910 — the first on the question of the Budget, and the second on that of restricting the powers of the House of Lords — reduced the Liberal majority in the Commons to such a degree that the ministry became dependent upon the Nationalist, as well as upon the Labour, group for support, nevertheless every session of Parliament since 1905 has been marked by an ever-increasing experimentation in social politics, an ever-growing record of significant achievement in political democracy and social reform.

[1] Percy Alden, Democratic England, p. 7.

CHAPTER I

WORKMEN'S COMPENSATION

[On March 26, 1906, Mr. Herbert J. Gladstone, as Home Secretary, introduced in the House of Commons the Government's bill for workmen's compensation in case of accident. His speech, given below (*Extract 1*), reviews the measures which had been enacted along similar lines in 1880, 1897, and 1900, but studiously avoids any mention of the failure of the Conservative measures of 1905.[1] The statement of Mr. Akers-Douglas (*Extract 2*) represents the favourable attitude of the Opposition, and that of Mr. G. N. Barnes (*Extract 3*), the position of the Labour party on the question. Mr. Joseph Chamberlain, whose speech (*Extract 4*) practically closed debate on first reading of the Bill, showed himself quite willing to go much further than the Liberal Government in legislating on the matter.

The Bill came up for second reading in the Commons on April 4. Sir Charles Dilke, the ardent Liberal, in moving an amendment demanding a recognition and guarantee of insurance sufficient to prevent the defeat of the legal expectation of compensation created under the law, called attention (*Extract 5*) to foreign experience and raised the fundamental issue of compulsory workmen's insurance. Mr. Gladstone, in reply, doubted whether any European country had really solved the problem, and pointed out the need of inquiry before preparing a scheme for Great Britain. In the course of the important debate on second reading the employer's point of view was ably presented by Mr. Montgomery, Conservative member for Somersetshire (*Extract 6*),

---

[1] Cf. supra, p. 14.

and that of the employed by Mr. Clynes, Labour member for Manchester (*Extract 7*).

On December 4 the Commons took up the Report stage of the Bill as amended by the Standing Committee, which had been begun on November 29. Insurance by small employers had been facilitated, and, by way of a compromise with the Labour members, workmen or their representatives were enabled to claim compensation for injuries resulting in death or disablement, even if attributable to their own misconduct. On December 5 a compromise was effected as to compensation for industrial diseases. Six such diseases were scheduled, but Mr. C. F. G. Masterman proposed an amendment tending to include within the operation of the clause sufferers from any disease incidental to their employment, on which Mr. J. C. Wedgewood, another Liberal, remarked that no disease but *delirium tremens* would be excluded. Ultimately an amendment giving power to the Home Secretary to extend the list of scheduled diseases was carried by 281 to 47. An amendment moved by Mr. Marks, Conservative member for Thanet, in Kent, extending the Act to domestic servants, was resisted by the Home Secretary, but supported from both sides of the House, and eventually this far-reaching change was accepted by the Prime Minister. This was a singularly profitable move both for the mover and for his party. Next day the Home Secretary proposed to empower aged or infirm workmen to contract with their employers for compensation below the ordinary rate, the object being to make it easier for such men to obtain employment. The Labour members protested, the Government left the amendment an open question, and it was rejected by 211 to 133.

The Bill passed third reading in the Commons, without division, on December 13, 1906, accompanied by the speech of the Home Secretary, foreshadowing a general scheme of national insurance (*Extract 8*), and the supporting speech of Mr. Joseph Walton (*Extract 9*).

The progress of the Bill through the House of Lords from December 13 to 19 was uneventful, as the support afforded it by the Unionists removed it from the field of partisan politics; and it received the royal assent on December 21.

Extract 10 is the Workmen's Compensation Act as thus finally promulgated in 1906. *Extract 11* is an amendatory measure enacted in 1909 in order to bring the principal Act into harmony with a treaty negotiated between the two great industrial countries of Great Britain and France, and is illustrative of the international character of the labour problem as well as suggestive of possibilities for international solutions.]

Extract 1

THE HOME SECRETARY ON WORKMEN'S COMPENSATION

(Mr. Herbert J. Gladstone, Secretary for the Home Department, Commons, March 26, 1906)

Mr. Gladstone [1] : . . . Up to 1880 there was the common law for the benefit of the workman, and in that year it was reinforced by the Employers' Liability Act, which continued in operation, with all the disadvantages attending the legal distinctions of negligence and common employment, until 1897, when a totally new departure was made with the Workmen's Compensation Act, founded on the doctrine laid down by the right hon. Gentleman, the Member for West Birmingham [Mr. Joseph Chamberlain], that, when a person on his own responsibility sets in motion an agency that creates risks for others, he ought to be similarly responsible for what he does. The acceptance of the liability of employers was made subject in 1897 to two considerations : first, the right of compensation was limited to the most dangerous employments ; and secondly, the liability was limited to those employers who could either afford

[1] Parliamentary Debates, Fourth Series, vol. 154, col. 886 sqq.

to pay directly or through insurance against the risk. Then in 1900 the Workmen's Compensation Act of that year was extended to agricultural labourers and gardeners. In that Act two of the main principles of the Act of 1897 were abandoned, because it was made to include two employments which are among the safest in the country; and in the second place, it included employment which exposed small farmers to very considerable risks on the ground that they would not be able to pay heavy compensation in case of serious injury to a workman, and might not insure, because the premium on insurance was out of all proportion to the risk.

The Government now think that the time has arrived for a wide extension of the Act of 1897 to every class of labour, and in the Bill a new principle is adopted which differentiates it from the Act of 1897. That Act excluded all classes of workmen who were not directly and expressly included; and it is now proposed to reverse this, and, subject to the definition of a workman in the Bill, all will be included who are not expressly excluded. The definition is important, as it is really a governing factor in the Bill. A workman includes any person not a police-constable, clerk, shop assistant, outworker, domestic servant, or a member of the employer's family dwelling in his house who works under contract for wages or serves under apprenticeship by way of manual labour or otherwise, and whether the contract is expressed or implied, oral or in writing. Under that definition certain classes of the community are excluded; but the House will observe that workmen employed in workshops, in transport service, fishermen, postmen, and seamen will be brought within the operation of the Act. With regard to seamen, the Committee which considered the subject two years ago recommended that their case should be dealt with under Section 207 of the Merchant Shipping Act, and hon. Members will know that under that Act provision was made for seamen injured during the voyage, but after landing they had to take their chance. The Government consider that the best and simplest plan would be to bring them under the Workmen's Compensation Act, and we propose, therefore, to deal with them in opposition to the proposal of the Committee. When a seaman lands after a voyage during which he has been partially or totally incapacitated, he will be able to claim under the Workmen's Compensation Act.

The difficulty of small employers which considerably hampered Parliament in 1897 is still with us. There are a number of small workshops throughout the country and a number of small employments in which an employer is practically a workman himself ; and, as hon. Members know, it is the small employer who, as a rule, neglects to insure and in case of serious injury is unable to pay very heavy compensation. According to the evidence given before the Committee, 25 per cent of the employers in the building trade do not insure at all, and probably the greater proportion of that 25 per cent consist of small employers. It does not always happen that small employers do not insure, for the report of the Committee mentioned stevedores as an important exception, who, though they paid a high premium, did as a rule insure. But, putting aside exceptions, small employers prefer to take the risk of accidents rather than to pay the minimum premium out of all proportion to the risks in their particular trades. The Committee spent a good deal of time on this question and pointed out that the successful working of the Act of 1897 was largely due to the organisation of the system of mutual insurance agencies and the action of the larger trade unions. When there was organised co-operation, the Act of 1897 had worked extremely well. But the Committee went on to point out that in industries where employers and workmen were not organised it was doubtful if the same results could be achieved, and it was difficult to say how far small employers would insure. It is dangerous to concede by law a right which in many cases will prove to be illusory ; and for that reason we propose that employers whose workmen do not exceed five in number shall not come under the operations of the Act. That limitation does not apply to agriculture, — the clause relating to agriculture provides that the test shall be one permanent workman, — and there are some other exceptions. Under this limitation there will no doubt be hardships and anomalies, but this Bill is not and cannot be final. There is no reason why different classes of workpeople, such as shop assistants and clerks, should be excluded from the Bill, but in certain cases small employers would have to pay a premium out of all proportion to the risk in their particular trade, and for that reason a large number would not insure at all. Then, if there were an accident, the employee would not have a substantial man to proceed against, and the employer probably would be ruined. The ultimate solution of the whole question is probably to be found in a scheme of compulsory insurance. When we have seen how this Bill works, fresh proposals might be made to make up proved deficiencies, to extend it to other classes, and to get rid of limitations; and some plan of cheap and easy insurance on a small scale through the medium of the Post Office might be possible. But we have not reached that point yet. There is one important limitation to the exclusion of workmen under the limit of five. It is provided that if the accident to a workman coming under the definition is attributable to the use by the employer of machinery driven by steam, water, or other mechanical power, or if the workman at the time of the accident was employed in the care or management of horses, mining, quarrying, or building operations, or in laying or repairing any electric line or works, the limit of five shall not apply in the case of such workman. The House will see that that is an important limitation of the exclusion, and I think it will agree that it is a valuable and practical application of the principle of workmen's compensation to cases which most require it, and which otherwise would be cut out by the limitation.

I have now dealt with the basis and scope of the Bill. One incidental advantage of the new form will be that our old friend, the "undertaker," will go out of workmen's compensation, and we get rid of the definition of included trades which has been so fruitful of litigation under the Act. Most of the proposals in this Bill are based wholly or in part on the valuable recommendations of the

Departmental Committee over which Sir Kenelm Digby presided. In the first place, we propose to extend workmen's compensation to industrial diseases. That involves a new departure. Of all the casualties to which the industrial army is unfortunately liable, those arising from disease are the most pitiable and disastrous. The Committee did not recommend that industrial diseases should be included in the Bill, but the Government thought the case was so strong that, although the difficulties were great, a strong effort ought to be made to surmount them. Therefore, we propose to include in the Bill the following diseases : anthrax, lead poisoning, mercury poisoning, phosphorus poisoning, arsenic poisoning, and ankylostomiasis. The clause which deals with this question contains the following general provision : Where a workman is certified to be suffering from disease, and thereby partially or totally disabled from earning full wages, and his disease is due to the nature of the employment on which he has been engaged during the previous twelve months, he is to be entitled to compensation, the compensation to be recovered from the employer who last employed him. But if the employer proves that the disease was, in fact, contracted or developed while the workman was in the service of another employer, or other employers, there is to be proportionate and collective responsibility. In these cases the limit of five is not applicable, and the Secretary of State is given powers by Provisional Order to extend this provision to other diseases.

We have given effect to the Committee's recommendations in respect of subcontracts, and the law will be amended to give the workman security for the recovery of compensation, the principal not to be liable, however, for accidents on premises which are not under his control or management. With regard to the payment of compensation, this is not made under the existing law until a fortnight has elapsed from the time of the accident. The Committee think that any interference with this provision of the law would involve a grave departure from the system of 1897. The Government have given serious consideration to this matter, knowing full

well that there is a strong objection to any interference with the
law as it stands. We have considered the case of industries which
are alleged already to be hampered by the cost of the Acts. The
Committee found that hitherto the pecuniary burden imposed by
the Acts upon the employers has not been excessive. On the other
hand, we have to remember that the employers have not yet come
to the point when compensation under the Act of 1897 will reach
its highest level, after which it will probably go down to a certain
extent. But since 1897, taking into account all available experience, the Government have come to the conclusion that trade has
not been hampered by the Act sufficiently to prevent what they
considered a further measure of justice. There was ample evidence
given to the Committee that large masses of men, women, and
children whose weekly earnings amounted to something between
5s. and 25s. a week are put to the most serious hardship by the
operation of the law as it stands. We have therefore come to the
conclusion that the two weeks shall be reduced to one. That is
the proposal in the Bill. Of course, it will put a certain increased
cost upon the employer. The cost has been variously estimated
by experts before the Committee at from 25 per cent up to 50 per
cent. I will not at this moment hazard an opinion as to the inci-
dence of that increased cost. A small proportion possibly may fall
upon wages, but it will probably be distributed between the proprietor and the customer — at any rate, it will be distributed upon
the resources of the trade without, as we think, doing any injury
at all to the trade, and it is a measure of justice which we cannot
leave out of this Bill.

Under the present law compensation is based on the wages received or agreed to be paid while the workman is in the service of
the same employer. But the effect of the law as it stands imposes
a great hardship on some classes of workmen, especially on those
engaged in casual labour. The Committee have given instances
of hardship which occur under the present law. A man earning
from 6s. to 7s. a day may be awarded 3s. 6d. a week. A case was

given in which a man went on for a night's work and, being injured, received only 2s. a week. Another more extreme case was
that of a man who in five days earned 30s. and then went on to a
fresh job and was injured in the first hour, and his compensation
was reckoned out at 3½d. per week. It is quite obvious that there
are great anomalies under the law as it stands which must be removed. Therefore, in the Bill, the Government have adopted the
recommendation of the Committee, which is founded, virtually,
upon the Employers' Liability Act standard. If a man has worked
with an employer for two continuous weeks or more, then his
compensation, when he is injured, will be founded on the wages he
is receiving in that employment, but if he has not worked for two
continuous weeks, then the court must have regard to the earnings which such workman would receive in the same trade, in the
same employment, and in the same district. In regard to the reassessment for partial incapacity, the proposal of the Bill is that the
weekly payment is not to exceed one half the difference between
the amount of the average weekly earnings before the accident
and the amount which the workman is earning or is fit to earn.
That is to say, if a man who is earning £2 a week is injured and
is awarded compensation at the rate of £1 a week, but on the
reassessment is found capable of earning £1 a week, he will
get 10s. a week compensation, so that he will be in a position
to earn 30s. a week. There is power under the Bill to commute
weekly payments which continued for not less than six months
for a lump sum not exceeding £500.

With regard to the question of aged persons and minors, the
Committee find that the Acts have largely increased the difficulties of old men finding and retaining employment, and the difficulty
is believed to be growing. They came practically to the same
conclusion with regard to infirm and maimed persons, and they
proposed that a lower rate of compensation should be payable in
regard to both these classes. The two cases of the aged person
and the infirm and maimed person appear to the Government to be

governed by somewhat different considerations. I confess that personally I am somewhat inclined to extend to both classes the proposals of the Committee, but the difficulties are undoubtedly rather more serious in the case of the infirm and maimed person. Other considerations arise which I will not mention now, and so, on the whole, the Government have decided only to deal with the recommendation of the Committee in its application to the aged person. After the age of sixty the employer is enabled to make special arrangements with the aged person, under which, in case of death, a maximum payment of £25 is payable and, in the case of injury and incapacity, weekly compensation with a maximum of 10s. a week. The Committee suggested 5s. The Government think that is too small an amount, and they, therefore, extend it to 10s. In the case of minors, again, very great hardships have arisen under the present law. A boy, for example, receiving 4s. a week, who is injured and incapacitated for life, cannot get more than 2s. a week compensation. The Bill provides that, where a minor is injured who earns less than 20s. a week, 100 per cent should be substituted for 50 per cent in respect of compensation based on his weekly earnings, but the weekly payment is not to exceed 10s. a week. If the case is reviewed within twelve months or more after the accident, the amount of the weekly payment may be increased to any amount not exceeding 50 per cent of the weekly sum which the workman would probably have been earning at the date of the review if he had remained uninjured, but not in any case more than £1 a week. The Bill authorises the payment into court by the employer of a lump sum in case of a fatal accident where dependants are left, to be invested at the discretion of the registrar. The Bill also deals with the case of widows, and provision is made, where there is evidence before the court that a widow who obtained compensation under the Act was prone to misconduct, for the court to apply the whole or part of the compensation, which otherwise would accrue to the widow, for the benefit of the other dependants.

I now come to the question of medical referees. As the law now stands, when there is an accident and a workman is injured, he has to submit himself to the employer's doctor, who reports to the employer. If there is disagreement, then there is no remedy but proceedings in the courts. If proceedings are taken under the Employers' Liability Act, medical evidence is taken, but it is not competent to bring a medical referee into court; but if they are taken under the Workmen's Compensation Act, after hearing the medical evidence, a medical referee may be appointed, and his judgment is final. But that leads to considerable delay and cost, and so under the Bill it is provided that if there is no agreement after injury between the employer and the workman, on the report of the employer's doctor, the employer or the workman, on payment of a fee, can apply to the court, and the registrar may at once appoint a medical referee, whose judgment will be final. And in case of review, either party in the same way can apply to the court, and the registrar will appoint a referee, whose judgment will be final. The Government hope that that provision will save a good deal of unnecessary cost and delay. Provision is also taken in the Bill that the Secretary of State may, with the sanction of the Treasury, appoint medical men to be referees under the Act, and, subject to Treasury regulations, remuneration and expenses may be paid to them out of public money.

There are various other minor points of detail, the consideration of which I propose to leave to another stage. The Government are aware that the change in the basis of the Act will bring out new conditions and new points, and they will welcome suggestions. They will have the benefit of the criticism and information of the House, and I have no doubt that the Bill in its passage through the House will be greatly improved and strengthened.

There is one important consideration on which I should like to touch, and that is the question of safety under the Workmen's Compensation Act. It was feared in 1897 that the adoption of the new principle would lead to more accidents. It is maintained by the Government, on the other hand, that the contrary result will probably ensue. The Committee find no evidence of any great improvement in the direction of safety to be placed to the credit of the Act, and their conclusion on the matter has reference to an important point which was raised in the evidence of Commander Smith with regard to the power of the court, under the Act of 1897, to set any fines imposed under the Factory and Workshop Act against the compensation due to the workman, and that that provision removed the Act from any penal operation. The Committee propose that that particular part of the clause should be repealed, and the Government have adopted that recommendation. The Committee say: "On the whole we feel unable to come to the conclusion that the operation of the Compensation Act of 1897 has had any marked or ascertainable effect, one way or the other, upon the safety of the workman."

Therefore, in considering this question anew, we must not flatter ourselves that by providing compensation we provide increased security for the workman. In my judgment that increased security will have to be found in the operation of other Acts, and more particularly, of course, in the operations of the Factory and Workshop Act and the Mines Regulation Act.

There is one further point which I think will give general satisfaction. The Bill which I propose to introduce is in the form of a consolidating Act, incorporating the Acts of 1897 and 1900, so that the House will have plainly before them, in more or less simple English, the whole statement of the case with regard to the compensation of workmen under the law. In these circumstances I venture on an appeal to the House. The Government are submitting the whole subject of workmen's compensation and are opening it all up, and as this is done for the convenience of the House, I hope that questions which are not only settled, but which are supposed to be satisfactorily settled, will not be unnecessarily reopened so as to hamper the progress of the Act. Our main object is to pass the Bill into law this session, and we offer it to the House in the hope that it will be of permanent practical benefit to all that are included within the scope of its provisions.

Extract 2

CONSERVATIVE REPLY TO THE HOME SECRETARY

(Mr. A. Akers-Douglas, Commons, March 26, 1906)

MR. AKERS-DOUGLAS[1]: I am sure I am voicing the opinion of the whole House when I congratulate the right hon. Gentleman upon the clearness and ability with which he has dealt with a very complicated subject. We have all listened to him with very great pleasure ; we have all felt the difficulty of his task and recognised the excellent manner in which he has discharged it. I do not think there is any difference of opinion as to the object to be aimed at. We all welcome a Bill to amend the Act of 1897. We feel that an Amendment of that Act is very much wanted. The Act, as the right hon. Gentleman has explained, was a new procedure in legislation in 1897, and for that reason it had to be to a certain extent experimental and tentative, and, therefore, we need not be surprised at the fact that after working eight or nine years it requires some considerable amendment. The experience of those eight or nine years, I think, on the whole, has been very satisfactory, but certainly the time has now come when we might deal with many matters which require amendment and, as the right hon. Gentleman proposes to do, very largely extend the Act in its operations towards the people who come under it. I have listened very carefully to the speech of the right hon. Gentleman, and I gather from him that not only is the Bill to be an amending, but a consolidating, Bill. I congratulate the right hon. Gentleman on this fact, and I

---

[1] Parliamentary Debates, Fourth Series, vol. 154, col. 895 sqq.

admire his courage in avoiding the temptation to legislate by reference. I know from the experience I had in introducing a measure
on this subject last year the very great difficulty of dealing with
it purely by an amending Bill, and I think that the right hon. Gentleman has taken a wise and, I am bound to say, a courageous
course in bringing in the Bill in the form he has done. I may assure him that, so far as I am concerned, and so far as my friends
on this side of the House are concerned, we will accept the suggestion that he has made to us in regard to not opening up
unnecessary subjects. . . .

I have no doubt the right hon. Gentleman has taken care to
consult employers of labour, especially on his own side of the
House, with regard to this extra burden which he is placing upon
them. I am anxious to give every reasonable facility to cover
reasonable cases in the interests of the employees, but we must
not in our desire to act generously to them either make the Act
unworkable or throw unreasonable cost upon industry. The Committee which sat under the chairmanship of Sir Kenelm Digby
took a great deal of evidence on this point. As to the additional
risk incurred and the cost of insurance, the General Accident Company thought that the additional premium required would be 35
per cent and the General Insurance thought it would be 50 per
cent. If the assurance companies still hold that these figures are
correct, we shall have seriously to consider whether such a scheme
would not throw too great a burden on the employer. I am most
anxious that the Act shall prove successful, and I hope that when
the Bill is in Committee this question of burden on the employers
will be carefully discussed. I do not want to press it now or on
the Second Reading, for I am anxious that the measure should
pass into law as quickly as possible; but details can always be
more usefully considered in Committee than on the floor of the
House. I am sure that hon. Members of the Labour party below
the gangway want only a measure which will be fair as between
man and man, and that they will endeavour by their criticisms and

Amendments to make it a workable measure and one likely to be accepted by all classes of employers and employed. Whether the right hon. the Home Secretary has gone too far or not in amending the Act of 1897, or in extending the benefits of the Act to further trades — the general principle being admitted — we must wait to see; but, so far as we could gather from the speech of the right hon. Gentleman, the measure is satisfactory, and I trust, therefore, that the House will agree to the First and Second Readings, leaving all these details to be considered fully in Committee.

Extract 3

LABOUR REPLY TO THE HOME SECRETARY

(*Mr. G. N. Barnes, Commons, March 26, 1906*)

MR. BARNES said [1] he wished to offer a few observations on the speech of the right hon. the Home Secretary and on the Bill which the right hon. Gentleman had asked leave to introduce into the House. First of all, on behalf of the Party with which he was identified, he welcomed the right hon. Gentleman's statement of the projected Bill as being, to a large extent at all events, satisfactory from their point of view; and he could promise that it would have a helpful and sympathetic consideration with a view to having it amended in their direction and passed into law. It seemed to him that the name of the Bill was to some extent a misnomer. The Bill would not compensate. It provided merely for a maintenance being given to a man who was injured. Therefore, it seemed to the Labour party that there should be some Amendment in the name of the Bill which would more accurately define what the Bill really was. On the whole, however, he felt satisfied that not only in its form but in its scope, as indicated in the speech of the right hon. Gentleman, the Bill would to a very large extent

[1] Parliamentary Debates, Fourth Series, vol. 154, col. 900 sqq.

meet the wishes of the Labour party. The Act of 1897 had been of inestimable benefit to a very large number of working people throughout the length and breadth of the country. With all its defects and blemishes it had proved one of the best bits of social legislation that had been put on the Statute Book in recent years. He wished to go a little further and to pay a well-merited tribute of indebtedness to one who was largely instrumental in getting that Act passed through Parliament. That right hon. Gentleman long ago contributed articles to magazines advocating what was then a novel principle in English law. He introduced that principle as an Amendment on the Bill of 1893, and had it afterwards successfully embodied in the Act of 1897. It was needless to say that reference was made to the right hon. Member for West Birmingham [Joseph Chamberlain]. He was all the more satisfied to pay that tribute of indebtedness to the right hon. Gentleman, for it was the vogue to jump upon his by no means prostrate form. A good deal had been said as to the deficiencies of the Act of 1897, but he believed that a great deal of the litigation and of the money which had found its way into the lawyers' pockets had been caused by the confusing lines between the " ins " and the " outs." He remembered the report of a debate eight or nine years ago in which it was predicted by hon. Gentlemen in this House, especially those who represented the mine-owners, that the Bill would lead to vast litigation ; and some even went the length of describing it as a " Lawyers' Employment Bill." He had had a good deal of experience in regard to the working of the Act of 1897, and had had the opportunity of hearing the testimony of others who had had more, and all he could say was that the cases which had been settled by the payment of money without litigation at all were from 90 to 95 per cent of the whole. From that point of view the Bill had been on the whole satisfactory ; but there was no reason why the 5 or 10 per cent of litigation should not also be reduced. In his belief, there would be no complete solution of the difficulty until all men, no matter what employment they were in, were included in the scope of the measure. It had been said that only dangerous trades were included in the last Act, but agricultural labourers were afterwards included, and no one would seriously contend that agriculture was a dangerous employment. He was sorry to hear that, while anyone employing more than five men was to be included in the Bill, all small employers having fewer than five employees were to be excluded. That would be a fruitful source of litigation and confusion which would benefit the lawyers and the agents of the insurance companies. He hoped that the Bill would be amended in these respects. He knew many small workshops where fewer than five men were employed under the most dangerous conditions — probably more dangerous than in large workshops. But it would be no good including them on paper only. Therefore, if they were to be included, there must be some provision whereby the money should be there when wanted. That carried with it some form of compulsory insurance. The right hon. Gentleman said that the time had not yet come for that. That remained to be seen. He was inclined to think that compulsory insurance would even now be necessary ; but if the Bill was carried further than its present scope, he was certain that compulsory insurance would be absolutely necessary. He knew that there were some who said that compulsory insurance, or insurance of any character, carried with it increased risk. There might be something in that argument, but, after all, the contention seemed to him to be advanced by those who strained at a gnat and swallowed a camel. . . .

Extract 4

MR. JOSEPH CHAMBERLAIN ON WORKMEN'S COMPENSATION

(*Commons, March 26, 1906*)

MR. CHAMBERLAIN [1]: . . . There was no desire to obstruct the Bill in any part of the House. But, in regard to the time before the compensation should commence to be paid, he would press the

[1] Parliamentary Debates, Fourth Series, vol. 154, col. 928 sqq.

representatives of the workingmen, both inside and outside the House, to consider very carefully whether a provision which at first sight might appear to be to the advantage of the workmen, might not ultimately be not so much to the disadvantage of the·manufacturer or the employer, as to the workman himself. They should not desire to press on the employer any expenditure which was not clearly in the interest of the workmen, because, after all, whatever political economists might say on the subject, they all knew that one of the factors in wages was the expense of production, and if the expense of production was raised beyond certain limits by legislation, it was conceivable that some part of that charge might be transferred by the employer on to the workmen. Before the Bill of 1897 was introduced, he consulted a large number of people acquainted with the principles of compensation insurance, some of the principal officials of the great friendly and benefit societies in this country, and representatives of insurance companies. They all pressed upon him that in the interests of the workman, as well as of the employer, a distinct and definite period should lapse before compensation was payable. The reason was that, after all, there was no great pressure for compensation where the accident was so slight as to be represented by no more than a fortnight's illness. In the second place, it was found by some of the friendly societies necessary to protect themselves by a delay before compensation became payable, in order to prevent fraud. He asked whether it was worth while putting fifty per cent more expense upon the employer in order merely to get compensation for the first fortnight's absence from work. He urged the representatives of the workmen to consider whether it was in their interests to press for an alteration in the law which would be found to be extremely unpopular and would place an increased charge on employers everywhere. When the Bill of 1897 was before the House he had returns furnished to him of the number of accidents which took place in every great trade in the country, and calculations were deduced from these returns as to what the operation of the

Bill would cost. At the time he believed that the statements made by the opponents of the Bill as to its cost were greatly exaggerated, and that had been proved to be the case, because after some years' experience of the working of the Act it was found that his original calculations were absolutely correct. He was informed that of late years there had been a considerable increase in the number of accidents. Why was that? [AN HON. MEMBER ON THE LABOUR BENCHES: Speeding up the machinery.] Well, if speeding up machinery had taken place, with the result of an increase in the number of accidents, then he for one was glad that means were provided for compensation. If the House reduced the close period, as it had been called, to seven days, he thought they would open the way to a great deal more litigation, and to that extent they would injure rather than benefit the working classes.

Extract 5

SIR CHARLES DILKE ON WORKMEN'S COMPENSATION

(*Commons, April 4, 1906*)

SIR CHARLES DILKE[1]: . . . The other day — and he dared say they would see the same to-day — the House seemed inclined to bless almost unanimously the principle of universal insurance, but, having done that, to take no steps towards giving it effect. How long was that to go on? It was no new question; it was a very old question. In 1883 Germany adopted her present law. He was not advocating the adoption of that law here. It was too bound up in other laws for it to be practicable here; but in 1883–1884 Germany and Austria called the attention of the world to the subject, and they adopted their law, admirable from their point of view, which so completely dealt with the question for them, and which had received only unimportant amendments of detail from

---

[1] Parliamentary Debates, Fourth Series, vol. 155, col. 523 sqq.

that time. Then the right hon. Member for West Birmingham [Mr. Joseph Chamberlain] brought the matter before this House, not on the lines of his subsequent Bill, which they were now amending, but on the lines of the Amendment. He moved an Amendment in 1893 to the Employers' Liability Bill, raising this very question. He moved that no amendment of the law could be satisfactory which did not provide compensation for workmen for all injuries. He made only one exception, and he stated that he had placed his Amendment upon the Paper with a view to telling the House an alternative system of dealing with the whole question. He quoted a conversation he had had with a well-known former Member, Mr. Knowles, who had just died, a great Tory employer, who was of opinion that universal liability was the only satisfactory settlement. The right hon. Member for West Birmingham added that universal liability meant universal insurance. Within the last few weeks it had been alleged that it was too soon to bring about so sudden a change, but 1893 was a good many years ago, and it was then already alleged that the thing was premature. The right hon. Member for West Birmingham asked the then Liberal Government, " Why do you not take this opportunity of completing your work ? " It was answered that public opinion was not prepared for so great a change, and he said, " How do you know that ? It is the duty of Government to lead and instruct public opinion. Opinion is making rapid strides in this direction." That was in 1893, and yet they had had nothing in that direction, although they raised these speeches and discussions against the right hon. Member for West Birmingham in 1897 and since. They were told that the Bill of 1897 was a tentative measure, and it was suggested that ultimately steps might be taken in their direction.

In 1898 France and Italy both suddenly adopted the very principle which he was now maintaining, a principle far ahead of that of 1897, of far more general satisfaction to the workmen, far more complete, and having the effect of giving far more money to the working-classes than any Bill in operation in this country or than the Bill now proposed. The late Secretary of State for the Colonies, Mr. Lyttelton, following the right hon. Member for West Birmingham, actually went so far as to suggest that the Workmen's Compensation Act was a handicap from which our competitors were free, but in France it was beyond all doubt five times more severe than it was here. There could also be no doubt that the benefits which it directly conferred upon the working-classes went further than our own. It was carried suddenly in Italy and France, and it was a compromise — such a compromise as they might expect to get in this country — between those who insisted on the individual liability of the employer, those who wanted to make the liability as little as possible, and those who wanted to make it a matter of State insurance. Those systems had been working close at hand in Europe satisfactorily from that time to this. . . .

His own main point was this : that by shutting their eyes for so long a time and giving the go-by to this question, they were not doing what the country expected and what so many hon. Members told the electors, namely, that they were going to work towards obtaining complete compensation for all workmen injured in all classes of trade. In this matter we had fallen into arrear as compared with other countries. Workmen's compensation treaties between France and Italy, Italy and Switzerland, and Italy and Germany were signed in 1904. Similar labour treaties were made between Austria and Germany in 1905 and between France and Belgium in 1906. Up to the present this country had not been able to come to any treaty engagement of that kind, and, therefore, they were unable to give or receive the advantages which all those States were conferring upon their workmen abroad. He appealed to the Government to give careful consideration to this subject in regard to which they were falling day by day more heavily into arrear. . . .

Extract 6

EMPLOYER'S ATTITUDE TOWARD WORKMEN'S COMPENSATION

(Mr. H. G. Montgomery, Commons, April 4, 1906)

MR. MONTGOMERY[1] asked the indulgence of the House for a few moments while he put before them the point of view of the employer. He wished to give employees the fullest measure of security, but at the same time the employer was entitled to know what amount of compensation he had to pay. At the present time he did not know. Unfortunately, he was one of those small employers of labour who, when the Act was introduced by the right hon. Gentleman the Member for West Birmingham [Joseph Chamberlain], joined with others in forming a mutual insurance of their own. He was sorry to say the speculation was a very bad one. They paid away a large sum in the first place in endeavouring to ascertain what the Workmen's Compensation Act meant. They had to fight a number of cases, and he was very much inclined to think that the ambiguity of the Act was a godsend to half the solicitors and barristers of this country. They had to defend a number of claims that ought never to have been brought. There were legal gentlemen who sent touts to the hospital in which an injured man was, telling him that if a claim were preferred under the Employers' Liability Act instead of under the Workmen's Compensation Act, the solicitor would be able to get a very much larger sum. As very often happened, the man was persuaded to make a claim under the Employers' Liability Act. He knew of an instance where a man had a sprained ankle, and they were willing to pay compensation under the Workmen's Compensation Act, but the tout at a hospital got hold of the man, and a claim was made under the Employers' Liability Act. In the end the jury gave a

1 Parliamentary Debates, Fourth Series, vol. 155, col. 548 sqq.

large sum, with the result that the firm had to pay £400 for a sprained ankle, whilst the man was said to be dancing a jig a few days after. He was told that the money did not all go to the workman, but that it was divided between solicitor and client. He was not sure that it was wise to give any workman a lump sum as compensation, because he was very often inclined to spend it in ways that he should not, and in a very liberal manner amongst his friends. He thought that the Act ought to cover every kind of accident that might possibly arise. He was in entire agreement with the extension of the Act, and he should like to see it extended to every form of service, even to the domestic who cleaned the doorstep in the morning. He noticed that it was provided in the Bill that if the employer could be proved to have been guilty of negligence, he would have to pay a larger sum, but if the employee was found guilty of negligence, it did not say that he should receive a less sum. He did not think that was fair, because what was sauce for the goose was also sauce for the gander. It had been proved over and over again that negligence was not wilful misconduct on the part of the employee. He knew a case where a man was engaged to feed a brick-making machine, and instead of putting the clay in with a shovel, as he ought to have done, he used his foot. On one occasion his foot was caught and he lost it. He received compensation and also got a wooden leg. Not more than two months after, the wooden leg found its way into the machine as well, and the man received a second measure of compensation. They could proceed against the employer for allowing the man to put his leg or wooden leg into the machine, but they should have an Act which would deal fairly between employer and employed. The House had been told that insurance companies did not make any money out of workmen's compensation. He was sorry to differ from the hon. Member for the St. Austell Division [Mr. William McArthur] on this point, because he believed that if the insurance was on a large scale, a large amount of profit could be made. A larger body of factory inspectors would be better able than anybody else to prevent accidents. If the Government would take this question up as a business matter and conduct it on business lines, he ventured to say that before two or three years had elapsed they would have made sufficient profit to take sixpence off the income tax and give every employee over seventy-five years of age an old age pension.

Extract 7

EMPLOYEE'S ATTITUDE TOWARD WORKMEN'S COMPENSATION

(Mr. J. R. Clynes, Commons, April 4, 1906)

MR. CLYNES[1] thought that they had heard too much about the small employer in this debate, and that some share of their pity should go out to those who suffered from injuries which this Bill proposed to meet. The debate had not supplied so far any reminder of the number of people injured and killed during their daily labour. He believed there were about 400 workpeople killed every month in this country, and about 7000 injured in one way or another. The first point which he desired to refer to was the insufficiency of the compensation proposed by the Bill. The compensation proposed was half the average earnings of the man. He submitted that if a man fairly needed all his wages when he was well, the family needed even more than the whole of the man's wages when he was ill. Let them take as an illustration a man earning 30s. a week who was disabled for three weeks. The man would lose £4 10s., and under the Bill he would receive as compensation only 30s. He submitted that that was not generous treatment, and they were entitled to call upon the Government to take a step in advance of the attitude assumed by the Government some years ago when the compensation law was first passed. They felt that the trades and industries generally could afford a greater strain. The profits of trading and the increase of the wealth of the

[1] Parliamentary Debates, Fourth Series, vol. 155, col. 1203 sqq.

well-to-do appeared to him to prove conclusively that a heavier burden for such a good reason could well be borne by the trades and industries of this country. He did not accept the suggestion that the small employers should be excluded from liability. He understood the Home Secretary to advocate the exclusion of small employers because they were indifferent and would not face their responsibilities. It had been said that such men were very often ignorant and did not do what the law called upon them to do. He had yet to learn that indifference to and ignorance of the law were sufficient reasons for escaping one's responsibilities in regard to the common law of the land, and in this matter he thought the Government should not exclude such a large number of workers as would be excluded if these small employers of labour were enabled to escape their responsibilities. The small employers of labour in respect of their profits and trading conditions knew how to combine, and if they could not singly accept the liability which the principle of this Bill proposed, then they might act in association in order to insure the lives and limbs of their workmen. He submitted also that sufficient reasons had not been given by the Secretary of State for the Home Department for the exclusion of domestic servants from the privileges of the Bill. Reference had been made by the right hon. Gentleman to the large number of domestic servants employed by working people. The Labour party made no plea that the wage-earners of the country should escape their liabilities in respect of injuries sustained by those whom they employed. If necessary, they should call upon the ordinary working-man to insure himself against the risk of accidents that might befall his domestic servant. He did not think they ought to exclude clerks from the operation of the Bill. They should not forget that there was a class of clerk who moved about large works and shipping yards amongst machinery in order to take down details, and he incurred almost as great a risk as the ordinary workingman. It had been said upon both sides of the House that it was not advisable to depart from the present limit of a fortnight, because of the

malingering there was or might be if workingmen were entitled
to compensation from the first day of injury. He would point out
that if a workingman went home and said he had been hurt, that
would not be taken as evidence of the injury, and his word would
not be taken as the foundation for the payment of compensation.
The doctor's evidence as to injury and incapacity would be required
before any workman could set up his title to compensation. He
thought the officers of the insurance company, the agents of the
employer, and all the things attaching to a workingman's condition of work would protect employers against the risk of having
to pay when a man was not disabled at all. There were many
points dealt with in this Bill which Labour Members warmly welcomed, but having accepted the payment of compensation as a
principle, and that industries must bear the cost of accidents and
deaths, he submitted that the House had had sufficient experience
of industrial life to justify it in going further in regard to the
amount of compensation, and in regard to the other items which
he had mentioned.

Extract 8

FORESHADOWING NATIONAL INSURANCE

*(Mr. Herbert J. Gladstone, Secretary of State for the Home
Department, Commons, December 13, 1906)*

MR. GLADSTONE[1]: . . . He had no occasion to detain the House
long upon this subject. The recent discussion extended over four
days, during which all the leading points of the Bill were fully discussed. But there was one matter upon which he desired to say a
few words. The House in its collective wisdom had shown an inveterate hostility to all the attempts of the Government to exempt
from the operation of this Bill the small employers. Now practically all classes of persons under contract of service, whether the
employment was dangerous or safe, were included in the purview

[1] Parliamentary Debates, Fourth Series, vol. 167, col. 693 sqq.

of this Bill. While 6,000,000 people were brought within the operation of the Act in 1897, and 1,000,000 in 1900, there were now 6,000,000 in addition. This great extension did involve benefit — he hoped great benefit — but it also, naturally, involved some danger to which this House should not shut their eyes. A number of small employers would be brought under the operation of this Act, and it was to be hoped that they would be raised to a sense of the duty imposed upon them by it — to a sense of the necessity which lay upon them to insure against the liability to which they would be exposed, in order to be in a position to meet it in compensating a workman who might be injured. Experience showed that a mass of these people would not insure, whatever steps were taken, and that experience was reinforced by the opinion expressed in the Committee which considered this question. It was pointed out that 24 per cent of those engaged in the building trades did not choose to insure, although the Act had been in operation for some six or seven years. If the Government required any pressure, this knowledge and this information from the Committee would hasten their desire to deal with the whole subject of national insurance in relation to the law of employers' liability. But in the meanwhile they would do the best they could, through Government agencies or otherwise, to warn employers, great and small, throughout the country, of the risks they were under, and also to tell the workpeople of this country what rights were given to them under this Act. . . .

Extract 9

THIRD READING OF WORKMEN'S COMPENSATION BILL

(Mr. Joseph Walton, Commons, December 13, 1906)

MR. WALTON [1]: . . . He felt sure that the 6,000,000 additional workers — men and women — to whom this measure did what was an act of justice in regard to this matter, would greatly appreciate

[1] Parliamentary Debates, Fourth Series, vol. 167, col. 708.

their inclusion within the scope of the measure. He had had no sympathy or support whatever from the Tory majority in the House, when he had introduced his Bill, but he gathered from speeches made by Members of the same political Party now sitting in Opposition that he might regard them as repentant sinners. It was indeed a death-bed repentance when they rose the other night and proposed the inclusion of 2,000,000 of domestic servants within the scope of the Bill. He welcomed that inclusion, but it was so hastily adopted by the House that he hoped, now that they were included, it was clearly understood that in case of accident they were to receive not only half their wages, but half the cost of their board and lodging as well, in case they were deprived of that, as that formed the greatest part of their earnings. He cordially supported the Bill.

Extract 10

WORKMEN'S COMPENSATION ACT, 1906

(6 Edw. 7, ch. 58)

An Act to consolidate and amend the Law with respect to Compensation to Workmen for Injuries suffered in the course of their Employment.   (21st December 1906)

Be it enacted by the King's most Excellent Majesty, by and with the advice and consent of the Lords Spiritual and Temporal, and Commons, in this present Parliament assembled, and by the authority of the same, as follows:

1. Liability of Employers to Workmen for Injuries

(1) If in any employment personal injury by accident arising out of and in the course of the employment is caused to a workman, his employer shall, subject as herein-after mentioned, be liable to pay compensation in accordance with the First Schedule to this Act.

(2) Provided that —

(*a*) The employer shall not be liable under this Act in respect of any injury which does not disable the workman for a period of at least one week from earning full wages at the work at which he was employed :

(*b*) When the injury was caused by the personal negligence or wilful act of the employer or of some person for whose act or default the employer is responsible, nothing in this Act shall affect any civil liability of the employer, but in that case the workman may, at his option, either claim compensation under this Act or take proceedings independently of this Act ; but the employer shall not be liable to pay compensation for injury to a workman by accident arising out of and in the course of the employment both independently of and also under this Act, and shall not· be liable to any proceedings independently of this Act, except in case of such personal negligence or wilful act as aforesaid :

(*c*) If it is proved that the injury to a workman is attributable to the serious and wilful misconduct of that workman, any compensation claimed in respect of that injury shall, unless the injury results in death or serious and permanent disablement, be disallowed.

(3) If any question arises in any proceedings under this Act as to the liability to pay compensation under this Act (including any question as to whether the person injured is a workman to whom this Act applies), or as to the amount or duration of compensation under this Act, the question, if not settled by agreement, shall, subject to the provisions of the First Schedule to this Act, be settled by arbitration, in accordance with the Second Schedule to this Act.

(4) If, within the time herein-after in this Act limited for taking proceedings, an action is brought to recover damages independently of this Act for injury caused by any accident, and it is

determined in such action that the injury is one for which the employer is not liable in such action, but that he would have been liable to pay compensation under the provisions of this Act, the action shall be dismissed; but the court in which the action is tried shall, if the plaintiff so choose, proceed to assess such compensation, but may deduct from such compensation all or part of the costs which, in its judgment, have been caused by the plaintiff bringing the action instead of proceeding under this Act. In any proceeding under this subsection, when the court assesses the compensation it shall give a certificate of the compensation it has awarded and the directions it has given as to the deduction for costs, and such certificate shall have the force and effect of an award under this Act.

(5) Nothing in this Act shall affect any proceeding for a fine under the enactments relating to mines, factories, or workshops, or the application of any such fine.

2. *Time for taking Proceedings*

(1) Proceedings for the recovery under this Act of compensation for an injury shall not be maintainable unless notice of the accident has been given as soon as practicable after the happening thereof and before the workman has voluntarily left the employment in which he was injured, and unless the claim for compensation with respect to such accident has been made within six months from the occurrence of the accident causing the injury, or, in case of death, within six months from the time of death:

Provided always that —

(a) The want of or any defect or inaccuracy in such notice shall not be a bar to the maintenance of such proceedings if it is found in the proceedings for settling the claim that the employer is not, or would not, if a notice or an amended notice were then given and the hearing postponed, be prejudiced in his defence by

the want, defect, or inaccuracy, or that such want,
defect, or inaccuracy was occasioned by mistake, absence from the United Kingdom, or other reasonable
cause ; and

(*b*) the failure to make a claim within the period above specified shall not be a bar to the maintenance of such
proceedings if it is found that the failure was occasioned by mistake, absence from the United Kingdom,
or other reasonable cause.

(2) Notice in respect of an injury under this Act shall give the
name and address of the person injured, and shall state in ordinary language the cause of the injury and the date at which the
accident happened, and shall be served on the employer, or, if
there is more than one employer, upon one of such employers.

(3) The notice may be served by delivering the same at, or
sending it by post in a registered letter addressed to, the residence
or place of business of the person on whom it is to be served.

(4) Where the employer is a body of persons, corporate or unincorporate, the notice may also be served by delivering the same
at, or by sending it by post in a registered letter addressed to, the
employer at the office, or, if there be more than one office, any one
of the offices of such body.

3. Contracting Out

(1) If the Registrar of Friendly Societies, after taking steps to
ascertain the views of the employer and workmen, certifies that
any scheme of compensation, benefit, or insurance for the workmen of an employer in any employment, whether or not such
scheme includes other employers and their workmen, provides
scales of compensation not less favourable to the workmen and
their dependants than the corresponding scales contained in this
Act, and that, where the scheme provides for contributions by the
workmen, the scheme confers benefits at least equivalent to those
contributions, in addition to the benefits to which the workmen

would have been entitled under this Act, and that a majority (to be ascertained by ballot) of the workmen to whom the scheme is applicable are in favour of such scheme, the employer may, whilst the certificate is in force, contract with any of his workmen that the provisions of the scheme shall be substituted for the provisions of this Act, and thereupon the employer shall be liable only in accordance with the scheme, but, save as aforesaid, this Act shall apply notwithstanding any contract to the contrary made after the commencement of this Act.

(2) The Registrar may give a certificate to expire at the end of a limited period of not less than five years, and may from time to time renew with or without modifications such a certificate to expire at the end of the period for which it is renewed.

(3) No scheme shall be so certified which contains an obligation upon the workmen to join the scheme as a condition of their hiring, or which does not contain provisions enabling a workman to withdraw from the scheme.

(4) If complaint is made to the Registrar of Friendly Societies by or on behalf of the workmen of any employer that the benefits conferred by any scheme no longer conform to the conditions stated in subsection (1) of this section, or that the provisions of such scheme are being violated, or that the scheme is not being fairly administered, or that satisfactory reasons exist for revoking the certificate, the Registrar shall examine into the complaint, and, if satisfied that good cause exist for such complaint, shall, unless the cause of complaint is removed, revoke the certificate.

(5) When a certificate is revoked or expires, any moneys or securities held for the purpose of the scheme shall, after due provision has been made to discharge the liabilities already accrued, be distributed as may be arranged between the employer and workmen, or as may be determined by the Registrar of Friendly Societies in the event of a difference of opinion.

(6) Whenever a scheme has been certified as aforesaid, it shall be the duty of the employer to answer all such inquiries and to

furnish all such accounts in regard to the scheme as may be made or required by the Registrar of Friendly Societies.

(7) The Chief Registrar of Friendly Societies shall include in his annual report the particulars of the proceedings of the Registrar under this Act.

(8) The Chief Registrar of Friendly Societies may make regulations for the purpose of carrying this section into effect.

4. Sub-contracting

(1) Where any person (in this section referred to as the principal), in the course of or for the purposes of his trade or business, contracts with any other person (in this section referred to as the contractor) for the execution by or under the contractor of the whole or any part of any work undertaken by the principal, the principal shall be liable to pay to any workman employed in the execution of the work any compensation under this Act which he would have been liable to pay if that workman had been immediately employed by him ; and where compensation is claimed from or proceedings are taken against the principal, then, in the application of this Act, references to the principal shall be substituted for references to the employer, except that the amount of compensation shall be calculated with reference to the earnings of the workman under the employer by whom he is immediately employed :

Provided that, where the contract relates to threshing, ploughing, or other agricultural work, and the contractor provides and uses machinery driven by mechanical power for the purpose of such work, he and he alone shall be liable under this Act to pay compensation to any workman employed by him on such work.

(2) Where the principal is liable to pay compensation under this section, he shall be entitled to be indemnified by any person who would have been liable to pay compensation to the workman independently of this section, and all questions as to the right to and amount of any such indemnity shall in default of agreement be settled by arbitration under this Act.

(3) Nothing in this section shall be construed as preventing a workman recovering compensation under this Act from the contractor instead of the principal.

(4) This section shall not apply in any case where the accident occurred elsewhere than on, or in, or about premises on which the principal has undertaken to execute the work or which are otherwise under his control or management.

5. *Provision as to Cases of Bankruptcy of Employer*

(1) Where any employer has entered into a contract with any insurers in respect of any liability under this Act to any workman, then, in the event of the employer becoming bankrupt, or making a composition or arrangement with his creditors, or if the employer is a company in the event of the company having commenced to be wound up, the rights of the employer against the insurers as respects that liability shall, notwithstanding anything in the enactments relating to bankruptcy and the winding up of companies, be transferred to and vest in the workman, and upon any such transfer the insurers shall have the same rights and remedies and be subject to the same liabilities as if they were the employer, so however that the insurers shall not be under any greater liability to the workman than they would have been under to the employer.

(2) If the liability of the insurers to the workman is less than the liability of the employer to the workman, the workman may prove for the balance in the bankruptcy or liquidation.

(3) There shall be included among the debts which under section one of the Preferential Payments in Bankruptcy Act, 1888, and section four of the Preferential Payments in Bankruptcy (Ireland) Act, 1889, are in the distribution of the property of a bankrupt and in the distribution of the assets of a company being wound up to be paid in priority to all other debts, the amount, not exceeding in any individual case one hundred pounds, due in respect of any compensation the liability wherefor accrued before the date of the receiving order or the date of the commencement of the

winding up, and those Acts and the Preferential Payments in Bankruptcy Amendment Act, 1897, shall have effect accordingly. Where the compensation is a weekly payment, the amount due in respect thereof shall, for the purposes of this provision, be taken to be the amount of the lump sum for which the weekly payment could, if redeemable, be redeemed if the employer made an application for that purpose under the First Schedule to this Act.

(4) In the case of the winding up of a company within the meaning of the Stannaries Act, 1887, such an amount as aforesaid, if the compensation is payable to a miner or the dependants of a miner, shall have the like priority as is conferred on wages of miners by section nine of that Act, and that section shall have effect accordingly.

(5) The provisions of this section with respect to preferences and priorities shall not apply where the bankrupt or the company being wound up has entered into such a contract with insurers as aforesaid.

(6) This section shall not apply where a company is wound up voluntarily merely for the purposes of reconstruction or of amalgamation with another company.

6. Remedies both against Employer and Stranger

Where the injury for which compensation is payable under this Act was caused under circumstances creating a legal liability in some person other than the employer to pay damages in respect thereof —

(1) The workman may take proceedings both against that person to recover damages and against any person liable to pay compensation under this Act for such compensation, but shall not be entitled to recover both damages and compensation ; and

(2) If the workman has recovered compensation under this Act, the person by whom the compensation was paid, and any person who has been called on to pay an indemnity

under the section of this Act relating to sub-contracting, shall be entitled to be indemnified by the person so liable to pay damages as aforesaid, and all questions as to the right to and amount of any such indemnity shall, in default of agreement, be settled by action, or, by consent of the parties, by arbitration under this Act.

7. *Application of Act to Seamen*

(1) This Act shall apply to masters, seamen, and apprentices to the sea service and apprentices in the sea-fishing service, provided that such persons are workmen within the meaning of this Act, and are members of the crew of any ship registered in the United Kingdom, or of any other British ship or vessel of which the owner, or (if there is more than one owner) the managing owner, or manager resides or has his principal place of business in the United Kingdom, subject to the following modifications:

(*a*) The notice of accident and the claim for compensation may, except where the person injured is the master, be served on the master of the ship as if he were the employer, but where the accident happened and the incapacity commenced on board the ship it shall not be necessary to give any notice of the accident:

(*b*) In the case of the death of the master, seaman, or apprentice, the claim for compensation shall be made within six months after news of the death has been received by the claimant:

(*c*) Where an injured master, seaman, or apprentice is discharged or left behind in a British possession or in a foreign country, depositions respecting the circumstances and nature of the injury may be taken by any judge or magistrate in the British possession, and by any British consular officer in the foreign country, and if so taken shall be transmitted by the person by whom they are taken to the Board of Trade, and such depositions or certified copies thereof shall in any proceedings for enforcing the claim be admissible in evidence as provided by sections 691 and 695 of the Merchant Shipping Act, 1894, and those sections shall apply accordingly:

(*d*) In the case of the death of a master, seaman, or apprentice, leaving no dependants, no compensation shall be payable, if the owner of the ship is under the Merchant Shipping Act, 1894, liable to pay the expenses of burial:

(*e*) The weekly payment shall not be payable in respect of the period during which the owner of the ship is, under the Merchant Shipping Act, 1894, as amended by any subsequent enactment, or otherwise, liable to defray the expenses of maintenance of the injured master, seaman, or apprentice:

(*f*) Any sum payable by way of compensation by the owner of a ship under this Act shall be paid in full notwithstanding anything in section 503 of the Merchant Shipping Act, 1894 (which relates to the limitation of a shipowner's liability in certain cases of loss of life, injury, or damage), but the limitation on the owner's liability imposed by that section shall apply to the amount recoverable by way of indemnity, under the section of this Act relating to remedies both against employer and stranger, as if the indemnity were damages for loss of life or personal injury:

(*g*) Subsections (2) and (3) of section 174 of the Merchant Shipping Act, 1894 (which relates to the recovery of wages of seamen lost with their ship), shall apply as respects proceedings for the recovery of compensation by dependants of masters, seamen, and apprentices lost with their ship as they apply with respect to proceedings for the recovery of wages due to seamen and apprentices; and proceedings for the recovery of compensation shall in such a case be maintainable if the claim is made within eighteen months of the date at which the ship is deemed to have been lost with all hands:

(2) This Act shall not apply to such members of the crew of a fishing vessel as are remunerated by shares in the profits or the gross earnings of the working of such vessel.

(3) This section shall extend to pilots to whom Part X of the Merchant Shipping Act, 1894, applies, as if a pilot when employed on any such ship as aforesaid were a seaman and a member of the crew.

8. *Application of Act to Industrial Diseases*

(1) Where —

> (i) the certifying surgeon appointed under the Factory and Workshop Act, 1901, for the district in which a workman is employed certifies that the workman is suffering from a disease mentioned in the Third Schedule to this Act and is thereby disabled from earning full wages at the work at which he was employed ; or
>
> (ii) a workman is, in pursuance of any special rules or regulations made under the Factory and Workshop Act, 1901, suspended from his usual employment on account of having contracted any such disease ; or
>
> (iii) the death of a workman is caused by any such disease ;

and the disease is due to the nature of any employment in which the workman was employed at any time within the twelve months previous to the date of the disablement or suspension, whether under one or more employers, he or his dependants shall be entitled to compensation under this Act as if the disease or such suspension as aforesaid were a personal injury by accident arising out of and in the course of that employment, subject to the following modifications :

> (*a*) The disablement or suspension shall be treated as the happening of the accident ;
>
> (*b*) If it is proved that the workman has at the time of entering the employment wilfully and falsely represented himself in writing as not having previously suffered from the disease, compensation shall not be payable ;

(*c*) The compensation shall be recoverable from the employer who last employed the workman during the said twelve months in the employment to the nature of which the disease was due :

Provided that —

    (i) the workman or his dependants if so required shall furnish that employer with such information as to the names and addresses of all the other employers who employed him in the employment during the said twelve months as he or they may possess, and, if such information is not furnished, or is not sufficient to enable that employer to take proceedings under the next following proviso, that employer upon proving that the disease was not contracted whilst the workman was in his employment shall not be liable to pay compensation ; and

    (ii) if that employer alleges that the disease was in fact contracted whilst the workman was in the employment of some other employer, and not whilst in his employment, he may join such other employer as a party to the arbitration, and if the allegation is proved that other employer shall be the employer from whom the compensation is to be recoverable ; and

    (iii) if the disease is of such a nature as to be contracted by a gradual process, any other employers, who during the said twelve months employed the workman in the employment to the nature of which the disease was due, shall be liable to make to the employer from whom compensation is recoverable such contributions as, in default of agreement, may be determined in the arbitration under this Act for settling the amount of the compensation;

(*d*) The amount of the compensation shall be calculated with reference to the earnings of the workman under the employer from whom the compensation is recoverable;

(*e*) The employer to whom notice of the death, disablement, or suspension is to be given shall be the employer who last employed the workman during the said twelve months in the employment to the nature of which the disease was due, and the notice may be given notwithstanding that the workman has voluntarily left his employment;

(*f*) If an employer or a workman is aggrieved by the action of a certifying or other surgeon in giving or refusing to give a certificate of disablement or in suspending or refusing to suspend a workman for the purposes of this section, the matter shall in accordance with regulations made by the Secretary of State be referred to a medical referee, whose decision shall be final.

(2) If the workman at or immediately before the date of the disablement or suspension was employed in any process mentioned in the second column of the Third Schedule to this Act, and the disease contracted is the disease in the first column of that Schedule set opposite the description of the process, the disease, except where the certifying surgeon certifies that in his opinion the disease was not due to the nature of the employment, shall be deemed to have been due to the nature of that employment, unless the employer proves the contrary.

(3) The Secretary of State may make rules regulating the duties and fees of certifying and other surgeons (including dentists) under this section.

(4) For the purposes of this section the date of disablement shall be such date as the certifying surgeon certifies as the date on which the disablement commenced, or, if he is unable to certify such a date, the date on which the certificate is given:

Provided that —

(*a*) Where the medical referee allows an appeal against a refusal by a certifying surgeon to give a certificate of disablement, the date of disablement shall be such date as the medical referee may determine ;

(*b*) Where a workman dies without having obtained a certificate of disablement, or is at the time of death not in receipt of a weekly payment on account of disablement, it shall be the date of death.

(5) In such cases, and subject to such conditions as the Secretary of State may direct, a medical practitioner appointed by the Secretary of State for the purpose shall have the powers and duties of a certifying surgeon under this section, and this section shall be construed accordingly.

(6) The Secretary of State may make orders for extending the provisions of this section to other diseases and other processes, and to injuries due to the nature of any employment specified in the order not being injuries by accident, either without modification or subject to such modifications as may be contained in the order.

(7) Where, after inquiry held on the application of any employers or workmen engaged in any industry to which this section applies, it appears that a mutual trade insurance company or society for insuring against the risks under this section has been established for the industry, and that a majority of the employers engaged in that industry are insured against such risks in the company or society and that the company or society consents, the Secretary of State may, by Provisional Order, require all employers in that industry to insure in the company or society upon such terms and under such conditions and subject to such exceptions as may be set forth in the Order. Where such a company or society has been established, but is confined to employers in any particular locality or of any particular class, the Secretary of State may for the purposes of this provision treat the industry,

as carried on by employers in that locality or of that class, as a separate industry.

(8) A Provisional Order made under this section shall be of no force whatever unless and until it is confirmed by Parliament, and if, while the Bill confirming any such Order is pending in either House of Parliament, a petition is presented against the Order, the Bill may be referred to a Select Committee, and the petitioner shall be allowed to appear and oppose as in the case of Private Bills, and any Act confirming any Provisional Order under this section may be repealed, altered, or amended by a Provisional Order made and confirmed in like manner.

(9) Any expenses incurred by the Secretary of State in respect of any such Order, Provisional Order, or confirming Bill shall be defrayed out of moneys provided by Parliament.

(10) Nothing in this section shall affect the rights of a workman to recover compensation in respect of a disease to which this section does not apply, if the disease is a personal injury by accident within the meaning of this Act.

9. *Application to Workmen in Employment of Crown*

(1) This Act shall not apply to persons in the naval or military service of the Crown, but otherwise shall apply to workmen employed by or under the Crown to whom this Act would apply if the employer were a private person:

Provided that in the case of a person employed in the private service of the Crown, the head of that department of the Royal Household in which he was employed at the time of the accident shall be deemed to be his employer.

(2) The Treasury may, by warrant laid before Parliament, modify for the purposes of this Act their warrant made under section one of the Superannuation Act, 1887, and notwithstanding anything in that Act, or any such warrant, may frame schemes with a view to their being certified by the Registrar of Friendly Societies under this Act.

10. *Appointment and Remuneration of Medical Referees and Arbitrators*

(1) The Secretary of State may appoint such legally qualified medical practitioners to be medical referees for the purposes of this Act as he may, with the sanction of the Treasury, determine, and the remuneration of, and other expenses incurred by, medical referees under this Act shall, subject to regulations made by the Treasury, be paid out of moneys provided by Parliament.

Where a medical referee has been employed as a medical practitioner in connection with any case by or on behalf of an employer or workman or by any insurers interested, he shall not act as medical referee in that case.

(2) The remuneration of an arbitrator appointed by a judge of county courts under the Second Schedule to this Act shall be paid out of moneys provided by Parliament in accordance with regulations made by the Treasury.

11. *Detention of Ships*

(1) If it is alleged that the owners of any ship are liable as such owners to pay compensation under this Act, and at any time that ship is found in any port or river of England or Ireland, or within three miles of the coast thereof, a judge of any court of record in England or Ireland may, upon its being shown to him by any person applying in accordance with the rules of the court that the owners are probably liable as such to pay such compensation, and that none of the owners reside in the United Kingdom, issue an order directed to any officer of customs or other officer named by the judge requiring him to detain the ship until such time as the owners, agent, master, or consignee thereof have paid such compensation, or have given security, to be approved by the judge, to abide the event of any proceedings that may be instituted to recover such compensation and to pay such compensation and costs as may be awarded thereon ; and any officer of customs or other officer to whom the order is directed shall detain the ship accordingly.

(2) In any legal proceeding to recover such compensation, the person giving security shall be made defendant, and the production of the order of the judge, made in relation to the security, shall be conclusive evidence of the liability of the defendant to the proceeding.

(3) Section 692 of the Merchant Shipping Act, 1894, shall apply to the detention of a ship under this Act as it applies to the detention of a ship under that Act, and, if the owner of a ship is a corporation, it shall for the purposes of this section be deemed to reside in the United Kingdom if it has an office in the United Kingdom at which service of writs can be effected.

12. Returns as to Compensation

(1) Every employer in any industry to which the Secretary of State may direct that this section shall apply shall, on or before such day in every year as the Secretary of State may direct, send to the Secretary of State a correct return specifying the number of injuries in respect of which compensation has been paid by him under this Act during the previous year, and the amount of such compensation, together with such other particulars as to the compensation as the Secretary of State may direct, and in default of complying with this section shall be liable on conviction under the Summary Jurisdiction Acts to a fine not exceeding five pounds.

(2) Any regulations made by the Secretary of State containing such directions as aforesaid shall be laid before both Houses of Parliament as soon as may be after they are made.

13. Definitions

In this Act, unless the context otherwise requires —

" Employer " includes any body of persons corporate or unincorporate and the legal personal representative of a deceased employer, and, where the services of a workman are temporarily lent or let on hire to another person by the person with whom the workman has entered into a contract of service or apprenticeship, the latter shall, for the purposes of this Act, be deemed to continue to be the employer of the workman whilst he is working for that other person ;

" Workman " does not include any person employed otherwise than by way of manual labour whose remuneration exceeds two hundred and fifty pounds a year, or a person whose employment is of a casual nature and who is employed otherwise than for the purposes of the employer's trade or business, or a member of a police force, or an outworker, or a member of the employer's family dwelling in his house, but, save as aforesaid, means any person who has entered into or works under a contract of service or apprenticeship with an employer, whether by way of manual labour, clerical work, or otherwise, and whether the contract is expressed or implied, is oral or in writing ;

Any reference to a workman who has been injured shall, where the workman is dead, include a reference to his legal personal representative or to his dependants or other person to whom or for whose benefit compensation is payable ;

" Dependants " means such of the members of the workman's family as were wholly or in part dependent upon the earnings of the workman at the time of his death, or would but for the incapacity due to the accident have been so dependent, and where the workman, being the parent or grandparent of an illegitimate child, leaves such a child so dependent upon his earnings, or, being an illegitimate child, leaves a parent or grandparent so dependent upon his earnings, shall include such an illegitimate child and parent or grandparent respectively ;

" Member of a family " means wife or husband, father, mother, grandfather, grandmother, step-father, step-mother, son, daughter, grandson, granddaughter, step-son, step-daughter, brother, sister, half-brother, half-sister ;

"Ship," "vessel," "seaman," and "port" have the same meanings as in the Merchant Shipping Act, 1894;

"Manager," in relation to a ship, means the ship's husband or other person to whom the management of the ship is entrusted by or on behalf of the owner;

"Police force" means a police force to which the Police Act, 1890, or the Police (Scotland) Act, 1890, applies, the City of London Police Force, the Royal Irish Constabulary, and the Dublin Metropolitan Police Force;

"Outworker" means a person to whom articles or materials are given out to be made up, cleaned, washed, altered, ornamented, finished, or repaired, or adapted for sale, in his own home or on other premises not under the control or management of the person who gave out the materials or articles;

The exercise and performance of the powers and duties of a local or other public authority shall, for the purposes of this Act, be treated as the trade or business of the authority;

"County court," "judge of the county court," "registrar of the county court," "plaintiff," and "rules of court," as respects Scotland, mean respectively sheriff court, sheriff, sheriff clerk, pursuer, and act of sederunt.

14. Special Provisions as to Scotland

In Scotland, where a workman raises an action against his employer independently of this Act in respect of any injury caused by accident arising out of and in the course of the employment, the action, if raised in the sheriff court and concluding for damages under the Employers' Liability Act, 1880, or alternatively at common law or under the Employers' Liability Act, 1880, shall, notwithstanding anything contained in that Act, not be removed under that Act or otherwise to the Court of Session, nor shall it be appealed to that court otherwise than by appeal on a question of law; and for the purposes of such appeal the provisions of the Second

Schedule to this Act in regard to an appeal from the decision of the sheriff on any question of law determined by him as arbitrator under this Act shall apply.

15. *Provisions as to existing Contracts and Schemes*

(1) Any contract (other than a contract substituting the provisions of a scheme certified under the Workmen's Compensation Act, 1897, for the provisions of that Act) existing at the commencement of this Act, whereby a workman relinquishes any right to compensation from the employer for personal injury arising out of and in the course of his employment, shall not, for the purposes of this Act, be deemed to continue after the time at which the workman's contract of service would determine if notice of the determination thereof were given at the commencement of this Act.

(2) Every scheme under the Workmen's Compensation Act, 1897, in force at the commencement of this Act shall, if re-certified by the Registrar of Friendly Societies, have effect as if it were a scheme under this Act.

(3) The Registrar shall re-certify any such scheme if it is proved to his satisfaction that the scheme conforms, or has been so modified as to conform, with the provisions of this Act as to schemes.

(4) If any such scheme has not been so re-certified before the expiration of six months from the commencement of this Act, the certificate thereof shall be revoked.

16. *Commencement and Repeal*

(1) This Act shall come into operation on the first day of July 1907, but, except so far as it relates to references to medical referees, and proceedings consequential thereon, shall not apply in any case where the accident happened before the commencement of this Act.

(2) The Workmen's Compensation Acts, 1897 and 1900, are hereby repealed, but shall continue to apply to cases where the accident happened before the commencement of this Act, except to the extent to which this Act applies to those cases.

17. Short Title

This Act may be cited as the Workmen's Compensation Act, 1906.

FIRST SCHEDULE

Scale and Conditions of Compensation

(1) The amount of compensation under this Act shall be —

    (a) Where death results from the injury —

        (i) if the workman leaves any dependants wholly dependent upon his earnings, a sum equal to his earnings in the employment of the same employer during the three years next preceding the injury, or the sum of one hundred and fifty pounds, whichever of those sums is the larger, but not exceeding in any case three hundred pounds, provided that the amount of any weekly payments made under this Act, and any lump sum paid in redemption thereof, shall be deducted from such sum, and, if the period of the workman's employment by the said employer has been less than the said three years, then the amount of his earnings during the said three years shall be deemed to be one hundred and fifty-six times his average weekly earnings during the period of his actual employment under the said employer;

       (ii) if the workman does not leave any such dependants, but leaves any dependants in part dependent upon his earnings, such sum, not exceeding in any case the amount payable under the foregoing provisions, as may be agreed upon, or, in default of agreement, may be determined, on arbitration under this Act, to be reasonable and proportionate to the injury to the said dependants; and

(iii) if he leaves no dependants, the reasonable expenses of his medical attendance and burial, not exceeding ten pounds ;

(b) where total or partial incapacity for work results from the injury, a weekly payment during the incapacity not exceeding fifty per cent of his average weekly earnings during the previous twelve months, if he has been so long employed, but if not then for any less period during which he has been in the employment of the same employer, such weekly payment not to exceed one pound: Provided that —

(a) if the incapacity lasts less than two weeks no compensation shall be payable in respect of the first week ; and

(b) as respects the weekly payments during total incapacity of a workman who is under twenty-one years of age at the date of the injury, and whose average weekly earnings are less than twenty shillings, one hundred per cent shall be substituted for fifty per cent of his average weekly earnings, but the weekly payment shall in no case exceed ten shillings.

(2) For the purposes of the provisions of this schedule relating to "earnings" and "average weekly earnings" of a workman, the following rules shall be observed :

(a) average weekly earnings shall be computed in such manner as is best calculated to give the rate per week at which the workman was being remunerated. Provided that where by reason of the shortness of the time during which the workman has been in the employment of his employer, or the casual nature of the employment, or the terms of the employment, it is impracticable at the date of the accident to compute the rate of remuneration, regard may be had to the average weekly amount which, during the twelve months previous to the accident, was being earned by a person in the same grade employed at the same work by the same employer, or, if there is no person so employed, by a person in the same grade employed in the same class of employment and in the same district ;

(*b*) where the workman had entered into concurrent contracts of service with two or more employers under which he worked at one time for one such employer and at another time for another such employer, his average weekly earnings shall be computed as if his earnings under all such contracts were earnings in the employment of the employer for whom he was working at the time of the accident ;

(*c*) employment by the same employer shall be taken to mean employment by the same employer in the grade in which the workman was employed at the time of the accident, uninterrupted by absence from work due to illness or any other unavoidable cause ;

(*d*) where the employer has been accustomed to pay to the workman a sum to cover any special expenses entailed on him by the nature of his employment, the sum so paid shall not be reckoned as part of the earnings.

(3) In fixing the amount of the weekly payment, regard shall be had to any payment, allowance, or benefit which the workman may receive from the employer during the period of his incapacity, and in the case of partial incapacity the weekly payment shall in no case exceed the difference between the amount of the average weekly earnings of the workman before the accident and the average weekly amount which he is earning or is able to earn in some suitable employment or business after the accident, but shall bear such relation to the amount of that difference as under the circumstances of the case may appear proper.

(4) Where a workman has given notice of an accident, he shall, if so required by the employer, submit himself for examination by a duly qualified medical practitioner provided and paid by the employer, and, if he refuses to submit himself to such examination, or in any way obstructs the same, his right to compensation, and to take or prosecute any proceeding under this Act in relation to compensation, shall be suspended until such examination has taken place.

(5) The payment in the case of death shall, unless otherwise ordered as herein-after provided, be paid into the county court, and any sum so paid into court shall, subject to rules of court and the provisions of this schedule, be invested, applied, or otherwise dealt with by the court in such manner as the court in its discretion thinks fit for the benefit of the persons entitled thereto under this Act, and the receipt of the registrar of the court shall be a sufficient discharge in respect of the amount paid in :

Provided that, if so agreed, the payment in case of death shall, if the workman leaves no dependants, be made to his legal personal representative, or, if he has no such representative, to the person to whom the expenses of medical attendance and burial are due.

[6–22. Various administrative details omitted.]

SECOND SCHEDULE

Arbitration, etc.

(1) For the purpose of settling any matter which under this Act is to be settled by arbitration, if any committee, representative of an employer and his workmen, exists with power to settle matters under this Act in the case of the employer and workmen, the matter shall, unless either party objects by notice in writing sent to the other party before the committee meet to consider the matter, be settled by the arbitration of such committee, or be referred by them in their discretion to arbitration as herein-after provided.

(2) If either party so objects, or there is no such committee, or the committee so refers the matter or fails to settle the matter within six months from the date of the claim, the matter shall be settled by a single arbitrator agreed on by the parties, or in the absence of agreement by the judge of the county court, according to the procedure prescribed by rules of court.

(3) In England the matter, instead of being settled by the county court, may, if the Lord Chancellor so authorises, be settled according to the like procedure, by a single arbitrator appointed by that judge, and the arbitrator so appointed shall, for the purposes of this Act, have all the powers of that judge.

(4) The Arbitration Act, 1889, shall not apply to any arbitration under this Act; but a committee or an arbitrator may, if they or he think fit, submit any question of law for the decision of the judge of the county court, and the decision of the judge on any question of law, either on such submission, or in any case where he himself settles the matter under this Act, or where he gives any decision or makes any order under this Act, shall be final, unless within the time and in accordance with the conditions prescribed by rules of the Supreme Court either party appeals to the Court of Appeal; and the judge of the county court, or the arbitrator appointed by him, shall, for the purpose of proceedings under this Act, have the same powers of procuring the attendance of witnesses and the production of documents as if the proceedings were an action in the county court.

(5) A judge of county courts may, if he thinks fit, summon a medical referee to sit with him as an assessor.

(6) Rules of court may make provision for the appearance in any arbitration under this Act of any party by some other person.

(7) The costs of and incidental to the arbitration and proceedings connected therewith shall be in the discretion of the committee, arbitrator, or judge of the county court, subject as respects such judge and an arbitrator appointed by him to rules of court. The costs, whether before a committee or an arbitrator or in the county

court, shall not exceed the limit prescribed by rules of court, and shall be taxed in manner prescribed by those rules and such taxation may be reviewed by the judge of the county court.

[8–18. Various details omitted.]

THIRD SCHEDULE

DESCRIPTION OF DISEASE	DESCRIPTION OF PROCESS
Anthrax	Handling of wool, hair, bristles, hides, and skins.
Lead poisoning or its sequelæ . . .	Any process involving the use of lead or its preparations or compounds.
Mercury poisoning or its sequelæ .	Any process involving the use of mercury or its preparations or compounds.
Phosphorus poisoning or its sequelæ	Any process involving the use of phosphorus or its preparations or compounds.
Arsenic poisoning or its sequelæ .	Any process involving the use of arsenic or its preparations or compounds.
Ankylostomiasis	Mining.

Extract 11

WORKMEN'S COMPENSATION (ANGLO-FRENCH CONVENTION) ACT, 1909

(9 Edw. 7, ch. 16)

An Act to authorise the making of such modifications in the Workmen's Compensation Act, 1906, in its application to French Citizens, as may be necessary to give effect to a Convention between His Majesty and the President of the French Republic.   (20th October 1909)

Whereas His Majesty the King and the President of the French Republic have concluded the Convention set out in the Schedule to this Act, but effect cannot be given to the Convention unless certain modifications are made in the Workmen's Compensation Act, 1906, so far as it applies to workmen who are French citizens.

Be it therefore enacted by the King's most Excellent Majesty, by and with the advice and consent of the Lords Spiritual and Temporal, and Commons, in this present Parliament assembled, and by the authority of the same, as follows :

I. His Majesty may, by Order in Council, make such modifications in the Workmen's Compensation Act, 1906, in its application to workmen who are French citizens, as appear to him to be necessary to give effect to the said Convention ; and the Workmen's Compensation Act, 1906, shall apply to such workmen, subject to the modifications contained in the Order.

II. This Act may be cited as the Workmen's Compensation (Anglo-French Convention) Act, 1909.

SCHEDULE

Convention signed at Paris the 3rd day of July 1909

ARTICLE I

British subjects who meet with accidents arising out of their employment as workmen in France, and persons entitled to claim through or having rights derivable from them, shall enjoy the benefits of the compensation and guarantees secured to French citizens by the legislation in force in France in regard to the liability of employers in respect of such accidents.

Reciprocally, French citizens who meet with accidents arising out of their employment as workmen in the United Kingdom of Great Britain and Ireland, and persons entitled to claim through or having rights derivable from them, shall enjoy the benefits of the compensation and guarantees secured to British subjects by the legislation in force in the United Kingdom of Great Britain and Ireland in regard to compensation for such accidents, supplemented as specified in Article 5.

ARTICLE 2

Nevertheless, the present Convention shall not apply to the case of a person engaged in a business having its headquarters in one of the two Contracting States, but temporarily detached for employment in the other Contracting State, and meeting with an accident in the course of that employment, if at the time of the accident the said employment has lasted less than six months. In this case the persons interested shall only be entitled to the compensation and guarantees provided by the law of the former State.

The same rule shall apply in the case of persons engaged in transport services and employed at intervals, whether regular or not, in the country other than that in which the headquarters of the business are established.

ARTICLE 3

The British and French authorities will reciprocally lend their good offices to facilitate the administration of their respective laws as aforesaid.

ARTICLE 4

The present Convention shall be ratified, and the ratifications shall be exchanged at Paris, as soon as possible.

It shall be applicable in France and in the United Kingdom of Great Britain and Ireland to all accidents happening after one month from the time of its publication in the two countries in the manner prescribed by their respective laws, and it shall remain binding until the expiration of one year from the date on which it shall have been denounced by one or other of the two Contracting Parties.

Nevertheless, the ratification mentioned in the preceding Article shall not take place till the legislation at present in force in the United Kingdom of Great Britain and Ireland in regard to workmen's compensation has been supplemented, so far as concerns accidents to French citizens arising out of their employment as workmen, by arrangements to the following effect:

(*a*) That the compensation payable shall in every case be fixed by an award of the County Court:

(*b*) That in any case of redemption of weekly payments the total sum payable shall, provided it exceeds a sum equivalent to the capital value of an annuity of 4 *l.* (100 fr.), be paid into Court, to be employed in the purchase of an annuity for the benefit of the person entitled thereto:

(*c*) That in those cases in which a lump sum representing the compensation payable shall have been paid by the employer into the County Court, if the injured workman returns to reside in France, or if the dependants resided in France at the time of his death or subsequently return to reside in France, the total sum due to the injured workman or to his dependants shall be paid over through the County Court to the *Caisse Nationale Française des Retraites pour la Vieillesse*, who shall employ it in the purchase of an annuity according to its tariff at the time of the payment; and further, that, in the case in which a lump sum shall not have been paid into Court, and the injured workman returns to reside in France, the compensation shall be remitted to him through the County Court at such intervals and in such way as may be agreed upon by the competent authorities of the two countries:

(*d*) That in respect of all the acts done by the County Court in pursuance of the legislation in regard to workmen's compensation, as well as in the execution of the present

Convention, French citizens shall be exempt from all expenses and fees :

(e) That at the beginning of each year His Majesty's principal Secretary of State for the Home Department will send to the *Département du Travail et de la Prévoyance sociale* a record of all judicial decisions given in the course of the preceding year under the legislation in regard to workmen's compensation in the case of French citizens injured by accident in the United Kingdom of Great Britain and Ireland.

CHAPTER II

TRADE UNIONISM

[In 1906 there were 1200 unions in Great Britain with a total membership of 2,113,806. They were recognised as legal associations by virtue of statutes enacted between 1871 and 1876, but the Taff Vale judgment had recently decided that they were corporations which could be sued with costs and damages for the action of any of their agents whenever such action had caused loss to other persons. How Mr. Balfour's Government failed in 1905 to pass into law a bill to protect the funds of the trade unions, which had been placed in jeopardy by that celebrated decision, has already been noted.[1] The judgment seriously threatened the future welfare of trade unionism because, with the financial danger ever before them, many workmen lost confidence in it.

One of the first steps taken, therefore, by the new Liberal Government was to present a measure intended to reverse the Taff Vale judgment and to allow reasonable liberty to the unions in the matter of "picketing." The bill was introduced in the House of Commons on March 28, 1906, by Sir John Walton, the Attorney-General (*Extract 12*), and was read a first time after a short debate, in which several Labour members expressed a strong preference for a solution of their own; and Sir Edward Carson, Lord Robert Cecil, and other staunch Conservatives protested against provisions tending to convert trade unions into what they described as a privileged class.

The Government proposed to limit the liability of trade union funds for damages to cases where the act complained of was that

---

[1] Cf. supra, p. 13.

77

of the executive committee of a union or of its authorised agent acting in accordance with its express or implied orders, or, at least, not contravening them. The Labour members, however, preferred that trade unions should not in any case be actionable for damages sustained through the conduct of their members, and a Bill embodying this provision was brought forward for second reading by Mr. W. Hudson, one of their number, representing Newcastle-on-Tyne. It was strongly opposed by Mr. F. E. Smith, who denied that trade unions had ever enjoyed the immunity now claimed for them and protested vigorously against the Bill as creating a class privilege. Mr. Keir Hardie, supporting the Labour Bill, put the difference between the Labour and the Ministerial measures neatly by declaring that trade unionists would not be satisfied with mere barbed-wire entanglements for the protection of their funds, but would insist upon their removal out of the range of the enemies' guns. The Prime Minister, after declaring that the suspicion formerly entertained of trade unions had given place to a general recognition that they were beneficial institutions, said that he had voted two or three times previously for Bills on the lines of that now under discussion, and he proposed to vote for the Labour Bill. This announcement was loudly cheered by the Labour members, and the Prime Minister proceeded to argue that the difference between the two bills was one of method rather than of principle. Subsequently, after application of the closure, the second reading of the Labour measure was passed by 416 to 66, several Ministers and some sixty or seventy other Liberals not voting.

The original Government Bill was read a second time on April 25. During the Committee Stage, the Attorney-General moved, on August 3, the addition of the special clause which had characterised the Labour Bill, prohibiting actions against unions, whether of workmen or masters, for the recovery of damages in respect of tortious acts. On the new clause Sir Edward Carson suggested that it might have run : " The king can do no wrong ; neither can trades unions." The Attorney-General defended the change at length, and, after a number of legal members had spoken, the clause was agreed to by 257 to 29 and the Bill was reported as amended — the Labour members' alternative Bill of course having been dropped.

The Bill passed through the various later stages against no little opposition, especially among the Lords, and finally received the royal assent on December 21. It was repeatedly affirmed that the Lords would have rejected the Bill altogether had they not feared the cumulative effect on the country of their rejection, in the same year, of the Education Bill and the Plural Voting Bill.

The Trade Unions and Trade Disputes Act, in its final form, is given as *Extract 13*. For convenience of reference, important portions of the Trade Union Acts, 1871 and 1876, and of the Conspiracy and Protection of Property Act, 1875, are inserted as *Extracts 14, 15,* and *16*, respectively.

It may be well to state at this point that trade unionism was subsequently affected by another remarkable judicial decision — the celebrated Osborne judgment, handed down by the House of Lords on December 21, 1909, the effect of which was to make it illegal to use the moneys of any trade union for paying members of Parliament. It had always been customary in the United Kingdom not to salary members of Parliament, with the result that the poor man had been either excluded from the House of Commons altogether or forced to accept financial aid from constituents or special friends. The greater number of the Labour members who entered the House in 1906 owed their places to funds advanced by workingmen, especially by trade unions. In consequence of the Osborne judgment, the Labour party felt that their very existence was imperilled, but the Liberal Government reassured them in part by securing statutory payment of all members (£400 per annum), beginning in 1911. In *Extract 17* are parts of two speeches delivered in the course of the debate on the payment of members, the one by Mr. Arthur Lee, a strong Conservative opponent, and the other by Mr. Ramsay Macdonald, the Labour leader.]

Extract 12

INTRODUCTION OF TRADE UNIONS AND TRADE DISPUTES BILL

(Sir John Walton, Attorney-General, Commons, March 28, 1906)

SIR JOHN WALTON [1]: . . . In their early days trade unions had to struggle against the ban of common law and repressive statutes. They were organisations which interfered with the perfect freedom of relationship between employers and employed and the free course of trade, and until a very recent period of our history this difficulty prevented any large extension of this industrial movement. In 1824 and 1825 repressive legislation disappeared; and in 1859 a declaration was made giving to these societies the right to exercise the faculty of persuasion, provided they did so in a reasonable and peaceful manner. In 1867 the pulse of the democracy was quickened by the Borough Franchise Act of that year, with the result that we had a Royal Commission followed by the charter of trade unionism of 1871, afterwards amplified and expanded by the supplementary Act of 1875. It is true that the legislation of 1871 and 1875 was limited in its scope. Its main aim was to remove the ban of the common law and the stigma of illegality from the operations of these bodies. It enabled them to register themselves, to frame rules, to amass property, to appoint agents, and to defend themselves and their funds from attack. It also created an important declaration limiting their criminal liability to those Acts only which are criminal if committed by individuals.

But in regard to their responsibility to the civil law, legislation is absolutely silent. That silence has led to serious controversy in determining the aim of Parliament in connection with that legislation. The House of Lords, which is the authoritative exponent of our law, and binds the High Court of Parliament as it binds every

[1] Parliamentary Debates, Fourth Series, vol. 154, col. 1295 sqq.

other Court in the realm, has pointed out that that silence does not disturb the liability under which these unions rested under the common law of the country, that the fact of registration made them suable in respect of wrongful conduct in the name of the organisation which was placed on the register, and that since the year 1883 the amalgamation of our systems of judicature as they existed under the common law and in Courts of equity made that liability enforceable by a form of action which up to that moment was only known in the Courts of Chancery.

The period of thirty years between 1871 and 1901 was a period of great material prosperity in regard to these unions. Their numbers increased, their branches spread, their wealth grew. The funds which were available to meet claims that might be made upon them induced actions to be brought in numerous quarters for the purpose of satisfying claims for redress for injuries attributed to conduct of which members of the community complained, and from 1892 onward a series of actions were successfully tried which at first took the form of actions for injunctions and afterwards of actions for damages. It is impossible to say that the result of this litigation did not create a serious situation. Trade unions are institutions which consist of the working-classes. Their funds represent the hard-earned savings of a large and most worthy section of the community, and they have been contributed in no small degree for the purpose of making provision against misfortune. This liability and its consequences have created a problem with which it is necessary that Parliament should deal, and which the Government have done their best to solve. In our opinion the law needs most careful examination, redefinition, and modification, and some of the general principles of the law require regulation in their application to these bodies.

In the first place, let me call attention to the law of conspiracy. The expression " conspiracy " is a little apt to shake timid nerves, and to suggest periods of our history when our Constitution was unstable and when sinister designs against the Crown and society

were incidents of our public life.   But conspiracy in law simply
means combination to violate the rights of another.   Combination is
a conspiracy or agreement, and the fact that its object is to violate
a right, constitutes it a criminal act and makes it subject to a claim
for damages on the part of the person whose right has been violated by the act so committed.   This is a part of our law which I
may describe as one of the blank spaces upon the juridical map.
There are a few rough tracks across it emanating from different
sources, and generally leading to different results.   The wary and
prudent litigant gives it as wide a berth as possible because it is the
region of judge-made law ; and when he is once lost in that area
it is not easy for him always to know exactly where he is or by
what means he will escape from it.

We propose that this region shall be carefully plotted out, that
its frontiers shall be limited, and that there shall be carried through
it a statutory highway which, so far, at any rate, as these organisations are concerned, may be safely travelled by the most unwary
traveller.   The legislation of 1875, while it defined the law of conspiracy in its criminal aspect, left that law, in so far as it is a department of civil jurisprudence, entirely untouched ; and the result
has been that this area has been the field of fierce struggles between disputants of legal eminence.   I doubt whether in our time
the serene judicial atmosphere has ever been so much disturbed
as it has been by different theories with regard to the law of
conspiracy. . . .

We propose to call in aid the principle which was established by
the Act of 1875.   It was there declared that the character of an
act committed by a trade union within the purview of the criminal
law should depend on the consideration of whether it was criminal
or not, assuming it to be the act of an individual.   And so we
say in regard to the applications of the civil law, that that act
shall be right or wrong, shall be lawful or unlawful, according as
it would be lawful or unlawful, judged on the assumption that it
has been committed by an individual and not by a combination ;

and I submit to the House that there is no other solution than that which I have suggested.

The next subject upon which I propose to say a few words is that of peaceful picketing, which I prefer to call the right of peaceful persuasion. What is the right of peaceful persuasion ? It is an essential part of the right to strike. How is it possible to strike unless you can persuade your fellows to join you ? How is it possible successfully to conduct a strike unless you may persuade men who are introduced from a distance not to interfere between the strikers and their employer ? The right to persuade those who would naturally join and swell your ranks, and the right to dissuade those who are brought in with a view to prevent the success of a strike, is absolutely essential for the effective conduct of an operation of that kind. The law at present is in a condition that I think I may fairly describe as impracticable, if not absurd. How does it stand ? It is held to be perfectly lawful to point out to the men what are the points of difference. You may either ask for information with regard to the strike, or you may give them information with regard to the nature of the conflict between the workman and the employer. But if you go one step further and so present the information you give them as to make your appeal in the nature of persuasion, you are then violating the law. The distinction is one which a legal mind may grasp ; but it is impossible to suppose that the distinction can be grasped by any advocate of a trade union who endeavours within the limits of the law as it now stands to give information to persons who are introduced from a distance and who are sought to be employed to take the places which the strikers have vacated. There are many illustrations in the decided cases which show that unless this part of the law is altered it is impossible to conduct a strike successfully.

Further, in enacting, as we purpose to enact in express terms, the right peaceably to persuade, we are not calling upon the House to make a new law. We are only reviving a law which is as old as the year 1859, because in that year there was a provision put into the statute upon this subject which was then passed, which attached an interpretation to a restrictive provision in an earlier Act. The statute used this language. It provided that no person should, by reason merely of his endeavouring peaceably, and in a reasonable manner, and without threats and intimidation, direct or indirect, to persuade, be deemed guilty of molestation or obstruction within the meaning of the Act of 1825, or should, therefore, be subject to prosecution or indictment for conspiracy. It may be said that the Act of 1875 repealed the Act of 1859. There is certainly no indication of repeal in that Act, and the history of the debates of that period shows that it was thought that the earlier provision held good. Therefore, in regard to this matter, we are only proposing to ask the House to take a step which occurs to us as eminently reasonable, as representing practical justice, and one which has the advantage of statutory precedent. . . .

Let me summarise in a word or two what we contend is the result of all this legislation. In the first place, we remove the fetter which is placed upon the operations of these unions by the action of conspiracy. We give them permission, so long as they observe the law as it affects individuals, to carry out their own policy upon lines which commend themselves to their favorable consideration, and we allow them to know beforehand whether the conduct which they propose to pursue will or will not be in conformity with the law. In the second place, we restore and give legislative sanction to the exercise of the right of peaceful persuasion. In the third place, we so define and regulate the application of the law of agency as to obviate the injustice which I have indicated and given illustrations of. We do that first of all by giving to each of these unions an authoritative and articulate organ. We allow them to speak through some defined agent. We allow them to delegate their authority subject to certain restrictions. We give them the right to disapprove of or repudiate acts which have been done in their name but without their approval or sanction.

I think that when this Bill is considered by the House, and dispassionately considered by every section of this House, it may be regarded as a satisfactory solution of a very complicated question. At all events it is an honest attempt to solve the question. We have sought, as far as we can, to do what we consider is justice to these organisations without inflicting injustice upon the community at large. It may be that the Bill will not commend itself to all sections of opinion in this House. It is very seldom that Acts of Parliament do, but it is undoubtedly the fact that some of the statutes which have been most successful have on their introduction offended Members on both sides. Compromise, however, is the genius of politics, although it is not a very pleasant lesson to learn. . . .

Extract 13

TRADE DISPUTES ACT, 1906

(*6 Edw. 7, ch. 47*)

An Act to provide for the regulation of Trades Unions and Trade Disputes. (21st December 1906)

Be it enacted by the King's most Excellent Majesty, by and with the advice and consent of the Lords Spiritual and Temporal, and Commons, in this present Parliament assembled, and by the authority of the same, as follows:

1. Amendment of Former Act

The following paragraph shall be added as a new paragraph after the first paragraph of section three of the Conspiracy and Protection of Property Act, 1875:

" An act done in pursuance of an agreement or combination by two or more persons shall, if done in contemplation or furtherance of a trade dispute, not be actionable unless the act, if done without any such agreement or combination, would be actionable."

2. *Peaceful Picketing*

(1) It shall be lawful for one or more persons, acting on their own behalf or on behalf of a trade union or of an individual employer or firm in contemplation or furtherance of a trade dispute, to attend at or near a house or place where a person resides or works or carries on business or happens to be, if they so attend merely for the purpose of peacefully obtaining or communicating information, or of peacefully persuading any person to work or abstain from working.

(2) Section seven of the Conspiracy and Protection of Property Act, 1875, is hereby repealed from "attending at or near" to the end of the section.

3. *Removal of Liability for Interfering with Another Person's Business*

An act done by a person in contemplation or furtherance of a trade dispute shall not be actionable on the ground only that it induces some other person to break a contract of employment or that it is an interference with the trade, business, or employment of some other person, or with the right of some other person to dispose of his capital or his labour as he wills.

4. *Prohibition of Actions of Tort against Trade Unions*

(1) An action against a trade union, whether of workmen or masters, or against any members or officials thereof on behalf of themselves and all other members of the trade union in respect of any tortious act alleged to have been committed by or on behalf of the trade union, shall not be entertained by any court.

(2) Nothing in this section shall affect the liability of the trustees of a trade union to be sued in the events provided for by the Trades Union Act, 1871, section nine, except in respect of any tortious act committed by or on behalf of the union in contemplation or in furtherance of a trade dispute.

5. *Short Title and Construction*

(1) This Act may be cited as the Trade Disputes Act, 1906, and the Trade Union Acts, 1871 and 1876, and this Act may be cited together as the Trade Union Acts, 1871 to 1906.

(2) In this Act the expression "trade union" has the same meaning as in the Trade Union Acts, 1871 and 1876, and shall include any combination as therein defined, notwithstanding that such combination may be the branch of a trade union.

(3) In this Act and in the Conspiracy and Protection of Property Act, 1875, the expression "trade dispute" means any dispute between employers and workmen, or between workmen and workmen, which is connected with the employment or non-employment, or the terms of the employment, or with the conditions of labour, of any person, and the expression "workmen" means all persons employed in trade or industry, whether or not in the employment of the employer with whom a trade dispute arises; and, in section three of the last-mentioned Act, the words "between employers and workmen" shall be repealed.

Extract 14

TRADE UNION ACT, 1871

(*34 & 35 Vict., ch. 31, in part*)

2. *Trade Union not Criminal*

The purposes of any trade union shall not, by reason merely that they are in restraint of trade, be deemed to be unlawful so as to render any member of such trade union liable to criminal prosecution for conspiracy or otherwise.

3. Trade Union not Unlawful for Civil Purposes

The purposes of any trade union shall not, by reason merely that they are in restraint of trade, be unlawful so as to render void or voidable any agreement or trust.

4. Trade Union Contracts

Nothing in this Act shall enable any court to entertain any legal proceeding instituted with the object of directly enforcing or recovering damages for the breach of any of the following agreements, namely,

1. Any agreement between members of a trade union as such, concerning the conditions on which any members for the time being of such trade union shall or shall not sell their goods, transact business, employ, or be employed :
2. Any agreement for the payment by any person of any subscription or penalty to a trade union :
3. Any agreement for the application of the funds of a trade union —
   (*a*) To provide benefits to members ; or
   (*b*) To furnish contributions to any employer or workman not a member of such trade union, in consideration of such employer or workman acting in conformity with the rules or resolutions of such trade union ; or
   (*c*) To discharge any fine imposed upon any person by sentence of a court of justice ; or,
4. Any agreement made between one trade union and another; or,
5. Any bond to secure the performance of any of the abovementioned agreements.

But nothing in this section shall be deemed to constitute any of the above-mentioned agreements unlawful. . . .

6. Registry of Trade Unions

Any seven or more members of a trade union may by subscribing their names to the rules of the union, and otherwise complying with the provisions of this Act with respect to registry, register such trade union under this Act, provided that if any one of the purposes of such trade union be unlawful such registration shall be void.

7. Buildings for Trade Unions

It shall be lawful for any trade union registered under this Act to purchase or take upon lease in the names of the trustees for the time being of such union any land not exceeding one acre, and to sell, exchange, mortgage, or let the same, and no purchaser, assignee, mortgagee, or tenant shall be bound to inquire whether the trustees have authority for any sale, exchange, mortgage, or letting, and the receipt of the trustees shall be a discharge for the money arising therefrom ; and for the purpose of this section every branch of a trade union shall be considered a distinct union.

8. Property of Trade Unions

All real and personal estate whatsoever belonging to any trade union registered under this Act shall be vested in the trustees for the time being of the trade union appointed as provided by this Act, for the use and benefit of such trade union and the members thereof, and the real or personal estate of any branch of a trade union shall be vested in the trustees of such branch, and be under the control of such trustees, their respective executors or administrators, according to their respective claims and interests, and upon the death or removal of any such trustees the same shall vest in the succeeding trustees for the same estate and interest as the former trustees had therein, and subject to the same trusts, without any conveyance or assignment whatsoever, save and except in the case of stocks and securities in the public funds of Great Britain and Ireland, which shall be transferred into the names of such new trustees ; and in all actions, or suits, or indictments, or summary proceedings before any court of summary jurisdiction, touching or concerning any such property, the same shall be stated to be the property of the person or persons for the time being holding the said office of trustee, in their proper names, as trustees of such trade union, without any further description.

9. *Actions by or against Trustees*

The trustees of any trade union registered under this Act, or any other officer of such trade union who may be authorised so to do by the rules thereof, are hereby empowered to bring or defend, or cause to be brought or defended, any action, suit, prosecution, or complaint in any court of law or equity, touching or concerning the property, right, or claim to property of the trade union; and shall and may, in all cases concerning the real or personal property of such trade union, sue and be sued, plead and be impleaded, in any court of law or equity, in their proper names, without other description than the title of their office; and no such action, suit, prosecution or complaint shall be discontinued or shall abate by the death or removal from office of such persons or any of them, but the same shall and may be proceeded in by their successor or successors as if such death, resignation, or removal had not taken place; and such successors shall pay or receive the like costs as if the action, suit, prosecution, or complaint had been commenced in their names for the benefit of or to be reimbursed from the funds of such trade union, and the summons to be issued to such trustee or other officer may be served by leaving the same at the registered office of the trade union.

10. *Limitation of Responsibility*

A trustee of any trade union registered under this Act shall not be liable to make good any deficiency which may arise or happen in the funds of such trade union, but shall be liable only for the moneys which shall be actually received by him on account of such trade union.

11. *Treasurers*

Every treasurer or other officer of a trade union registered under this Act, at such times as by the rules of such trade union he should render such account as herein-after mentioned, or upon being required so to do, shall render to the trustees of the trade union, or to the members of such trade union, at a meeting of the trade union, a just and true account of all moneys received and paid by him since he last rendered the like account, and of the balance then remaining in his hands, and of all bonds or securities of such trade union, which account the said trustees shall cause to be audited by some fit and proper person or persons by them to be appointed ; and such treasurer, if thereunto required, upon the said account being audited, shall forthwith hand over to the said trustees the balance which on such audit appears to be due from him, and shall also, if required, hand over to such trustees all securities and effects, books, papers, and property of the said trade union in his hands or custody ; and if he fail to do so the trustees of the said trade union may sue such treasurer in any competent court for the balance appearing to have been due from him upon the account last rendered by him, and for all the moneys since received by him on account of the said trade union, and for the securities and effects, books, papers, and property in his hands or custody, leaving him to set off in such action the sums, if any, which he may have since paid on account of the said trade union ; and in such action the said trustees shall be entitled to recover their full costs of suit, to be taxed as between attorney and client.

12. Penalties

If any officer, member, or other person being or representing himself to be a member of a trade union registered under this Act, or the nominee, executor, administrator, or assignee of a member thereof, or any person whatsoever, by false representation or imposition obtain possession of any moneys, securities, books, papers, or other effects of such trade union, or, having the same in his possession, wilfully withhold or fraudulently misapply the same or wilfully apply any part of the same to purposes other than those expressed or directed in the rules of such trade union, or any part thereof, the court of summary jurisdiction for the place in which the registered office of the trade union is situate, upon a complaint made by any person on behalf of such trade union, or by the registrar, or in Scotland at the instance of the procurator fiscal of the court to which such complaint is competently made, or of the trade union, with his concurrence, may, by summary order, order such officer, member, or other person to deliver up all such moneys, securities, books, papers, or other effects to the trade union, or to repay the amount of money applied improperly, and to pay, if the court think fit, a further sum of money not exceeding twenty pounds, together with costs not exceeding twenty shillings ; and, in default of such delivery of effects, or repayment of such amount of money, or payment of such penalty and costs aforesaid, the said court may order the said person so convicted to be imprisoned, with or without hard labour, for any time not exceeding three months : Provided, that nothing herein contained shall prevent the said trade union, or in Scotland Her Majesty's Advocate, from proceeding by indictment against the said party ; provided also, that no person shall be proceeded against by indictment if a conviction shall have been previously obtained for the same offence under the provisions of this Act.

13. Registry of Trade Union

With respect to the registry, under this Act, of a trade union, and of the rules thereof, the following provisions shall have effect :

(1) An application to register the trade union and printed copies of the rules, together with a list of the titles and names of the officers, shall be sent to the registrar under this Act :

(2) The registrar upon being satisfied that the trade union has complied with the regulations respecting registry in force under this Act, shall register such trade union and such rules :

(3) No trade union shall be registered under a name identical with that by which any other existing trade union has

been registered, or so nearly resembling such name as to be likely to deceive the members or the public:

(4) Where a trade union applying to be registered has been in operation for more than a year before the date of such application, there shall be delivered to the registrar before the registry thereof a general statement of the receipts, funds, effects, and expenditure of such trade union in the same form, and showing the same particulars as if it were the annual general statement required as herein-after mentioned to be transmitted annually to the registrar:

(5) The registrar upon registering such trade union shall issue a certificate of registry, which certificate, unless proved to have been withdrawn or cancelled, shall be conclusive evidence that the regulations of this Act with respect to registry have been complied with:

(6) One of Her Majesty's Principal Secretaries of State may from time to time make regulations respecting registry under this Act, and respecting the seal (if any) to be used for the purpose of such registry, and the forms to be used for such registry, and the inspection of documents kept by the registrar under this Act, and respecting the fees, if any, to be paid on registry, not exceeding the fees specified in the second schedule to this Act, and generally for carrying this Act into effect.

14. Rules of Registered Trade Unions

With respect to the rules of a trade union registered under this Act, the following provisions shall have effect:

(1) The rules of every such trade union shall contain provisions in respect of the several matters mentioned in the first schedule to this Act:

(2) A copy of the rules shall be delivered by the trade union to every person on demand on payment of a sum not exceeding one shilling.

15. Registered Office of Trade Unions

Every trade union registered under this Act shall have a registered office to which all communications and notices may be addressed; if any trade union under this Act is in operation for seven days without having such an office, such trade union and every officer thereof shall each incur a penalty not exceeding five pounds for every day during which it is so in operation.

Notice of the situation of such registered office, and of any change therein, shall be given to the registrar and recorded by him: until such notice is given the trade union shall not be deemed to have complied with the provisions of this Act.

16. Annual Returns

A general statement of the receipts, funds, effects, and expenditure of every trade union registered under this Act shall be transmitted to the registrar before the first day of June in every year, and shall show fully the assets and liabilities at the date, and the receipts and expenditure during the year preceding the date to which it is made out, of the trade union; and shall show separately the expenditure in respect of the several objects of the trade union, and shall be prepared and made out up to such date, in such form, and shall comprise such particulars, as the registrar may from time to time require; and every member of, and depositor in, any such trade union shall be entitled to receive, on application to the treasurer or secretary of that trade union, a copy of such general statement, without making any payment for the same.

Together with such general statement there shall be sent to the registrar a copy of all alterations of rules and new rules and changes of officers made by the trade union during the year preceding the date up to which the general statement is made out, and a copy of the rules of the trade union as they exist at that date.

Every trade union which fails to comply with or acts in contravention of this section, and also every officer of the trade union, so failing, shall each be liable to a penalty not exceeding five pounds for each offence.

Every person who wilfully makes or orders to be made any false entry in or any omission from any such general statement, or in or from the return of such copies of rules or alterations of rules, shall be liable to a penalty not exceeding fifty pounds for each offence.

17. Registrars

The registrars of the friendly societies in England, Scotland, and Ireland shall be the registrars under this Act.

The registrars shall lay before Parliament annual reports with respect to the matters transacted by such registrars in pursuance of this Act.

18. Fraud

If any person with intent to mislead or defraud gives to any member of a trade union registered under this Act, or to any person intending or applying to become a member of such trade union, a copy of any rules or of any alterations or amendments of the same other than those respectively which exist for the time being, on the pretence that the same are the existing rules of such trade union, or that there are no other rules of such trade union, or if any person with the intent aforesaid gives a copy of any rules to any person on the pretence that such rules are the rules of a trade union registered under this Act which is not so registered, every person so offending shall be deemed guilty of a misdemeanor. . . .

Extract 15

TRADE UNION ACT, 1876

(39 & 40 Vict., ch. 22, in part)

1. Title

This Act and the Trade Union Act, 1871, herein-after termed the principal Act, shall be construed as one Act, and may be cited together as the "Trade Union Acts, 1871 and 1876," and this Act may be cited separately as the "Trade Union Act Amendment Act, 1876." . . .

9. *Membership of Minors*

A person under the age of twenty-one, but above the age of sixteen, may be a member of a trade union, unless provision be made
in the rules thereof to the contrary, and may, subject to the rules
of the trade union, enjoy all the rights of a member except as
herein provided, and execute all instruments and give all acquit-
tances necessary to be executed or given under the rules, but shall
not be a member of the committee of management, trustee, or
treasurer of the trade union.

10. *Nomination*

A member of a trade union not being under the age of sixteen
years may, by writing under his hand, delivered at, or sent to, the
registered office of the trade union, nominate any person not being an officer or servant of the trade union (unless such officer or
servant is the husband, wife, father, mother, child, brother, sister,
nephew, or niece of the nominator), to whom any moneys payable
on the death of such member not exceeding fifty pounds shall be
paid at his decease, and may from time to time revoke or vary such
nomination by a writing under his hand similarly delivered or sent ;
and on receiving satisfactory proof of the death of a nominator,
the trade union shall pay to the nominee the amount due to the
deceased member not exceeding the sum aforesaid.

11. *Change of Name*

A trade union may, with the approval in writing of the chief
registrar of Friendly Societies, or in the case of trade unions registered and doing business exclusively in Scotland or Ireland, of the
assistant registrar for Scotland or Ireland respectively, change its
name by the consent of not less than two thirds of the total
number of members.

No change of name shall affect any right or obligation of the
trade union or of any member thereof, and any pending legal

proceedings may be continued by or against the trustees of the trade union or any other officer who may sue or be sued on behalf of such trade union notwithstanding its new name.

12. Amalgamation

Any two or more trade unions may, by the consent of not less than two thirds of the members of each or every such trade union, become amalgamated together as one trade union, with or without any dissolution or division of the funds of such trade unions, or either or any of them ; but no amalgamation shall prejudice any right of a creditor of either or any union party thereto. . . .

14. Dissolution

The rules of every trade union shall provide for the manner of dissolving the same, and notice of every dissolution of a trade union under the hand of the secretary and seven members of the same, shall be sent within fourteen days thereafter to the central office herein-before mentioned, or, in the case of trade unions registered and doing business exclusively in Scotland or Ireland, to the assistant registrar for Scotland or Ireland respectively, and shall be registered by them : Provided, that the rules of any trade union registered before the passing of this Act shall not be invalidated by the absence of a provision for dissolution. . . .

16. Definition of "Trade Union"

The term " trade union " means any combination, whether temporary or permanent, for regulating the relations between workmen and masters, or between workmen and workmen, or between masters and masters, or for imposing restrictive conditions on the conduct of any trade or business, whether such combination would or would not, if the principal Act had not been passed, have been deemed to have been an unlawful combination by reason of some one or more of its purposes being in restraint of trade.

Extract 16

CONSPIRACY AND PROTECTION OF PROPERTY ACT, 1875

(38 & 39 Vict., ch. 86, in part)

3. Conspiracy, and Protection of Property

An agreement or combination by two or more persons to do or procure to be done any act in contemplation or furtherance of a trade dispute between employers and workmen shall not be indictable as a conspiracy if such act committed by one person would not be punishable as a crime.

Nothing in this section shall exempt from punishment any persons guilty of a conspiracy for which a punishment is awarded by any Act of Parliament.

Nothing in this section shall affect the law relating to riot, unlawful assembly, breach of the peace, or sedition, or any offence against the State or the Sovereign.

A crime for the purposes of this section means an offence punishable on indictment, or an offence which is punishable on summary conviction, and for the commission of which the offender is liable under the statute making the offence punishable to be imprisoned either absolutely or at the discretion of the court as an alternative for some other punishment.

Where a person is convicted of any such agreement or combination as aforesaid to do or procure to be done an act which is punishable only on summary conviction, and is sentenced to imprisonment, the imprisonment shall not exceed three months, or such longer time, if any, as may have been prescribed by the statute for the punishment of the said act when committed by one person.

4. Breach of Contract by Persons employed in Supply of Gas or Water

Where a person employed by a municipal authority or by any company or contractor upon whom is imposed by Act of Parliament the duty, or who have otherwise assumed the duty of supplying any city, borough, town, or place, or any part thereof, with gas or water, wilfully and maliciously breaks a contract of service with that authority or company or contractor, knowing or having reasonable cause to believe that the probable consequences of his so doing, either alone or in combination with others, will be to deprive the inhabitants of that city, borough, town, place, or part, wholly or to a great extent of their supply of gas or water, he shall on conviction thereof by a court of summary jurisdiction, or on indictment as herein-after mentioned, be liable either to pay a penalty not exceeding twenty pounds or to be imprisoned for a term not exceeding three months, with or without hard labour.

Every such municipal authority, company, or contractor as is mentioned in this section shall cause to be posted up, at the gasworks or waterworks, as the case may be, belonging to such authority or company or contractor, a printed copy of this section in some conspicuous place where the same may be conveniently read by the persons employed, and as often as such copy becomes defaced, obliterated, or destroyed, shall cause it to be renewed with all reasonable despatch.

If any municipal authority or company or contractor make default in complying with the provisions of this section in relation to such notice as aforesaid, they or he shall incur on summary conviction a penalty not exceeding five pounds for every day during which such default continues, and every person who unlawfully injures, defaces, or covers up any notice so posted up as aforesaid in pursuance of this Act, shall be liable on summary conviction to a penalty not exceeding forty shillings.

5. *Breach of Contract involving Injury to Persons or Property*

Where any person wilfully and maliciously breaks a contract of service or of hiring, knowing or having reasonable cause to believe that the probable consequences of his so doing, either alone or in combination with others, will be to endanger human life, or cause serious bodily injury, or to expose valuable property whether real or personal to destruction or serious injury, he shall on conviction thereof by a court of summary jurisdiction, or on indictment as herein-after mentioned, be liable either to pay a penalty not exceeding twenty pounds, or to be imprisoned for a term not exceeding three months, with or without hard labour.

6. *Penalty for Neglect by Master*

Where a master, being legally liable to provide for his servant or apprentice necessary food, clothing, medical aid, or lodging, wilfully and without lawful excuse refuses or neglects to provide the same, whereby the health of the servant or apprentice is or is likely to be seriously or permanently injured, he shall on summary conviction be liable either to pay a penalty not exceeding twenty pounds, or to be imprisoned for a term not exceeding six months, with or without hard labour.

7. *Penalty for Intimidation or Annoyance*

Every person who, with a view to compel any other person to abstain from doing or to do any act which such other person has a legal right to do or abstain from doing, wrongfully and without legal authority —

1. Uses violence to or intimidates such other person or his wife or children, or injures his property ; or,
2. Persistently follows such other person about from place to place ; or,

3. Hides any tools, clothes, or other property owned or used by such other person, or deprives him of or hinders him in the use thereof ; or,

4. Watches or besets the house or other place where such other person resides, or works, or carries on business, or happens to be, or the approach to such house or place ; or,

5. Follows such other person with two or more other persons in a disorderly manner in or through any street or road,

shall, on conviction thereof by a court of summary jurisdiction, or on indictment as herein-after mentioned, be liable either to pay a penalty not exceeding twenty pounds, or to be imprisoned for a term not exceeding three months, with or without hard labour.

Attending at or near the house or place where a person resides, or works, or carries on business, or happens to be, or the approach to such house or place, in order merely to obtain or communicate information, shall not be deemed a watching or besetting within the meaning of this section.

8. *Reduction of Penalties*

Where in any Act relating to employers or workmen a pecuniary penalty is imposed in respect of any offence under such Act, and no power is given to reduce such penalty, the justices or court having jurisdiction in respect of such offence may, if they think it just so to do, impose by way of penalty in respect of such offence any sum not less than one fourth of the penalty imposed by such Act. . . .

16. *Saving Clause*

Nothing in this Act shall apply to seamen or to apprentices to the sea service. . . .

Extract 17

LABOUR AND THE PAYMENT OF MEMBERS OF PARLIAMENT

(Mr. Arthur Lee and Mr. Ramsay Macdonald, Commons, August 10, 1911)

Motion moved by Mr. David Lloyd George, Chancellor of the Exchequer,

That, in the opinion of this House, provision should be made for the payment of a salary at the rate of four hundred pounds a year to every Member of this House, excluding any Member who is for the time being in receipt of a salary as an officer of the House, or as a Minister, or as an officer of His Majesty's Household.

MR. LEE[1]: . . . I claim, and that is my argument, that the representatives of the people are entirely in a different category from servants of the State; they are not servants even of their constituencies. They are free representatives of their constituencies; at any rate, they have been in the past and I hope they will so remain. It is further not essential they should give their whole time to the business of Parliament. It is well known many of the most useful and influential Members of this House have not given their whole time. If a change of this kind is desired I maintain the people ought to be consulted with regard to it, because at least it is they who have to pay. I feel strongly it is not fair, at any rate it is highly undesirable, to hold out this bait to men who have in their hands the power to confer this pecuniary benefit upon themselves. It is a temptation which may warp their judgment. It is a temptation, not to poor men only, but even to well-to-do and to rich men as well, because, whatever a man's income may be, whether it is £100 or £10,000 a year, his commitments and responsibilities are probably in proportion. And I

---

[1] Parliamentary Debates, Commons, Fifth Series, vol. 29, col. 1366 sqq.

venture to say there is no man, even well-to-do or rich, to whom an additional £400 would not be a real convenience. It certainly would be in my case. I say it is asking too much of human nature to bring a motion of this kind before the House and to expect a majority of Members will seriously resist the proposal when it means an injury to their financial interests. It is so very much easier to welcome an inflow of money than its outflow. Therefore I recognise this proposal is bound to have a fatal popularity within the walls of Parliament, but I also venture to think it will be justly and greatly unpopular outside.

Above all, I object to it because I believe it will sound the death-knell of that system of voluntary service which has been the chief and unique glory of British public life. I have spoken strongly because I feel more strongly on this particular subject than on almost any other in the whole range of politics. In every election address I have issued, and in the numberless speeches I have made to my constituents, I have expressed my repugnance to the proposal that Members of Parliament should be paid for their work as representatives of the constituencies, and the objections I felt to it when the proposal was only in an academic form have been deepened and confirmed by the effect which the near realisation in a concrete form of this proposal has already had upon the House of Commons. I have, in the eleven years I have been in this House, seen many regrettable incidents, but I cannot recall any more repellent or humiliating spectacle than the House of Commons, the very day after it has taken into its own hands by force supreme and exclusive control over the nation's finances,[1] hungrily seizing without even a decent interval upon the first opportunity after the Bill is passed to help themselves out of the pockets of the taxpayers. The Government in this matter appears to be insatiable. Not content in this week with dragging the Crown through the mire of party politics, not content with destroying the legislative authority of the other House of Parliament, they are now proposing to

[1] Cf. infra, ch. ix.

destroy the moral authority of the House of Commons as well. It is because I love the House of Commons and am proud of it that I wish the votes of my hon. Friends on this side to save it, if possible, from this wanton and unnecessary humiliation. . . .

MR. RAMSAY MACDONALD : . . . It is a profound mistake for the hon. Gentleman to assume that you have not got payment of Members now. You have payment of Members now ; you have payment by the classes to whom the Members belong. I wish to refer to a significant expression which the hon. Gentleman used. He said :

> If this is done, it cannot be undone. The reason why it cannot be done is this : When we who sit on this side of the House come into office, we will not be able to move that this Resolution be no longer operative, because they will tell us we are driving our opponents out of the House.

But if the undoing of this Resolution would be driving their opponents out of the House, is not the failure to pass it keeping your opponents out of the House ?

MR. LEE : I said we should be accused of driving some hon. Members out of the House. I say that I think this principle will bring in a certain new style of Member.

MR. RAMSAY MACDONALD : But it surely cannot bring a worse type of Member than my hon. Friends. Let me say quite frankly that I doubt if there are two Members who would be here if they were not paid to be here, and therefore my remark is a perfectly proper one. Consequently, I repeat my argument that the persons who are going to come in are not going to be persons of low moral character, they are not going to be undesirable persons, but they are going to be the type of men who cannot get in here now, because when you are in here you have to live on your wits by being a company promoter, a lawyer, a half-pay officer, the son of a rich father, or that rich father himself. Consequently the people who are going to be driven out are not people who are undesirable, but people who are representative, and that is the point. Until the door is sufficiently opened by my right hon. Friend's Resolution, these people cannot come here unless they are Members of the Irish party, or Members of our own party. There is one point that I will deal with in a second. I must deal with it, because probably nobody else can deal with it in the same way. The hon. Member said something about the Osborne Judgment. There was no attempt at bargaining over that. He said at the beginning that the principle involved in the payment of Members must be justified or condemned. That ground is a totally different one from that upon which the Osborne decision has got to be justified or condemned. I accept every word my hon. Friend said in that respect. The trade unionists were driven by the sheer necessity of the circumstances to lay their heads and their funds together for the purpose of paying certain out-of-pocket expenses for the men. Theoretically, I have never justified that. I am not going to do it now. All I say is that if this House neglected to do its duty, then things had to be strained in order that the representative character of this House should be maintained. I welcomed certain things that happened which compelled this House to face its own responsibilities, to turn its eyes away from trade unions for the fulfilling of the responsibilities which this House ought to do itself.

We have said all along that we desire the reversal of the Osborne Judgment, not that trade unions may pay Members, but that they may be able to do certain other things. We desire the payment of Members, because we maintain that this House, with its changed functions, widened field of operations, increased nearness to the lives of the common people must be representative of the common people, and that their representatives ought not to be asked to come here as the private and secret pensioners of political parties, having their election expenses paid by the party opposite, or the party on this side, and when they are sent out into the country to take part at bye-elections receiving fees in order to enable them to remain here — kept here on secret party funds, the subscribers to which cannot be published in the light of open day. I say that is the sort of thing that is going to degrade workingmen. That

is the sort of thing that is going to degrade not only the workingman, but the professional man, or the labourer. The man who
comes in under these circumstances, belonging to either party, is
the man who is going to degrade public life and lower the character of the House. If we are going to come here, we are going to
be paid by the State for services done for the State in the open
light of day, our constituencies knowing precisely what we get,
how we get it, and examining our operations here in justification
of the way we get it. It is because I believe that will raise the
dignity of the House, rather than lower it, it is because I believe
that when we are paid we shall feel as proud as we do now of being Members of this House, sharing in its discussions, and taking
part in its work, that I will give my heartiest support to the Resolution moved by my right hon. Friend.

CHAPTER III

CHILD WELFARE

[Mr. Asquith, addressing the Commons on April 18, 1907, said: "There is nothing that calls so loudly or so imperiously as the possibilities of social reform. . . . First of all there is the child for whom heredity and parental care have perhaps done nothing or worse than nothing. And yet it is the raw material, upon the fashioning of which depends whether it shall add to the common stock of wealth and intelligence and goodness, or whether it shall be cast aside as a waste product in the social rubbish heap. . . .[1]

When Queen Victoria ascended the throne, hardly one act of Parliament really represented the protective interest which Mr. Asquith meant that the State should take in the welfare of the young, and members of Parliament had long showed themselves very chary about interfering with what many honest people thought to be exclusive rights and liberties of parents. Aside from partial factory and mines regulation, there was little State action, even in education, until the seventies. In the year 1869–1870, the total cost of education to the public in the form of Parliamentary grants — for of course there was then no rate-aid — was £721,000. But various subsequent educational acts widened the sphere of State control until by 1906–1907 the amount spent on education from Parliamentary grants and local rates reached £25,144,000.

While the Unionists were still in office, an important Interdepartmental Commission on Physical Deterioration was appointed.

[1] Mr. Asquith was urging social legislation in favour of the aged as well as of the child. Cf. infra, p. 136.

The report of this Commission,[1] published on July 28, 1904, contained some fifty-three recommendations, a large proportion of which were concerned with child life. Children in all schools and factories should periodically be weighed and measured; the results, together with the weekly reports of medical officers to Boards of Guardians, should be forwarded to a new advisory council, which would thus collect valuable data; overcrowding should be dealt with in the worst districts by fixing a standard (of two persons per room for tenements of one, two or three rooms) not to be exceeded after a certain date; persons displaced might be transferred to labour colonies, and their children sent to public nurseries or boarded out; factory and workshop inspection should be stricter and include medical inspection; building by-laws and the provision of open spaces should receive further attention; special attention should be paid to milk supply, and standards fixed to check the adulteration of all foods; provision should be made by the local authorities for dealing with underfed children — possibly by the school preparing food given by private benevolence, but no special system was specified; hygiene and the effects of alcoholism should be well taught in schools, and cookery continuation classes were urged; cleanliness should be pressed upon the children, notably as to teeth, eyes, and ears; in country districts the school curriculum should be made suitable for country children, who should not go to school too young; attention should be paid to children's games and boys' and girls' clubs, and juvenile smoking should be repressed. Generally the Report contemplated greatly increased State and municipal action in conjunction with private benevolence, and for the benefit in the main of the rising generation.

Towards the fulfilment of this programme, the Liberal Government from their victory in 1906, together with their Labour allies, worked steadily, and in carrying out most of the important measures the Conservatives coöperated. On February 22, 1906, a bill was introduced in the House of Commons by Mr. W. T. Wilson, a Labour

[1] Annual Register, 1904, p. 195.

member, dealing with the provision of meals for necessitous children in elementary schools. Mr. Wilson moved second reading of the bill on March 2 (*Extract 18*). It was opposed by Mr. Harold Cox, Liberal member for Preston[1] (*Extract 19*), and by others, as lessening parental responsibility and tending to lower wages, but Mr. Augustine Birrell, President of the Board of Education, in a happy speech (*Extract 20*) approved of the measure in behalf of the Government. The bill was subsequently passed in an amended form in both Houses and received the royal assent on December 21. This statute, known as the Education (Provision of Meals) Act, 1906, is given below as *Extract 21*.

This was only a beginning of the legislation affecting children. In 1907 the Education Act contained special provisions for play centres and for free medical inspection of children. To decrease the alarming infant mortality and secure proper medical care for young children, Lord Robert Cecil, a distinguished Conservative member of the House of Commons, introduced a bill on April 23 (*Extract 22*), which was eventually enacted as the Notification of Births Act. In the same year the Probation of Offenders Act dealt with juvenile offenders along reformatory rather than punitive lines.

The Children Act, which Mr. Herbert Samuel, Under-Secretary of State for the Home Department, introduced on February 10, 1908, and which passed third reading in the Commons on October 19 and in the Lords on November 30, and received the royal assent on December 21, dealt with practically every phase of infant and child life, protection of infants and little children, treatment of children in reformatories and industrial schools, the question of juvenile crime, children's courts and probation officers. A slight idea of the nature and scope of this Act may be gathered from Mr. Samuel's remarks on First Reading (*Extract 23*).

The health and general welfare of children, as well as of adults, were in the minds of the framers and advocates of the Housing and Town Planning Act of 1909.[2]]

[1] Mr. Cox frequently voted with the Unionist minority. [2] Cf. infra, ch. vii.

Extract 18

PROVISION OF MEALS FOR SCHOOL CHILDREN

(Mr. W. T. Wilson, Commons, March 2, 1906)

MR. WILSON [1] said he did not think anyone in the House would doubt that a very large number of children went to school without food, or underfed, and the object of the Bill was to provide that meals should be given to such children. Of course, differences of opinion might arise in the House as to who should be responsible for the feeding of the children. Some hon. Members might say that it was the duty of the parents to see that their children were fed, but when they considered the amount of wages that some parents earned, they must be satisfied that it was an absolute impossibility for them properly to feed and clothe their families. There were hundreds of thousands of families in this country whose weekly income did not exceed 18s., and he thought the House would agree that if the children in these families averaged more than three, it was almost impossible for them to be fed as they ought to be. Taking 18s. as the average rate of wages of a very large number of unskilled workers in this country — and he was sorry to say that during the last three years many skilled workers had not earned more than 18s. a week — and taking the average family as consisting of three children, taking the rent at 4s. 6d. a week, and allowing three meals per head per day at 1½d. per head per meal, it would be seen that the whole of the wages were gone, and nothing was left for clothing, fire, and the hundred and one things required in a household. Therefore, children whose parents were in that position should at least be fed. It was not the fault of the children that they were there, and if the parents through force of circumstances were unable to feed them properly, the State should see that they were fed.

[1] Parliamentary Debates, Fourth Series, vol. 152, col. 1390 sqq.

The State recognised that it was to its best interests that the children should be educated, and it was only right that the children should be in a fit condition to receive instruction. Better results would then accrue from education. The education authority was the proper authority to deal with the question. He went further and said that even in cases where the parents of children were earning sufficient to provide them with food, if the education authority thought it would be to the best interests of the State that those children should be fed, they should have the power to feed them and to make a charge upon the parents afterwards. In many of the industrial centres both fathers and mothers were working during the day, and if the children had the opportunity of having meals supplied by the authority, they would be quite willing to pay for such meals. Even if the parents were unable to pay, they should not be pauperised by accepting such assistance. He asked the House to look at the matter from a strictly business standpoint. Everyone must have noticed the very large number of what he might term human weeds among the children who attended the schools of the State. The present system which permitted children to attend school in an underfed condition was the means of, he was almost going to say, manufacturing undesirables; but undoubtedly it was to a great extent responsible for physical deterioration. If that deterioration could be arrested by providing children with food, they would have done something which would be beneficial to the nation in the future. No one would deny that if a child went to school with a full stomach, it was in a better condition to receive instruction, and would be more fitted to take its place in life.

The fact that children attended school underfed was also responsible for mental deterioration. He was convinced that the presence of a large number of inmates of lunatic asylums and epileptic homes could be traced to the fact that in their early days they were underfed. No one would deny, too, that underfeeding had a tendency to create disease. He was sure that their being underfed was a direct incentive to crime on the part of children.

In the opinion of some who were opposed to the State feeding of children reliance ought to be placed upon charity. They had relied upon charity too long as it was. . . . Charity was not a reliable source from which to provide meals for children, and therefore he asked the Government to accept the Bill to provide underfed school children with at least one good meal a day. If this was done he felt sure the nation would appreciate it. From a business point of view the money would be well invested, because not only would the children be better equipped for fighting the battle of life, but it would be found in the near future that the expenditure on prisons, workhouses, and asylums was considerably reduced, and therefore the money invested would be returned with interest. He moved the Second Reading of the Bill, because he believed it would be to the best interests and the welfare of the nation, and he asked the House in the name of humanity and Christianity to adopt the Bill.

Extract 19

OPPOSITION TO PROVISION OF MEALS

(Mr. Harold Cox, Commons, March 2, 1906)

MR. Cox [1] said he should like to move the following Amendment to the Provision of Meals Bill:

That it is undesirable to proceed further with a measure which would diminish the responsibility of the parents for the maintenance of their children, and would tend to lower the wages of the poorer classes.

His reason for objecting to this Bill was that it dealt only with a symptom instead of with the disease itself. People saw that a certain number of children going to school were badly fed. They were horrified at the fact, and they proceeded at once to expostulate, but the remedy they suggested was merely to feed these particular children. But, surely, when a child was sent to a school improperly

1 Parliamentary Debates, Fourth Series, vol. 152, col. 1413 sqq.

fed it meant that there must be something wrong in the home of the child. Obviously, then, the first thing to do was to ascertain what was wrong with the homes — in other words, before they dealt with the problem of the school children they must make inquiry at the homes as to what was the cause of the underfeeding of the children.

This Bill provided no machinery for such an inquiry. Yet experience proved conclusively that where inquiry did take place, then those symptoms which appeared to be so serious at first sight turned out to be comparatively unimportant in relation to other and graver diseases. He would take the case of Johanna Street School. The hon. Member for North Camberwell and other investigators about twelve months ago visited that school, and complained that a number of children were underfed. That complaint was dealt with by the Board of Guardians, who instructed their superintending relieving officer to inquire into the actual homes of the children and ascertain the causes of the underfeeding. What did he find? In the first place, the parents in all the houses whence underfed children came were instructed to apply to the relieving officer if they wanted food. Only in one case was any application made. That alone seemed to dispose of the fact that it was impossible for the parents to feed their children. That was not all. They found in many cases that the incomes of the families ranged from 20s. up to as much as 72s. a week.

AN HON. MEMBER: These facts were subsequently challenged.

MR. COX said at any rate they had them on the authority of the Lambeth Board of Guardians. But what was more important still was that in many houses where parents were asked why children were sent to school without a proper meal, the answer was something to this effect, " Oh, we heard that other children were getting meals for nothing and we thought ours might do the same."

They would have to begin not with the child, but with the family. They had to ask what was wrong in the family. Two things might be wrong in the family. Either the family might

be honest but poor through adverse circumstances, or it might
be drunken and dishonest. In the first event it was their duty
to relieve the family as a whole, and not to pick out one child.
In the second event, it might, in extreme cases of drunkenness
or other serious vice, be necessary to remove the children from
the family altogether. In the majority of cases, however, it would
be sufficient to screw up the parents to a realisation of the duty
that they owed to their children. The simplest way of accom-
plishing that object, and certainly the least expensive, would be
to placard the doors of the houses of parents who wilfully sent
their children to school underfed with the simple announcement,
" These people send their children to school without feeding them."

AN HON. MEMBER : What a statesmanlike suggestion that is !

MR. COX said he could quite understand hon. Gentlemen on the
other side objecting to his proposal, for he gathered from some
of their speeches this afternoon that their object was to relieve
parents of all their responsibilities.

. . . The effect of this Bill would be to create a body of
workingmen who, instead of helping their fellows and standing
alone, would be sponging upon their fellow workers. What would
be the effect on the child ? [AN HON. MEMBER : It would be
better fed.] If they took the child away from the home, they
would in the first place lower the standard of the home. [" No,
no."] That might seem a striking statement to make, but it was
borne out by the experience of people who spent their lives in
working among the poorer classes. The duty of providing for a
child was one of the greatest bonds in keeping up the standard of
a home. A woman was ashamed to be drunk in the presence of
her child. Take away the child and that motive for self-restraint
was gone. He had been told of the case of a poor woman with
an illegitimate child, who was working honourably to maintain it.
Some charitable people thought it was very hard upon her to have
to keep a child out of her scanty wages, and so they relieved her
of her burden and took the child away. What was the result ?

That poor woman, with no longer any stimulus to exertion or motive for maintaining a higher standard, dropped gradually down to the lowest depths of degradation.

MR. J. WARD on a point of order said there was no suggestion of taking the children away from the parents.

MR. SPEAKER : I think the hon. Member's observations were in order. I see no reason to interfere.

MR. COX said he was sorry he was not making his argument clear to his hon. Friend, but he was pointing out that if they were to give meals, they must also give boots and clothing. Then they must begin to ask under what conditions the child lived, and what kind of rooms it slept in, was it washed before it was put to bed, and did it sleep in a decent cot at night. [" Hear, hear," from·the Labour Benches, and cries of " Why not ? "]

MR. CROOKS : We should do it ; we should not ask.

MR. COX : Then the hon. Member's colleague had been a little slow in taking his point. When they had asked themselves these questions they were driven to say, " We must take this child away. We must house it somewhere else, where it can get better air, etc." They would house it in a beautiful building, with sanitary walls, and provide neat little beds arranged in rows all exactly alike. They would feed it well at long tables with others and clothe it well, but there would be no holidays for that child. It would always live in this great barrack. [" Why ? "] If the home was unfit for it in school-time, it was unfit for it in holiday time, and it would be a crime to send it back to the home from which they had rescued it. It would always live in this barrack with never a holiday and never a sight of the ordinary human relationships that mankind enjoyed.

AN HON. MEMBER : Is that in the Bill ?

MR. COX : It is a consequence of the Bill. They had got, he said, to think in all these social problems of where they were drifting. His hon. Friend the Member for Merthyr Tydfil [Mr. Keir Hardie] was far-sighted enough to see where he was going, but there were a great many Members on both sides of the House who did not see where they were going [" Oh, oh "], and where this Bill would lead to. When they had got these children fed and clothed, did they imagine they had made the children happy? Was there not something else which every child wanted — something that could not be provided by any Act of Parliament? Was there not love of home and parents? It was that love they were going to destroy, and when they had destroyed it, they would put nothing in its place. They could not. Did they think they would have solved the problem of poverty? They would have only made more people willing to accept dependence upon others. It was not by such methods as these that they would raise the mass of the people to a better condition. In the long run they could only raise people by teaching them to raise themselves, but the effect of this Bill would be to encourage people to degrade themselves.

Extract 20

GOVERNMENT ADVOCACY OF PROVISION OF MEALS

(*Mr. Augustine Birrell, President of the Board of Education, Commons, March 2, 1906*)

MR. BIRRELL[1] said they had had an interesting and profitable discussion, and many speeches had been made by new Members, who had shown an almost alarming capacity for taking an active part in the debates. It was a subject which touched all of them, this of hungry children in schools. Most Members of the House, he suspected, were fathers, all of them had been children, and some of them had been teachers, and in all these capacities they knew that to attempt to teach a hungry child, faint and weak, the elements of learning, either divine or human, was an act of

[1] Parliamentary Debates, Fourth Series, vol. 152, col. 1440 sqq.

cruelty. They also knew that to attempt anything of the kind at the expense of either the taxpayer or the ratepayer was a waste of public money.

This was, therefore, in the first place an educational question. He protested in the name of the teachers against so odious a duty being imposed upon them as the attempt to teach hungry children. He knew quite well how generously teachers had approached the task, how kindly they had attempted to discharge it, and what a heavy tax it too often was upon their slender resources to try and mitigate the evils and the hardships that came under their attention. There was the hungry child; they must either feed it or turn it away; and as the Minister for Education he could not be responsible for the latter alternative. As everybody was agreed that the child could not be taught before it was fed, then fed it had to be.

The next question was, By what agency was the feeding to be done? It appeared to him that the proper agency, in the first instance, to see that this primary step was taken was the education authority itself. As to whether or not local education authorities should have the power, if so disposed, to try the experiment of providing food for a considerable number of the children who might avail themselves of it, endeavouring to be repaid the cost of the meals, he reminded the House that that course had been adopted for many years in Paris, in connection with the *cantines scolaires*, and had worked exceedingly well.

There was one advantage of teaching poor children what a good dinner was, that it raised their own standard very much, and created in their youthful stomachs a divine dissatisfaction with their lot. He could conceive no greater service to posterity than to raise the standard of living in the children of the present day. Therefore he should be sorry to forbid by law a local authority trying the experiment of feeding children upon a larger scale than would be necessary if it were to be confined to necessitous children. In Paris 10,500,000 meals were given in 1904;

of those it was difficult to ascertain what proportion were given gratuitously, but it was certain that a very large proportion were given in exchange for payment. He thought that what Paris could do London ought to be able to do, especially after the visit of the County Councillors to the French capital. There it was found possible to combine a good system of feeding the children, which should be gratuitous to those whose parents stood in need of it without in any way interfering with payment by those who could afford to pay. That was the only reason why he should be rather sorry were the local authority to be prohibited from attempting to do something of the same sort as was done in Paris.

That being so, the question became one rather of detail. What means were to be employed to see that they were not imposed upon? Of course, parental responsibility was a great ideal, but how it could really be destroyed either by free meals being given to very poor children or by meals being given to children for which they paid, he was at a loss to conceive. He was not one of those who loved the phrase "the children of the State." It was a phrase which grated upon his ear. The State could not have any children. The mace on the table might as well beguile its ample leisure by the hope of a child. Man was born of a woman, and not of the Local Government Board, and anything which in any way interfered with the family as the unit of our civilisation was greatly to be deplored.

On what rate was the burden to fall? Was it more convenient it should fall on the education rate or on the poor rate? Whether the education rate or the Poor Law rate was the better fund to bear the burden when they failed to recover the cost was a question which might fairly be considered by the Committee to which he hoped the Bill would be referred. He hoped the Committee would take into consideration the whole question as to how local authorities might work the powers conferred by this Bill. Charity was not to be sneezed at, but it required to be steady and well-organised, otherwise it was apt to be sporadic, fanciful, and fitful. He hoped, too, that local education authorities would fully consider whether they could not properly utilise voluntary agencies and organise and receive contributions from them in aid of the rate or any other relief they might think necessary to establish. He did not suppose for a moment that any popularly-elected body, with ratepayers behind it, would be anxious to increase the burden of the rates, or that they would desire to discourage the assistance of charitable persons in the community. He thought it was not much use saying that this question was part of a far greater question — everything was part of a greater question. Everything was part and parcel of education. From the teacher's point of view, boots were not so important as that the child should be fed. This was a practical problem which presented itself every day in almost every school in the great towns, and we had to deal with the problem. He was quite content to leave posterity to deal with a great many other problems which might arise.

Extract 21

EDUCATION (PROVISION OF MEALS) ACT, 1906

(*6 Edw. 7, ch. 57*)

An Act to make provision for Meals for Children attending Public Elementary Schools in England and Wales.

(21st December 1906)

Be it enacted by the King's most Excellent Majesty, by and with the advice and consent of the Lords Spiritual and Temporal, and Commons, in this present Parliament assembled, and by the authority of the same, as follows:

1. Special Power of Local Education Authority

A local education authority under Part III of the Education Act, 1902, may take such steps as they think fit for the provision of meals for children in attendance at any public elementary school in their area, and for that purpose —

(*a*) may associate with themselves any committee on which the authority are represented, who will undertake to provide food for those children (in this Act called a " school canteen committee "); and

(*b*) may aid that committee by furnishing such land, buildings, furniture, and apparatus, and such officers and servants as may be necessary for the organisation, preparation, and service of such meals;

but, save as herein-after provided, the authority shall not incur any expense in respect of the purchase of food to be supplied at such meals.

2. Recovery of the Cost of Meals

(1) There shall be charged to the parent of every child in respect of every meal furnished to that child under this Act such an amount as may be determined by the local education authority, and, in the event of payment not being made by the parent, it shall be the duty of the authority, unless they are satisfied that the parent is unable by reason of circumstances other than his own default to pay the amount, to require the payment of that amount from that parent, and any such amount may be recovered summarily as a civil debt.

(2) The local education authority shall pay over to the school canteen committee so much of any money paid to them by, or recovered from, any parent as may be determined by the authority to represent the cost of the food furnished by the committee to the child of that parent, less a reasonable deduction in respect of the expenses of recovering the same.

3. Power of Local Education Authority to defray the Cost

Where the local education authority resolve that any of the children attending an elementary school within their area are unable by reason of lack of food to take full advantage of the education provided for them, and have ascertained that funds other than public funds are not available or are insufficient in amount to defray the cost of food furnished in meals under this Act, they may apply to the Board of Education, and that Board may authorise them to spend out of the rates such sum as will meet the cost of the provision of such food, provided that the total amount expended by a local education authority for the purposes of this section in any local financial year shall not exceed the amount which would be produced by a rate of one halfpenny in the pound over the area of the authority, or, where the authority is a county council (other than the London County Council), over the area of the parish or parishes which in the opinion of the council are served by the school.

4. Provisions as to Disfranchisement

The provision of any meal under this Act to a child and the failure on the part of the parent to pay any amount demanded under this Act in respect of a meal shall not deprive the parent of any franchise, right, or privilege, or subject him to any disability.

5. Application of Education Acts

(1) The powers of a local education authority under this Act shall be deemed to be powers of that authority under the Education Acts, 1870 to 1903, and the provisions of those Acts as to the manner in which the expenses of a local education authority are to be charged and defrayed, and as to borrowing, and as to the manner in which the amount which would be produced by any rate in the pound is to be estimated, shall apply to expenses incurred and

money borrowed under this Act, and to the estimate of the produce of any rate in the pound for the purposes of this Act.

(2) Any expression to which a special meaning is attached in the Education Acts, 1870 to 1903, shall have the same meaning in this Act, except that for the purposes of this Act the expression " child " shall, notwithstanding anything in section forty-eight of the Elementary Education Act, 1876,[1] include any child in attendance at a public elementary school.

6. · Provision as to Teachers

No teacher seeking employment or employed in a public elementary school shall be required as part of his duties to supervise or assist, or to abstain from supervising or assisting, in the provision of meals, or in the collection of the cost thereof.

7. Application to Scotland

This Act shall not apply to Scotland.

8. Title

This Act may be cited as the Education (Provision of Meals) Act, 1906.

Extract 22

INTRODUCTION OF NOTIFICATIONS OF BIRTH BILL, 1907

(Lord Robert Cecil, Commons, April 23, 1907)

LORD R. CECIL [2] in moving for leave to introduce a Bill to provide for the early notification of births, said that he had taken the unusual course of asking leave under the ten minutes rule, because of the very great gravity of the evil with which the Bill, however

---

[1] 39 & 40 Vict., ch. 79.
[2] Parliamentary Debates, Fourth Series, vol. 172, col. 1582 sqq.

imperfectly and however modestly, attempted to deal. At the present moment 120,000 infants under one year of age died in this country every year, and it was no exaggeration to say that of these 60,000 might be saved if proper measures were taken. Such a state of things required the very earnest consideration of the House, for it amounted to this, that out of every 1000 children born in this country 145 died without reaching the age of one year; and there were particular localities in which as many as 250, 300, or even 400 out of every 1000 born died at that early age. It was no exaggeration to say that half of them might be saved; for the rate in some of our Colonies was no higher than seventy per 1000, and in some of our own counties it was not higher than eighty-four.

The seriousness of the question was not diminished by the fact that while the general death-rate in this country had been much diminished as the result of sanitary measures, the infantile death rate remained practically stationary. That he attributed mainly to two causes — neglect by mothers of their own health before the birth of their children, and neglect of the children's health immediately after they were born. He did not suggest for a moment that the neglect was due to wickedness or even to carelessness exactly, but it was in most cases due to ignorance, which was a far more potent cause of infantile mortality than the more commonly assigned causes of parental poverty and intemperance.

Something could be done to remedy this state of affairs by the provision of skilled assistance to mothers in the early days of motherhood, and many health societies throughout the country had charged themselves with this duty. Remarkable results had been achieved in Huddersfield from the creditable efforts of the ex-mayor. But under the existing registration law six weeks might elapse before registration, and one-third of the children dying in the first year of life died in the first six weeks; so that these children were dead before the societies to which he referred could know that they had been born. It was solely with a view to remedy this defect that he had been asked to introduce this Bill. It provided that within forty-eight hours of the birth of every child a notification was to be made in the simplest way, it being specially provided that it might be made by post card, and the duty of notifying a birth was thrown, in the first place, on the father of the child and, failing him, on any one who had been in attendance on the mother. The Bill further required that notification of children stillborn should be made as well as of those born alive.

He urged the House to consider the seriousness of the evil which the Bill was designed, he would not say to cure, but in some degree to mitigate. This was a non-Party question, and he ventured to hope that the Bill would be regarded as absolutely non-contentious. It was supported by hon. Members in all quarters of the House, and he hoped its promoters would have the sympathetic support of the Government and that the measure might be passed into law before the close of the present session.

Extract 23

INTRODUCTION OF CHILDREN BILL, 1908

(Mr. Herbert Samuel, Under-Secretary of State for the Home Department, Commons, February 10, 1908)

Mr. Samuel [1] in asking leave to bring in a Bill " to consolidate and amend the law relating to the protection of children and young persons, reformatory and industrial schools, and juvenile offenders, and otherwise to amend the law with respect to children and young persons," said : This is the first reading of a Bill to which we can give no narrower title than that of " Children Bill." The present law for the protection of children and the treatment of juvenile offenders is in some confusion. It is spread over a large number of statutes, and it urgently needs consolidation. Experience has shown the need of a considerable number of amendments and

1 Parliamentary Debates, Fourth Series, vol. 183, col. 1432 sqq.

extensions of the law. The Government have decided not to introduce a series of small Bills in successive years, but to ask Parliament
to enact, in one large and comprehensive measure, a thorough codification and amendment of the law relating to children. A Bill of
this scope could not, in a crowded session like this, expect to pass
into law unless it commanded, more or less, the favour of all sections in the House, and we have, therefore, excluded from it all
the subjects which might properly be described as controversial.
Even the question of children in public-houses, with regard to which
there is a general measure of assent, we have thought it wiser to
defer to be dealt with in the Licensing Bill. The question of the
employment of children, whether in factories or elsewhere, raises
important industrial questions on which, unhappily, there is not
complete agreement. The question of education naturally belongs to the Education Acts, and there are other subjects which
we might have liked to include but which we have been obliged to
omit. But, even with these omissions, the Bill is a somewhat vo-
luminous one. It contains 119 clauses, covers seventy pages, and
consolidates twenty-two statutes and parts of many others, together
with a number of new provisions. . . .

The Bill extends to the whole of the United Kingdom. Through
all its parts uniform definitions run. A child is a person under the
age of fourteen years; a young person is a person above the age
of fourteen and under the age of sixteen. The first part of the
Bill embodies the Infant Life Protection Act, 1897, which was
passed to stop the evils of baby farming, and for the protection of
the lives of infants put out to nurse. That Act has been found in
practice ineffective in many respects. There are many holes through
which evil-disposed persons may escape its control, but, by a series
of detailed amendments we stop these holes and strengthen the
control of the Act. . . .

The second part of the Bill re-enacts the Prevention of Cruelty
to Children Act, 1894, with a large number of amendments mainly
designed to strengthen the law and to facilitate the action of those

societies which are doing such admirable work in the three kingdoms for the prevention of cruelty to children. I will mention only
two of the chief provisions proposed in this part of the Bill. Every
year some 1600 infants meet their deaths from overlying, a waste
of infant life which should easily be preventible and which ought
not to be allowed to continue. We propose, in such cases, since
the offence is not one of wilful cruelty, but of negligence, to make
the penalty a light one, except where drunkenness can be proved.
An equal number of children are killed year by year from burns
and scalds, owing to their being left in rooms with unguarded fires.
We impose in such cases also a similar penalty, except where it
can be shown that reasonable precautions were taken.

The proposals of the third part of the Bill deal with an evil,
growing in extent, most deleterious to child life, and for which
public opinion almost universally demands a remedy. I refer to
the evil of juvenile smoking. The Committee on Physical Deterioration recommended a legislative remedy, and a Committee of
the House of Lords, appointed in 1906 specially to examine this
question, after hearing much medical and other evidence, made a
unanimous and a very emphatic recommendation in the same sense.
Many countries throughout the world have already legislated on
this subject. We propose to prohibit the sale of cigarettes and
cigarette paper to children under the age of sixteen, to prohibit
persons under the age of sixteen from smoking in streets and public
places, and to make them liable for the first offence to no more
than a reprimand, but for subsequent offences to a light fine. We
also allow, and this will probably prove a more effective provision,
the police and other authorised persons to confiscate the tobacco
which is being used by those little boys who are found smoking
in streets and public places. We have a provision also for dealing
with such automatic machines for the sale of cigarettes as are found
to be extensively used by juveniles.

The fourth part of the Bill consolidates the nineteen statutes
which now contain the law relating to reformatory and industrial

schools. The changes we propose are too many and too minute to deal with now, but I would like to mention that it has been suggested that the age for committal to a reformatory should be raised above the present figure of sixteen, and to explain that we are not adopting that suggestion only because we consider that it is inadvisable to mix older offenders with smaller boys and girls, and because my right hon. Friend the Home Secretary hopes to introduce a Bill establishing a new class of reformatories for these older offenders.

There are in the Bill a number of miscellaneous clauses, of which I will only mention two. From time to time cases of cruelty and neglect are discovered in so-called homes for children which are fraudulent institutions, conducted by persons who live on the charitable contributions which are intended for the destitute children whom they have collected. There is no right of entry under the present law to such institutions, and the Bill provides that, where a home is kept for destitute children and is supported by charitable contributions, there shall be a right of entry for persons authorised by the Secretary of State. Regard will be had in the selection of such persons to the religious denomination by which such homes are being maintained. The other clause is one designed to solve the difficult and long-standing problem of the vagrant child. There are some hundreds of children who are now continually taken about the country, deprived of any opportunity of schooling, educated only in vagabondage, and denied many of the most elementary benefits of civilised life. We propose a clause which, we hope, will stop that once and for all. We adapt the machinery of the Compulsory Education Acts, which are at present found to be inapplicable to these cases, to meet the requirements of the vagrant child.

The last part of the Bill, which has to do with juvenile offenders, is based upon three main principles. The first is that the child offender ought to be kept separate from the adult criminal, and should receive at the hands of the law a treatment differentiated to suit his special needs — that the courts should be agencies for the rescue as well as the punishment of children. We require the establishment throughout the country of juvenile courts — that is to say, children's cases shall be heard in a court held in a separate room or at a separate time from the courts which are held for adult cases, and that the public who are not concerned in the cases shall be excluded from admission. In London we propose to appoint by administrative action a special children's magistrate to visit in turn a circuit of courts. Further, we require police authorities throughout the whole of the country to establish places of detention to which children shall be committed on arrest, if they are not bailed, and on remand or commitment for trial, instead of being committed to prison. A great many towns have already provided places of detention, and we require that this practice should be made universal. We anticipate that a Treasury grant will be made for the maintenance of children, in places of detention, on remand.

The second principle on which this Bill is based is that the parent of the child offender must be made to feel more responsible for the wrong-doing of his child. He cannot be allowed to neglect the up-bringing of his children, and having committed the grave offence of throwing on society a child criminal, wash his hands of the consequences and escape scot free. We require the attendance in court of the parent in all cases where the child is charged, where there is no valid reason to the contrary, and we considerably enlarge the powers, already conferred upon the magistrates by the Youthful Offenders Act of 1901, to require the parent, where it is just to do so, to pay the fines inflicted for the offence which his child has committed.

The third principle which we had in view in framing this part of the Bill is that the commitment of children in the common gaols, no matter what the offence may be that is committed, is an unsuitable penalty to impose. The child is made to feel for the rest of his life that he is regarded as a criminal and belongs to the criminal classes, and at the same time that vague dread of the unknown penalties of imprisonment, which is one of the most powerful deterrents of crime, becomes useless and nugatory. After consultation with many of the chief judicial and legal authorities of the country, the Government have come to the conclusion that the time has now arrived when Parliament can be asked to abolish the imprisonment of children altogether, and we extend this proposal to the age of sixteen, with a few carefully defined and necessary exceptions. Many methods will still be left in the hands of the courts for dealing with delinquent children, but where none of the ordinary methods are suitable, our Bill will permit the committal of the child for a short period, under Home Office rules and a proper system of classification, to the places of detention which have to be provided for remand cases. Such committals we anticipate will be exceedingly few, and a similar Treasury grant will be in respect of them. . . .

CHAPTER IV

OLD AGE PENSIONS

[Together with the problem of child welfare, that of the aged and infirm pressed for solution. Since 1834 the Government had dealt with the problem along three different lines. Up to 1871 there was an indiscriminate use of general workhouses for all classes of the indigent aged, modified to a slight extent by supplying doles as outdoor relief. An even harsher method of dealing with these people was instituted in 1871 : namely, that of applying a workhouse test, the assumption being that the deserving could maintain themselves out of their own savings, or be maintained by their relatives, aided by charitable gifts, and that only the undeserving would apply for admission to the workhouses. As a result of the investigations and reports of the Royal Commissioners of 1893–1895, a new policy was adopted, at least in theory, — either outdoor relief fully adequate to all the deserving aged, or good comfortable quarters in some institution. The actual operation of each of these policies had been far from satisfactory ; and the labour interests began to urge partial solutions along more radical lines.

Mr. Joseph Chamberlain succeeded in pledging the Unionist party to support the principle of old age pensions, but failed to control a majority sufficient to pass such a measure through Parliament; and the only contribution to the subject by the Balfour Government was the constitution of a Poor Law Commission to study and report upon the whole problem of the aged and infirm.

Very soon after the assembling of the Parliament in 1906, a resolution was introduced by Labour members asking for the provision of old age pensions from public funds. The Chancellor of the Exchequer expressed the complete sympathy of the Liberal Government with the proposed reform, but intimated that he could not then provide the necessary funds. In the course of the debate Mr. John Burns said that in his judgment perhaps the best, simplest, and fairest scheme would be one under which every person would receive 5s. a week at sixty-five years of age; the Poor Law Commission would report before long, and then the Government would be in possession of sufficient information to justify their making a beginning, and it was their intention to take the matter up as soon as that should be possible. The resolution was carried unanimously.

Agitation in favour of old age pensions continued throughout 1907. On May 10 of that year a bill was introduced by Mr. W. H. Lever, providing for a pension of 5s. a week payable, upon personal application, to persons sixty-five years of age and upwards, from funds supplied nine-tenths by the Exchequer and one-tenth by local taxation. A graduated system of income tax, beginning with a charge of 2d. in the pound on every man earning 20s. weekly and not necessarily stopping at 1s. in the pound in the case of the rich man, would furnish sufficient funds. An amendment to reject Mr. Lever's Bill was negatived 232 to 19, but the proposal never got by second reading in the Commons.

On April 18, 1907, Mr. Asquith, in making the customary Budget statement as Chancellor of the Exchequer, pledged the Ministry to deal with old age pensions during the next session of Parliament (*Extract 24*). A year later Mr. Asquith succeeded Sir Henry Campbell-Bannerman as Prime Minister and First Lord of the Treasury, and Mr. David Lloyd George was transferred from the Presidency of the Board of Trade to the office of Chancellor of the Exchequer. Mr. Asquith, however, made the Budget statement on May 7, 1908, in the course of which he took occasion to revert to the social problem, especially to old age pensions (*Extract 25*).

The Government measure was presented to the Commons on May 28, 1908. Its second reading was moved by Mr. Lloyd George on June 15 (*Extract 26*), and opposed by Mr. Harold Cox (*Extract 27*) and Lord Robert Cecil (*Extract 28*), who endeavoured unsuccessfully to pass an amendment condemning expenditure of " taxpayers' money in giving subsidies to persons selected by arbitrary standards of age, income, and character."

When the Committee stage of the Bill was begun in the House of Commons on June 23, many of the Conservatives took up an attitude of grave suspicion if not downright hostility, and several of them proposed amendments, which, had they been adopted, would have defeated the objects of the measure. Amendments moved by Lord Robert Cecil and Mr. Bowles, altering the wording of the first clause so as to stamp the measure as experimental, were rejected respectively by 293 to 55 and 341 to 103, there being some cross-voting. Another amendment, moved by Mr. Bowles, suspending the pension in the absence of the pensioner from the United Kingdom, was ultimately rejected by 376 to 101, it being explained by Mr. Lloyd George that short absences would not disqualify, though permanent removal would involve forfeiture. An amendment moved by Viscount Castlereagh, embodying the principle of a sliding scale according to means, was opposed by the Labour members as insufficient, though they would accept a scale ranging from 10s. to 15s. per week. Lord Robert Cecil proposed another amendment, providing that the scheme should be contributory under regulations to be made by the Treasury. This was rejected by 346 to 86 after a speech by Mr. Buxton, Postmaster-General, repeating the Ministerial objections to the contributory principle (*Extract 26*).

Then the Unionists resorted to moving amendments to the Bill which would largely increase its cost. Thus, an amendment moved by Mr. Mildmay directed the pension authority to disregard sums under £40 annually, received in consideration of previous payment, from a friendly society or trade union; and Mr. Chaplin met an objection against distinguishing between various forms of thrift by moving to extend the amendment so as to cover all other approved provision against old age, sickness, or infirmity. This was supported by several Opposition and Labour members, whereupon the Chancellor of the Exchequer said that the Opposition thought they were putting the Government into a hole. Their policy had been to move wild, illogical, irrational amendments, regardless of the cost, in order to say to every class in turn, "We voted for you and those wicked radicals voted against you." Later, he said that Mr. Mildmay's amendment would add 100,000 pensioners and £1,300,000 annually to the cost; Mr. Chaplin's £2,600,000. The amendment, in the form given it by Mr. Chaplin, was rejected by 243 to 113.

The thinly-veiled hostility of the Unionists to the Government Bill was displayed in the Commons on the occasion of the third reading on July 9 when Mr. Arthur J. Balfour offered his sceptical apology (*Extract 29*), to which the Labourites replied eloquently through Mr. William Crooks (*Extract 30*). On the final division, only 12 Unionists voted for the Bill, 11 voted against it, and 140 abstained.

What the Lords would do with the Old Age Pensions Bill was for some time problematical. Introduced in their House on July 10, it came up for second reading ten days later. The Earl of Wemyss in a remarkable speech (*Extract 31*) at once moved an amendment declaring such legislation unwise pending the issue of the Report of the Poor Law Commission. All manner of financial and moral reasons were assigned against the Government measure by various speakers, among whom were the Earl of Cromer, Viscount St. Aldwyn, Lord Avebury, and the Earl of Halsbury. Lord Rosebery, while profoundly disquieted as to the effect of the Bill, urged the Lords (*Extract 32*) not to incur the risk of a dispute with the House of Commons by rejecting a measure that was largely fiscal. Two prominent Churchmen, the archbishop of Canterbury, and the bishop of Ripon, defended the Bill (*Extract 33*).

Lord Lansdowne, the Tory leader, expressed grave opposition to the measure, but counselled its adoption as good party tactics. It must be borne in mind that it was in 1908 that the Lords rejected the important Licensing Bill which had passed the lower House with large majorities.

The Old Age Pensions Bill passed third reading in the House of Lords on July 30, and after the House of Commons had rejected various Lords' amendments, the measure received the royal assent on August 1, 1908. It is given below as *Extract 34.*

An important amendment was enacted in 1911, clarifying and extending several provisions of the major Act. It is inserted as *Extract 35.*]

Extract 24

PROMISE OF OLD AGE PENSIONS

(Mr. H. H. Asquith, Chancellor of the Exchequer, Commons, April 18, 1907)

MR. ASQUITH [1] : . . . It is, I think, a mistake to treat the annual Budget as if it were a thing by itself, and not, as it is, or as it certainly ought to be, an integral part and a necessary link in a connected and coherent chain of policy. In my opinion, and I think it is an opinion that will be shared by a great number of hon. Gentlemen opposite, the country has reached a stage in which, whether we look merely at its fiscal or at its social exigencies, we cannot afford to drift along the stream and treat each year's finance as if it were self-contained. The Chancellor of the Exchequer, in other words, ought to budget, not for one year, but for several years. It is in that spirit that the proposals which I am going presently to submit to the Committee have been conceived, and it is from that point of view that I ask they shall be judged.

[1] Parliamentary Debates, Fourth Series, vol. 172, col. 1175 sqq.

What, then, are the lines for financial progress which this Government, and a majority in this House, are bound by their pledges and by their convictions to pursue? First and foremost, we are under an immediate obligation, often insisted upon when we sat upon the other side in the last Parliament, and reiterated certainly by me over and over again at the general election after which I had assumed the office of the Chancellor of the Exchequer — an immediate obligation of reinstating and improving the national credit. . . . A substantial and exceptional effort to effect a further reduction in the Debt is, for the moment, one of the paramount duties of the Government.

But behind and beyond this there lies the whole still unconquered territory of social reform. Social reform may be regarded, according to the point of view from which you look at it, as a luxury or as a necessity, but in any case it is expensive. It has to be paid for. Someone must be prepared to meet the bill. Well, now, this is a House of Commons which was elected more clearly and definitely than any other House in our history in the hope and belief on the part of the electors that it would find the road and provide the means for social reform. No doubt social reform is a phrase vague in itself, which carries different meanings to different minds. But there are some things which it certainly means to all of us who sit upon this side of the House, and I fancy to a good many who sit opposite. I myself, for instance — if I may refer to myself — am not what is called a Socialist. I believe in the right of every man face to face with the State to make the best of himself, and, subject to the limitation that he does not become a nuisance or a danger to the community, to make less than the best of himself. This world is much too full of wrong-doing, and of injustice, and of unmerited suffering; but, in my judgment, the way of escape is not to be found in any solution, or so-called solution, which, by slowly but surely drying up the reservoir which gives vitality to human personality and human purpose, will in the long run leave the universe a more sterile place. I say this in no polemical spirit, not at

all, but simply by way of emphasising the fact that to all of us —
people like myself, who may be regarded by some of my hon. friends
below the gangway as a lukewarm Moderate — there is nothing
that calls so loudly or so imperiously as the possibilities of social
reform. Just let me, in order to make plain what I am going to
say, invite the House to look at two sets of figures in our modern
community, whose appeal is irresistible.

First of all there is the child[1] for whom heredity and parental
care have perhaps done nothing or worse than nothing. And yet it
is the raw material, upon the fashioning of which depends whether
it shall add to the common stock of wealth and intelligence and
goodness, or whether it shall be cast aside as a waste product in
the social rubbish heap. The State has long recognised that it cannot pass by that appeal with folded arms. It has put the child to
school, it keeps the child at school, and (much as it shocks some
excellent people) after the legislation of last year, if the poor body
of the child is benumbed with cold or pinched with hunger so that
it can get no benefit from its lessons, it will even go so far as to
help to provide it with bread. Does the House realise what the
recognition of that means on the part of the State, what every one
of us now agrees is a duty, though it was neglected and passed by
generation after generation by humane and far-sighted statesmen?
Does anyone realise what the performance of that duty has cost
this community? Let me give two or three figures which I think
very striking. In the year 1869–70, the last year of what I may
call the old system, the total cost of education to the public in the
form of Parliamentary grants — for of course there was no rate-aid
at that time — was £721,000. What was it in the year 1906–7?
Your Parliamentary grants, if you add the Exchequer contributions,
as you ought to, were £13,359,000; sums raised by local rates
were £11,785,000; a total of £25,144,000. That is what it has
cost the State to recognise its duty to the children of the community. I do not say that every penny or every pound of that money

[1] Cf. supra, p. 107.

is well or wisely spent. I rejoice to think that we have at the head of the Board of Education my right hon. Friend the President, a severe economist, who subjects the whole of this expenditure to a most searching review. But this I do say, that there is not a man who sits on either side of the House who is prepared substantially to recede from the performance of this enormous duty. Well, that is one thing.

There is another thing, nearer the other end of the journey of life, which makes an equally strong, though hitherto an unavailing, appeal both to the interest and to the conscience of society — I mean the figure of the man or woman who, perhaps, spent out with a life of unrequited labour, finds himself confronted in old age, without fault or demerit of his own, with the prospect of physical want and the sacrifice of self-respect. Sir, I never gave, nor, so far as I know, did any of my colleagues on this Bench give, any pledge at the elections on the subject of what is called old age pensions. We knew something of the magnitude of the problem, and we thought it wrong to raise expectations without the knowledge that they could be met. Nor do I now commit myself or any of my colleagues to any specific scheme, although both my right hon. Friend the Prime Minister and myself have laid down certain conditions to which, in our judgment, any practical proposal must conform. Whatever is done in this matter, as I have said before in this House, must be done by steps and stages, and cannot be achieved at a single blow. But this I do say, and I wish to say it with all the emphasis of which I am capable, speaking for the whole of my colleagues who sit upon this Bench, that in the sphere of finance we regard this as the most serious and the most urgent of all the demands for social reform ; and that it is our hope — I will go further and say it is our intention, before the close of this Parliament, yes, before the close of the next session of this Parliament, if we are allowed to have our way (it is a large " if ") — to lay the firm foundations of this reform. . . .

Extract 25

RENEWED PROMISE OF OLD AGE PENSIONS

(*Mr. H. H. Asquith, Prime Minister and First Lord of the Treasury, Commons, May 7, 1908*)

MR. ASQUITH [1]: . . . Last year, in introducing the Budget, I said that this Parliament and this Government had come here pledged to social reform, and I pointed to two figures in our modern society that make an especially strong and, indeed, an irresistible appeal, not only to our sympathy, but to something more practical, a sympathy translated into a concrete and constructive policy of social and financial effort. One is the figure of a child. I reminded the House that in less than forty years — since 1870 — you have added to your annual provision for the education of the children of this country out of taxes and rates an annual sum of over £24,000,000 sterling. There is not one of us who would go back upon that.

The other figure is the figure of old age, still unprovided for except for casual and unorganised effort, or, by what is worse, invidious dependence upon Poor Law relief. I said then that we hoped and intended this year to lay firm the foundations of a wiser and a humaner policy. With that view, as the Committee may remember, I set aside £1,500,000, which was temporarily applied to the reduction of debt, and I anticipated that that other £750,000 which, through the activity of the Inland Revenue, has been swept into the old Sinking Fund of last year, would also be available. I propose now to show how we intend to redeem the promises which I then made.

I need not remind the Committee that this question in one shape or another has been before the country now for the best part of thirty years. The first schemes that were put forward proceeded

[1] Parliamentary Debates, Fourth Series, vol. 188, col. 445 sqq.

on the footing either of compulsory or voluntary insurance, accompanied and fortified by State aid. The Royal Commission on the Aged Poor in 1895 reported adversely to all the proposals which had up to that time been made. There followed a series of inquiries into schemes for granting immediate pensions to the aged and deserving poor. There was Lord Rothschild's Committee, there was a Select Committee of this House presided over by the right hon. Gentleman the Member for Wimbledon in 1899, and there was Sir Edward Hamilton's Departmental Committee of 1900, and again a Select Committee of this House in 1903. Much valuable information was accumulated and classified in the course of these inquiries, with the result, I think, that all the material facts may now be said to have been ascertained. But up to this moment nothing has been done, nothing at all.

In the meantime other countries have been making experiments. The German system, which is one of compulsory State-aided assurance, has been in existence since 1889. Under it pensions averaging a little over £16 13s. a year are paid to insured persons of the age of seventy and upwards. The State contribution amounts to less than 40 per cent of the whole, and it would seem that in 1907 not more than 126,000 persons out of a population of over 52 millions were in receipt of old age pensions.

More instruction, I think, for our purposes is to be derived from the legislation initiated in Denmark in 1891, in New Zealand in 1898, and subsequently in New South Wales and Victoria. These systems, though differing widely in their details, have several important features in common. In the first place, they do not depend for their application upon either voluntary or compulsory contribution on the part of the pensioner. In the next place, they are limited in all cases to persons whose income or property is below a prescribed figure; and, thirdly, in all cases they impose some test or other, varying in stringency and in complexity, of character and desert in regard to such matters, for instance, as past criminality or pauperism. Although both in Denmark and in New Zealand the expenditure upon the pensions has, in the course of time, exhibited a tendency to increase beyond the original estimate, yet the cost of administration has turned out to be relatively small, amounting in New Zealand in 1907 to not more than 1.67 per cent; and I think I may say that in none of these communities is there any dissatisfaction either with the principles or with the working of the law, and certainly no disposition to go back to the state of things which prevailed before old age pensions were set up.

His Majesty's present Government came into power and went through the last general election entirely unpledged in regard to this matter, not that they were insensible to its importance or to its urgency, but they felt it right to enter into no binding engagement until they had had full time to survey the problem in all its aspects, and — what is still more important — to lay a solid financial foundation for any future structure it might be possible to raise. It was accordingly not until we had seen our way to make some substantial provision for the reduction of the national liabilities that I found myself able to announce in the Budget of last year that this year it was our intention to make a beginning — and more than a beginning I never promised — in the creation of a sound and workable scheme. . . .

Extract 26

SECOND READING OF OLD AGE PENSIONS BILL

(Mr. David Lloyd George, Chancellor of the Exchequer, Commons, June 15, 1908)

MR. LLOYD GEORGE [1]: . . . The scheme is necessarily an incomplete one. We have never professed that it was complete and dealt with the whole problem; we wished it to be treated as an incomplete one, and to be considered as such. It is purely the first step, and I may even say that it is necessarily an experiment.

[1] Parliamentary Debates, Fourth Series, vol. 190, col. 564 sqq.

The second observation I should like to make is this, that those who have criticised most severely the disqualifications which we have introduced into the Bill are those who are opposed to the principle of the payment of old age pensions at the expense of the State at all. Therefore I should invite hon. Members to consider very cautiously those criticisms when they recollect the quarter from which in the main they have come.

The first general criticism is that this is a non-contributory scheme. I am not sure that that is not the effect of the Amendments of the noble Lord the Member for Marylebone [Lord Robert Cecil] and my hon. Friend the Member for Preston [Mr. Harold Cox] — these two anarchist leaders.[1] I demur altogether to the division of the schemes into contributory and non-contributory. So long as you have taxes imposed upon commodities which are consumed practically by every family in the country there is no such thing as a non-contributory scheme. You tax tea and coffee, sugar, beer, and tobacco, and you get a contribution from practically every family in the land one way or another. So, therefore, when a scheme is financed out of public funds it is as much a contributory scheme as a scheme which is financed directly by means of contributions arranged on the German or any other basis. A workman who has contributed health and strength, vigour and skill, to the creation of the wealth by which taxation is borne has made his contribution already to the fund which is to give him a pension when he is no longer fit to create that wealth. Therefore I object altogether to the general division of these schemes into contributory and non-contributory schemes.

There is, however, a class of scheme which is known as a contributory one. There is the German scheme, in which the workmen pay into a fund. It is rather a remarkable fact that most social reformers who have taken up this question have at first favoured contributory schemes, but a closer examination has almost invariably led them to abandon them on the ground that they are unequal

---

[1] Cf. infra, *Extracts 27* and *28*.

in their treatment of the working class, cumbersome, and very expensive, and in a country like ours hopelessly impracticable. . . .
Let me give you now two or three considerations why, in my judgment, a contributory scheme is impossible in this country. In the
first place, it would practically exclude women from its benefits.
Out of the millions of members of friendly societies there is but
a small proportion, comparatively, of women. Another consideration is that the vast majority are not earning anything and cannot
pay their contributions. The second reason is that the majority of
the workingmen are unable to deflect from their weekly earnings
a sufficient sum of money to make adequate provision for old age
in addition to that which they are now making for sickness, infirmity, and unemployment. I do not know what the average
weekly wage in this country is; we have not had a wage census
since 1886. I hope the Board of Trade will soon be able to pub-
lish the result of the wages census initiated some months ago, but
I do not suppose we shall have the Returns in time for our debates
on this Bill. The average weekly wage in 1886 was 24s. 9d., and
57 per cent of the working classes in this country were earning
25s. or less. It is quite clear, therefore, that out of such wages
they cannot make provision for sickness, for all the accidents and
expenses of life, and also set aside a sufficient sum to provide a
competence for old age as well. Take the agricultural labourer
with his 15s. or 16s. a week. How can he set aside 4d. a week
for a period of forty years, in addition to what he has to set aside
already for the purpose of sickness or infirmity? . . .

The provision which is made for the sick and unemployed is
grossly inadequate in this country, and yet the working classes
have done their best during fifty years to make provision without
the aid of the State. But it is insufficient. The old man has to
bear his own burden, while in the case of a young man who is
broken down and who has a wife and family to maintain, the suffering is increased and multiplied to that extent. These problems
of the sick, of the infirm, of the men who cannot find means of

earning a livelihood, though they seek it as if they were seeking for alms, who are out of work through no fault of their own, and who cannot even guess the reason why, are problems with which it is the business of the State to deal; they are problems which the State has neglected too long. In asking the House to give a second reading to this Bill, we ask them to sanction not merely its principle, but also its finance, having regard to the fact that we are anxious to utilise the resources of the State to make provision for undeserved poverty and destitution in all its branches.

Extract 27

OPPOSITION TO OLD AGE PENSIONS BILL

(*Mr. Harold Cox, Commons, June 15, 1908*)

MR. COX[1] moved an Amendment declaring:

While it is desirable that the State should organise aid for the unfortunate by establishing and assisting a general system of insurance against the principal risks of life, it is unjust to spend the taxpayers' money in giving subsidies to persons selected by arbitrary standards of age, income, and character.

He said he was not opposed on general grounds to the organisation of a system of old age pensions, but he was strongly opposed to the particular scheme which the Government had put forward, because he held that the scheme was unjust in principle, and as a consequence was necessarily unjust in almost every one of its details. That arose from the fact that if they started with a false principle, they were bound to set up arbitrary distinctions which must act harshly upon particular individuals and give a favour to one man while they refused the same favour to another man who had an equal title to it. Why should they start by saying that people over the age of seventy were entitled to a pension any

1 Parliamentary Debates, Fourth Series, vol. 190, col. 596 sqq.

more than by saying, for instance, that all people afflicted with blindness should receive a pension? He would take a more striking case — that of a woman who was left a widow with a young family. What did the Government do for her? All the Government did for her was to tax the food of her children in order that they might have money to give pensions to old people who were possibly much better off than she was. That was the essence of the scheme. Taxes would be kept on the necessaries of life in order to provide pensions for old people.

The whole idea of giving pensions instead of leaving people to draw relief from the Poor Law was that the Poor Law was humiliating. They had heard that stated in all the speeches in favour of the Bill. What were they going to do for the man over sixty and under seventy? Was he to go on suffering humiliation, or was he to starve? There was as much humiliation in receiving Poor Law relief at sixty as at seventy years of age. The Chancellor of the Exchequer in the somewhat extraordinary speech which he had delivered that afternoon seemed to be apologising in almost every sentence for his scheme. In fixing the age limit at seventy, the Government were flying in the face of experience. What had the trade unions done? The Amalgamated Society of Engineers provided pensions which were drawable at the age of fifty-five in cases where on account of infirmity or old age a member was unable to obtain the ordinary wages of his trade. . . . The Prime Minister, speaking a night or two ago at the National Liberal Club in regard to the payment of 5s. to people over seventy, said, " It will, without any offence to their self-respect or to their proper pride, without any feeling of humiliation, put at least half a million of old folk, the veterans of our industrial army, entirely beyond the reach of pecuniary anxiety and care." What kind of a world did the Prime Minister live in? He wondered whether his right hon. Friend had ever tried to live in London on 5s. a week, and if he had found himself entirely beyond the reach of pecuniary anxiety and care. Why! he would not get a single room for less than 3s., and then he would have 2s. left for food or clothing. There were a great many people who, even if they had the money, could not take care of themselves. . . . In particular there was evidence of the effect of drink on the old age pension question. So serious was that evil in Australia that it was recommended by the Royal Commission that it should be made a penal offence to give or serve drink to old age pensioners.

AN HON. MEMBER : For giving one glass of beer to an old man?

MR. COX said there was exactly the same difficulty in our own country. He had a letter from the master of a workhouse near London, where they had a good many Army pensioners. . . . He might mention that he had frequently called the attention of the Secretary for War to this scandal, but as yet nothing had been done. If old age pensions were paid as a right, the man might claim to be treated as other individuals in regard to the right to buy a glass of beer. . . .

The question he asked hon. Members opposite was, " Do you propose to give honourable pensions to men who dishonour our common humanity, and provide these pensions by taxing men who honestly earn their living ? " He challenged them to go on a platform and say that that was what they meant. That was a dilemma from which there was no possibility of escape as long as they had a non-contributory system. They must either give honourable pensions to any number of blackguards, or have an investigation of character which would be painful to all the honest people. The only escape from that dilemma was by contributory pensions. The money then belonged of right to the pensioner, and there was no need for an inquiry into character. . . .

A phrase constantly used in this matter was that old age pensions were to be given as a right, and not as a charity, as a recompense for previous services to the State. Did hon. Members below the gangway agree with that ? [" Hear, hear."] They did ; then they would be willing to accept some test to prove that there had been previous service to the State. Otherwise they would be throwing dust in the eyes of the public. He hoped he might say without offence that they had already been misleading the public by confusing the difference between the pension given to Lord Cromer and old age pensions which they demanded for everybody.

An Hon. Member : Why ?

Mr. Cox said he was sorry his hon. Friend could not see the difference between giving a pension to a man like Lord Cromer, who had done great service to the State, and to a man with regard to whom they would not take the trouble to ascertain whether he had done anything at all.

An Hon. Member : Lord Cromer had a big salary.

Mr. Cox said that as regarded that it sometimes happened that when a trade union secretary, who had drawn what was for him a substantial salary and had served his society well, at the end of his time retired, he received a handsome present from his society. That was exactly what the State had done to Lord Cromer. . . . [Mr. Cox then sketched the German contributory scheme and queried as to whence money was coming for a non-contributory scheme.]

Personally he lived by what he earned, and he would be ashamed if he did not make a fair contribution to the cost of the government of the country. He was quite sure that was the opinion of most Englishmen. He observed with great pleasure that hon. Members below the gangway had consistently supported the proposal that the income tax should be extended downwards so that every man, however poor, might make some contribution in proportion to his means. But while they held that sound view they unfortunately also held a view that was very alluring, but which he thought was ultimately deceptive — the view that they could through the Budget redress the inequalities of fortune. It was very alluring. When one saw the hideous inequalities which existed at present, the horrible contrast between great riches and abject poverty, one was greatly tempted to say, " We will redress this injustice by means of taxation." If they could do it he would be in favour of doing it, but he did not think it could be done, for the proposal involved subsidising the industries of the country which were not paying a sufficient wage at present, and giving money to people not in return for the work they did but because they were poor. That meant that they were going to treat poverty as a permanent institution, and the necessary consequence was that they would create a vast number of dependants. The man who earned his living was independent. He could face his master as a man because he gave his work in return for his wages. But if they were going to give a man something in return for nothing, they made him a dependant. He ceased to be an independent citizen and became a dependant on the will of some official or of some committee of elected persons consisting either of superior persons with charitable inclinations or of inferior persons with axes to grind. But whichever it was, he was a dependant, and no longer a free man as he was before. Therefore he held that the true ideal to set before them was to raise wages. That was the problem of all problems, because on that depended everything. On that depended housing, the feeding of children, and old age.

What he objected to in all these schemes of State charity was that instead of aiming at the abolition of poverty they tended to perpetuate poverty by treating it as a permanent institution. In the same way if they were going to argue that because wages were low in certain industries, those wages must be supplemented at the expense of the taxpayer, it meant they were going to say certain industries were parasitic and must be subsidised by the taxpayer. What would be the result? People would begin to say, " If you are going to have parasitic industries paid for by the taxpayer, why should we not pay for them in the simplest way, by putting a duty on foreign goods?" The free-trade objection to a protectionist tariff was that it created parasitic industries, and the good industries of the country were taxed for the benefit of the bad industries. Thus by admitting the principle of a subsidy to badly-paid industries they were giving away the free-trade case. That was a danger which he thought had not been sufficiently faced.

Some weeks ago the Chancellor of the Exchequer, apropos of nothing in particular, had described him as a champion of lost causes. He was not quite sure that he knew what that meant. For the past eight or nine years he had devoted the greater part of his life to fighting for free trade. Was that a lost cause? When he listened to the speeches of his right hon. Friend he was sometimes tempted to fear that he thought so. Personally he did not share that opinion. He had too much confidence in the ultimate common-sense of his countrymen to believe that there could be anything more than an ephemeral success for the strange movement which had captured the imagination and temporarily imprisoned the intelligence of hon. Gentlemen opposite. Even were it otherwise, even if he thought free trade were indeed a lost cause, he for one would not cease fighting for it. For he was not ashamed to confess that the principles of free trade were to him a living faith. In saying that he was not referring only to the application of those principles to the business of international buying and selling, though that alone was no little matter. It was no little matter that the teeming population of these islands was free to draw its sustenance from every quarter of the globe. It was no little matter that our manufacturers and captains of industry were free to assemble here every type of raw material that the world produced and every kind of machine and mechanical device that other brains had invented or other hands had fashioned, and thus aided were to build up, here in these little islands, vast and flourishing industries. That alone was no little matter. But there was something even more than that. So far as the relations of the citizens of a country to one another and to their Government were concerned, the essential principle of free trade, stated in its simplest terms, was fair play all around — the principle which required the State to give equal consideration to all its subjects and which forbade the State to give gratuitous favours either to

particular industries or to particular individuals. That principle
he held to be of priceless value. In all the complexities, in all
the temptations, of political life, it would enable them to steer a
straight course and maintain unblurred upon their banner the device
" Equal justice between man and man." He begged to move.

Extract 28

A CONSERVATIVE OPPONENT TO THE GOVERNMENT BILL

(*Lord Robert Cecil, Commons, June 15, 1908*)

LORD ROBERT CECIL,[1] in seconding the amendment, said the
Chancellor of the Exchequer had referred to him as an anarchist. He preferred to describe his form of political belief as a
reasonable trust in personal freedom and personal liberty. But
he imagined that it was not only in this country that the bureau-
crat had always thought that he who differed from him was an
anarchist. He presumed the Chancellor of the Exchequer was
really, if one might attribute such a defect to so eminent a person,
making a confusion between anarchism and individualism. They
did not appear to be in every respect identical. In the main question of principle that they had to discuss, it was fair to say that
those who differed from the Government differed because they
were of a more individualistic tendency than was shown in the
immediate proposals of the Government. He did not wish to attempt to define socialism and individualism, but there were two
very distinct principles on which they might proceed in approaching
this question of old age pensions. There was the principle that it
was primarily the duty of everybody to provide for his own old age,
and provide for himself generally. That was the principle that he
himself held, and he quite admitted that they were entitled to add
to that, that where for some reason or another the individual was
unable to provide for himself, it was reasonable for the State

1 Parliamentary Debates, Fourth Series, vol. 190, col. 613 sqq.

to come in and give assistance to that individual. That was the principle on which the contributory system rested. . . .

They were now in a position to state shortly what the real proposal of the Government was. It was to make an enormous gift of money, originally stated to be between £6,000,000 and £7,000,000, to a very large section of the working classes who were possessed of very large electoral power. In the last Parliament they constantly heard it said, he thought very unwisely, by hon. Members opposite that the Party to which he had the honour to belong was in the habit of giving doles to various classes. Why was not that said of this Bill ?

MR. JOHN WARD : It is following your precedent.

LORD R. CECIL said that the hon. Member would not find any precedent for a gift of £6,000,000 or £7,000,000 to any particular class of the community. He did not say that it was necessarily wrong ; all he wished to do was to call the attention of the House to the fact that this was a definite gift of 6,000,000 or 7,000,000 golden sovereigns out of the money of the general taxpayers to a particular class who possessed very large electoral power. The only reason why this was not described as a dole by hon. Members opposite was that this particular class happened to have a very large voting power in the country. Let the House remember that this was only the beginning. He was using the ordinary thin end of the wedge argument, but he would remind hon. Members what had been said by Ministers in recommending this scheme. The Prime Minister had stated that it was avowedly and professedly a temporary measure and that there was no finality about it. The scheme began at £6,000,000 and it had now risen to £7,500,000, and the Chancellor of the Exchequer had shown that it might automatically rise, unless something further was done, to £11,000,000.

The Chancellor of the Exchequer had pledged himself to the proposition that it was not right for the State to require any contribution from those whom it was intended to assist. It did not need any violent stretch of the imagination to guess what would happen the next time the Government got in some little difficulty

in regard to one of its measures — it might be the Licensing Bill
or the Education Bill. They knew what had happened at recent
bye-elections and they could easily imagine what would happen in
the future. The Government would be able to say that 5s. a week
for people over seventy was ridiculous and it ought to be extended
to people over sixty-five years of age, and the pensions ought to be
10s. a week. Having stated that, perhaps the bye-elections would
go a little bit better for the Government. He thought the right
hon. Gentlemen might be trusted in this matter, but any ordinary
Government which had this great opportunity for wholesale persuasion of the electors at the expense of the taxpayer must go on
extending gifts as long as the finances of the country permitted it.
. . . He did not wish to be an alarmist, but he felt that with the
vast responsibilities of this country they had in the last resort only
the national character to depend on. They had no right to assume
that during the next twenty-five years they would have so peaceful
a course to steer. No one who looked even from outside at the
present international situation could fail to see certain elements of
difficulty and danger in the future. And if they had to enter upon
a great life and death struggle, as might well happen, and they had
weakened the fibre of their people by a system and by a policy of
which this was only the beginning, then the statesmen in the House
of Commons who had sanctioned that miserable backsliding from
the true statesmanship of Empire would have much to answer for.
He begged to second.

Extract 29

SCEPTICISM ON OLD AGE PENSIONS

(Mr. Arthur J. Balfour, Commons, July 9, 1908)

MR. BALFOUR[1]: . . . I think that neither the actual provisions
of this Bill nor the mode in which the Government have allowed it
to be discussed gives us the smallest security that one of the greatest

[1] Parliamentary Debates, Fourth Series, vol. 192, col. 175 sqq.

and most costly experiments in social legislation is going to be tried under circumstances that will give any hope of permanent success. There are three main questions raised by the scheme. The first is, Will this Bill work according to its avowed objects? Is the machinery of the Bill, in other words, going to give pensions on the plan that the Government say is desirable? The second is, How is it going to affect the broader and wider problems of social reform? And the third is, How is it going to affect the national finances? These are the three problems that every man in this House, no matter in which quarter he may sit, should really consider if he wants to estimate the value of the legislative experiment the Government are now trying.

The first point is whether the Bill is really going to work out according to the theory of its framers; and, if it does, what will be its results? The theory of its framers is a very simple one. They say that, pending the acquisition of further national resources, they must limit their Bill to pensions for persons seventy years of age, and, to put it broadly, of good character. How is this Bill going to attain these two objects? How is the machinery going to limit the Bill to persons of seventy and to persons of good character? And will the machinery work smoothly, justly, and to public advantage? I cannot really believe that the Government have thoroughly thought out the method in which their own machinery is going to work. Take the first of the two conditions, that of age. That is one of the subjects we have discussed. We have not had an opportunity of discussing the age as between seventy and sixty-five, because that was shut out by the closure, but we have discussed on more than one occasion the machinery by which the age of seventy is to be arrived at. I do not think that by any statement the Government have shown a clear idea of the difficulties by which that investigation is surrounded or the means by which those difficulties are to be surmounted. In the first place, who are the investigators? They are officers of the Inland Revenue, a single committee for each county and large borough, and ultimately the President of the

Local Government Board. For the life of me I cannot see that an investigation can be carried out by any of these three bodies. I made some remarks in Committee with regard to the Inland Revenue officers which I believe have given pain to those most estimable public officers. If I have said anything that gave them pain I most heartily withdraw it. They are a most valuable body of men and carry out duties of great responsibility with perfect uprightness and great efficiency. But I ask whether the most admirable performance of the duties of the Inland Revenue either gives a man the training or provides him with the machinery by which this kind of investigation is to be carried out. Take the case of an unskilled labourer in London. He reaches an age that he himself thinks is either seventy or very nearly so. He believes that he has worked hard all his life, and that if anybody deserves a pension he does. He applies to the Inland Revenue officer and says, " My name is O'Grady."

Mr. John Wilson : Make it Smith, and then you are safe.

Mr. Balfour. I chose an Irish name for a particular reason which will appear directly. He says, " My age is seventy, and I desire to be supplied with a pension. I come from Cork." The Inland Revenue officer says, " What proof have you that you are seventy ? " He has no proof. Why should he have a proof ? I do not believe I should know my own age if it were not that tactless friends are constantly reminding me of it. Most assuredly a dock labourer who left Cork thirty years ago may very well be excused if he has not proof of his age, since he was born in a country where there was no registration of births at the time when he was presumably born. How is this unfortunate official going to investigate in the City of Cork whether Mr. O'Grady working at the docks is or is not seventy years of age ? The thing appears to be wholly impossible, and there is no machinery for doing it. The county committee to which he refers are no better off than himself, and if they refer to the head of the Local Government Board he is no better off. The machinery cannot be found and will not be supplied. . . .

If the difficulties with regard to age are overwhelming, what are we to say with regard to the investigation as to character? None of us are without some misgivings as to the enormous power given to an Imperial officer and to a local committee to form a judgment on the way in which the poorer classes of the community have carried out their life's duty. It is not a pleasant thing to have to do, and if it is done honestly and conscientiously it will be a very painful duty thrown on those who may have to do it. Here, again, we really have very little means of obtaining assistance. Do not let us consider the country village where everyone's character is known. There may be an opportunity for favouritism or vindictive attacks on unpopular persons, but the facts will be known and may be fairly and properly judged upon. But how can the facts be known with regard to the great floating population of the huge industrial centres? . . .

Will its operation be confined to persons over seventy, and of virtuous character? I do not believe for one moment that it will. We are very good-natured people, particularly so when we are dealing with other people's money; and the duty of excluding anybody from the benefits of the Act will be a painful and also an expensive one. Every committee which declares a person in its district or county or borough to be ineligible for a pension has to do that which is very painful from the point of view of humanity, and very disagreeable from the point of view of the local purse. When humanity and economy are on one side, I think they are too strong for any legislative dykes which the Government may raise against them, and I do not believe that the dykes that the Government have raised will keep out the waters of expenditure for one moment. Hon. Gentlemen below the gangway greatly regretted that they could not discuss their Amendment for reducing the age from seventy to sixty-five. I do not think it will make very much difference. I believe that under this Bill everybody who desires a pension and can show a decent appearance of being seventy will probably be found eligible by a kindly Imperial officer and a charitable county committee.

That raises one or two points of very great importance. The first point touches on what I have described as the second great question raised by this Bill — namely, its future effect on social reform. If you are going to use, as I am sure you are going to use, this Bill as a mere method of giving pensions at the taxpayers' expense to persons in declining years, and who have not got a very black mark against their character, how will you prevent its becoming a mere part of the outdoor relief system of the country? You cannot do it. It is quite true that you have got a different machinery for allocating the money, but to suppose that the ordinary citizen is going nicely to distinguish between what he gets through the Imperial officer and the committee and what he gets through the relieving officer and the board of guardians, and to regard one as discreditable and the other as creditable, is really trespassing upon our credulity. . . . The truth is, the Government must be perfectly well aware that they ought to have taken this question of old age pensions as part of the general problem of poverty. You cannot divorce the two. If only for the purpose of distinguishing pension from Poor Law relief you must consider the two together. . . .

This really brings me to the last of the three points I wished to touch upon — namely, the relation of this measure to our national finances. I confess that I look on this whole question with considerable alarm. The hon. Member for Newcastle-under-Lyme [Mr. Wedgwood] explained that after all no great burden would be cast on our national finances, because the money was now paid by the charitable and through the Poor Law, and there was not much difference whether the burden was thrown on the Exchequer by this Bill or whether it was left to be paid sporadically and uncertainly, partly by Poor Law machinery and partly by the private machinery of charity. I think that the hon. Member is profoundly mistaken. It makes the whole difference where the money comes from. The mere fact that there is money to be got somewhere does not make it easy for the Chancellor of the Exchequer to get it. . . . The Government here shows what the public are to get, but they have not yet been shown how they are to pay for it. But there is a divergence of opinion even among the members of the Government. The Prime Minister assured us more than once that the Government had considered the point, and that they clearly saw their way to provide the necessary funds by means of free-trade finance. This method of carrying it out is a secret which the Prime Minister has kept not only from the Opposition, but from his colleague the Chancellor of the Exchequer. I think that is carrying secrecy too far. I think that in the comity of the Cabinet the late Chancellor of the Exchequer should have told the present Chancellor of the Exchequer how, within the limits of free-trade finance, £6,500,000 are to be found next year and £7,500,000 the year after. It is not going to be £7,500,000 either. If my interpretation of the situation is correct, you will get to £11,500,000 almost immediately, and how within the limits of free-trade finance are you to get £11,500,000? There is no great information either to be got from the present Chancellor of the Exchequer, according to what he has already told the City, and if he has kept the secret from the high financial authorities of the City, it is not likely that he will tell his critics in the House. I do not ask him, therefore, to tell us, if he does not know. But again I ask, Where, within the limits of free-trade finance, are £6,500,000, £7,500,000, or £11,500,000 to be obtained? . . .

I regret the hasty course which the Government have taken, but the responsibility must lie with them. The Government alone have the opportunity of estimating the resources at their disposal for carrying it out. They, and they alone, have the machinery for making some comparative survey of all the needs of the State. On them lies the responsibility. The Bill does not satisfy the demands of those who claim the right to old age pensions, and on the other hand it so burdens and cripples the national resources that we may find it impossible to meet other obligations not less pressing, not less connected with the safety of the State and the well-being of the poorer members of the State.

Extract 30

LABOUR DEFENCE OF OLD AGE PENSIONS

(Mr. William Crooks, Commons, July 9, 1908)

MR. CROOKS [1]: I apologise to the House for intervening in the debate at this late hour. What astonished me in the course of the discussion is the different grounds hon. Gentlemen above the gangway have taken. First they wanted a proper universal scheme ; then they wanted certain qualifications put in ; then the mover of the Amendment to-day deplored that there were so many qualifications in order that a poor man might get a certificate of character before he could secure a pension. Now they regret the failure of their efforts to put in still more qualifications.

I have read somewhere that life is a comedy to a thinking man and a tragedy to a feeling man. That is all the difference in the world. We have had an exhibition of thinking without feeling. I have felt pretty keenly about the whole business — listening to the flippancy which one expects at some kind of Tory meeting. In a pamphlet which I wrote ten years ago I anticipated that whenever a scheme of old age pensions was considered in the House of Commons it would be called " a glorified outdoor relief." So is every kind of pension that is paid out of the taxpayers' pockets. We have been told by opponents of the Bill about inquisitorial examinations of claimants for a pension. It is very good of these hon. Gentlemen, I admit it. Is it not the case that hon. and right hon. Gentlemen who receive pensions from His Majesty's Government are obliged to declare in writing their impecuniosity ? How dreadfully lowering and degrading it must be to a man whose private income would be wealth beyond the dreams of avarice to an ordinary poor man in this country ! Yet, he has the nerve to write to somebody and to declare his impecuniosity before he gets

[1] Parliamentary Debates, Fourth Series, vol. 192, col. 193 sqq.

his £1200 a year! No man reads him a little homily on thrift. No man says a word about it. There is nothing degrading about pensions at all, except when they get down to 5s. a week; they are not awfully degrading, but the reward for services to the State — that is, if they are anything between £1200 and £4000 a year. They then add to the dignity and importance of His Majesty's subjects. . . .

There is a Poor Law Commission sitting now, and that would be a reason for doing nothing, because when the late Government wished to do nothing, they appointed a Royal Commission. I have illustrated the fact, I think, before. It is the case of the man who once saw a lot of coloured cooked eggs on a barrow, and he said, "What are those eggs, guv'nor?" "Oh, they are partridge eggs." "Do you think a hen would bring them off?" "Yes, I should think so." "Then how much for a sitting?" "1s. 6d. and a share of your luck." About four weeks after he turned up again and gazed wistfully at the stall, and the man recognised him and said: "Well, what luck?" "Oh, you never saw anything like it in your life. The hen, she sat and sat, and I am blowed if she did not cook them." There has never been an Old Age Pension Commission or a Poor Law Commission which did not well cook their reports before bringing them to this House. The regulations of the Board have amended Poor Law relief out of all knowledge. They told us to give outdoor relief generously, and in giving it to old and deserving people we should not rake up the past. I was a guardian and I wished to do it generously. Some said, "They do not want old age pensions; you want to make the workhouse more comfortable." Well, we did that, and what was the result? I was put on trial and very nearly got time. . . .

I once said, and I repeat, that no man should sit in this House without having served first for ten years as a Poor Law guardian. He would then know something about human nature. It is not perfect. There are a good many sides to it, but most people who apply for relief are very human, and I do not think they very much object to these inquisitorial examinations as to their character. We were challenged by the hon. Member for Preston [Mr. Harold Cox], who said, " Would you go on any public platform and declare that you are in favour of giving a pension of 5s. per week to a drunken, thriftless, worthless man or woman ? " My reply is very prompt to that. A man of seventy with nothing in the world to help him is going to cut a pretty shine on 5s. per week, whether his character be good or bad. What could he do with it ? It is not enough to keep him in decency, and he would be well punished for not taking care when he had the opportunity if he had to live on 5s. per week. Who are you, to be continually finding fault ? Who amongst you has such a clear record as to be able to point to the iniquity and wickedness of an old man of seventy ? I said before, and I repeat, if a man is foolish enough to get old, and if he has not been artful enough to get rich, you have no right to punish him for it. It is no business of yours. It is sufficient for you to know he has grown old.

After all, who are these old men and women ? Let me appeal to the noble Lord the Member for Marylebone [Lord Robert Cecil]. They are the veterans of industry, people of almost endless toil, who have fought for and won the industrial and commercial supremacy of Great Britain. Is their lot and end to be the Bastille of the everlasting slur of pauperism ? We claim these pensions as a right. Ruskin, I think, read you a little homily on the subject — " Even a labourer serves his country with his spade and shovel as the statesman does with his pen, or the soldier with his sword." He has a right to some consideration from the State. Here in a country rich beyond description there are people poverty-stricken beyond description. There can be no earthly excuse for the condition of things which exists in this country to-day. If it be necessary to have a strong Army and Navy to protect the wealth of the nation, do not let us forget that it is the veterans of industry who have created that wealth ; and let us accept this as an instalment to bring decency and comfort to our aged men and women.

Extract 31

OPPOSITION TO THE BILL IN THE HOUSE OF LORDS

(*Earl of Wemyss, Lords, July 20, 1908*)

THE EARL OF WEMYSS,[1] who had given notice of an Amendment—

That pending the Report of the Royal Commission now inquiring into the principles and working of the existing Poor Law it would be unwise to enter upon the consideration of a Bill establishing the far-reaching principle of State Old Age Pensions —

said : . . . Last Thursday the *Times*, in a leading article, recommended your Lordships to pass the second and even the third. reading of the Bill, not on account of any merit it has, but for your own sake, and for the good of your Lordships' House. In the same article, however, there was a sentence which blew all this to smithereens, and I commend it to the notice of your Lordships' House. The sentence ran — " But the real objection to the Bill is that it is fundamentally on wrong lines, and is, in fact, not a pension but a Bill giving indefinite extension of outdoor relief."

It is on that ground that I venture to ask your Lordships whether it is wise to go on with the Bill. I want your Lordships to consider, supposing this to be right, what indefinite extension of outdoor relief means.

I should like to take your Lordships back seventy years. In 1834 the Poor Law, which had existed from the time of Elizabeth, had, by mismanagement and lax administration, produced such a state of things that it was given in evidence before the Poor Law Commission of that date that labourers said, " Damn work ! Blast work ! Why should I work when I can get 10s. from the rates for doing nothing."

The Commission, on which the Bishop of London and the Bishop of Carlisle sat, reported that all this was due to lax administration, and that stringency in administering the law was necessary. There may be people who say that the law has been too stringent and too harsh, but those two Bishops evidently did not think so. What has happened since then ? From that time better administration has prevailed, outdoor relief has been restricted, and the independence of the people has been restored. If, from sentimental motives, Parliament passes this Bill, I hold that you will establish a system of demoralisation amongst the working classes, that you will do away with thrift, that families will cease to regard it as an obligation to maintain those of their members whose working days are passed, and that self-reliance will be diminished.

I see in his place my noble friend Lord Rosebery. He, as Chancellor of the University of Glasgow, delivered the other day a most admirable speech, in the course of which he spoke strongly of the need of self-reliance. What he said is so much to the point that I will, with your Lordships' permission, read it. The noble Earl said : " The State invites us every day to lean upon it. I seem to hear the wheedling and alluring whisper, ' Sound you may be, we bid you be a cripple. Do you see? Be blind. Do you hear ? Be deaf. Do you walk ? Be not so venturesome. Here is a crutch for one arm ; when you get accustomed to it, you will soon want another — the sooner the better.' The strongest man if encouraged may soon accustom himself to the methods of an invalid ; he may train himself to totter, or to be fed with a spoon. . . . Every day the area for initiative is being narrowed, every day the standing ground for self-reliance is being undermined ; every day the public infringes — with the best intentions, no doubt — on the individual ; the nation is being taken into custody by the State." And at the end the noble Earl said, " It was self-reliance that built the Empire ; it is by self-reliance, and all that that implies, that it must be welded and continued." Those are wise words, which I humbly recommend to the attention of your Lordships. . . .

I could, if I wished to detain your Lordships, give you unlimited quotations against this Bill. All those who have given their lives

to the care of the poor and are interested in thrift and other societies are all hostile to the Bill, as it at present stands. I will not
quote those authorities, but will be satisfied by reading to your
Lordships an extract from a circular issued by the Charity Organisation Society, of which many of your Lordships are members,
and which has done excellent work during the last thirty years.
That society has issued a circular against the Bill in which they
assert that — " Neither the Bill, nor anything like the Bill, has ever
been demanded by, or received the sanction of, the electors. To
delay the passing of the Bill can do no serious injury to the country and will enable the nation to consider calmly the policy of a
measure which, for good or bad, produces a social revolution."
That is an accurate description of the Bill, and I think it would be
wise if your Lordships were to postpone consideration of it until
all possible information is obtained. For what are you doing ? You
will be tying a millstone round the neck of the country and involving
it in an expenditure in the end of nearly £30,000,000 a year.

On the very day last week when this Bill passed through the
other House there was in France a Commission of the Senate sitting considering a Pension Bill, and that Commission, in spite of
the wish of the French Government that the Bill should proceed
and that they should report upon it, declined to do so until all the
information that could possibly be obtained was before them. My
Lords, we are told, *Fas est ab hoste doceri*, but I venture to suggest
that your Lordships might also learn from a friend. I should like
to see the *entente cordiale* of Shepherd's Bush carried to your Lordships' House ; and that you should act as wisely, as moderately,
and as reasonably as the French Commission are doing. Let me
further remind your Lordships of that splendid French maxim
Fais ce que doit advienne que pourra, and urge your Lordships to
act upon it. I have nothing more to add. I intend to stick to my
guns and to divide your Lordships if I can get a teller, and I have
secured one. What success we shall have in the division lobbies I
do not know, but, at any rate, whatever the result may be, one

thing is certain — that all the common-sense and the sense of what is right and reasonable in dealing with such a question as this will be found with the minority. I beg to move the Amendment standing in my name.[1]

Extract 32

DANGER OF DISPUTE WITH THE HOUSE OF COMMONS

(Earl of Rosebery, Lords, July 20, 1908)

THE EARL OF ROSEBERY [2] : . . . I believe this is the most important Bill by a long way that has ever been submitted to the House of Lords during the forty years that I have sat in it. I view its consequences as so great, so mystic, so incalculable, so largely affecting the whole scope and fabric of our Empire itself, that I rank it as a measure far more vitally important than even the great Reform Bills which have come before this House. I confess, to come at once to the Amendment of my noble friend, whom we heard with so much pleasure in such vigour at an age so greatly surpassing the ordinary span of man, that, if you take that Amendment in pure logic, it is extremely difficult to say anything against it. My noble friend says that you should wait for the Report of the Poor Law Commission before coming to a decision upon this Bill. His Majesty's Government have been a little unfortunate, owing to their enthusiasm for legislation, in more than once being unable to await pending inquiries before they proceeded to carry legislation into effect ; and I do not know that on any occasion they have been so unfortunate as they have been with regard to this Bill. . . . But when I come to the practical bearings of my noble friend's Amendment I feel much greater doubts, and I must tell him at once that I shall not be able to accompany him and his teller into the lobby which they have projected for themselves. I

---

[1] The Amendment of Earl Wemyss was eventually rejected by a vote of 123 to 16.
[2] Parliamentary Debates, Fourth Series, vol. 192, col. 1379 sqq.

cannot do so for very clear and obvious reasons. The first is that the Bill is an almost purely financial measure, coming up from the House of Commons with the almost unanimous support of that House after a division which, I think, only mustered ten against it in its final stage, and which had no division against it at all on its second reading. [Viscount St. Aldwyn here whispered to the noble Earl.] I am wrong, but at any rate an almost equally insignificant division on the second reading.

A financial Bill coming up with this practical unanimity from the House of Commons it may be within your legal prerogative to reject, but I am quite sure it is equally impolitic for you to do so. More than this, it comes with the assent of both political parties. No one can forget — we have been more than once reminded of it to-night — that the question was started by Mr. Chamberlain somewhere about 1894 or 1895, and therefore if you sit on the cross benches and you are not pledged to either party in this matter, you must feel, quite impartially, that this proposal comes as a principle equal to both parties. . . .

The first responsibility of every country and every nation is national defence. I confess this prospect fills me with despair. I understand that the Government already acknowledge some liability in respect of an increase in the Navy for next year; and I strongly suspect that, in spite of the somewhat ambiguous proceedings of which we have read, they do not expect any material reduction in the Army. Surely the moment is ill-chosen for undertaking this vague experiment, so prodigal of expenditure, and I would ask the Government — I say it in no spirit of hostility, but in a spirit of earnest and deep anxiety — to meet some of the points raised in this debate, and to assure us that, in furthering and not opposing this boon which they offer to the old of the United Kingdom, we are not dealing a blow at the Empire which may be almost mortal, and that we are not embarrassing and encumbering our finances to a degree of which no man now living, however young he may be, will see the limit or the end.

Extract 33

AN ANGLICAN BISHOP ON OLD AGE PENSIONS

(*Bishop of Ripon, Lords, July 20, 1908*)

THE LORD BISHOP OF RIPON [1]: . . . My Lords, there is something in nations which is of more importance to them than mere financial prosperity. The accumulation of the power of wealth which enables nations to raise a considerable revenue through taxation, gives the stamp, as it were, of prosperity, but the best asset of a nation is a manly, vigorous, and numerous race, and the best asset of the race is that the character of its men and women shall never be impaired. A Frenchman once wrote a book concerning what he called the superiority of the Anglo-Saxon race, and in the course of that book he pointed out what he believed to be the one essential factor which contributed to that superiority. He said that in all the history of English life one spirit had prevailed, and that was the spirit of self-reliance. He turned to his countrymen and said, "The danger which we are in to-day is that we are not rearing our population to self-reliant habits." He drew the picture of the little farmer in Normandy who would stint himself and live in an unclean and even unwholesome dwelling in order that he might leave a sufficient sum to his children. He pointed then to the English farmer who, he said, so far from crippling himself in order that his sons may be well started in the world, takes the strong and independent line and says, "I made my way in the world and I expect my sons to do the same." "In other words," said the French writer, "the race across the Channel has educated its children in the habits of self-reliance, and to this habit is largely due the superiority and the strength of that race."

Now I cannot help asking myself, and I feel sure that is the thought which has been passing through many minds to-night,

[1] Parliamentary Debates, Fourth Series, vol. 192, col. 1389 sqq.

whether we are not in danger, not now, not to-day, but in the future, of dealing with this question of financial support in such a way that we undermine that spirit of self-reliance out of which the strength and the power of the British race has largely grown. That seems to me to be by far the most important question involved. It is character which makes, as it were, for the generous strength of a race, and it is character alone which can give them the security for true and abiding riches. Therefore it is that I cannot help asking myself whether there may not be a danger of its being weakened in the future.

I speak not of those of seventy years of age who are to receive the benefit of this measure. Their characters are formed, their conditions are settled. We are going forward to-night and saying : " Let us help them, let us give to them something which will ease their later years, and if a few have not deserved, well, we will at any rate with large-heartedness forget those who were weak and deal largely and generously with this matter before us, for all these men or women of seventy naturally appeal to the pity and sympathy of our hearts." But when I look beyond and ask whether it is conceivable that we may begin so to hold out the thought that men may be able to receive from the State that which in olden days they won by their own strong labours, self-denial, and thrift, then I am apprehensive lest we should, in attempting to do a good, do a great and grievous wrong, robbing ourselves and our children of that which is the best inheritance, the inheritance of a sturdy, strong, self-reliant manhood, that will take upon itself the responsibilities of life and be equal, therefore, to the responsibilities of Empire. I think none of us can shut our eyes to the fact that there are among us people who are very ready to shirk responsibility, and I, for one, would feel that the whole system and condition of English life had lost its meaning and value if once we should act in such a fashion as to remove responsibility, and the sense of responsibility, from the people of this country. We are in this world for responsibility ; through responsibility we grow and rise to the height of character which Divine Providence intended us to reach. Let us not, by any action of ours, weaken that which is the best thing we can preserve, the character of the population, for out of that, and out of that alone, will spring the strength and the stability of the nation.

Extract 34

OLD AGE PENSIONS ACT, 1908

(*8 Edw. 7, ch. 40*)

An Act to provide for Old Age Pensions.　(1st August 1908)

Be it enacted by the King's most Excellent Majesty, by and with the advice and consent of the Lords Spiritual and Temporal, and Commons, in this present Parliament assembled, and by the authority of the same, as follows :

1. Right to receive Old Age Pension

(1) Every person in whose case the conditions laid down by this Act for the receipt of an old age pension (in this Act referred to as statutory conditions) are fulfilled, shall be entitled to receive such a pension under this Act so long as those conditions continue to be fulfilled, and so long as he is not disqualified under this Act for the receipt of the pension.

(2) An old age pension under this Act shall be at the rate set forth in the schedule to this Act.

(3) The sums required for the payment of old age pensions under this Act shall be paid out of moneys provided by Parliament.

(4) The receipt of an old age pension under this Act shall not deprive the pensioner of any franchise, right, or privilege, or subject him to any disability.

2. *Statutory Conditions for Receipt of Old Age Pension*

The statutory conditions for the receipt of an old age pension by any person are —

(1) The person must have attained the age of seventy:

(2) The person must satisfy the pension authorities that for at least twenty years up to the date of the receipt of any sum on account of a pension he has been a British subject, [and has had his residence, as defined by regulations under this Act, in the United Kingdom] [1]:

(3) The person must satisfy the pension authorities that his yearly means as calculated under this Act do not exceed thirty-one pounds ten shillings.

3. *Disqualification for Old Age Pension* [2]

(1) A person shall be disqualified for receiving or continuing to receive an old age pension under this Act, notwithstanding the fulfilment of the statutory conditions —

(*a*) While he is in receipt of any poor relief (other than relief excepted under this provision), and, until the thirty-first day of December nineteen hundred and ten unless Parliament otherwise determines, if he has at any time since the first day of January nineteen hundred and eight received, or hereafter receives, any such relief: Provided that for the purposes of this provision —

(i) any medical or surgical assistance (including food or comforts) supplied by or on the recommendation of a medical officer; or

(ii) any relief given to any person by means of the maintenance of any dependant of that person in any lunatic asylum, infirmary, or hospital, or the payment of any expenses of the burial of a dependant; or

---

[1] Repealed by the Old Age Pensions Act, 1911. Cf. infra, p. 178.
[2] Cf. amendments in the Old Age Pensions Act, 1911. Cf. infra, p. 179.

(iii) any relief (other than medical or surgical assistance, or relief herein-before specifically exempted) which by law is expressly declared
not to be a disqualification for registration as
a parliamentary elector, or a reason for depriv-
ing any person of any franchise, right, or
privilege;

shall not be considered as poor relief:

(b) If, before he becomes entitled to a pension, he has habitually
failed to work according to his ability, opportunity, and
need, for the maintenance or benefit of himself and those
legally dependent upon him:

Provided that a person shall not be disqualified under
this paragraph if he has continuously for ten years up to
attaining the age of sixty, by means of payments to
friendly, provident, or other societies, or trade unions,
or other approved steps, made such provision against old
age, sickness, infirmity, or want or loss of employment
as may be recognised as proper provision for the purpose
by regulations under this Act, and any such provision,
when made by the husband in the case of a married
couple living together, shall as respects any right of the
wife to a pension, be treated as provision made by the
wife as well as by the husband:

(c) While he is detained in any asylum within the meaning of
the Lunacy Act, 1890, or while he is being maintained in
any place as a pauper or criminal lunatic:

(d) During the continuance of any period of disqualification
arising or imposed in pursuance of this section in consequence of conviction for an offence.

(2) Where a person has been before the passing of this Act,
or is after the passing of this Act, convicted of any offence, and
ordered to be imprisoned without the option of a fine or to suffer
any greater punishment, he shall be disqualified for receiving or

continuing to receive an old age pension under this Act while he is detained in prison in consequence of the order, and for a further period of ten[1] years after the date on which he is released from prison.

(3) Where a person of sixty years of age or upwards having been convicted before any court is liable to have a detention order made against him under the Inebriates Act, 1898, and is not necessarily, by virtue of the provisions of this Act, disqualified for receiving or continuing to receive an old age pension under this Act, the court may, if they think fit, order that the person convicted be so disqualified for such period, not exceeding ten years, as the court direct.

4. Calculation of Means [2]

(3) If it appears that any person has directly or indirectly deprived himself of any income or property in order to qualify himself for the receipt of an old age pension, or for the receipt of an old age pension at a higher rate than that to which he would otherwise be entitled under this Act, that income or the yearly value of that property shall, for the purposes of this section, be taken to be part of the means of that person.

5. Mode of paying Pensions

(1) An old age pension under this Act, subject to any directions of the Treasury in special cases, shall be paid weekly in advance in such manner and subject to such conditions as to identification or otherwise as the Treasury direct.

(2) A pension shall commence to accrue on the first Friday after the claim for the pension has been allowed, or, in the case of a claim provisionally allowed, on the first Friday after the day on which the claimant becomes entitled to receive the pension.

---

[1] Amended in 1911 to read "two."
[2] Subsections (1) and (2) of section 4 were repealed by the Act of 1911. For the substitutions, cf. infra, p. 177.

6. *Old Age Pension to be Inalienable*

Every assignment of or charge on and every agreement to assign or charge an old age pension under this Act shall be void, and, on the bankruptcy of a person entitled to an old age pension, the pension shall not pass to any trustee or other person acting on behalf of the creditors.

7. *Determination of Claims and Questions*

(1) All claims for old age pensions under this Act and all questions whether the statutory conditions are fulfilled in the case of any person claiming such a pension, or whether those conditions continue to be fulfilled in the case of a person in receipt of such a pension, or whether a person is disqualified for receiving or continuing to receive a pension, shall be considered and determined [1] as follows :

(*a*) Any such claim or question shall stand referred to the local pension committee, and the committee shall (except in the case of a question which has been originated by the pension officer and on which the committee have already received his report), before considering the claim or question, refer it for report and inquiry to the pension officer :

(*b*) The pension officer shall inquire into and report upon any claim or question so referred to him, and the local pension committee shall, on the receipt of the report of the pension officer and after obtaining from him or from any other source if necessary any further information as to the claim or question, consider the case and give their decision upon the claim or question :

(*c*) The pension officer, and any person aggrieved, may appeal to the central pension authority against a decision of the local pension committee allowing or refusing a claim for

---

[1] The character of such questions is defined in the Old Age Pensions Act, 1911, section 6. Cf. infra, p. 180.

pension or determining any question referred to them within the time and in the manner prescribed by regulations under this Act, and any claim or question in respect of which an appeal is so brought shall stand referred to the central pension authority, and shall be considered and determined by them :

(*d*) If any person [1] is aggrieved by the refusal or neglect of a local pension committee to consider a claim for a pension, or to determine any question referred to them, that person may apply in the prescribed manner to the central pension authority, and that authority may, if they consider that the local pension committee have refused or neglected to consider and determine the claim or question within a reasonable time, themselves consider and determine the claim or question in the same manner as on an appeal from the decision of the local pension committee :

(2) The decision of the local pension committee on any claim or question which is not referred to the central pension authority, and the decision of the central pension authority on any claim or question which is so referred to them, shall be final and conclusive.

8. *Administrative Machinery*

(1) The local pension committee shall be a committee appointed for every borough and urban district, having a population according to the last published census for the time being of twenty thousand or over, and for every county (excluding the area of any such borough or district) by the council of the borough, district, or county.

The persons appointed to be members of a local pension committee need not be members of the council by which they are appointed.

(2) A local pension committee may appoint such and so many sub-committees, consisting either wholly or partly of the members of the committee as the committee think fit, and a local pension

[1] Cf. Act of 1911, section 6, subsection (6), infra, p. 182.

committee may delegate, either absolutely or under such conditions as they think fit, to any such sub-committee any powers and duties of the local committee under this Act.

(3) The central pension authority shall be the Local Government Board, and the Board may act through such committee, persons, or person appointed by them as they think fit.

(4) Pension officers shall be appointed by the Treasury, and the Treasury may appoint such number of those officers as they think fit to act for such areas as they direct.

(5) Any reference in this Act to pension authorities shall be construed as a reference to the pension officer, the local pension committee, and the central pension authority, or to any one of them, as the case requires.

9. Penalty for False Statements [1]

(1) If for the purpose of obtaining or continuing an old age pension under this Act, either for himself or for any other person, or for the purpose of obtaining or continuing an old age pension under this Act for himself or for any other person at a higher rate than that appropriate to the case, any person knowingly makes any false statement or false representation, he shall be liable on summary conviction to imprisonment for a term not exceeding six months, with hard labour.

(2) If it is found at any time that a person has been in receipt of an old age pension under this Act while the statutory conditions were not fulfilled in his case or while he was disqualified for receiving the pension, he or, in the case of his death, his personal representative, shall be liable to repay to the Treasury any sums paid to him in respect of the pension while the statutory conditions were not fulfilled or while he was disqualified for receiving the pension, and the amount of those sums may be recovered as a debt due to the Crown.

[1] Important amendments of this section in the Old Age Pensions Act, 1911, sections 6 and 7. Cf. infra, pp. 180–183.

10. Regulations and Expenses

(1) The Treasury in conjunction with the Local Government Board and with the Postmaster-General (so far as relates to the Post Office) may make regulations for carrying this Act into effect, and in particular —

(a) for prescribing the evidence to be required as to the fulfilment of statutory conditions [and for defining the meaning of residence for the purposes of this Act] [1]; and

(b) for prescribing the manner in which claims to pensions may be made, and the procedure to be followed on the consideration and determination of claims and questions to be considered and determined by pension officers and local pension committees or by the central pension authority, and the mode in which any question may be raised as to the continuance, in the case of a pensioner, of the fulfilment of the statutory conditions, and as to the disqualification of a pensioner; and

(c) as to the number, quorum, term of office, and proceedings generally of the local pension committee and the use by the committee, with or without payment, of any offices of a local authority, and the provision to be made for the immediate payment of any expenses of the committee which are ultimately to be paid by the Treasury.

(2) The regulations shall provide for enabling claimants for pensions to make their claims and obtain information as respects old age pensions under this Act through the Post Office, and for provisionally allowing claims to pensions before the date on which the claimant will become actually entitled to the pension, and for notice being given by registrars of births and deaths to the pension officers or local pension committees of every death of a person over seventy registered by them, in such manner and subject to

---

[1] Repealed by the Act of 1911.

such conditions as may be laid down by the regulations, and for making the procedure for considering and determining on any claim for a pension or question with respect to an old age pension under this Act as simple as possible.

(3) Every regulation under this Act shall be laid before each House of Parliament forthwith, and, if an address is presented to His Majesty by either House of Parliament within the next subsequent twenty-one days on which that House has sat next after any such regulation is laid before it, praying that the regulation may be annulled, His Majesty in Council may annul the regulation, and it shall thenceforth be void, but without prejudice to the validity of anything previously done thereunder.

(4) Any expenses incurred by the Treasury in carrying this Act into effect, and the expenses of the Local Government Board and the local pension committees under this Act up to an amount approved by the Treasury, shall be defrayed out of moneys provided by Parliament.

11. Application to Scotland, Ireland, and the Scilly Isles

(1) In the application of this Act to Scotland, the expression " Local Government Board " means the Local Government Board for Scotland; the expression " borough " means royal or parliamentary burgh; the expression " urban district " means police burgh; the population limit for boroughs and urban districts shall not apply; and the expression " Lunacy Act, 1890," means the Lunacy (Scotland) Acts, 1857 to 1900.

(2) In the application of this Act to Ireland, the expression " Local Government Board " means the Local Government Board for Ireland; ten thousand shall be substituted for twenty thousand as the population limit for boroughs and urban districts; and the expression " asylum within the meaning of the Lunacy Act, 1890," means a lunatic asylum within the meaning of the Local Government (Ireland) Act, 1898.

(3) In the application of this Act to the Isles of Scilly, those isles shall be deemed to be a county and the council of those isles the council of a county.

12. Commencement and Title

(1) A person shall not be entitled to the receipt of an old age pension under this Act until the first day of January nineteen hundred and nine and no such pension shall begin to accrue until that day.

(2) This Act may be cited as the Old Age Pensions Act, 1908.

SCHEDULE

MEANS OF PENSIONER	RATE OF PENSION PER WEEK	
Where the yearly means of the pensioner as calculated under this Act —	s.	d.
Do not exceed £21	5	o
Exceed £21, but do not exceed £23 12s. 6d. . . .	4	o
Exceed £23 12s. 6d., but do not exceed £26 5s. . .	3	o
Exceed £26 5s., but do not exceed £28 17s. 6d. . .	2	o
Exceed £28 17s. 6d., but do not exceed £31 10s. . .	1	o
Exceed £31 10s.	No pension	

Extract 35

OLD AGE PENSIONS ACT, 1911

(*1 & 2 Geo. 5, ch. 16*)

An Act to amend the Old Age Pensions Act, 1908.

(18th August 1911)

Be it enacted by the King's most Excellent Majesty, by and with the advice and consent of the Lords Spiritual and Temporal, and Commons, in this present Parliament assembled, and by the authority of the same, as follows :

1. *Calculation of Date of attaining Specified Age*

For the purposes of the Old Age Pensions Act, 1908 (in this Act referred to as " the principal Act "), a person shall be deemed, according to the law in Scotland as well as according to the law in England and Ireland, to have attained the age of seventy or sixty on the commencement of the day previous to the seventieth or six-tieth anniversary, as the case may be, of the day of his birth.

2. *Calculation of Means*

(1) In calculating, for the purpose of the principal Act, the means of a person, account shall be taken of —

(*a*) the yearly value of any property belonging to that person (not being property personally used or enjoyed by him) which is invested, or is otherwise put to profitable use by him, or which, though capable of investment or profitable use, is not so invested or put to profitable use by him, the yearly value of that property being taken to be one-twentieth part of the capital value thereof ;

(*b*) the income which that person may reasonably expect to re-ceive during the succeeding year in cash, excluding any sums receivable on account of an old age pension under this Act, and excluding any sums arising from the invest-ment or profitable use of property (not being property personally used or enjoyed by him), that income, in the absence of other means for ascertaining the income, being taken to be the income actually received during the pre-ceding year ;

(*c*) the yearly value of any advantage accruing to that person from the use or enjoyment of any property belonging to him which is personally used or enjoyed by him, except furniture and personal effects in a case where the total value of the furniture and effects does not exceed fifty pounds ; and (*d*) the yearly value of any benefit or privilege enjoyed by that person :

Provided that, where under paragraph (*a*) of the foregoing provisions the yearly value of any property is taken to be one-twentieth part of the capital value thereof, no account shall be taken under any other of those provisions of any appropriation of that property for the purpose of current expenditure.

(2) In calculating the means of a person being one of a married couple living together in the same house, the means shall be taken to be half the total means of the couple.

(3) The foregoing provisions of this section shall be substituted for subsections (1) and (2) of section four of the principal Act.

3. Provisions as to Nationality and Residence

Notwithstanding anything in the principal Act —

(1) the condition as to nationality imposed by paragraph (2) of section two of the principal Act shall not be required to be fulfilled in the case of a woman who satisfies the pension authorities that she would, but for her marriage with an alien, have fulfilled the condition, and that, at the date of the receipt of any sum on account of a pension, the alien is dead, or the marriage with the alien has been dissolved or annulled, or she has, for a period of not less than two years up to the said date, been legally separated from, or deserted by, the alien :

(2) it shall be a statutory condition for the receipt of an old age pension by any person, that the person must satisfy the pension authorities that for at least twelve years in the aggregate out of the twenty years up to the date of the receipt of any sum on account of a pension he has had his residence in the United Kingdom :

Provided that for the purposes of computing the twelve years' residence in the United Kingdom under this provision —

(*a*) any periods spent abroad in any service under the Crown, the remuneration for which is paid out of moneys provided by Parliament, or as the wife or servant of a person in any such service so remunerated ; and

(*b*) any periods spent in the Channel Islands or the Isle of Man by a person born in the United Kingdom ; and

(*c*) any periods spent abroad by any person during which that person has maintained or assisted in maintaining any dependant in the United Kingdom ; and

(*d*) any periods of absence spent in service on board a vessel registered in the United Kingdom by a person who before his absence on that service was living in the United Kingdom ; and

(*e*) any periods of temporary absence not exceeding three months in duration at any one time ;

shall be counted as periods of residence in the United Kingdom.

4. *Amendments of Section 3 of Principal Act*

(1) Any rule of law and any enactment, the effect of which is to cause relief given to or in respect of a wife or relative to be treated as relief given to the person liable to maintain the wife or relative, shall not have effect for the purposes of section three of the principal Act (which relates to disqualification).

(2) Two years shall be substituted for ten years as the further period of disqualification under subsection (2) of section three of the principal Act, both as respects persons convicted before the passing of this Act, and, as respects persons convicted after the passing of this Act, in cases where the term for which a person has been ordered to be imprisoned without the option of a fine does not exceed six weeks.

(3) Any person in receipt of an old age pension who is convicted of any offence which is mentioned in or deemed to be mentioned or included in the First Schedule to the Inebriates Act, 1898, shall, if not subject to disqualification under the principal Act, be disqualified for receiving or continuing to receive an old age pension for a period of six months after the date of his conviction, unless the court before whom he is convicted direct to the contrary.

5. Limitations with Respect to the Payment of Old Age Pensions

A sum shall not be paid on account of an old age pension —
- (a) to any person while absent from the United Kingdom ; or
- (b) if payment of the sum is not obtained within three months after the date on which it has become payable.

6. Amendments with Respect to Questions as to Old Age Pensions

(1) It is hereby declared that a question may be raised at any time —

- (a) whether at any time or during any period a person has been in receipt of an old age pension when the statutory conditions were not fulfilled, or when he was disqualified for receiving the pension ; and

- (b) whether a person has been at any time or during any period in receipt of a pension at a certain rate when his means exceeded the amount which justified the payment of a pension at that rate, and, if so, at what rate the pension, if any, should have been paid ; and

- (c) whether a person who is in receipt of a pension at a certain rate is, having regard to his means, entitled to a pension at a higher or a lower rate, and, if so, at what rate the pension (if any) should be paid ;

and that an application may be made at any time to alter or revoke a provisional allowance of a claim for a pension.

(2) Section seven of the principal Act shall apply to any such question or application as it applies to the questions mentioned in that section.

(3) Any such question may be raised notwithstanding that the decision of the question involves a decision as to the correctness of a former decision of the local pension committee or central pension authority as the case may be, but, where by a later decision a former decision is reversed, a person who has received any sums on account of an old age pension in accordance with the former decision shall, notwithstanding anything in subsection (2) of section nine of the principal Act, in the absence of any fraud on his part, be entitled to retain any sum so received up to the date of the later decision which he would have been entitled to retain but for the reversal of the former decision.

(4) Where a question is raised as to the disqualification of a person to receive an old age pension and it is alleged that the disqualification has arisen since the person has been in receipt of the pension, and that the disqualification is continuing at the time the question is raised, or, if it has ceased, has ceased less than three weeks before that time, the payment of the pension shall be discontinued, and no sum shall be paid to the pensioner on account of the pension after the date on which the question is raised : Provided that, if the question is decided in favour of the pensioner, he shall be entitled to receive all sums which would have been payable to him if the question had not been raised.

(5) If the decision on any question involves the discontinuance of an old age pension, or the reduction of the rate at which the pension is paid, or if, in a case where the payment of the pension has been discontinued on the raising of the question, the question is not decided in favour of the pensioner, the person in respect of whose pension the decision is given shall not be entitled to receive a pension or to receive a pension at a rate higher than that determined by the committee or authority, as the case may be, notwithstanding any change of circumstances, unless he makes a fresh

claim for the purpose and the claim is allowed, or, in a case where he alleges that he is entitled to receive a pension at a higher rate, raises a question for the purpose and the pension is allowed at a higher rate.

(6) It is hereby declared that a pension officer, if dissatisfied with any refusal or neglect of a local pension committee to consider a claim or determine a question, has, under paragraph (*d*) of subsection (1) of section seven of the principal Act, a right to apply to the central pension authority as a person aggrieved within the meaning of that provision.

7. *Amendments of Section 9 of the Principal Act*

(1) Subsection (2) of section nine of the principal Act shall apply, with the necessary modifications, to cases where an old age pension is received at a higher rate than that appropriate to the case as it applies to cases where a person has been in receipt of an old age pension while the statutory conditions were not fulfilled.

(2) For the purposes of subsection (2) of section nine of the principal Act and this section, any decision of the local pension committee under section seven of the principal Act on any question which is not referred to the central pension authority and the decision of the central pension authority on any question which is referred to them under that section shall be conclusive proof of any matters decided by the committee or the authority.

A copy of any decision of the local pension committee or central pension authority, if authenticated in manner provided by regulations to be made for the purpose under section ten of the principal Act, shall be received in evidence.

(3) Where any person who is in receipt of an old age pension is liable to repay to the Treasury any sums under subsection (2) of section nine of the principal Act in consequence of the finding of a local pension committee, or of the central pension authority

in the case of a question referred to them, the Treasury shall be entitled, without prejudice to their powers under that subsection, to direct the deduction of those sums from any sums to which that person becomes entitled on account of an old age pension, in manner to be provided by regulations to be made for the purpose under section ten of the principal Act:

Provided that, in the case of a personal representative, the deduction shall only be made from any sums to which that person becomes entitled as a personal representative.

(4) A court of summary jurisdiction in Ireland shall have the same power as a court of summary jurisdiction in England, in the case of a person convicted for an offence under subsection (1) of section nine of the principal Act, to impose a fine not exceeding twenty-five pounds instead of imprisonment, if they think that the justice of the case would be better met by a fine than by imprisonment.

8. Saving for Existing Pensioners

The provisions of this Act modifying the statutory conditions for the receipt of an old age pension shall not operate —

    (a) so as to disentitle any person who is in receipt of such a pension at the time of the commencement of this Act to continue to receive his pension; or

    (b) so as to reduce the rate of pension to which such a person is entitled.

9. Title and Commencement

(1) The enactments mentioned in the schedule to this Act are hereby repealed to the extent specified in the third column of that schedule.

(2) Any reference in this Act to the principal Act or any enactment therein shall, unless the context otherwise requires, be construed as references to that Act or enactment as amended by this Act.

(3) This Act shall be read as one with the principal Act, and may be cited as the Old Age Pensions Act, 1911; and this Act and the principal Act may be cited together as the Old Age Pensions Acts, 1908 and 1911.

SCHEDULE

Enactments Repealed

SESSION AND CHAPTER	SHORT TITLE	EXTENT OF REPEAL
8 Edw. 7, ch. 40	The Old Age Pensions Act, 1908	In paragraph (2) of section two the words " and has had his residence as defined by regulations under this Act in the United Kingdom "; subsections (1) and (2) of section four; and the words " and for defining the meaning of residence for the purposes of this Act " in paragraph (a) of subsection (1) of section ten

CHAPTER V

THE UNEMPLOYED

[On February 17, 1909, a formidable series of subjects for social legislation was supplied by the publication of the Report of a Poor Law Commission which had been appointed in December, 1905, with Lord George Hamilton as chairman. The Commission contained a number of high authorities on the subjects with which it dealt, including various Poor Law officials, Mr. C. S. Loch of the Charity Organisation Society, Professor Smart of Glasgow, and three well-known women — Miss Octavia Hill, Mrs. Bosanquet, and Mrs. Sidney Webb. It held over 200 meetings, heard 1300 witnesses, sent out special investigators, and visited many unions and institutions in the three kingdoms; and its evidence and other material filled forty volumes. The Report volume was the largest ever issued by a British Royal Commission; and the mere summary of its contents occupied three pages of the *London Times*. The very brief synopsis that appeared in the "Annual Register" is given below (*Extract 36*).

On May 19, 1909, Mr. Pickersgill, a Liberal Member of Parliament, called attention to the Minority Report of the Poor Law Commission and moved a resolution declaring the urgency of " steps for the decasualisation of casual labour and for the absorption of the surplus labour thereby thrown out of employment; also to regularise the demand for labour, to develop trade union insurance against the risks of unemployment, and to establish training colonies and detention colonies." The motion was seconded by Mr. Percy Alden and supported by Mr. Ramsay Macdonald, the Labour leader.

Then Mr. Winston Churchill, President of the Board of Trade, took the opportunity to set forth a Government scheme of labour exchanges and unemployment insurance (*Extract 37*). The scheme was welcomed as of far-reaching importance by Mr. F. E. Smith on behalf of the Opposition (*Extract 38*), and by Mr. Arthur Henderson on behalf of the Labour party (*Extract 39*). Mr. Pickersgill's motion was withdrawn, and the Labour Exchanges Bill was introduced the next day by Mr. Churchill, the insurance plan being deferred until another session.

The second reading of the Labour Exchanges Bill on June 16, 1909, gave rise to an interesting debate. Sir F. Banbury, Unionist member for London, doubted the utility of the exchanges and argued that the loans to unemployed men to enable them to take work at a distance would lead merely to idle travelling. Mr. Pointer, a new Labour member, referred to the successful working of the system in Berlin, urged that the age of leaving school should be raised and scientific and technical instruction given, and declared that working overtime robbed unemployed men of work. He suggested that employers should contribute towards the travelling expenses of men who found employment through the exchanges. Mr. Chiozza Money, the Liberal, urged that the railways should carry such men at a reduced rate. Mr. Renwick, Unionist member from Newcastle-on-Tyne, condemned the Bill, declaring that it would degrade labour, and the exchanges would be a sort of hiring fair. Mr. Roberts, a Labourite from Norwich, warned the House that while the Bill would assist the organisation of labour, unemployment would continue until collective superseded individual ownership. Mr. Bonar Law, the prominent Unionist, while approving the Bill in principle, thought there was too much centralisation, and the measure was too much of a blank cheque — the Government were introducing their Bill first and preparing their plan afterwards; if eloquent speeches alone would cure unemployment, the Government would do it; otherwise they must wait for some other Government.

Second reading was agreed to on June 16 and third reading on July 29. The progress of the Bill through the House of Lords (July 30–August 5) was uneventful; and the royal assent was registered on September 20. The Labour Exchange Act, 1909, is inserted as *Extract 40*.

For the provisions of the Natural Insurance Act of 1911 affecting unemployment, see infra, Chapter X.]

Extract 36

REPORT OF POOR LAW COMMISSION, 1909

(Résumé from the "Annual Register")

The Report of the Poor Law Commission,[1] published on February 17, 1909, contained a majority and a minority report. The former, signed with some reservations by fourteen of the eighteen Commissioners, was largely statistical and historical, dealing with the history of Poor Law administration before and since 1835, the causes of and remedies for unemployment, and the reorganisation of charity; and it made 239 recommendations as to reform.

Briefly, the majority of the Commissioners held that the Local Government Board should have more direction and initiative in assisting local authorities in relief; and that these latter should be entirely reorganised. Boards of Guardians should be abolished and replaced by a " Public Assistance Authority " in each county or county borough, with Public Assistance Committees under it with delegated powers, one Committee (in the first instance) in each existing union area. The poor rate would be a county or county borough rate. The Public Assistance Authority would be a committee of the County or County Borough Council, half being appointed from outside it, and consisting of persons experienced in " public assistance " (the recommendations avoided the terms

[1] Annual Register, 1909, pp. 9 sqq.

" poor " and " charity "), and one-third retiring each year. Women were to be eligible under either head. The Public Assistance Committees were to be appointed by the authority, and to include representatives of the local Urban and Rural District Councils, and of the Local Voluntary Aid Committees of which the Report contemplated the formation. Of these Public Assistance Committees at least one-third should ordinarily be women, and the members should be experienced in " public assistance." One-third should retire annually, but should be re-eligible. For London the general scheme was modified as follows : half of that half of the Public Assistance Authority which was to consist of non-members of the County Council " skilled in public assistance " was to be appointed by the Local Government Board, so as to secure representation of the medical and legal professions, employers and workmen, hospitals and charities, etc. ; and the Public Assistance Committees would contain some borough councillors. The poor rate, moreover, was to be made uniform throughout London.

The Public Assistance Committees in each area were to take their powers from the Authority ; they were to inquire into cases for assistance, administer aid in conjunction with the Voluntary Aid Committees, and supervise the public charitable institutions within their areas. These would be of seven kinds, the old workhouses being abolished : institutions for (1) children, (2) the aged and infirm, (3) the sick, (4) able-bodied men, (5) able-bodied women, (6) vagrants, and (7) the feeble-minded and epileptic. · In each subordinate area, alongside the Public Assistance and Voluntary Aid Committees, there was to be a Labour Exchange and a State-aided organisation of unemployment insurance. The unemployed would be dealt with by the Public Assistance Authority ; but those who required detention and discipline would be transferred to Labour Colonies under the Home Department.

The Commission, while admitting many exceptions, found the work of Boards of Guardians generally unsatisfactory, and concluded that general workhouses, the consequence of the existing small areas, were often ill-administered and normally demoralising. Out-relief was given in doles, 'and often inadequately, and sometimes " subsidised dirt, disease and immorality." The elective system failed to get a sufficiency of competent guardians, and little interest was taken in the elections. It was claimed by the Commission that their scheme would insure the co-operation of local and private charity with the public authorities ; members of the Public Assistance bodies would sit on the Voluntary Aid Committees and Councils, and vice versa, and the Charity Commission would receive widened powers and be affiliated to the Local Government Board. In each county or county borough the Voluntary Aid Committees would be under a council, formed under a scheme approved by the Charity Commission, and containing, besides members of the Public Assistance Authority, trustees of endowed charities, representatives of registered voluntary charities, trade associations, friendly societies and co-opted persons ; this body would advise, and collect funds for, the Voluntary Aid Committees in its area ; and these latter would aid cases unsuitable for public assistance, or referred to them by the Public Assistance Committee of their area. They would investigate, aid, visit, and register cases, and would be eligible for grants from the Public Assistance Authority, but would also raise money by subscription. Disfranchisement on account of public assistance would be confined to those assisted for more than three months in the qualifying year, and reception of medical relief should not disfranchise. Careful classification of the recipients of relief, now officially to be described as " necessitous," not " destitute," and different treatment of the different classes, were throughout contemplated, and the appointment of a temporary commission under the Local Government Board was recommended to bring the new system into working.

One of the most impressive portions of the Majority Report dealt with unemployment and the efforts hitherto made to relieve it. It was pointed out that in spite of improvements in economic conditions, machinery and the stress of competition demanded more skill than most workmen possessed, and tended to throw out men at an increasingly early age. Thus there was a mass of casual unskilled labor, swelled by the skilled men thrown out of work by changes in manufacture ; there were no means of getting such men fresh employment, and the total amount of the unskilled labour was unknown. The workhouse and labour-yard tended to produce inefficiency and degrade the efficient ; outdoor relief, unemployed relief funds, and municipal relief works were similarly unsatisfactory and tended to concentrate instead of dispersing inefficient casual labour ; the Unemployed Act of 1905, while useful in that it prepared for a diagnosis of the evil and a classification and dispersal of the unemployed, had in fact perpetuated the old evils of provision for the casual labourer by relief works and had failed to continue to attract charitable funds. The Commission saw remedies for unemployment : (1) in better education, a higher age for leaving school, and means for diverting boys from unskilled occupations ending with manhood (an evil on which special stress was laid), by technical training, and advice to parents ; (2) in a national system of Labour Exchanges, in the "regularisation of employment" by public bodies (in getting their own work done at slack times) and in Unemployment Assurance, which should be voluntary, and conducted by trade unions and provident organisations subsidised by the State. For the various classes of unemployed various treatment was proposed, including detention for the loafers and emigration.

The Minority Report of 500 pages, signed by four Commissioners, — the Rev. H. Russell Wakefield, Mr. F. Chandler, Mr. George Lansbury, and Mrs. Sidney Webb, — started from the same basic conceptions as the majority, but went a good deal further and produced a more systematised and uniform scheme. Holding that the regular "destitution authorities" — the Boards of Guardians — were having their work overlapped and encroached on by "specialised authorities," i.e., the Education, Health and Asylums Committees of the County and Borough Councils, and the Old

Age Pensions Committees, and also by unsystematised charitable work of various descriptions, the minority held that the functions of the Guardians (and the poor law functions of the Scottish Parish Councils) should be transferred to the County or County Borough Council and exercised through its Committees. The provision for the able-bodied and the non-able-bodied requiring relief should be wholly separated, the latter being dealt with by the Committees of the Council; and under each County or County Borough Council there should be a registrar of Public Assistance with a staff, who should register cases requiring relief, assess and recover the charges made by Parliament for the purpose, and sanction the grants of "Home Aliment" proposed by the committee. The various committees would be under separate Government departments. The duty of organising the national labour market so as to prevent or minimise unemployment should be laid on a special Ministry of Labour, which should arrange a ten years' programme of Government work, to cost £4,000,000 a year, but to be undertaken only in "the lean years of the trade cycle," and carried out by ordinary labour paid at ordinary local rates.

The chances of acceptance of the Minority Report were obviously remote.[1] Towards the vast schemes of the Majority Report a beginning was made during the session of 1909 by the Labour Exchanges Bill; the rest was left for future years.

Extract 37

GOVERNMENT PROPOSALS ON UNEMPLOYMENT

(Mr. Winston Churchill, President of the Board of Trade, Commons, May 19, 1909)

MR. CHURCHILL[2]: I am indebted to my hon. Friend [Mr. Pickersgill] whose Motion occupies the Paper this evening for the opportunity which his Motion affords of making some statement

[1] Cf. Annual Register, 1909, pp. 9 sqq.
[2] Parliamentary Debates, Commons, Fifth Series, vol. 5, col. 499 sqq.

upon the subject of unemployment and the measures to be taken to cope with that problem on behalf of the Government.

There are three Departments in the State which are in the main concerned with the Motion which the hon. Member has brought forward. They are the Home Office, the Local Government Board, and the Board of Trade, and each Department is concerned with a different part of that problem. The Home Office is concerned with the regulatory and disciplinary aspect, with the Factory Acts, and so on. The Board of Trade is concerned with the organisation of industry, so far as the Government may properly concern itself with the organisation of industry, and the Local Government Board is the Department which deals with relief, with curative and relieving processes apart from the functions of the other two Departments that I have mentioned.

And it is with the organisation section of the problem that it will be my duty to deal as President of the Board of Trade, and any suggestions or proposals which I may submit in the course of this Debate are concerned with organisation, and with organisation alone. They do not extend to other aspects of the problem, in some of which my right hon. Friend is deeply and actively concerned at the present time, but only with this one aspect of organisation ; and the proposals which I shall venture to submit to the House must not, I ask, be judged as if they were an attempt to cover the whole field of these larger questions, but must only be judged in so far as they deal with that particular sphere which falls to the province of the Board of Trade.

The first proposal which I think emerges from the argument of the hon. Gentleman is the proposal to establish a system of labour exchanges, and I hope to ask the House to-morrow for permission to introduce a Bill for the establishment of a national system of labour exchanges.

There is high authority for such a measure. The Majority and Minority Reports of the Poor Law Commission, differing in so much, agreeing in so little, are agreed unanimously in advocating a system of labour exchanges as the first step which should be taken in coping with the problem of poverty and unemployment. Conferences were held in London the other day by delegates who represented 1,400,000 trade unionists who passed a resolution in favour of this policy. The Central (Unemployed) Body, who are equally concerned in these matters, have approved of that policy. The delegates of the Labour party who went to Germany a few months ago returned greatly impressed with the exchanges which they saw at work in Germany. Economists as diverse in their opinions as Professor Ashley, of Birmingham, and Professor Chapman, of Manchester — leading exponents of Tariff Reform and of Free Trade — have all publicly testified in favour of such proposals; and several prominent Members of the Front Opposition Bench have in public, either in evidence before the Commission or in speeches in the country, expressed themselves as supporters of such a policy. The argument from authority is reinforced by the argument from example, because as early as 1904 Germany, Austria, Switzerland, France, and Belgium all exhibited the system of public labour exchanges and public labour bureaux in full working order; and since 1904 Norway has also adopted some application of that system. Mr. Bliss, who was sent over by the Government of the United States to investigate the conditions and methods of dealing with unemployment in European countries last year, has, in the May bulletin for last year of the Washington Bureau of Labour, surveyed the whole field of unemployment organisations in European countries and has come to the conclusion that a principal element in the methods by which that difficulty may be successfully treated lies in the establishment of public labour exchanges; and he draws great attention to the rapid and successful development in the last fifteen years of the system in Germany. So we not only have the practical consensus of opinion of all authorities, irrespective of party, irrespective of the point of view in this country in favour of such a system, but we have the evidence of the successful practice of the greatest industrial community on the Continent and its continuous extension in different forms and under different circumstances to many other countries of the Continent of Europe.

With such argument from authority and example it is hardly necessary to submit the case upon its merits, but there are two general defects in the industrial position of this country which are singled out by the Royal Commission, the lack of mobility of labour and the lack of information about all these questions of unemployment. For both of these defects the policy of labour exchanges is calculated to afford a remedy. Modern industry is national. The facilities of transport and communication knit the country together as no country has ever been knitted before. Labour alone has not profited by this improved organisation. The method by which labour obtains its market to-day is the old method, the demoralising method of personal application, hawking labour about from place to place, and treating a job as if it were a favour — looking at it as if it were a favour, as a thing which places a man under an obligation when he has got it. Labour exchanges will increase the mobility of labour, but to increase the mobility of labour is not to increase the movement of labour. To increase the mobility of labour is only to render the movement of labour, when it has become necessary, less painful. The movement of labour when it is necessary should be effected with the least friction, the least suffering, the least loss of time and of status to the individual who is called upon by the force of economic conditions to move. It would be a great injustice to the policy of labour exchanges if it were supposed that it would be the cause of sending workmen gadding about from pillar to post throughout the country, whereas the only result of the policy will be, not to make it necessary for any man to move who does not need to move to-day, but to make it easy for him to move the moment the ordinary economic events arise which make the movement necessary.

There is another thing in connection with labour exchanges. They will not to any large extent create new employment. In so far as facilities for getting labour on particular occasions sometimes lead to extra men being taken on, they will increase employment. That, however, is only a very small result. They will not directly add to the volume of employment. I never contemplated that they should. It would be to invest the policy with an air of humbug if we were to pretend that labour exchanges are going to make more work. They are not. What they are going to do is to organise the existing labour, to reduce the friction which has attended the working of the existing economic and industrial system; by reducing the friction of that system we cannot help raising the general standard of economic life.

As to lack of information, labour exchanges must afford information of the highest value in the sphere of social subjects on which we are lamentably ill-informed. In proportion as this system comes to be used, it will afford us accurate contemporary information about the demand for labour, both as to the quantity and the quality of that demand, as between one trade and another, and as between one district and another, and as between one season and another, and one cycle and another. It will enable us to tell workmen in search of work where to go, and it will also enable us, which is not the least important, to tell them where not to go. Over and over again at the present time men are led by the rumours of work. They crowd into a district, to find that there is no gratification of their hope, and, if there is gratification, it is wholly insufficient for the numbers who have been led to make that desultory pilgrimage. In association with the school employment bureaux which so many educational authorities are now starting in Scotland, and to a lesser extent in England, we hope that the system of labour exchanges will have the effect of enabling us to guide to some extent a new generation into the trades· which are not overstocked and which are not declining, and to prevent the exploitation of boy labour, to which the hon. Member for Leicester [Mr. Ramsay Macdonald] has referred.

So far as local and accidental unemployment is concerned, by which I mean unemployment in one place when there is a demand for labour in another, the labour exchanges will undoubtedly diminish that evil. They are, further, the only method of grappling with the evils of casual employment, which are singled out by the Royal Commission as being the original fountain of so many of the greatest evils in our social life. We hope that they will help to the process of dovetailing one seasonal trade into another, so that people who are always slack at a particular season in one trade may acquire in some cases a secondary trade which is only brisk at that season, and which will enable them to obtain a uniform average in the economy of their domestic life.

Labour exchanges, by dispensing with the need of wandering in search of work, will render it for the first time possible to deal stringently with vagrants. I am quite sure that those who know the sort of humiliation to which the genuine workingman is subject, by being very often indistinguishable from one of the class of mere loafers and vagrants, will recognise as of great importance any steps which can sharply and irretrievably divide the two classes in our society.

Lastly, labour exchanges are indispensable to any system of unemployment insurance, or, indeed, I think to any other honourable method of relieving unemployment, since it is not possible to make the distinction between the vagrant and the loafer on the one hand and the bona fide workman on the other, except in conjunction with some elaborate and effective system of testing willingness to work such as is afforded by the system of labour exchanges.

I shall to-morrow have an opportunity of asking the permission of the House to introduce this Bill, and we present it to the House as a piece of social machinery, nothing more and nothing less, the need of which has long been apparent, and the want of which has been widely and cruelly felt by large numbers of our fellow countrymen. I said a little earlier that we might profit by the example of Germany, but we may do more, we may improve on the example of Germany. The German system of labour exchanges, although co-ordinated and encouraged by the State and by the Imperial Government, is, nevertheless, mainly municipal in its character. Starting here with a clear field, and with the advantage of experience and of experiments in other lands, we may, I think, begin at a higher level and on a larger scale than has been done in any other country up to the present time. The utility of a system of labour exchanges, like the utility of any other market, increases with its range and scope, and we propose, as the first principle of our system of labour exchanges, to adopt a plan which shall be uniform and national in its character, and in that we are supported both by the Minority and Majority Reports of the Royal Commission on the Poor Law.

During the last few months a Departmental Committee has been sitting at the Board of Trade elaborating details of this scheme, and I am glad to tell the House and the hon. Members who moved and seconded this Motion that those details are now very far advanced. We should propose, if the House assent to the Bill, to divide the whole country into about ten divisions, each with a Divisional Clearing House, and presided over by a divisional chief, and all co-ordinated with a National Clearing House in London. Distributed amongst those ten divisions will be between 30 and 40 first-class labour exchanges in towns of 100,000 or upwards, and about 45 second-class labour exchanges in towns between 50,000 and 100,000, and 150 minor offices and sub-offices, third-class labour exchanges, with waiting rooms, will be established in the smaller centres. The control of this system will be exercised by the Board of Trade. In order to secure absolute impartiality as between capital and labour, we propose that a joint Advisory Committee should be established in every principal centre, on which representatives of the workers and representatives of the employers shall meet in equal numbers under an impartial chairman. . . .

If Parliament should assent to the Bill this Session without undue delay I should hope to bring this system of Labour Exchanges into simultaneous operation all over the country so far as practicable in the early months of next year. Temporary premises will be engaged in the first instance everywhere, but at the same time I think it very important that we should have permanent premises. A building programme is being prepared by which we will erect so many labour exchanges every year until in about ten years, so far as first-class exchanges are concerned, we shall be permanently housed. This has been all worked out in very careful detail.

The expense of this system will no doubt be considerable. The ordinary working of the system will not be less than about £170,000 per year, and during the period when the building is going on the expenditure will rise to about £200,000 per year, not ever above £200,000 during the next ten years. We hope that the labour exchanges will become industrial centres in each town. We hope they will become a labour market, we hope they will become an office where the Trade Board will hold its meetings as a natural course, and that they will be open to trade unions, with whom we desire to co-operate in every way on the closest and frankest terms, while preserving our impartiality between capital and labour. We hope that the trade unions will keep their vacant book in some cases at the exchanges. We hope that the structure of those exchanges will be such as to enable us to have rooms which can be let to trade unions at a rent for benefit and other meetings so as to avoid the necessity under which all but the strongest unions lie at the present time — of conducting their meetings in licensed premises. The exchanges may in some cases afford facilities for washing, clothes mending, and for non-alcoholic refreshments to persons who are attending them. Separate provision will be made for men and for women, and for skilled and unskilled labour. Boy labour will be dealt with in conjunction with the local education authority, because we have no intention of allowing the commercial side to override the educational side in regard to young people. Travelling expenses can be advanced on loan, it is contemplated, to workmen by whom situations have been procured if the Management Committee think fit.

I do not want to go into all the details. They have been studied very carefully, and I shall be prepared when we are at closer quarters on the Bill to give the fullest information and to discuss without restraint of any kind all those special aspects and points to which I have referred.

So much for the policy of labour exchanges. That is a policy complete in itself. It would be considerable if it stood alone, but it does not stand alone. As my right hon. Friend the Chancellor of the Exchequer has announced in his Budget speech, the Government propose to associate with the policy of labour exchanges unemployment insurance. The hon. Member who moved this Motion has referred particularly to the Minority Report. He knows that the Minority Report advocates a system of compulsory labour exchanges, that no person shall engage any man for less than a month except through a labour exchange. That is not the proposal we are making. We are making a proposal of voluntary labour exchanges. I am quite ready to admit that no system of voluntary labour exchanges by itself deals adequately with the evils and difficulties of casual labour, but there is one reason against compulsory labour exchanges at the present time. My hon. Friend foresaw it. To establish a system of compulsory labour exchanges, to eliminate casual labour, to divide among a certain proportion of workers all available employment would absolutely and totally cast out a surplus of unemployed, before you have made preparation for dealing with that surplus, would be to cause an administrative breakdown, and could not fail to be attended with the gravest possible disaster. Therefore until poor law reform, which falls to the Department of my right hon. Friend Mr. Burns, and with which he and those who are working with him are engaged, has made further progress, to establish a compulsory system of labour exchanges would naturally increase and not diminish the miseries with which we are seeking to cope. We have, therefore, decided that our system of labour exchanges shall be voluntary in its character. For that very reason there is a great danger, to which

I have never shut my eyes, that the highest ranks of labour, skilled workers, members of strong trade unions, would not think it necessary to use the exchanges, but would use the very excellent apparatus which they have established themselves, that this expensive system of exchanges which we are calling into being would come to be used only by the poorest of the workers in the labour markets and, consequently, would gradually relapse and fall back into the purely distress machinery, not economic machinery, from which we are labouring to extricate and separate it. It is for that reason, quite apart from the merits of the scheme of unemployment insurance, that the Government are very anxious to associate with their scheme of labour exchanges a system of unemployment insurance. If labour exchanges depend for their effective initiation or inauguration upon unemployment insurance being associated with them, it is equally true to say that no scheme of unemployment insurance can be worked except in conjunction with some apparatus for finding work and testing willingness to work, like labour exchanges. The two systems are complementary ; they are man and wife ; they mutually support and sustain each other.

So I come to unemployment insurance. It is not practicable at the present time to establish a universal system of unemployment insurance. It would be risking the policy to cast one's net so wide. We, therefore, have to choose at the very outset of this subject between insuring some workmen in all trades and insuring all workmen in some trades. That is the first parting of the ways upon unemployment insurance. In the first case we can have a voluntary and in the second case a compulsory system. If you adopt a voluntary system of unemployment insurance, you are always exposed to this difficulty. The risk of unemployment varies so much between man and man, according to their qualities ; character, circumstances, temperament, demeanour towards their superiors — these are all factors ; and the risk varies so much between man and man that a voluntary system of unemployment insurance which the State subsidises always attracts those workers who are most likely to be unemployed. That is why all voluntary systems have broken down when they have been tried, because they accumulate a preponderance of bad risks against the insurance office, which is fatal to its financial stability. On the other hand, a compulsory system of insurance, which did not add to the contribution of the workers a substantial contribution from outside, has also broken down, because of the refusal of the higher class of worker to assume unsupported a share of the burden of the weaker members of the community. We have decided to avoid these difficulties. Our insurance scheme will present four main features. It will involve contributions from the workpeople and from the employers; those contributions will be aided by a substantial subvention from the State; it will be insurance by trades, following the suggestion of the Royal Commission; and it will be compulsory within those trades upon all, unionist and non-unionist, skilled and unskilled, workmen and employers alike. The hon. Member for Leicester [Mr. Ramsay Macdonald] with great force showed that to confine a scheme of unemployment insurance merely to trade unionists would be trifling with the subject. It would only be aiding those who have been most able to aid themselves, without at the same time assisting those who hitherto under existing conditions have not been able to make any effective provision.

To what trades ought we, as a beginning, to apply our system of compulsory contributory unemployment insurance? There is a group of trades well marked out for this class of treatment. They are trades in which unemployment is not only high, but chronic, for even in the best of times it persists; where it is not only high, and chronic, but marked by seasonal and cyclical fluctuations, and wherever and howsoever it occurs it takes the form not of short time or of any of those devices for spreading wages and equalising or averaging risks, but of a total, absolute, periodical discharge of a certain proportion of the workers. These are the trades to which, in the first instance, we think the system of unemployment insurance ought to be applied. The group of trades which we contemplate to be the subject of our scheme are these : house building and works of construction, engineering, machine and tool making, ship and boat building, vehicles, sawyers, and general labourers working at these trades.

MR. RAMSAY MACDONALD : Is the engineering civil engineering or mechanical ?

MR. CHURCHILL : The whole group of mechanical engineering trades. That is a very considerable group of industries. They comprise, according to the last Census Reports, two and a quarter millions of adult workers. Two and a quarter millions of adult workers are, roughly speaking, one-third of the adult population of these three kingdoms engaged in purely industrial work ; that is to say, excluding commercial, professional, agricultural, and domestic occupations. Of the remaining two-thirds of the adult industrial population, nearly one-half are employed in the textile trades, in mining, on the railways, in the merchant marine, and in other trades, which either do not present the same features of unemployment which we see in the precarious trades, or which, by the adoption of short time or other arrangements, avoid the total discharge of a proportion of workmen from time to time. So that this group of trades to which we propose to apply the system of unemployment insurance, roughly speaking, covers very nearly half of the whole field of unemployment. That half, on the whole, is perhaps the worst half. The financial and actuarial basis of the scheme has been very carefully studied by the light of all available information. The report of the actuarial authorities whom I have consulted leaves me no doubt that, even after all allowance has been made for the fact that unemployment may be more rife in the less organised and less highly skilled trades than in the trade unions who pay unemployment benefits, — that is a fact which is not proved, and which I am not at all convinced of, — there is no doubt whatever that a financially sound scheme can be evolved which, in return for moderate contributions, will yield adequate benefits. I am not going to offer figures of contributions or benefits to the House at this

stage, though I should not be unable to do so. I confine myself
to stating that we propose to aim at a scale of benefits which is
somewhat lower both in amount and in duration than those which
the strongest trade unions pay at the present time. Nevertheless,
they will be benefits which will afford substantial weekly payments
for a period which will cover by far the greater part of the period
of unemployment of all unemployed persons in this great group of
insured trades. In order to enable such a scale of benefits to be
paid it is necessary that we should raise something between 5d.
and 6d. — rather nearer 6d. than 5d. — per man per week. That
sum, we propose, should be made up by contributions, not necessarily equal, between the workman, the employer, and the State.
For such a sacrifice — and it is not, I think, an exorbitant one,
which, fairly adjusted, will not hamper industry nor burden labour,
nor cause an undue strain upon the public finances — we believe
it possible to relieve a vast portion of the industrial population of
these islands from that haunting dread and constant terror which
gnaws out the very heart of their prosperity and content.

The relation of the insurance scheme towards the unions must
be most carefully considered. We hope that there will be no difficulty, as the discussion on this subject proceeds, in showing that we
safeguard all the institutions which have made voluntary efforts
in this direction from anything like the unfair competition of a
national insurance fund. More than that, we believe that the proposals which we shall make, when they are brought forward in
detail, will act as a powerful encouragement to all voluntary agencies to adopt and extend the system of unemployment insurance.
Yes, but the House may say, What is the connection of all this
with labour exchanges? I must apologise for detaining the House
so long —

MR. JOHN WARD: This is the most interesting part of your
speech.

MR. CHURCHILL: But the machinery of the insurance office has
been gone into with great detail, and we propose as at present

advised to follow the German example of insurance cards or books, to which stamps will be affixed every week. For as soon as a man in an insured trade is without employment, if he has kept to the rules of the system, all he will have to do is to take his card to the nearest labour exchange, which will be responsible, in conjunction with the insurance office, either for finding him a job or paying him his benefits.

I am very glad, indeed, to have availed myself of the opportunity which my right hon. Friend has given me to submit this not inconsiderable proposal in general outline, so that the Bill for labour exchanges which I will introduce to-morrow may not be misjudged as if it stood by itself, and was not part of a considered, co-ordinated, and connected scheme to grasp with this hideous, crushing evil which has oppressed for so long the mind of everyone who cares about social reform.

We cannot deal with the insurance policy this Session for five reasons. We have not the time now. We have not got the money yet. The finances of this insurance scheme have got to be adjusted and interwoven with the finances of the other schemes which my right hon. Friend the Chancellor of the Exchequer is engaged upon now for dealing with various forms of invalidity and other insurance. In the next place, labour exchanges are the necessary preliminary. We must get the apparatus of the labour exchanges into working order before this system of insurance can effectually be established or worked. Lastly, no such novel departure as a compulsory, contributory unemployment insurance in a particular trade could possibly be adopted without a very much fuller degree of consultation and negotiation with the parties concerned than has been possible to us under the conditions of secrecy under which we have necessarily been working.

In the autumn the Board of Trade will confer with all the parties affected by the proposals which I have outlined to-night, and we shall endeavour, while not making the production of our proposals contingent upon their agreement, to secure as wide and as large a measure of agreement as possible of all these parties, in order that all our proposals may be received with as much consent as possible when next Session they are presented in their final form.

One word more. The prospect and pressure of these considerable duties have involved some rearrangement of the Labour Department of the Board of Trade. I propose that that Department should be divided in the future into three distinct sections. The first section will deal with wages questions, arbitration, conciliation, and with the Trade Boards, which will be set up under the Trade Boards Bill if it should pass into law. The second section will deal with statistics, special inquiries, and with the *Labour Gazette.* The third section will be occupied with labour exchanges and unemployment insurance work in conjunction. One of the functions of the last section will be to act as a kind of intelligence bureau, watching the continual changes of the labour market here and abroad, and suggesting any measure which may be practicable, such as co-ordination and distribution of Government contracts and municipal work, so as to act as a counterpoise to the unemployment of the labour market, and it will also, we trust, be able to conduct examinations of schemes of public utility, so that such schemes, if decided upon by the Government and the Treasury, can be set on foot at any time with knowledge and consideration beforehand, instead of the haphazard, hand-to-mouth manner with which we try to deal with these emergencies at the present time.

That is a part of the policy I have unfolded to-night, which has not reached the same stage of maturity as the other subjects with which I have attempted to deal. I have only attempted to foreshadow them in the vaguest terms. . . . I have not trespassed at all upon the other no less important or scarcely less important branches of this problem, and I am quite certain this Parliament will gladly exert what strength remains to it in attempting to cope with these hideous problems of social disorganisation and chaos which are marring the happiness of our country, and which, unless grappled with, may fatally affect its strength and its honour.

Extract 38

CONSERVATIVE POSITION ON UNEMPLOYMENT

(Mr. F. E. Smith, Commons, May 19, 1909)

Mr. Smith[1]: Nobody listening to the speech of the right hon. Gentleman will make any complaint of the length at which he dealt with this extremely important subject. He dealt with it in a manner which I think all sections of the House will admit was worthy of the importance of the subject. Perhaps, representing as I do a Liverpool Constituency, in which there is a great deal of casual labour, I may make one or two observations on the subject of the Resolution before the House before I venture to address one or two remarks to the compulsory insurance proposals which the right hon. Gentleman has outlined.

So far as casual employment is concerned, the Resolution which the House has now under consideration, I think probably all Members of the House, wherever they sit, will agree that even a mere superficial analysis would suggest the drawing of a distinction between cyclical fluctuations of unemployment which are produced by general depression, and, in the second place, local and sectional fluctuations produced by causes only merely local and, therefore, more susceptible of local treatment. If one gives one's attention for a moment to the case of cyclical fluctuations in trade, he will at once find that he is face to face with the great question as to what is the particular system in any particular country which is best qualified to deal with the general difficulty of the depression in trade. I do not propose to embarrass this debate at this stage with the discussion of that question. I do not seek to introduce the subject of Tariff Reform, or the subject of afforestation, or the subject of labour colonies. Every one of these is extremely controversial, and the value of any of them, if urged as a practical contribution to the

[1] Parliamentary Debates, Commons, Fifth Series, vol. 5, col. 512 sqq.

debate, would be hotly canvassed in some particular section of the House. Perhaps, therefore, it will be better to pass by for the purposes of a limited debate the whole general question of cyclical fluctuation of unemployment, the reason of which it is extremely difficult to discover, and, therefore, it is better to deal with the question of local and sectional fluctuation, and see from this how far the proposals indicated by the right hon. Gentleman in the Bill he is about to introduce are likely to present anything in the nature of a cure or at all events a palliation for this local and sectional fluctuation.

I come from a constituency where casual labour is present. I have given some careful attention to the subject and to the work of the local labour exchanges in foreign countries, and I have no hesitation in accepting the view which the right hon. Gentleman has placed before the House that without undue sanguineness you may look forward to labour exchanges to furnish considerable palliative. It is extremely important that the House should clearly understand what is the nature of the gain which they may reasonably count upon these labour exchanges to furnish. . . .

Let us take a simple illustration, and then reduce it to a concrete case. Take the case of one employer who employs ten men on Monday and another who employs ten men in the same class of employment on Tuesday. If there is no such organisation as that contemplated by the labour exchanges, the result will be you will have twenty men partially employed on those two days. The express object of the organisation and the labour exchanges is that instead of having twenty men partially employed, you will have ten men fully employed. It is quite true that the labour is decasualised, and I am one of those who contemplate the economic consequences as a whole that society. gets by the decasualisation of the whole of that labour. But it is very important that all engaged in attempting to suggest remedies for unemployment should realise what would be involved in the decasualisation of that labour in order to measure the admitted gains with the disadvantages, which cannot certainly be disputed. It follows that decasualisation of the kind contemplated in this Resolution replaces ten half-employed men by five fully-employed men. If you are going to decasualise labour in that way, if you are going to see that the men who are doing that constant amount of labour shall have it more widely distributed, it follows that you are going to replace ten half-employed men by five fully-employed men.

The right hon. Gentleman stated very modestly that conclusion when he said that he did not claim that labour exchanges would add to employment. I think he might have stated it more strongly, because not only will the establishment of labour exchanges not add to employment, but if they are to serve the only purpose which they can economically serve, the necessary consequence of their establishment must be actually to diminish employment. I recognise that, and although I do so, I still do not hesitate to say that the Bill which the right hon. Gentleman is going to produce is one well worth introducing and worthy of the support of the House. The reason which I venture to offer to the House for that view is that, in my opinion, it is far better in the interests of society as a whole that you should have ten men fully paid and fully nourished than twenty men partially paid and partially nourished. It is clear that under this system you will not be able to supply even partial labour for as large a number of workers as you find partial work for to-day, and you are bound to increase the number of men who will have to appeal for corrective treatment or outdoor relief. I think it is important that those who are pressing forward this proposal to start labour exchanges should realise that the inevitable economic consequence of establishing those exchanges will be that you will diminish the number of men who can find work of any kind, although you are going to give them a larger living wage.

The right hon. Gentleman has touched upon a much more difficult question in regard to compulsory insurance. Now, Sir, I do not desire for a single moment to underrate the difficulties of compulsory insurance, but I do not think that the right hon. Gentle-man will find himself confronted with very serious opposition from these benches, because during the discussions on old age pensions my hon. Friends here on this side of the House pressed upon the Government that compulsory contributions would be a reasonable basis for the system. We were told that there was something un-English in such a proposal — that is, the proposal of compul-sory contribution. Speaking for myself, I was never convinced by that argument, and I am unable to see why if the working classes would never consent to a system of compulsory contributions for old age pensions, the Government are entitled to suppose that they will consent to compulsory contributions to provide against unemployment. Speaking for myself, I am convinced that the true and only method lies on the lines which the right hon. Gentleman has indicated. I do not think that compulsory contribution to any-thing can be easily made. But I do venture to think that the pro-posal which the right hon. Gentleman has suggested to the House is such that all sections of the House may unite in supporting it. It is a proposal, whether popular or unpopular, which will conduce to the interests of the working classes.

Extract 39

LABOUR PARTY'S ATTITUDE TOWARD UNEMPLOYMENT

(*Mr. Arthur Henderson, Commons, May 19, 1909*)

MR. HENDERSON [1] : . . . I have risen for the purpose of giving a very general but a very hearty welcome to the statement which the President has made. I regret exceedingly that the House was not much fuller to listen to what, in my opinion, has been, so far as the great majority of the people in all our constituencies are concerned, one of the most important, and what I believe

[1] Parliamentary Debates, Commons, Fifth Series, vol. 5, col. 518 sqq.

will prove to be one of the most far-reaching, statements which have been delivered during the time I have been associated with Parliament. I also rejoice at the statement made by the hon. and learned Member for the Walton Division [Mr. F. E. Smith]. He concluded by urging that this question should be kept as far as possible on purely non-party lines. I think this is an excellent beginning, for there is no social question that touches so vitally the condition in which so many of our people are compelled to live as this great problem of unemployment, and I think of all questions this is the one that every section in this House should strive to keep entirely apart from party bias. It is the problem upon which we should centre the whole of our attention, in order to find the best and most practical remedy.

We on these Benches may be pardoned if we feel slightly gratified at the statement that the President has addressed to the House. I think that statement contains the germs of some proposals for which we have been striving in the Labour party for a good many years past. I think we may feel almost ready to congratulate ourselves that at last the Government have made a beginning in taking out — I will put it in a very rough form — the Right to Work Bill in penny numbers. I know the President would not admit that. It would scarcely do for him to make such an admission having regard to the attitude which the Government have always taken up when this Bill of ours has been before the House, but I think our Bill contained labour exchanges. It contained a form of maintenance in the absence of work. I think our Bill made some reference to insurance, and we are gratified to find that at last a beginning is to be made, if not in the adoption of the complete scheme, one which goes a long way in the direction that we have suggested for some time past.

When I come to look at the two main principles which have been outlined to us to-night, I am personally very pleased to find that the Government are going to set up what I hope will be a complete system of co-ordinating labour exchanges. I am well aware of the objection which can be lodged against labour exchanges. They do not provide, in a strict sense, work for the unemployed. The only thing they do is, if there is a position going, it does not necessitate the demoralising tramping system, which, in my judgment, has done more to reduce the status of the workmen of this country than anything else I know of. I venture to say that some men have been compelled, in consequence of the difficulty of obtaining information as to the condition of the labour market in other districts than those in which they reside, to begin the tramping system, and in beginning that system they have begun the demoralisation of their own lives, and have gone so far down that they have never again been able to get back to the former standard of their manhood. The German system, which, I believe, the President of the Board of Trade is very closely following, is, in my judgment, excellent, and it is almost impossible to describe to the House the difference of the condition of the unemployed workmen in Germany and the condition that you find them in in this country. I believe that it is very largely due to the fact that they have been able to remain at home and to ascertain the actual condition of the labour market, and that, if they have to move, they have been assisted to move with their families, and have thus been kept free from much of the demoralising associated with unemployment in our own country.

As to the second proposal outlined, I must say that, whilst I give to it a very cordial welcome, I regret that the Government have not seen their way clear to make the scheme much more comprehensive. What I fear is that the scheme of insurance that has been outlined will be largely prejudiced because some of the worst trades in our present recurring periods of unemployment are not to be included. Probably I may be answered by the Government that in their scheme they have only included such trades as enable them to get proper information upon which to base the actuarial cost that would be incurred. But the Government at present especially should not lose sight of the fact that some of the trades not so highly organised, some of the trades which in days gone by were not so hard hit by unemployment as they are to-day, will feel very strongly because they are left entirely out of any provision in connection with this State insurance scheme. I should like to learn at the earliest possible moment — for I did not notice anything in the speech of the President of the Board of Trade on this point — whether this scheme that is going to be set up is going to be regarded as purely temporary, and whether there is going to be taken in the Bill provision for its easy extension, provided that there is a desire expressed on the part of the other trades hardly hit by unemployment that they should be included without the necessity of going through the very long delay that often takes place in the process of passing another Bill through both Houses of Parliament.

MR. CHURCHILL: I may state that the Government contemplate taking power for the extension of the system in the event of its succeeding — after all, that is the important point — to other trades and industries suitable for it, provided that Parliament approves of that extension and that money is available.

MR. HENDERSON : I am delighted to hear the statement made by the right hon. Gentleman. I think this will assist in modifying very considerably the feeling of opposition that might have arisen in connection with some of the trades that are not for the moment included in the scheme. I have no doubt we will be told during subsequent discussion that this is going to be a costly scheme. Having regard to the fact that workmen are going to be included and will have to contribute, that the employers will have to contribute, and that the State itself is going to be associated with what I venture to hope will be a very generous contribution, I have no hesitation in saying that while the scheme may be to a certain extent costly, the cost is not excessive.

There are other proposals that have been brought before the House for the purpose of assisting to remedy this great unemployed problem, as to which I do not say a single word of a controversial character; but I have heard it suggested in this House and in the country that we ought to go in for a larger naval programme in order to assist in solving the unemployed problem. When I consider this scheme of insurance I have no hesitation in saying that, though it may be costly, it will be much more permanent in character for good than any large scheme or programme of armaments for the purpose of assisting the solution of this great social problem. We welcome this scheme, not because we consider it is a complete remedy for this problem. We welcome it because we believe it is a beginning, and that it asserts in another form than that outlined in our Bill the recognition by the State of its obligations to make some provision for the relief and for the maintenance of those who have been suffering so seriously from unemployment in recent years, and on these grounds we shall give it a general and most hearty support. And our only regret is that the President has not seen his way to announce to the House that not only the labour exchange portion of the scheme but the insurance portion will be forced through Parliament during the present Session.

Extract 40

LABOUR EXCHANGES ACT, 1909

(9 Edw. 7, ch. 7)

An Act to provide for the establishment of Labour Exchanges and for other purposes incidental thereto.

(20th September 1909)

Be it enacted by the King's most Excellent Majesty, by and with the advice and consent of the Lords Spiritual and Temporal, and Commons, in this present Parliament assembled, and by the authority of the same, as follows:

1. *Power of Board of Trade*

(1) The Board of Trade may establish and maintain, in such places as they think fit, labour exchanges, and may assist any labour exchanges maintained by any other authorities or persons, and in the exercise of those powers may, if they think fit, co-operate with any other authorities or persons having powers for the purpose.

(2) The Board of Trade may also, by such other means as they think fit, collect and furnish information as to employers requiring workpeople and workpeople seeking engagement or employment.

(3) The Board of Trade may take over any labour exchange (whether established before or after the passing of this Act) by agreement with the authority or person by whom the labour exchange is maintained, and any such authority or person shall have power to transfer it to the Board of Trade for the purposes of this Act.

(4) The powers of any central body or distress committee, and the powers of any council through a special committee, to establish or maintain, under the Unemployed Workmen Act, 1905, a labour exchange or employment register shall, after the expiration of one year from the commencement of this Act, not be exercised except with the sanction of, and subject to any conditions imposed by, the Local Government Board for England, Scotland, or Ireland, as the case may require, and that sanction shall not be given except after consultation with the Board of Trade.

2. *Regulations and Management*

(1) The Board of Trade may make general regulations with respect to the management of labour exchanges established or assisted under this Act, and otherwise with respect to the exercise of their powers under this Act, and such regulations may, subject to the approval of the Treasury, authorise advances to be made by way of loan towards meeting the expenses of workpeople travelling

to places where employment has been found for them through a labour exchange.

(2) The regulations shall provide that no person shall suffer any disqualification or be otherwise prejudiced on account of refusing to accept employment found for him through a labour exchange where the ground of refusal is that a trade dispute which affects his trade exists, or that the wages offered are lower than those current in the trade in the district where the employment is found.

(3) Any general regulations made under this section shall have effect as if enacted in this Act, but shall be laid before both Houses of Parliament as soon as may be after they are made, and, if either House of Parliament within the next forty days during the session of Parliament after any regulations have been so laid before that House resolves that the regulations or any of them ought to be annulled, the regulations or those to which the resolution applies shall, after the date of such resolution, be of no effect, without prejudice to the validity of anything done in the meantime under the regulations or to the making of any new regulations.

(4) Subject to any such regulations, the powers of the Board of Trade under this Act shall be exercised in such manner as the Board of Trade may direct.

(5) The Board of Trade may, in such cases as they think fit, establish advisory committees for the purpose of giving the Board advice and assistance in connexion with the management of any labour exchange.

3. Penalties for making False Statements

If any person knowingly makes any false statement or false representation to any officer of a labour exchange established under this Act, or to any person acting for or for the purposes of any such labour exchange, for the purpose of obtaining employment or procuring workpeople, that person shall be liable in respect of each offence on summary conviction to a fine not exceeding ten pounds.

4. Expenses of the Board of Trade

The Board of Trade may appoint such officers and servants for the purposes of this Act as the Board may, with the sanction of the Treasury, determine, and there shall be paid out of moneys provided by Parliament to such officers and servants such salaries or remuneration as the Treasury may determine, and any expenses incurred by the Board of Trade in carrying this Act into effect, including the payment of travelling and other allowances to members of advisory committees and other expenses in connexion therewith, to such amount as may be sanctioned by the Treasury, shall be defrayed out of moneys provided by Parliament.

5. Interpretation

In this Act the expression "labour exchange" means any office or place used for the purpose of collecting and furnishing information, either by the keeping of registers or otherwise, respecting employers who desire to engage workpeople and workpeople who seek engagement or employment.

6. Short Title

This Act may be cited as the Labour Exchanges Act, 1909.

CHAPTER VI

SWEATED LABOUR

[How to remove the worst evils resulting from long hours and low wages had disturbed the minds of British statesmen for a long time. Many philanthropists like Oastler, Hobhouse, Sadler, Kingsley, and the Earl of Shaftesbury laboured to improve the situation; and a Select Committee of the House of Lords made an elaborate investigation extending over the years 1888 to 1890. The Report of this Select Committee, which aroused a good deal of public interest and sympathy, stated, among other things, that without being able to assign an exact meaning to sweating, the evils known by that name were: (1) an unduly low rate of wages; (2) excessive hours of labour; (3) an unsanitary state of the houses in which work was carried on.

The situation with regard to low wages was summed up by the Select Committee as follows:

It may be said that the inefficiency of the workers, early marriages, and the tendency of the residuum of the population in large towns to form a helpless community, together with a low standard of life and the excessive supply of unskilled labour, are the chief factors in producing sweating. Moreover, a large supply of cheap female labour is available by the fact that married women working at unskilled labour in their homes, in the intervals between attending to their domestic duties, and not wholly supporting themselves, can afford to work at what would be starvation wages to unmarried women. Such being the conditions of the labour market, abundant materials exist to supply the unscrupulous employer with his wretched dependent workers.[1]

[1] Fifth Report from the Select Committee of the House of Lords on the Sweating System (1890), p. cxxxv.

After the publication of the report, an Anti-Sweating League was formed with the purpose of securing the parliamentary enactment of a minimum wage for workers in sweated industries and trades. Prior to 1906 several unsuccessful attempts were made to prevail upon the Unionist party to sponsor some form of minimum wage bill.

On February 21, 1908, Mr. George Toulmin introduced in the House of Commons a bill designed to establish wages boards with power to fix the minimum wage for workers in certain scheduled trades, the Home Secretary having power to add to the schedule. The Boards would be composed of representatives of employers and employed in equal numbers, with a chairman chosen by the members or nominated by the Home Secretary. Payment of the minimum wage would be enforced through the factory inspectors, the payment of less being punished by imprisonment. Mr. Toulmin gave some pitiable instances of underpayment and stated that a similar law worked well in Australia. The Bill was opposed by many Unionists, including Sir F. Banbury, as the thin end of the Socialistic wedge, but it was accepted in principle by several Unionists and Tariff Reformers, including Mr. Lyttelton, and also by Mr. Herbert Gladstone, the Home Secretary, whose suggestion that it be referred to the Select Committee on Home Work, was adopted.

Early in 1909 two attempts, independent of the Government, were made to deal with the problem of sweating : Mr. H. H. Marks, a Unionist and Protectionist, unsuccessfully moved on March 23 for leave to bring in a bill providing that when a minimum rate of wages in any trade had been established by law or custom, it should be protected from the competition of goods produced abroad by sweated or lower-paid labour ; and Mr. Hills, another Unionist, moved the second reading of a bill on March 26 to create wages boards of employers and employed to fix a minimum wage for tailoring, dressmaking, shirtmaking and certain other trades, to be designated by the Home Secretary. The debate on this Bill was eventually adjourned pending the debate on the Government Bill, which had been introduced by Mr. Winston Churchill, President of the Board of Trade, on March 24 (*Extract 41*), and which proceeded along similar lines, save that the administrative machinery provided for in Mr. Churchill's Bill was by devolution of powers from the Board of Trade, while Mr. Hills' measure began from below.

The second reading of the Government Bill (the Trade Boards Bill) was moved by Mr. H. J. Tennant, the Parliamentary Secretary to the Board of Trade, on April 28 (*Extract 42*). He reminded the House of the prevalence of the evils of sweating established by the Home Work Committee of 1908, and declared that the Bill would apply only to exceptional industries, unorganised, immobile, and carried on under unhealthy economic conditions. It was an experiment and a revolution, the first modern proposal of Government machinery for settling and enforcing the rate of wages. He called attention to the action taken by Continental Governments, and thought some agreement with them might be reached. Mr. Lyttelton supported the Bill in a sympathetic speech, but with some reservations, chiefly as to the powers to be given to the Board of Trade; Mr. Marks renewed his effort to raise the Tariff Reform issue, and after other speeches Mr. Balfour insisted (*Extract 43*) on certain difficulties, especially that set up by foreign competition, but supported the second reading; to these Mr. Churchill replied that other nations were taking steps to deal with sweating, and that wages might be raised without affecting prices, to which, indeed, the wages paid often bore no relation. Mr. T. F. Richards, a workingman member of Parliament, urged (*Extract 44*) that the measure be made more comprehensive.

It may be added that the Bill went to a Standing Committee, and was reported to the House and read a third time on July 16. A Labour attempt was made unsuccessfully to provide for the inclusion of other trades besides those scheduled; and the foreign competition question was again raised unsuccessfully by Mr. H. H. Marks. The Bill was extended by a provision that an employer convicted of paying wages below the minimum rate might also be ordered to make up the deficient wages ; and a clause relating to sub-contracting was dropped. In the House of Lords, the Bill passed second reading on August 30 and third reading on September 20 ; on the former occasion, Lord Hamilton of Dalzell expressed the Government view (*Extract 45*) and the Marquess of Salisbury that of the Opposition (*Extract 46*). Royal assent was accorded the Bill on October 20.

The Bill, enacted as the Trade Boards Act, 1909, is *Extract 47*.]

Extract 41

INTRODUCTION OF THE TRADE BOARDS BILL

(*Mr. Winston Churchill, President of the Board of Trade, Commons,
March 24, 1909 ; Sir Frederick Banbury, ibid.*)

MR. CHURCHILL [1]: . . . The central principle of the Trade Boards Bill is the establishment of Trade Boards in certain trades where the evils known as sweating prevail, and the fixing by those particular Boards of a minimum standard of wages, and the enforcement by those Trade Boards of that minimum when fixed.

The Trade Boards set up under this Bill will exercise other functions besides their particular statutory functions of fixing a minimum rate of wages. They will be a centre of information, and I hope they will become the foci of organisation. As centres of information they may as time goes on be charged with some other aspects of the administration of the work of the trades, with the question of the training of the workers, and also they will be able to afford information upon the subject of unemployment. They will generally be not merely boards for the purpose of fixing the minimum rate of wages, for that is their primary purpose, but boards designed to nourish, as far as possible, the interests of the

[1] Parliamentary Debates, Commons, Fifth Series, vol. 2, col. 1787 sqq.

workers, the health, and the state of the industry of each particular trade in which they operate.

The trades which will be scheduled under the Bill, and to which the Bill will at once apply, are these : the tailoring trade, — but let me say that after very careful examination we have arrived at a correct definition of those portions of the tailoring trade to which the Act should apply, that is, the ready-made and wholesale be-spoke, — the trade of cardboard-box making, machine-made-lace and finishing trade, and the ready-made-blouse-making trade. Those are the trades that are scheduled under the Bill for a beginning ; but power is taken in the Bill to extend the provisions of the Bill to other trades by an Order which acquires validity when it has lain on the table of the House unchallenged for thirty days. So much for the scope of the Bill.

There are two methods by which Trade Boards may be called into being. You may make local Trade Boards in the different districts. Then you may federate all those Trade Boards and form a Central Council; or, on the other hand, you can have a Trade Board which would give the duties and power to local Trade Boards or local committees, which are set up in the particular districts by the trade. Having to choose between the principle of devolution and federation of local bodies into a central body, we have chosen devolution from the central body. It is of very great importance that the balance should be held evenly between one district and another in some of those trades. Therefore, I felt any assistance of this character must be gripped and co-ordinated strictly from the centre in each trade.

The Trade Board, having been formed in any trade, establishes a district trade committee. The district trade committee will consist of local representatives of the employers and of the workmen, and a proportionate number of the Central Trade Board. The Trade Board itself will also be composed of the representatives of the employers and of the workers, and the Trade Board in any trade will have three expert paid official members, salaried official members, and, I trust, where women are largely employed, at least one of those members shall always be a woman. Those official members are the link we are relying on to couple together and strengthen the local organisations and to procure, with a general view to that harmony of action which is essential, that the provisions of this Bill are really to be useful and effective. The official members of the Central Trade Boards will also be members of the district trade committees, and the official member of the district trade committee will occupy the chair whenever that committee meets.

Great latitude is taken by the Board of Trade in regard to the processes by which those Trade Boards are called into existence. We give power by any method — by election, and where the materials for election do not exist, and those who have studied this question know that in many cases they do not exist, we take the power to proceed . . . as circumstances may direct. . . .

The Bill applies, indeed is indispensable, not only to home workers, but to factory workers, and that is obviously necessary. To screw up by those special and artificial means the position of the home worker, while leaving the factory untouched, would be to improve the lot of the home worker by a process which in practice would be very harsh. The Bill allows the different treatment to be applied simultaneously to the home workers and factory workers in any district. A minimum time-rate will be the general basis, and to that minimum time-rate all piece-rates will be referred. It will be open to the Trade Boards to fix the general minimum piece-rates in regard to articles more or less standard in their character and regularly produced. It will be open to an employer to go to the Trade Board and ask for a special minimum in regard to any special class of work he has on hand. It will be open for the Trade Board to fix different piece-rates and in some cases different time-rates for the whole of the factory workers in any particular district. All these rates will be co-ordinated as between district and district by the general division of the Trade Board.

Now, I have dealt with the scope, and I have dealt with the machinery, and I propose to deal with the procedure. The district trade committee — that is, the local body in session, with its official members — recognises minimum time piece-rates. The Trade Board of the whole trade considers those in all their bearings from a central point of view, and, after an interval to hear objections, amends, approves, and finally prescribes. Thereupon the minimum, when prescribed by the Trade Board, will become obligatory on Government and municipal contractors, and in all cases the wages specified are recoverable as a civil debt in the absence of a written contract to the contrary. The rates will be posted in a manner similar to the notices under the Factory Acts, and a white list, accessible to the public, will be formed of manufacturers voluntarily agreeing to be bound under penalties to observe the minimum rate. No one who does not appear on that list will be eligible for any Government contract.

By such methods it is hoped by the Board of Trade, and some who have studied the question, that there will be in the first instance a healthy trade opinion from the beginning, and that, beginning, an organisation will be formed which, with a certain backing of solid support within the trade committees, will act on the state of minimum wage which we are anxious to enforce. At any time not less than six months after the minimum rates have been prescribed, the Board of Trade may, on the application of the Trade Board, make an order, making those rates obligatory by law on all persons. It may then use, to enforce the rates, the powers which we are going to ask Parliament to confer upon us by the Act. I say at the outset that the enforcement will be effective in proportion as there is a strong element of support among the workers and among the employers in the trade committees. But it is also necessary, and I could not be responsible for the Act without that necessity being made, that full powers of enforcement, not only by investigation and complaint, but also by inspection, should rest in the hands of the authorities who administer the Act. The use of such powers must depend upon the circumstances of each particular varying trade and on each particular varying district, but that those powers should be made in the Act is in our judgment essential.

I therefore take powers which authorise entry to factories, to workshops and places where work is being carried on, at all reasonable and suitable times. The powers which the Act confers provide for investigation of the complaints by a thoroughly efficient system of inspection by officers who will devote their whole time to the work and who will be appointed with the sanction of the Board of Trade to work under Trade Boards in each particular trade and under the local committees in each particular district. Arrangements are made in the Bill to utilise the services of the factory inspectors of the Home Office, who are also engaged in covering ground not far removed from that which we are now entering. In order that we may not have to come to Parliament again for the fullest power to give effect to these proposals by clauses in the Bill, we ask the House to enable the powers which the Board of Trade have under this Act to be transferred if necessary to the Home Office for administration by the Home Office. That gets over any difficulty of a subsequent demand upon Parliament for further powers and places in the hands of the authorities many channels through which to enforce the Act, and the power of choosing from a variety of measures that which will attain the most favourable result.

I have now unfolded the main outlines of the Bill. The principles on which we are proceeding are to endeavour to foster organisation in trades in which, by reason of the prevalence of exceptionally evil conditions, no organisation has yet taken root, and in which, in consequence, no parity of bargaining power can be said to exist; to use these organisations, when formed, as instruments to determine minimum standards below which the wages paid ought not to be allowed to fall; to rally to the side of these minimum standards all the healthy elements in the trade;

and, finally, if and when this has been achieved, to protect the good employers — and there are always good employers in the worst of trades — who are anxious to pay a proper rate of wages from being undercut, and to protect them by compulsory powers which are no doubt far-reaching in their character, which I also think will be found to be properly safeguarded in their use. I hope the House will now accord me permission to introduce the Bill. The difficulties which confront those who attempt to deal with these questions are no doubt great; but there is a very large measure of sympathy and interest in such efforts, not by any means confined to one side or one quarter of the House, and I am confident that Parliament will not grudge the time and labour which the consideration of these questions and the attempt to legislate upon them will most certainly require.

MR. SPEAKER: The question is that leave be given to bring in the Bill. Does any Member rise to oppose?

SIR FREDERICK BANBURY: Yes, Sir; certainly. The right hon. Gentleman has given utterance to some elaborate sentences to explain the principles which actuated His Majesty's Government in introducing this Bill. The right hon. Gentleman might have saved the time of the House, and made his position more clear, if he had said that the principles which actuated His Majesty's Government were to be found in a complete surrender to the Socialist party. The right hon. Gentleman told us that the object of his Bill — and I call the attention of the hon. Member for Preston to this — is to screw up by artificial methods the position of the worker. And he also said something about power to protect the worker and about fixing the minimum wages, and finished up by saying, " So much for the scope of the Bill." I think the scope is very large, because, as I understand, there is not a single trade in the country which may not be brought within the provisions of the Bill. It seems that one effect of this Bill will be to provide employment for certain people at the expense of the State at a time when the finances of the State are as bad as they can possibly be; another will be to put a final nail in the coffin of the trade of this country. [Laughter.] Hon. Members laugh. Do they suppose that people here in England will be able to cope with all the provisions which the right hon. Gentleman has indicated? Are they aware that employers abroad are not hampered by any of these restrictions which it is sought to impose upon employers in this country? The result will be that the few remaining trades in this country— [Laughter.] I do not consider this a laughing matter. I think the position of this country is extremely grave, not only in regard to its trade, but in regard also to many other matters. I cannot admit that it is a laughing matter to interfere with the trade of the country. It may be right, or it may be wrong, but it is a serious question, and one which will have to be dealt with with gravity, even in this House of Commons.

Extract 42

SECOND READING OF THE TRADE BOARDS BILL

(Mr. H. J. Tennant, Parliamentary Secretary of the Board of Trade, Commons, April 28, 1909)

MR. TENNANT[1]: It is a singular coincidence that on April 28, 1890, exactly nineteen years ago to this day, the Select Committee of the House of Lords, called Lord Dunraven's Committee, made a Report. That Committee sat over a long period, and examined no less than 291 witnesses. It reported that sweating had been known for fifty years. It referred to "a rate of wages inadequate to the necessities of the workers or disproportionate to the work done." It reported that the state of things which existed involved excessive hours of labour and insanitary state of houses. The Committee also said:

---

[1] Parliamentary Debates, Commons, Fifth Series, vol. 4, col. 342 sqq.

These evils can hardly be exaggerated. The earnings of the lowest classes of workers are barely sufficient to sustain existence. The hours of labour are such as to make the lives of the workers periods of almost ceaseless toil, hard and often unhealthy.

The Committee concluded with the impressive remark:

We make these statements on evidence of the truth of which we are fully satisfied, and we feel bound to express our admiration of the courage with which the sufferers endure their lot, of the absence of any desire to excite pity by exaggeration, and of the almost unbounded charity they display towards each other in endeavouring by gifts of food and other kindnesses to alleviate any distress for the time being greater than their own.

All, or nearly all, of the recommendations of that Committee have been embodied in new legislation. Has there been any considerable improvement in the interval? Let us hope that there has. Miss Squire, a very competent inspector of factories, says that the conditions have been largely improved since that Committee sat, but in spite of this and of the great prosperity enjoyed by the bulk of the nation, the Home Work Committee reported last year that there was " no doubt whatever that the number of sweated individuals is very large, and that it is still true that the evils of sweating are very great." That Committee also reported:

The earnings of a large number of people are so small as alone to be insufficient to sustain life in a most meagre manner, even when the workers toil hard for extremely long hours, that the conditions under which they live are altogether pitiable and distressing, and that sufficient evidence has been put before us to show that sweating still exists to such a degree as to call urgently for the interference of Parliament.

The Bill which I am now asking the House to read a second time is an attempt to deal with these conditions of labour. The principle of this legislation was introduced to this House by my right hon. Friend the Member for the Forest of Dean [Sir Charles Dilke], who has been the author of so many schemes for social progress. May I felicitate him on the important stage which has been reached now by a measure which I know is near his heart.

It is a pleasure to me to reflect that I have been associated with him from the beginning in this legislation — in this and many other endeavours in the direction of industrial improvement. . . .

Our remedy is only intended to apply to a very limited extent. It is a remedy which has reference to low wages, and does not deal with the question whether State action can, or ought to, control wages. The general rates of wages throughout the country will be settled by other means than this Bill — that is, by economic forces. It is generally accepted that State interference with the remuneration for labour can only be justified in exceptional cases where two fundamental conditions are absent — I mean the mobility of labour in its true sense and effective organisation. It is only in those two cases that we propose to apply this legislation. Indeed, the application of this measure is very limited. It is intended to be applied exclusively to exceptionally unhealthy patches of the body politic where the development has been arrested in spite of the growth of the rest of the organism. It is to the morbid and diseased places — to the industrial diphtheritic spots — that we should apply the antitoxin of Trade Boards.

Incidentally, may I say, that these spots are not peculiar to this country. The same evils exist in other industrial countries—France, Germany, Austria, and the United States of America. The House will be familiar with the theory and practice of the pocket-money wage earner. A girl may wish to have a little work to do, although she may possibly live in a very comfortable home. Wages with her are not the primary consideration. She simply wants to supplement her income, and she is not particular as to the rate of wages that she may get. Thus we have the paradox that the same result is achieved by the ignorant whim of the comparatively well-to-do person and by the dire necessity of the starving. Both accept work at sweated rates, and the result is sweated trade. The trade becomes a parasitic trade, feeding upon other industries and trades in the country and on the wealth of the nation, for in such a case the wages bill of the sweated industry is largely paid by the relatives with whom the worker lives, by the poor law, by the community who subscribe to hospitals and asylums, by charity, and by a proportion of the cost of old age pensions. I think I may say that such a trade is a parasitic trade, when we hear the argument, " Is it not better that you should give the girl some work rather than no work — that she should be sweated rather than starved ? " To that I reply, " No, a hundred times No." In the first place the argument is false, because starvation is not an alternative, but usually an accompaniment of sweating, and I agree with the witness who gave evidence before the Royal Commission on Labour, that it is easier to starve without the work. One of the best results of this Bill will be the recognition of the inefficient and unemployable by the State. It is far more humane, far safer, and far cheaper that the nation should recognise and deal with these sweated workers. If the girl is sweated, rather than go to the poor law she drags others down with her into this industrial abyss.

It is to combat these evils that we are introducing this Bill. It is at once an experiment and a revolution — a new step in the social progress. These conditions which are now familiar to the House demand drastic treatment and, therefore, I feel that no apology will be expected of me because we are introducing a drastic measure. Parliament, quite two generations ago, enacted that payment of wages should take place in the coin of the realm. Parliament has also decreed that Government contractors shall pay a definite and standard rate of wages, and great authorities like the London County Council have decided that their contractors must pay a minimum rate of wages. This is the first occasion, certainly in modern Parliamentary times, in which any Government has proposed machinery, first for deciding, and secondly for enforcing, a legal rate of wages. To that extent the proposal is new — to that extent the proposal is a revolution.

Now, may I address myself to the hon. Baronet the Member for the City of London, who said that such a Bill as this is going to alter the whole system on which the fabric of British trade has been built up. He says it is going to do little or not much good to the workers. Now I assume that the argument is based on the assumption that if you raise the rate of wages, you necessarily increase prices. I should like to quote an extract from an interesting Report written by Mr. Ernest Aves (quoted in the Report of the Home Work Committee). He says:

Some of the fallacies, mainly traceable to an assumed fixity in the determining conditions — personal and economic — which underlie this assumption in its application to certain industries are recalled by Victorian experience, and the extent to which the combined view is held that special boards have increased wages and have not increased cost is of practical significance, since it is found to prevail in several of those trades in which the evil of underpayment is apt to be most prevalent. The special boards themselves may or may not have sent wages up to the extent often assumed or even at all. The fact remains that in several trades in which wages have tended upwards there is much testimony to the fact that neither cost nor price have been similarly affected, and in some instances it has been admitted that they have tended in the opposite direction.

I have expressly avoided dealing with the Australian experiment because I am perfectly aware that the conditions in this country are so entirely different from those in Victoria; but I do think I am entitled to say, at any rate, that it has been proved that the assumption that invariably and inevitably an increase of prices must take place with an increase of wages is not a fact. Well, again, I should like to remind the House that an increase of wages brings increased efficiency, and increased efficiency brings an increase not only in quality but in quantity. There is no doubt that it further stimulates resource on the part of manufacturers and the inventive genius of the people who give their minds to mechanics.

SIR FREDERICK BANBURY: As the hon. Gentleman has referred to me, I should like to say that I never stated that an increase of wages must be accompanied by an increase of price. What I said was that unless an increase of wages was accompanied by an increase of price, an industry might disappear.

MR. TENNANT : I am endeavouring to show there are many things upon which an industry can draw before it becomes extinct. The Home Work Committee found material difference existing in the rates usually paid by different employers in the same town at the same moment for the same work. Again, I would like to remind the House that high wages do not carry with them high prices. That is proved by the sweated trades. Certainly low wages do not necessarily carry with them low prices. That was certainly proved in the cotton and the iron and steel trades of this country, where you have in many cases existing minimum rates of wages which have not been found to raise prices. Furthermore, there are certain profits of the middleman — exorbitant profits, as some of us think — which will disappear. Trade Boards in their establishment will bring together not only the workpeople but the employers. They may possibly find it convenient to make arrangements — they may, at any rate, have a chance to make arrangements — by which they will be able to avoid some of the very violent competition which they now wage against each other, and they may be able to effect considerable economy. It may also be urged that they will also endeavour to raise prices. If they do so they will only do it temporarily, because there is sufficient capital to set up new factories or workshops, and that will soon bring back prices to their old level.

I think I have demonstrated that the experience which we have, at any rate, has shown that normally a rise of wages does not bring about a rise in price. It is ridiculous to assume that a rise in wages must bring about an increase in price. But suppose it does, let us imagine what will be the result. Will the worker be harmed by a reduced demand for a dearer article ? Unless the decrease in the demand is very great, I say this, with great conviction, that it would be better that the worker should be employed on a lesser demand, with reasonable hours of work at a fair rate of wages, than on a great demand with long hours at sweated rates of wages. [Ironical cheers.] I suppose what is running in the minds of the

hon. Gentlemen who cheer is that you are going to invite foreign competition from abroad. [An Hon. Member: That is it.]
Then I say to those hon. Gentlemen who cheer, remember that
these Trade Boards are composed of the best representatives of the
trades that the Board of Trade can find, and they will be and ought
to be the guardians of the interests of the trade, as they are both
employers and employees, dependent upon the prosperity of the
trade. Look at the great staple industries, I say, again. Look at
the cotton trade, where the wages are highest. They compete
against the same trade in India and Japan, where the wages are
lowest, and they are not afraid of foreign competition. They have
never found it difficult to compete against India and Japan in the
neutral markets of the world.

But let us consider what other nations are doing. For instance,
take Germany. Germany has an elaborate Factory Code, and she
held an exhibition in Berlin similar in character to our Sweated
Industries Exhibition. There is at the present moment a Committee
of the Reichstag considering the further limitation of home work,
and it is proposed to empower the Federal Council, and also the
local police, to make rules requiring all home workers to be furnished with a wage-book, or labour ticket, and to see that in every
room in which home work is carried on there should be posted
a statement of the wages to which each worker is entitled. The
Governments of Bavaria and Baden have recently made investigations into these industries through their factory inspectors, and the
reports which have been published as a result contain various
recommendations as to their legal regulation. The measures suggested by the Bavarian Report (1907) include: (1) the obligation to
employ wage-books or tickets; (2) the extension to all home workers
of the insurance laws; (3) obligatory registration; (4) the fixing of
minimum rates of wages with allowances for rent, light, heating,
and time lost in fetching and delivering work; (5) inspection of the
dwellings used for domestic industry. That is beyond any proposals
that we offer by Bill, and those are the proposals of Germany.

Austria is also making certain proposals, which I have not time to go into, but there was held in 1906 a conference under the auspices of the International Association for Labour Legislation at Geneva, where certain resolutions were passed in regard to the social conditions of home workers, the industrial condition of workers in Europe having regard to the competition with foreign nations, and the finding of a legislative remedy. Arising out of that meeting there has been held, in conformity with the resolution passed at Geneva, an inquiry in France in regard to what is called the French lingerie trade, which is famous all over the world and very expensive. That inquiry has elicited the fact that 56 per cent of the home workers in this white lingerie trade work an average of more than ten hours a day, at rates of pay not exceeding 1½d. an hour, and 50 per cent of them have net earnings of less than £16 per annum.

I think I have said enough to show that public conscience on the Continent of Europe has been aroused with regard to the evils of the sweating system, and it will not be very difficult for us to arrive at an agreement with foreign nations similar to that which has recently been carried out in the Bill of last year for the prohibition of the importation or use of white phosphorus in matches. If prices are not raised, it leaves me free to assert that competition in the markets of the world is an unreal and negligible bogey, and what objection have hon. Gentlemen then to this legislation? Is it going to be asserted, as I have heard it asserted, that it will be so difficult to enforce that enforcement will be impossible, and evasion will be the rule rather than the exception? I think that argument implies want of grasp of the principle which underlies this Bill, and that is, that the determinations are not going to be exaggerated beyond what the trade will bear by those who are dependent upon the trade for a livelihood. The decisions of the Trade Boards will be in harmony with and representative of trade opinion. I will ask the House whether evasion is a reason for inaction. We know that new principles have been carried out in the law of this country in regard to work and wages. The provisions as to particulars and truck are evaded to a great extent and to an injurious degree, but I am sure that hon. Members below the gangway will bear me out when I say that enormous good has resulted from those enactments, and are we going to deny the indubitable benefits of this legislation simply because we are afraid that for some of those who are most in need of it our intentions may be frustrated? I cannot help thinking that that is not good argument.

There are certain criticisms which have been made upon the details of this legislation. They are largely Committee points, but there are one or two which I think I ought to advert to. The hon. Member for Durham said that he objects to the centralising organisation embodied in the Bill, and my right hon. Friend the Member for the Spen Valley said it was doubtful policy to appoint committees throughout the country and co-ordinate the whole. I say that, after all, this Bill carries all that my right hon. Friend the Member for the Spen Valley would wish, because the district trade committee will make suggestions which will go forward to the Central Trade Boards, and I maintain that the suggestions of the district trade committees will be seldom altered by the Central Trade Boards. The right hon. Gentleman said that " wages should be fixed in the first instance between the workers and their employers in the localities, and that the co-ordination should come afterwards." That is, I think, exactly what we have done, because, so far from the localities being debarred from making their own suggestions for the government of their own local trade, we have provided by clause 12 that " no such minimum rate . . . and no variation or cancellation of (it) . . . shall have effect unless either the rate has been recommended by the district trade committee or an opportunity has been given to the committee to report thereon to the Trade Board, and the Trade Board have considered the report (if any) made by the committee." It seems to me that the principle of local government could not be given wider application. The hon. Member for Durham and others have also complained of the optional character of the Bill. I do not know whether by that he alludes to the setting up of the Trade Boards or to making their determinations compulsory. Probably both. [AN HON. MEMBER : Both.] On the question of setting up the Trade Boards, I think there is very little indeed to be said. The Board of Trade are the proper authority to set up these bodies, and I can assure the hon. Gentleman that it is the intention of the Board of Trade to set them up. The word " may " is inserted in the Bill to be on the safe side in case that it is found impossible to set them up in any particular trade, and in order that we shall not be guilty of a legal offence if we fail to achieve the impossible. I think the House will believe in the integrity of our intentions, and I trust it will not withhold its concurrence from our prudential motive.

With regard to making the determination compulsory, the Board of Trade is the authority responsible to Parliament, and that being so, it should retain to itself the last word in the matter. I think an arrangement can be arrived at between hon. Gentlemen below the gangway and ourselves, which we practically came to yesterday, by which we may arrive at a working agreement. I think I have shown that the evil with which we are attempting to deal is a real evil, that it is of old standing, and that it clamours for remedy. I have also shown that our remedy has the same inspiration and the same objective as was possessed by the old reformers, and proceeds upon lines parallel with those which have led the State to interfere with the control of the hours of labour and the conditions of safety and sanitation. Our remedy only gives statutory sanction to principles and methods adopted in numberless cases by voluntary agreement, which have been attended with the greatest possible success. I do not anticipate from this legislation either dislocation of trade, damage to employers, or diminution of employment. Our proposals are very limited in their application, they are limited to those plague spots of industry which, without drastic treatment, will continue, as they have continued for three quarters of a century, feeding upon the national wealth, supplying recruits to our hospitals, asylums, and workhouses, and swelling the ranks of the unemployed, and being the forcing grounds of the unemployable. When I am told that this legislation will subvert the foundations upon which the commercial supremacy of this country is based, I decline to believe that the commercial supremacy of this or any other country rests upon sweated labour. If I am told capital will not stand it, I answer there is another and a greater capital with greater claims upon us. It is against the drain upon this capital that this effort we are making to-day is directed; against this waste we protest — I mean the life capital of the nation.

Extract 43

SWEATED LABOUR AND FOREIGN COMPETITION

(Mr. Arthur J. Balfour, Commons, April 28, 1909)

MR. BALFOUR[1]: . . . The broad fact remains that the rate of wages you fix for one part of the country might or might not be suitable to another. And it seems to me that the difficulties which will be thrown upon the Board of Trade will be very great. While those difficulties will undoubtedly have the result of restricting the area over which this Bill could be properly allowed to extend, that difficulty is nothing compared with the competition between British and foreign sweated industries. Cases will clearly arise in this country, unless you are very careful, in which the only result of fixing a rate of wages would be to drive the industry out of this country, and send it to another country. I admitted the truth of the statement that the result of raising wages was not in many instances to increase the price. The whole machinery of production may be improved, and the whole raising of wages of production may be improved. These wages are not fixed by competition,

[1] Parliamentary Debates, Commons, Fifth Series, vol. 4, col. 384–385.

but it is a forced sale of value. It is not competition value. It is a forced sale value. It is grossly unfair of anyone to say that a forced sale represents the true value of the article sold. A forced sale never gives a true market rate of wages. Therefore, I do not think that if this Bill is properly worked, it will interfere with anything that can truly be said to be a fair market rate of wages.

But at the same time there are cases in which the raising of wages does not diminish the cost, there may be and must be cases where the industry is not carried on so economically when the wages are raised. How are you going to deal with these cases? You really cannot dismiss that as a Protectionist crotchet. Whatever your views on Protection may be, you are now interfering not with the fair value of wages but with the cost at which certain articles may be introduced. You ought to interfere all round. I do not think how you can refuse to do so. Your only possible alternative would be not merely to restrict the operation of the Bill to those industries to which the right hon. Gentleman the Member for the Forest of Dean [Sir Charles Dilke] has referred, but to take into account the conditions under which those industries are carried on in foreign countries, and to ask yourselves whether those industries are carried on under sweated labour. If you think that the raising of wages in this country will make the cost of production greater, you are driven to the inevitable conclusion that you are going to hand over the trades to foreign sweated labour. You are absolutely bound to make provision to deal with that difficulty. Under this Bill the only provision you can make is to exclude the industry in question from the beneficent operations of this measure. That is a very unpleasant alternative. But the Government must face it. No answer has been given, or can be given, and the House must either reconcile itself to finding some method of regulating between home and foreign productions in the special industries or exclude them from the operation of the Bill. . . .

Extract 44

A LABOUR VIEW OF THE TRADE BOARDS BILL

(Mr. T. F. Richards, Commons, April 28, 1909)

Mr. Richards[1]: I regret exceedingly that someone who has had some practical experience of the sweating industry has not had an opportunity to present his view to the House. With the exception of myself, who belong to the boot and shoe industry, and the hon. Member for East Leeds, who belongs to the furnishing trade, I am not aware that any other hon. Member has any direct association with this particular industry. So far as we are concerned we regret exceedingly that we are not in the schedules. I certainly should have liked to see the boot and shoe industry in the schedule for more reasons than one. So far as the East End of London is concerned, there are 24,000 operatives employed in this industry. Whilst we in the trade unions can protect ourselves, the Hebrew workers of our industry cannot protect themselves. They have no association, simply and solely because their wages are so small that they have not sufficient means to contribute to an association, and I want, if I possibly can, to take this sweating question away from the manufacturers for the time being.

We do not complain in our particular trade of sweated wages paid by manufacturers. What we complain of is the sweater, the middleman, the ex-operative, who goes to the employer and takes our work and pays just what wages he thinks fit, and by that means eases the direct manufacturer of playing the part which he ought to do in manufacturing his own goods direct. In my own industry fifteen or twenty years ago in Leicester we were so disgusted at the sweating that was in operation, where one man often took work out and employed five, six, seven, eight, or nine boys or youths whom he sweated, that we asked the manufacturers to make

[1] Parliamentary Debates, Commons, Fifth Series, vol. 4, col. 393 sqq.

structural alterations to their premises, and allow us to go inside, because we were home workers at the time. They demurred for a time, but we threatened to strike simply and solely because we were strong enough to strike. But I am pleased to say that the employers allowed us to go indoors.

Some members have said that this Bill will kill home work altogether. I think it is going to check home work, and I should like to see home work checked if we operatives cannot get a living wage. In respect of the statement of one of my friends from Ireland, who made the suggestion that the Irish members do not want this Bill to apply to Ireland, we have to-day received a letter with a request from the Irish Trade Union Congress, that we will do everything we possibly can to oppose the idea that this should be excluded from Ireland. The Irish trade unionists know full well that there is sweating in Ireland the same as in every other part of the country, and it is this middle sweater that I am concerned about.

For the last fifteen years my work has been to do nothing else than to settle disputes between our members and employers, and I challenge contradiction when I say that our manufacturers are desirous of paying good wages, but they do want us to do our utmost to bring everyone up to the same standard. That is their trouble. So far as the men are concerned, in my own industry we have little to complain of where the men are organised. In the East End of London it was my duty only two months ago to go down and find a poor Hebrew, an alien I admit. He was not naturalised. He was working there. He showed me his book, and in a month he had not earned £2 5s., and that very day he had received a 3d. reduction. I said, "Why do you stand to it?" He said: "What shall I do? I have a wife and four children. What am I to do?" His wages were insufficient to subscribe to an organisation which would defend him, and this Wages Board Bill I hope will be utilised to assist cases of that kind.

This has not always been the case. There are other parts of the United Kingdom where this idea prevails, and so far as our factories are concerned now it applies very largely to females. Unfortunately the females in our industry when they get married leave the factory and work at home, and as a consequence they accept 2s. 6d., 5s., or 7s. 6d. Generally speaking, 10s. is about as high a wage as they get. Under the circumstances we might do something to improve the wages in this particular. Our boards of arbitration in London and in Leicester grant permits so that the operative shall not be persecuted. In case of illness or of general weakness the board of arbitration, which is composed of employers and employed, grant a permit for the persons who work outdoors, but at the same time they take into consideration that that person has an adequate wage for the work that he or she performs, and this is the point that we are considering. We want these people to have something upon which they can adequately and comfortably exist.

I was astounded yesterday to see that case with reference to the Territorial Army clothing. I have some facts and information in my possession that the Government might render assistance in that particular and not encourage work of this kind to be given out without enforcing the Trade Union Rates of Wages Resolution of this House. I think the Government would do well to strengthen it in that particular. So far as we as trade unions are concerned we are endeavouring to the best of our ability to bring other countries up to our own standard because we have intercommunication and international trade union conferences, and I hope by that means we shall make the improvement that we think is necessary in this way. I do not think for a moment that anyone will be persecuted if only we adopt the policy which these boards of arbitration do, namely, that if a person happens to be aged or infirm or feeble and cannot work inside a factory, he ought to have an opportunity of working outdoors. We have been told by the representative from Birmingham that we might kill this trade. We ought to kill a trade which will not give an adult man or woman after working 60 hours a week more than 5s. or 6s. I have no love or regard for trades of that description; they ought to come under the general purview of this nation as a whole. I know full well that so far as my own trade is concerned there is not a single manufacturer with whom I have come in contact who complains that because we have got men working indoors, because we have raised wages in many cases, it has checked their methods of manufacture, and I refuse to believe that it is likely to check the method of manufacture in these industries. I am satisfied in my own mind that if the Bill is given an opportunity, and boards are set up with an equal number of representatives of workmen and of manufacturers, there will be no injustice perpetrated or perpetuated on the trade or on the operatives.

Extract 45

THE LORDS' DEBATE — A LIBERAL VIEW

(Lord Hamilton of Dalzell, Lords, August 30, 1909)

LORD HAMILTON OF DALZELL [1]: My Lords, the main object of this Bill is the establishment of a minimum rate of wages in certain trades in which what is termed sweating is well known to exist. The establishment by statute of a minimum rate of wages is, I suppose, a novel expedient, but your Lordships are aware that regulation of the conditions of labour in certain trades is by no means new, and that ever since the passing of the First Factory Act Parliament has from time to time agreed to legislation having that object. Only last year your Lordships agreed to a Bill limiting the hours of labour in mines. I have lived all my life amongst miners, and I never doubted for a moment that the passing of that Bill was a right and a just measure ; but I confess that I had an uneasy feeling, not with regard to those whom the Bill affected, but with regard to those who were not included in it. I felt, and I think many of your Lordships may have felt, that besides the

[1] Parliamentary Debates, Lords, Fifth Series, vol. 2, col. 974 sqq.

miners — and I am sure we do not grudge them their good luck — there were many other people, helpless people, with no political or other organisation, who stood in equal need of help. Therefore I am glad, and I believe your Lordships will be glad, that the case of those poor and helpless people is now to be dealt with. But I admit that that is a sentimental consideration, and it is a consideration which is, perhaps, out of place in dealing with a Bill which is not based upon sentiment but upon hard solid facts.

I think the facts are well known to us all. Everyone knows what sweating is, and everyone acknowledges it to be a great evil. It is not a new thing. It has been known to exist and its existence has been noted for the last fifty years or more. I do not suppose that during the last twenty years there is any feature of our social system which has been so much inquired into, so much spoken about, and so much written about as the evil of sweating ; and the Government are of opinion that the time has now come when the only practical remedy should be applied. It is not only in this country that sweating has excited attention. It has excited attention in practically every civilised country, and in Germany, in particular, I understand that legislation on this subject is imminent. I would commend that fact to anyone who may be afraid that by legislation of this sort trade in this country may be driven abroad ; and I would point out that even if we do move a little faster in this matter than other countries, and if we do take the lead, as in a matter of this sort I think we ought to take the lead, we shall probably not maintain that lead indefinitely, because other countries are moving, and moving very fast, in the same direction.

I shall not attempt to coin a new definition of " sweating." There are many such in circulation already, but I will take what I believe to be the ordinary meaning of the word — the payment by an employer to his workpeople of a wage which is insufficient to purchase for them the necessaries of life ; and in bringing forward this Bill I would simply ask your Lordships whether or not you consider that such wages ought to continue to be paid. I do not think that there can be more than one answer to such a question. It is already, to our credit as a nation, a punishable offence in this country to allow an animal which is dependent upon us to starve, and it does not seem very much to ask that the same principle should be extended to human beings. When an insufficient wage is paid, something approaching starvation must take place, perhaps not actually in the matter of food, but in poorness of clothing, poorness of lodging, and bad quality of food — that is, unless the insufficient wages are supplemented from some other source. There are cases, of course, in which the wages are so supplemented. In some cases that may be done by charitable relief, perhaps rather misplaced charitable relief, and even I believe by Poor Law relief in some form or another. I think it might fairly be said that a trade which cannot exist without such assistance must be a thoroughly rotten one and a trade of which we should be well rid.

But, as a matter of fact, there is not the slightest reason to suppose that any trade will either be killed or driven abroad by this Bill, and I do not think that any better proof of that is needed than the warm support which has been given to this Bill by almost all of those, both masters and men, connected with the trades mentioned in the Schedule. What we imagine will happen will be that a levelling-up process will take place. The best class of employer, the man who pays fair wages now, will continue to pay fair wages; the second class of employer, the man who we have reason to believe would like to pay fair wages but is afraid of having his prices undercut by the class immediately below him, will be enabled to pay fair wages; and the third class of employer, the genuine sweater, will have to pay fair wages whether he likes it or not. There is one source from which wages may be supplemented which I have not mentioned, and which falls under a rather different heading. There are certain people, principally women, who wish to earn a little money but are not really dependent on the trade for their living, such as girls living at home with their family or married women who have no children to look after. It sometimes happens that for the purpose of earning a few shillings, a little spending money, such people are willing to accept considerably less than the market rate of wages, and it may perhaps be said that if both parties are agreeable to that arrangement, there is no reason to interfere. But I think, my Lords, that it is necessary to look a little deeper than that, and if we do, it will be seen that it is far from right that those people, for the purpose of earning a little pocket money, should drag down the level of wages and inflict serious injury on people who have to depend on the trade for their living. There is no reason why these people should not be paid at the same rate as any other people doing the same work. If their work is worth having, it must be worth paying for. If they only devote part of their time to this work, they will naturally not earn as much in a day as a person of equal ability who devotes the whole day to the work. But the point is that the rate should be the same. There is no reason why it should not be, and therefore we do not propose to make any exception in those cases.

Four trades have been selected for the purposes of the Bill, and they are set out in the Schedule. They are certain parts of the tailoring trade, the paper-box-making trade, certain parts of the commoner lace- and net-finishing trade, and certain parts of the chain-making trade. Those are all trades in which sweating is acknowledged to exist. There are provisions in the Bill to enable its extension to other trades, and it is the intention that trades carried on under similar circumstances shall be included. That will be done on the initiative of the Board of Trade and will be carried out by means of a Provisional Order Bill. Thus your Lordships will see that the control of Parliament in the case of the inclusion of a new trade is absolutely maintained. What will happen will be this. The Board of Trade will say that in their opinion the Act ought to be extended to a certain trade, and a Provisional Order will be promoted in the ordinary way and passed through Parliament with the object of carrying that out. It will rest entirely with Parliament to say whether or not that Bill should pass. I should like to say here, as strongly as possible, that it is not fair, as has been done, to describe this Bill as being the thin end of a wedge. The scope of the Bill is absolutely defined, and there is no intention of using its provisions as a general means of regulating wages in all trades. If your Lordships will turn to subsection (2) of Clause 1, you will see that it is not possible that the Bill should be so used. In that subsection the Board of Trade are only given power to make a Provisional Order "if they are satisfied that the rate of wages prevailing in any branch of the trade is exceptionally low." It will therefore be seen that the machinery for including a new trade can only be set in motion if those exceptional circumstances can be shown to exist. . . .

Extract 46

THE LORDS' DEBATE — A CONSERVATIVE VIEW

(Marquess of Salisbury, Lords, August 30, 1909)

THE MARQUESS OF SALISBURY [1]: My Lords, I am sure your Lordships will all be of opinion that in the interesting observations which the noble Lord opposite has just made he has not said one word too much in commiserating the position of those unfortunate women who are the victims of this sweated labour. There is no spectacle more deplorable than that of these unfortunate workers, not themselves able to fight their way through life in a manner which men might do, and subject to most adverse conditions both of work and of wages. Nothing that the noble Lord has said, nothing that any of your Lordships can say, will be an exaggeration of the pitifulness of the cases of which testimony was given before the Select Committee of the House of Commons.

But, my Lords, I thought, if I may be allowed to criticise the general tenor of the noble Lord's remarks, that he made too light of the difficulty of dealing with this subject. He said the procedure

[1] Parliamentary Debates, Lords, Fifth Series, vol. 2, col. 979 sqq.

of the Bill was simple. I am sure that I agree with him, but, even if the procedure of the Bill is simple, certainly the subject matter with which the Bill deals is not simple, but, on the contrary, very complicated. It would be a mistake if your Lordships thought that the mass of home workers are sweated. The evidence appears to be conclusive in the other direction. Apparently, the majority of home workers are persons, no doubt working at a very low standard in the industrial scale, but perfectly able to look after themselves, and, in a sense, well-to-do. But there is a minority, a very considerable minority, a deplorable minority, in connection with whom those conditions do not obtain. Unfortunately, it is impossible to legislate with regard to one set of workers — namely, those whom we pity — without affecting the case of those workers who are perfectly well-to-do, and, in a measure, quite satisfied with the present conditions of their life. That is the first difficulty, and it is a very great difficulty.

There is a second difficulty which pertains, not to the generality of the workers, but to those very workers whom we are here to-day to pity, and, if possible, to succour. It would be a cruel kindness if by any legislation to which your Lordships' House gave assent we were to add to the sufferings of these poor workers one further crushing disaster — namely, to take away from them the only work they have. Therefore, we must walk very warily, and I confess I regretted the tone of confidence which I think was the feature of the noble Lord's speech. He was only following the example of his chief. I noticed that the President of the Board of Trade, speaking in another place and upon another Bill, — the Labour Exchanges Bill, — sketched a picture of a sort of universal condition of Trade Boards. When he was advocating the necessary expense for the edifices under the Labour Exchanges Bill he spoke as though there would be a Trade Board meeting in every such building, which he put forward as a reason for its existence. That may be, or may not be, an ultimate development, but at the present moment the matter is only experimental, and I hope your

Lordships will treat it as experimental. Whether hereafter this experiment may be a success, and whether your Lordships will agree under the provisions of the Bill to extend its operation to other trades, are matters in which we need not inquire at the present moment. Let us first see how this experiment succeeds before we cast our eyes further afield.

I confess that I see no way out of the main proposition which the Government have put before your Lordships' House. As far as I myself am concerned, I assent to the establishment of these Trade Boards, whose principal function is to fix a minimum rate of wages. I do so because the ordinary trade remedy for these evils appears to be impracticable — I mean the union of the workers. That is the proper remedy wherever it can be applied, and that is the remedy one would like to see applied in these cases. They know much better — I am speaking of employer and employed — what is good for them than any Trade Board which the ingenuity of the Government or of your Lordships' House can construct. But, unfortunately, the evidence is almost conclusive that these women have not made sufficient progress in the arts of citizenship to be able to combine in a trade union, and until they do I presume we must be content with this procedure, not so good and not so effective as the other would have been. . . .

Extract 47

TRADE BOARDS ACT, 1909

(*9 Edw. 7, ch. 22*)

An Act to provide for the establishment of Trade Boards for certain Trades.   (20th October 1909)

Be it enacted by the King's most Excellent Majesty, by and with the advice and consent of the Lords Spiritual and Temporal, and Commons, in this present Parliament assembled, and by the authority of the same, as follows :

ESTABLISHMENT OF TRADE BOARDS FOR TRADES TO WHICH THE
ACT APPLIES

1. Application of Act to Certain Trades

(1) This Act shall apply to the trades specified in the schedule to this Act and to any other trades to which it has been applied by Provisional Order of the Board of Trade made under this section.

(2) The Board of Trade may make a Provisional Order applying this Act to any specified trade to which it does not at the time apply if they are satisfied that the rate of wages prevailing in any branch of the trade is exceptionally low, as compared with that in other employments, and that the other circumstances of the trade are such as to render the application of this Act to the trade expedient.

(3) If at any time the Board of Trade consider that the conditions of employment in any trade to which this Act applies have been so altered as to render the application of this Act to the trade unnecessary, they may make a Provisional Order that this Act shall cease to apply to that trade.

(4) The Board of Trade may submit to Parliament for confirmation any Provisional Order made by them in pursuance of this section, but no such Order shall have effect unless and until it is confirmed by Parliament.

(5) If, while a Bill confirming any such Order is pending in either House of Parliament, a petition is presented against any Order comprised therein, the Bill, so far as it relates to that Order, may be referred to a select committee, or, if the two Houses of Parliament think fit so to order, to a joint committee of those Houses, and the petitioner shall be allowed to appear and oppose as in the case of Private Bills.

(6) Any Act confirming a Provisional Order made in pursuance of this section may be repealed, altered, or amended by any subsequent Provisional Order made by the Board of Trade and confirmed by Parliament.

2. *Establishment of Trade Boards for the Particular Trades*

(1) The Board of Trade shall, if practicable, establish one or more Trade Boards constituted in accordance with regulations made under this Act for any trade to which this Act applies or for any branch of work in the trade.

Where a Trade Board is established under this Act for any trade or branch of work in a trade which is carried on to any substantial extent in Ireland, a separate Trade Board shall be established for that trade or branch of work in a trade in Ireland.

(2) Where a Trade Board has been established for any branch of work in a trade, any reference in this Act to the trade for which the Board is established shall be construed as a reference to the branch of work in the trade for which the Board has been established.

3. *General Duties of Trade Boards*

A Trade Board for any trade shall consider, as occasion requires, any matter referred to them by a Secretary of State, the Board of Trade, or any other Government department, with reference to the industrial conditions of the trade, and shall make a report upon the matter to the department by whom the question has been referred.

MINIMUM RATES OF WAGES

4. *Duties and Powers of Trade Boards with Respect to Minimum Rates of Wages*

(1) Trade Boards shall, subject to the provisions of this section, fix minimum rates of wages for timework for their trades (in this Act referred to as minimum time-rates), and may also fix general minimum rates of wages for piecework for their trades (in this Act referred to as general minimum piece-rates), and those rates of wages (whether time- or piece-rates) may be fixed so as to apply universally to the trade, or so as to apply to any special process

in the work of the trade or to any special class of workers in the trade, or to any special area.

If a Trade Board report to the Board of Trade that it is impracticable in any case to fix a minimum time-rate in accordance with this section, the Board of Trade may so far as respects that case relieve the Trade Board of their duty.

(2) Before fixing any minimum time-rate or general minimum piece-rate, the Trade Board shall give notice of the rate which they propose to fix and consider any objections to the rate which may be lodged with them within three months.

(3) The Trade Board shall give notice of any minimum time-rate or general minimum piece-rate fixed by them.

(4) A Trade Board may, if they think it expedient, cancel or vary any minimum time-rate or general minimum piece-rate fixed under this Act, and shall reconsider any such minimum rate if the Board of Trade direct them to do so, whether an application is made for the purpose or not:

Provided that the provisions of this section as to notice shall apply where it is proposed to cancel or vary the minimum rate fixed under the foregoing provisions in the same manner as they apply where it is proposed to fix a minimum rate.

(5) A Trade Board shall on the application of any employer fix a special minimum piece-rate to apply as respects the persons employed by him in cases to which a minimum time-rate but no general minimum piece-rate is applicable, and may as they think fit cancel or vary any such rate either on the application of the employer or after notice to the employer, such notice to be given not less than one month before cancellation or variation of any such rate.

5. Order giving Obligatory Effect to Minimum Rates of Wages

(1) Until a minimum time-rate or general minimum piece-rate fixed by a Trade Board has been made obligatory by order of the Board of Trade under this section, the operation of the rate shall be limited as in this Act provided.

(2) Upon the expiration of six months from the date on which a Trade Board have given notice of any minimum time-rate or general minimum piece-rate fixed by them, the Board of Trade shall make an order (in this Act referred to as an obligatory order) making that minimum rate obligatory in cases in which it is applicable on all persons employing labour and on all persons employed, unless they are of opinion that the circumstances are such as to make it premature or otherwise undesirable to make an obligatory order, and in that case they shall make an order suspending the obligatory operation of the rate (in this Act referred to as an order of suspension).

(3) Where an order of suspension has been made as respects any rate, the Trade Board may, at any time after the expiration of six months from the date of the order, apply to the Board of Trade for an obligatory order as respects that rate ; and on any such application the Board of Trade shall make an obligatory order as respects that rate, unless they are of opinion that a further order of suspension is desirable, and, in that case, they shall make such a further order, and the provisions of this section which are applicable to the first order of suspension shall apply to any such further order.

An order of suspension as respects any rate shall have effect until an obligatory order is made by the Board of Trade under this section.

(4) The Board of Trade may, if they think fit, make an order to apply generally as respects any rates which may be fixed by any Trade Board constituted, or about to be constituted, for any trade to which this Act applies, and while the order is in force any minimum time-rate or general minimum piece-rate shall, after the lapse of six months from the date on which the Trade Board have given notice of the fixing of the rate, be obligatory in the same manner as if the Board of Trade had made an order making the rate obligatory under this section, unless in any particular case the Board of Trade, on the application of any person interested, direct to the contrary.

The Board of Trade may revoke any such general order at any time after giving three months' notice to the Trade Board of their intention to revoke it.

6. *Penalty*

(1) Where any minimum rate of wages fixed by a Trade Board has been made obligatory by order of the Board of Trade under this Act, an employer shall, in cases to which the minimum rate is applicable, pay wages to the person employed at not less than the minimum rate clear of all deductions, and if he fails to do so shall be liable on summary conviction in respect of each offence to a fine not exceeding twenty pounds and to a fine not exceeding five pounds for each day on which the offence is continued after conviction therefor.

(2) On the conviction of an employer under this section for failing to pay wages at not less than the minimum rate to a person employed, the court may by the conviction adjudge the employer convicted to pay, in addition to any fine, such sum as appears to the court to be due to the person employed on account of wages, the wages being calculated on the basis of the minimum rate, but the power to order the payment of wages under this provision shall not be in derogation of any right of the person employed to recover wages by any other proceedings.

(3) If a Trade Board are satisfied that any worker employed, or desiring to be employed, on time-work in any branch of a trade to which a minimum time-rate fixed by the Trade Board is applicable is affected by any infirmity or physical injury which renders him incapable of earning that minimum time-rate, and are of opinion that the case cannot suitably be met by employing the worker on piece-work, the Trade Board may, if they think fit, grant to the worker, subject to such conditions, if any, as they prescribe, a permit exempting the employment of the worker from the provisions of this Act rendering the minimum time-rate obligatory, and, while

the permit is in force, an employer shall not be liable to any penalty for paying wages to the worker at a rate less than the minimum time-rate so long as any conditions prescribed by the Trade Board on the grant of the permit are complied with.

(4) On any prosecution of an employer under this section, it shall lie on the employer to prove by the production of proper wages sheets or other records of wages or otherwise that he has not paid, or agreed to pay, wages at less than the minimum rate.

(5) Any agreement for the payment of wages in contravention of this provision shall be void.

7. *Limited Operation of Minimum Rate which has not been made Obligatory*

(1) Where any minimum rate of wages has been fixed by a Trade Board, but is not for the time being obligatory under an order of the Board of Trade made in pursuance of this Act, the minimum rate shall, unless the Board of Trade direct to the contrary in any case in which they have directed the Trade Board to reconsider the rate, have a limited operation as follows:

(*a*) In all cases to which the minimum rate is applicable an employer shall, in the absence of a written agreement to the contrary, pay to the person employed wages at not less than the minimum rate, and, in the absence of any such agreement, the person employed may recover wages at such a rate from the employer;

(*b*) Any employer may give written notice to the Trade Board by whom the minimum rate has been fixed that he is willing that that rate should be obligatory on him, and in that case he shall be under the same obligation to pay wages to the person employed at not less than the minimum rate, and be liable to the same fine for not doing so, as he would be if an order of the Board of Trade were in force making the rate obligatory; and (*c*) No contract involving employment to which the minimum rate is applicable shall be given by a Government department or local authority to any employer unless he has given notice to the Trade Board in accordance with the foregoing provision :

Provided that in case of any public emergency the Board of Trade may by order, to the extent and during the period named in the order, suspend the operation of this provision as respects contracts for any such work being done or to be done on behalf of the Crown as is specified in the order.

(2) A Trade Board shall keep a register of any notices given under this section :

The register shall be open to public inspection without payment of any fee, and shall be evidence of the matters stated therein :

Any copy purporting to be certified by the secretary of the Trade Board or any officer of the Trade Board authorised for the purpose to be a true copy of any entry in the register shall be admissible in evidence without further proof.

8. *Special Provision for Piece-work Employees*

An employer shall, in cases where persons are employed on piece-work and a minimum time-rate but no general minimum piece-rate has been fixed, be deemed to pay wages at less than the minimum rate —

(*a*) in cases where a special minimum piece-rate has been fixed under the provisions of this Act for persons employed by the employer, if the rate of wages paid is less than that special minimum piece-rate ; and

(*b*) in cases where a special minimum piece-rate has not been so fixed, unless he shows that the piece-rate of wages paid would yield, in the circumstances of the case, to an ordinary worker at least the same amount of money as the minimum time-rate.

9. Prevention of Evasion

Any shopkeeper, dealer, or trader, who by way of trade makes any arrangement express or implied with any worker in pursuance of which the worker performs any work for which a minimum rate of wages has been fixed under this Act, shall be deemed for the purposes of this Act to be the employer of the worker, and the net remuneration obtainable by the worker in respect of the work after allowing for his necessary expenditure in connection with the work shall be deemed to be wages.

10. Consideration of Complaints

(1) Any worker or any person authorised by a worker may complain to the Trade Board that the wages paid to the worker by any employer in any case to which any minimum rate fixed by the Trade Board is applicable are at a rate less than the minimum rate, and the Trade Board shall consider the matter and may, if they think fit, take any proceedings under this Act on behalf of the worker.

(2) Before taking any proceedings under this Act on behalf of the worker, a Trade Board may, and on the first occasion on which proceedings are contemplated by the Trade Board against an employer they shall, take reasonable steps to bring the case to the notice of the employer, with a view to the settlement of the case without recourse to proceedings.

CONSTITUTION, PROCEEDINGS, ETC. OF TRADE BOARDS

11. Constitution of Trade Boards

(1) The Board of Trade may make regulations with respect to the constitution of Trade Boards which shall consist of members representing employers and members representing workers (in this Act referred to as representative members) in equal proportions and of the appointed members. Any such regulations may be made so as to apply generally to the constitution of all Trade Boards, or

specially to the constitution of any particular Trade Board or any particular class of Trade Boards.

(2) Women shall be eligible as members of Trade Boards as well as men.

(3) The representative members shall be elected or nominated, or partly elected and partly nominated as may be provided by the regulations, and in framing the regulations the representation of home workers on Trade Boards shall be provided for in all trades in which a considerable proportion of home workers are engaged.

(4) The chairman of a Trade Board shall be such one of the members as the Board of Trade may appoint, and the secretary of the Trade Board shall be appointed by the Board of Trade.

(5) The proceedings of a Trade Board shall not be invalidated by any vacancy in their number, or by any defect in the appointment, election, or nomination of any member.

(6) In order to constitute a meeting of a Trade Board, at least one third of the whole number of the representative members and at least one appointed member must be present.

(7) The Board of Trade may make regulations with respect to the proceedings and meetings of Trade Boards, including the method of voting; but subject to the provisions of this Act and to any regulations so made Trade Boards may regulate their proceedings in such manner as they think fit.

12. Establishment of District Trade Committees

(1) A Trade Board may establish district trade committees consisting partly of members of the Trade Board and partly of persons not being members of the Trade Board but representing employers or workers engaged in the trade and constituted in accordance with regulations made for the purpose by the Board of Trade and acting for such area as the Trade Board may determine.

(2) Provisions shall be made by the regulations for at least one appointed member acting as a member of each district trade committee, and for the equal representation of local employers and local

workers on the committee, and for the representation of home workers thereon in the case of any trade in which a considerable proportion of home workers are engaged in the district, and also for the appointment of a standing sub-committee to consider applications for special minimum piece-rates and complaints made to the Trade Board under this Act, and for the reference of any applications or complaints to that sub-committee.

(3) A Trade Board may refer to a district trade committee for their report and recommendations any matter which they think it expedient so to refer, and may also, if they think fit, delegate to a district trade committee any of their powers and duties under this Act, other than their power and duty to fix a minimum time-rate or general minimum piece-rate.

(4) Where a district trade committee has been established for any area, it shall be the duty of the committee to recommend to the Trade Board minimum time-rates and, so far as they think fit, general minimum piece-rates, applicable to the trade in that area, and no such minimum rate of wages fixed under this Act and no variation or cancellation of such a rate shall have effect within that area unless either the rate or the variation or cancellation thereof, as the case may be, has been recommended by the district trade committee, or an opportunity has been given to the committee to report thereon to the Trade Board, and the Trade Board have considered the report (if any) made by the committee.

13. Appointed Members of Trade Boards

(1) The Board of Trade may appoint such number of persons (including women) as they think fit to be appointed members of Trade Boards.

(2) Such of the appointed members of Trade Boards shall act on each Trade Board or district trade committee as may be directed by the Board of Trade, and, in the case of a Trade Board for a trade in which women are largely employed, at least one of the appointed members acting shall be a woman :

Provided that the number of appointed members acting on the same Trade Board, or the same district trade committee, at the same time, shall be less than half the total number of members representing employers and members representing workers.

APPOINTMENT OF OFFICERS AND OTHER PROVISIONS FOR ENFORCING ACT

14. Appointment of Officers

(1) The Board of Trade may appoint such officers as they think necessary for the purpose of investigating any complaints and otherwise securing the proper observance of this Act, and any officers so appointed shall act under the directions of the Board of Trade, or, if the Board of Trade so determine, under the directions of any Trade Board.

(2) The Board of Trade may also, in lieu of or in addition to appointing any officers under the provisions of this section, if they think fit, arrange with any other Government department for assistance being given in carrying this Act into effect, either generally or in any special cases, by officers of that Department whose duties bring them into relation with any trade to which this Act applies.

15. Powers of Officers

(1) Any officer appointed by the Board of Trade under this Act, and any officer of any Government department for the time being assisting in carrying this Act into effect, shall have power for the performance of his duties —

(*a*) to require the production of wages sheets or other record of wages by an employer, and records of payments made to outworkers by persons giving out work, and to inspect and examine the same and copy any material part thereof;

(*b*) to require any person giving out work and any outworker to give any information which it is in his power to give with respect to the names and addresses of the persons to whom the work is given out or from whom the work is received, as the case may be, and with respect to the payments to be made for the work ;

(*c*) at all reasonable times to enter any factory or workshop and any place used for giving out work to outworkers ; and

(*d*) to inspect and copy any material part of any list of outworkers kept by an employer or person giving out work to outworkers.

(2) If any person fails to furnish the means required by an officer as necessary for any entry or inspection or the exercise of his powers under this section, or if any person hinders or molests any officer in the exercise of the powers given by this section, or refuses to produce any document or give any information which any officer requires him to produce or give under the powers given by this section, that person shall be liable on summary conviction in respect of each offence to a fine not exceeding five pounds; and, if any person produces any wages sheet, or record of wages, or record of payments, or any list of outworkers to any officer acting in the exercise of the powers given by this section, knowing the same to be false, or furnishes any information to any such officer knowing the same to be false, he shall be liable, on summary conviction, to a fine not exceeding twenty pounds, or to imprisonment for a term not exceeding three months, with or without hard labour.

16. Officers to Produce Certificates when Required

Every officer appointed by the Board of Trade under this Act, and every officer of any Government Department for the time being assisting in carrying this Act into effect, shall be furnished by the Board or Department with a certificate of his appointment, and when acting under any or exercising any power conferred upon him by this Act shall, if so required, produce the said certificate to any person or persons affected.

17. Power to take and conduct Proceedings

(1) Any officer appointed by the Board of Trade under this Act, and any officer of any Government Department for the time being assisting in carrying this Act into effect, shall have power in pursuance of any special or general directions of the Board of Trade to take proceedings under this Act, and a Trade Board may also take any such proceedings in the name of any officer appointed by the Board of Trade for the time being acting under the directions of the Trade Board in pursuance of this Act, or in the name of their secretary or any of their officers authorised by them.

(2) Any officer appointed by the Board of Trade under this Act, or any officer of any Government Department for the time being assisting in carrying this Act into effect, and the secretary of a Trade Board, or any officer of a Trade Board authorised for the purpose, may, although not a counsel or solicitor or law agent, prosecute or conduct before a court of summary jurisdiction any proceedings arising under this Act.

SUPPLEMENTAL

18. Regulations as to Mode of giving Notice

(1) The Board of Trade shall make regulations as to the notice to be given of any matter under this Act, with a view to bringing the matter of which notice is to be given so far as practicable to the knowledge of persons affected.

(2) Every occupier of a factory or workshop, or of any place used for giving out work to outworkers, shall, in manner directed by regulations under this section, fix any notices in his factory or workshop or the place used for giving out work to outworkers which he may be required to fix by the regulations, and shall give notice in any other manner, if required by the regulations, to the persons employed by him of any matter of which he is required to give notice under the regulations :

If the occupier of a factory or workshop, or of any place used for giving out work to outworkers, fails to comply with this provision, he shall be liable on summary conviction in respect of each offence to a fine not exceeding forty shillings.

19. Regulations to be laid before Parliament

Regulations made under this Act shall be laid as soon as possible before both Houses of Parliament, and, if either House within the next forty days after the regulations have been laid before that House resolve that all or any of the regulations ought to be annulled, the regulations shall, after the date of the resolution, be of no effect, without prejudice to the validity of anything done in the meantime thereunder or to the making of any new regulations. If one or more of a set of regulations are annulled, the Board of Trade may, if they think fit, withdraw the whole set.

20. Interchange of Powers between Government Departments

(1) His Majesty may, by Order in Council, direct that any powers to be exercised or duties to be performed by the Board of Trade under this Act shall be exercised or performed generally, or in any special cases or class of cases, by a Secretary of State, and, while any such Order is in force, this Act shall apply as if, so far as is necessary to give effect to the Order, a Secretary of State were substituted for the Board of Trade.

(2) Any Order in Council under this section may be varied or revoked by any subsequent Order in Council.

21. Expenses

There shall be paid out of moneys provided by Parliament —

(1) Any expenses, up to an amount sanctioned by the Treasury, which may be incurred with the authority or sanction of the Board of Trade by Trade Boards or their committees in carrying into effect this Act; and

(2) To appointed members and secretaries of Trade Boards and to officers appointed by the Board of Trade under this Act such remuneration and expenses as may be sanctioned by the Treasury; and

(3) To representative members of Trade Boards and members (other than appointed members) of district trade committees any expenses (including compensation for loss of time), up to an amount sanctioned by the Treasury, which may be incurred by them in the performance of their duties as such members; and

(4) Any expenses, up to an amount sanctioned by the Treasury, which may be incurred by the Board of Trade in making inquiries, or procuring information, or taking any preliminary steps with respect to the application of this Act to any trade to which the Act does not apply, including the expenses of obtaining a Provisional Order, or promoting any Bill to confirm any Provisional Order made under, or in pursuance of, the provisions of this Act.

22. Title and Commencement

(1) This Act may be cited as the Trade Boards Act, 1909.

(2) This Act shall come into operation on the first day of January nineteen hundred and ten.

SCHEDULE

Trades to which the Act applies without Provisional Order

1. Ready-made and wholesale bespoke tailoring and any other branch of tailoring in which the Board of Trade consider that the system of manufacture is generally similar to that prevailing in the wholesale trade.

2. The making of boxes or parts thereof made wholly or partially of paper, cardboard, chip, or similar material.

3. Machine-made lace and net finishing and mending or darning operations of lace curtain finishing.

4. Hammered and dollied or tommied chain-making.

CHAPTER VII

THE HOUSING AND LAND PROBLEM

[An early obvious phase of the Industrial Revolution was the remarkably sudden growth of manufacturing towns and cities, out of all proportion to the increase of the rural population. And this rush of thousands of countrymen to the cities at once precipitated the gravest municipal problems. Properly to house the new multitudes was no easy task. The meanest, ugliest dwellings were hastily constructed; dingy tenements arose; new sections were built up without provision for open spaces or parks — in fact, without plan or design of any sort, save to house the working classes with the least possible outlay of time and money. A Ruskin might cry out against the ugliness, the filth, and the dirt of a growing industrial town of the mid-century and against the disease, even the vice and crime that these engendered — those who owned the land and had the capital for building must profit to the full themselves, and besides, the workingmen were too poor to afford anything else.

Overcrowding became the rule of the day and the cause of many municipal ills. In 1901 the Census Commissioners described as overcrowded 392,000 tenements in which 2,667,000 persons were living, that is to say, 8.2 per cent of the whole population of England and Wales. In the industrial towns of the United Kingdom " more than half a million people live in dwellings of only one room. To-day in London, with all its immense wealth, nearly two-thirds of the whole population live in dwellings of not more than four rooms in all, while in Glasgow, famous for its splendid municipal enterprises, no less than one-fifth of the people live in one-room dwellings, and more than half the people have houses of not more than two rooms."[1]

To deal with the problem, several steps must be taken. In the first place, the slums and older insanitary dwellings in the heart of the town must be removed, and the newer tenements must be constructed with an eye to health, comfort, and beauty. Open spaces and parks, places for real sunlight, playgrounds and recreation centres, must be provided. Then, in the second place, there must be adequate control of urban growth, so that as the town stretches out into the country the workingmen's dwellings may not be dreary, monotonous piles of brick, but pleasant cottages amply relieved by trees and shrubs and grass. If these steps are to be taken, it is essential also that every municipality should have plenty of cheap land at its disposal and likewise cheap and rapid transit facilities.

Then, too, in the United Kingdom the problem has been complicated still further by the fact that the ownership of the land in the country as well as in the city has been in the hands of the few.[2] The peasant has not had a direct, personal interest in the land, and the consequence has been to draw him too readily to the city and to hinder any urban resident from settling in the country. To break down land monopoly everywhere must be a policy of any government bent upon social reform.

In 1884 an important Housing Commission was appointed with Sir Charles Dilke, an enthusiastic reformer, as Chairman, and with such members as King Edward VII, then Prince of Wales, Cardinal Manning, and Lord Salisbury. Its exhaustive report made clear, among other things, that pauperism and crime, drunkenness, physical degeneration, disease, and high death rates were all bound up with the problem of housing. Several definite recommendations of the Commission were embodied in the Housing of the Working Classes Act of 1890 and in subsequent legislation.

---

[1] Percy Alden, Democratic England, p. 170. Cf. also Mr. Seebohm Rowntree's book, "Poverty," and the investigations of Mr. Charles Booth among the poor of London.   [2] Cf. supra, pp. 5, 6.

But it was not until 1909 that serious attempts were made to grapple with practically all forms of the housing problem. It was against the land monopoly that many provisions of the celebrated Lloyd George Budget[1] of that year were directed, notably the tax on the unearned increment and the proposals for land development.

Already, in 1907, the Liberal Government had succeeded in securing the enactment of an important Small Holdings and Allotments Bill.[2] In 1909, in addition to the Budget, a Housing and Town Planning Act and a Development Act were passed.

The Housing and Town Planning Bill was introduced on February 17, 1909, and when it reached second reading on April 5, Mr. John Burns, President of the Local Government Board, said (*Extract 48*) that it was an almost exact reproduction of a Bill considered in Grand Committee in 1908. It proposed that the existing law which enabled local authorities to provide new houses should be obligatory, and increased facilities would be given for the acquisition of land for housing on small-holding terms. Loans would be obtainable for periods up to eighty years at the minimum rate of interest possible, and the Housing Acts would be consolidated into one. The law with regard to closing orders and demolition of buildings unfit for habitation would be strengthened and simplified, and landlords would be required to keep holdings in all respects reasonably fit for human habitation. As to town planning, there was no fear that open spaces and parks would be affected. The measure provided, moreover, that every county council should have a medical officer devoting all his abilities and services to public health and sanitation ; and underground and cellar dwellings and back-to-back houses would be abolished.

[1] Cf. infra, ch. viii.

[2] This measure " to consolidate the enactments with respect to small holdings and allotments in England and Wales " (7 Edw. 7, ch. 54, August 28, 1907) should be read in conjunction with the various Irish Land Laws and with the Small Landholders Act for Scotland (1 & 2 Geo. 5, ch. 49, December 16, 1911). All these Acts, in one way or another, illustrate social politics, but lack of space has precluded their incorporation in this volume.

Mr. Lyttelton, in behalf of the Opposition, gave general support to the Bill, though he complained that it was largely "legislation by reference," and he did not think the Local Government Board should coerce a county council, or that the provisions as to compulsory purchase were sound. Moreover, the Local Government Board should have an increased staff to work the Bill. Two Unionist members for rural constituencies, Mr. Lane-Fox and Mr. Hicks-Beach, respectively, moved and seconded an amendment declining to impose the cost of housing, a natural service, on local rates, but eventually this was rejected by 128 to 20 after closure, and the second reading agreed to.

The Housing and Town Planning Bill was disposed of in the Commons on August 30 and 31, after various Opposition members had unsuccessfully moved amendments restricting the powers conferred on the Local Government Board, altering the proposed land purchase procedure, saving lands held by railway companies and similar undertakings from compulsory purchase, and preventing local authorities from extending their schemes outside their own jurisdiction. A clause requiring local authorities to hold a quinquennial survey and inspection of small dwelling-houses and register the results, carried against the Government in Grand Committee, was debated independently of party lines and struck out by 121 to 95.

In the House of Lords the Bill was generally welcomed on its second reading on September 14, when Earl Beauchamp explained the measure in detail (*Extract 49*). The Earl of Onslow thought there would be too much governmental supervision and insisted upon the dangers of bureaucracy (*Extract 50*). The fate of the quinquennial survey clause was deplored by the Bishop of Birmingham (*Extract 51*) and by the Primate.

But the Lords, already in conflict with the Commons over the Budget, began to perceive dangers in the Housing and Town Planning Bill, and drastic alterations were proposed that materially weakened the measure. Of the changes effected in Committee

Stage, September 22–23, the most important (1) substituted a costlier plan of land purchase borrowed from the Port of London Act; (2) subjected housing orders to the control of either House; (3) permitted back-to-back houses if the medical officer of health certified their ventilation satisfactory; (4) exempted the land of railway and other statutory companies from compulsory purchase under the Bill; (5) relieved the County and County Borough Councils from the proposed compulsion by the Local Government Board; and (6) interfered with the town planning clauses by setting up the machinery of Provisional Orders which might be dealt with and defeated by either House.

The Bill was further amended by the Lords on Report on October 4, in a manner displeasing to its supporters. Some feeling was excited by the attitude of the Duke of Northumberland towards the proposals made to secure the fitness of cottages for habitation and the closing of insanitary dwellings, inasmuch as certain miners' cottages on his estate at Walbottle, Northumberland, leased to a mining company, had been closed as insanitary by order of the County Bench. " Walbottle " was heard of for some time afterwards at Liberal meetings. The Bill was further amended very considerably on third reading a week later.

The measure, as it finally received the royal assent on December 3, is a very long and technical one, but a number of its most salient provisions are given as *Extract 52.*

The Development Bill, the success of which had been repeatedly linked with that of the Budget,[1] was introduced on August 26 and reached second reading on September 6. It provided: (1) That grants on loans might be made by the Treasury, aided by an Advisory Board, towards forestry, agriculture, rural industries and transport, harbours, canals, fisheries, and other modes of economic development. The fund would be provided (*a*) by annual Parliamentary grants; (*b*) by five annual grants, each of £500,000

---

[1] The Chancellor of the Exchequer had referred to its purposes in his Budget speech on April 29, 1909. Cf. infra, *Extract 58*, pp. 366–369.

charged on the Consolidated Fund; (*c*) by interest and, in certain cases, profits on grants or loans. (2) It constituted a Road Board of one paid and four unpaid members, which would either itself construct new loans or make grants and loans to the highway authorities for the purpose. Its own roads would primarily be motor roads with no speed limit, and it would have compulsory powers of acquisition not only of land for new roads, but of land for 220 ft. on each side, of which it would get the increment. The expenses would be covered partly by this and by charges on non-motor traffic on the new roads or for private roads through this strip, and partly by the duties on motor spirit and motor cars. Its work was to have reference to the state and prospects of employment.

Lord Robert Cecil bitterly opposed the second reading (*Extract 53*), declaring that the Bill would produce political corruption and that it exhibited megalomania. Mr. David Lloyd George, the Chancellor of the Exchequer, replied to Lord Robert in a characteristically caustic speech (*Extract 54*); and subsequently Mr. G. N. Barnes expressed an interesting Labour view of the matter (*Extract 55*). Eventually the second reading was carried after closure by 137 to 17, and the necessary financial resolution was also carried after the defeat by 105 to 6 of an amendment limiting the grant of £500,000 to one year.

Stormy scenes marked all the later stages of the Development Bill in the House of Commons. Conservative discontent with its provisions was obvious. On the Report Stage, on October 7, Unionists unsuccessfully moved amendments (1) to secure greater Parliamentary control over the Development Commission by abolishing the annual grant of £500,000 out of the Consolidated Fund; (2) to limit the amounts payable in a year to England, Scotland, and Ireland respectively to 80, 11, and 9 per cent of the total sum advanced; (3) to secure greater independence for the Commissioners; (4) to restrict the number of the members of the Road Board to five; (5) to deprive the Board of power to construct new roads. The Bill was then read a third time.

In the Lords, second reading was passed on October 14, after an excellent summary of the general principles underlying the measure by Earl Carrington, President of the Board of Agriculture (*Extract 56*). Efforts were made to amend the Bill, but the Commons declined to accept any amendments, and the Lords yielded. The Bill received the royal assent on December 3, and is given below as *Extract 57*.]

Extract 48

GENERAL PRINCIPLES OF THE HOUSING AND TOWN PLANNING BILL

(*Mr. John Burns, President of the Local Government Board, Commons, April 5, 1909*)

MR. BURNS [1]: The Bill that we ask the second reading of to-day is the Government's Housing and Town Planning Bill, which was read a second time on May 12 of last year. After the Bill received its second reading, it was committed to the Grand Committee upstairs. This Bill was most favourably received both in this House on the second reading and in the country both before and since, and for twenty-three days it stood upstairs the ordeal of criticism and improvement. After the twenty-three days upstairs, the Bill was reported to the House of Commons on December 3 last, but the Government considered, mainly in deference to the general view that was then expressed, and because of the demands made upon its time for other measures that had an equal claim, that it was impracticable to pass such an important Bill last Session ; and the Prime Minister promised that, as the Bill was not passed last year, it should be re-introduced as early as possible in the Session of 1909. This has now been done, and, I submit, in extension of

[1] Parliamentary Debates, Commons, Fifth Series, vol. 3, col. 733 sqq.

the Prime Minister's promise, that the new Bill which we submit to-day is almost an exact reproduction of last year's Bill, except those Amendments which were added in the Committee, with a few deletions, which were effected on the initiative of the Government and generally approved by the Committee upstairs. . . .

The main and essential feature of the Bill is that Part III of the Housing of the Working Classes Act, 1890, which enables local authorities to provide new houses for the working classes, and which is now only adoptive, shall be put in force throughout the country. This is an important, a serious and necessary, and, I believe, a practical step that housing reformers have been asking for for some years.

Beyond that the Bill gives increased facilities for the acquisition of land for housing the working classes on small holdings terms. Such conditions under which land can be acquired for small holdings have been so recently before both Houses of Parliament — and have secured, I believe, the cordial assent of both branches of Parliament; and it is, at any rate, equally necessary that the acquisition of land for what is equally necessary for the improvement of the country, namely, land for the housing of the working classes, should be under similar conditions — that it is not necessary for me to labour those conditions at any length.

The third improvement is that the provisions in this Bill enable loans to be obtained through the Public Works Loans Commissioners for periods up to eighty years, with the minimum rate of interest possible, and I think desirable.

The fourth provision is that not only will the new Bill, when it becomes an Act, be better enforced by improved machinery than the existing Acts now are, but existing Acts will be embodied in this Bill; and at the end of the Session the whole of the Housing Acts, consolidated into one intelligible and practical working measure, will, I trust, enable the housing of the working classes to be secured by machinery that will act more easily, more promptly, and more efficiently, and at less cost, than now prevails.

The fifth point is that this Bill strengthens and simplifies the present law as regards closing orders, and the demolition of insanitary property unfit for human habitation.

The sixth point of the Bill is that it extends, in Clauses 14 and 15, to houses of a higher rental value than at present, an implied condition in the contract for letting that the houses are fit for human habitation. It is not only that we should be content with the present law which says that when a landlord lets a house or tenement to an intending occupant, at the time of entry for occupation the house shall be fit for human habitation. What we want is to maintain that house in a condition fit for human habitation so long as human beings reside therein. Small though that point is, if vigorously enforced, which we believe under the machinery of this Bill it will be, that small but necessary point will, I trust, create a revolution in the minor conditions of the house, especially in our large towns and cities. Clause 15 throws upon the landlord the responsibility of keeping the house reasonably fit. Now all these very objects are secured and achieved by the process of machinery set forth in this Bill. So far as the House is concerned this Bill is a distinct advance on the existing law. These proposals are moderate, reasonable, practical, and nothing has given the Government greater pleasure than the general way in which they have been accepted, so far as the House is concerned. I cordially commend that portion of the Bill to the House.

The next portion of the Bill is that portion which deals with town planning. This is a new department in the legislation of this country. I regret that it has come so late. No one can go through the East End of London, or to places like Liverpool, Leeds, Manchester, and Glasgow, and see the effect on the physique, morale, happiness, and comfort of men, women, and children, through lack of some such condition as this one hundred, or at least fifty, years ago, but will come to one definite conclusion, that, late though it is, it is better late than never, and that the House of Commons should not lose this opportunity of giving to communities, especially to growing and industrial communities, the opportunity of consciously shaping their own development in a better way than has occurred in the past. I have lately been spending week ends in visiting thirty or forty unemployed works in the East End of London, particularly in close proximity to open spaces, and if Members who do not know the East End of London had been with me, I could have pointed out in a practical way how, even close to places like West Ham Park, Hainault Forest, the western portion of Epping Forest, and Hackney Marshes, and by the River Lea and other places, if we had had this Bill forty or fifty years ago, the amenities of these parks and open spaces could have been enormously added to by maintaining a balance between them and the houses built in their neighbourhood. It is not fair or just to our poor that in many cases you build, as you do, close by a river or a canal, which might be made a pleasurable and healthy amenity by the adoption of a proper system of laying out roadways; it is not fair, I say, that streets should be put the wrong way on, that roads should be formed at the wrong angle, that they should be placed where the sun rarely reaches, but where the wind does always, or where ventilation is denied them, and where the line of greatest resistance is pursued in neglecting those natural and physical opportunities which, under the Town Planning Bill, could be profitably exploited for the whole community — to the benefit not only of the present generation, but particularly of children who are cursed, many of them, in their habitations and environment. This portion of the Bill has met with a favourable reception. It has had a little criticism, but I trust that before June the measure, the town planning portion of it particularly, will be on the Statute Book.

I come to one or two portions of the measure which have been rather misunderstood or unintentionally misrepresented. If town planning is to be a success, as we all agree it should be, it is essential that the central body should have more control than it now has. I can understand some hon. Members saying that what has prevented town planning in the past has been where special, personal, or local interests have been so anxious to satisfy prejudices or selfish objects that it has been impossible for local owners, with a local authority of limited views, sometimes consisting not always of the most disinterested personnel, to come to the agreement that would be arrived at if the central authority intervened. And it is universally admitted on both sides of the House that for this purpose the Local Government Board ought to have more power to intervene, first by way of local inquiry, secondly by making surveys and investigations, separating the goats from the sheep, and seeing that the community do not suffer because litigious owners or prejudiced councillors happen to be at loggerheads, not about the·interests of the locality as a whole, but about some pettifogging local or personal grievance which is very often allowed to stand in the way of a good owner developing his property, or of public-spirited companies doing the right thing — the local authorities being influenced, as alone they ought to be influenced, for the benefit of the community they serve. We think that the Local Government Board, as the central authority, ought to exercise a wider control, and for this control the Department has taken no more power than is essential for the proper purposes of this Bill.

Some of the powers of this Bill have been misunderstood, others have been exaggerated, and one or two are suspected on minor details. May I say to all who do not agree with me as to the proposals of this Bill, whether as to parks or open spaces, roads or other points of detail, that they will find the Local Government Board as amenable and susceptible to reason and advice in the Committee of this House as they were in Grand Committee upstairs. It would be ridiculous if, on minor points in a Bill like this, we should be suspected of dragging in proposals, as has been represented, to grab commons, to filch open spaces, to appropriate parks, and, generally speaking, not to rest content until the houses of West Ham and Poplar are in the middle of Kensington Gardens or in the centre of Wimbledon Common. Yet, that is the kind of representation we receive. As a matter of fact, the people who make that kind of suggestion in the newspapers forget that the Local Government Board is pre-eminently a body more concerned in regard to parks and open spaces than any other person or authority could be in this country. First, it has the care of the public health, and no town or city can possess health without open spaces and pleasant environment. Last year alone, the Local Government Board, which is suspected in some quarters of having designs to build on every common, on every open space or commonable piece of land, sanctioned £300,000 for the purchase of additional parks and open spaces. When it is suggested that we have fell designs on commons, my answer is: that out of £230,000 spent out of the unemployed fund last winter, £130,000 was expended in adding to parks and open spaces, and beautifying those which already existed. To suggest that we want to filch commons and run away with parks and open spaces is absurd. What differences there are between my Department and one or two hon. Members are open to consideration and adjustment. Of course, I do not hope to please every Member whose mind is filled with open spaces, but I do say that there is nothing in these proposals but what one can come to an agreement upon.

I now come to the third portion of the Bill. That is the portion which deals with the medical officers of health. It is a very important part of the measure. We have sixty-two county councils in the country, and, up to recently, only half of them have had medical officers. I do not think that this country, which for the last hundred years has led the world in public sanitation, should remain longer under the reproach of not having in every county of England and Wales a whole-time medical officer. And we have decided that every county council shall have a whole-time medical officer, devoting all his abilities and services to public health and sanitation. Bearing in mind the special provisions of this Bill, we also say that this in itself, especially when the terms and conditions under which the medical officer serves are to be approved by the Local Government Board, should give some satisfaction to the members of a useful and honourable profession, which has a right to be protected against, at times, the capricious local interference which prevents them from doing their duty to the body politic as well as they ought to be allowed to do it. . . .

There are one or two other things to which I must refer before I sit down. The first is with regard to underground dwellings. We are taking steps to abolish underground and cellar dwellings altogether. Personal and public opinion in the last few years has moved rapidly, and the proposals of the Bill practically terminate underground and cellar dwellings for human habitation for the future. We are also seeking to obtain power to prohibit back-to-back dwellings. [" Oh."] I notice that one Member of the House says " Oh." That confirms the fact, perhaps, that representations as to back-to-back houses have only been received from one district. I do not believe that back-to-back houses ought to exist at all. So far as this Bill is concerned no back-to-back houses are to be allowed in future. And we are supported in that proposal, I see, in a little handbill entitled " Fresh Air and Ventilation," published by the National Association for the Prevention of Consumption and Other Forms of Tuberculosis. I find in that leaflet they say that "back-to-back houses and cellar tenements are unfit for human habitation." And that is our view, and no injustice is done to any community or to any owner or to any interest when, if this Bill be passed, we say that no more back-to-back houses shall be allowed in future. If we wanted arguments against back-to-back houses, I should like, if time permitted, to read one of the most remarkable little books I ever read dealing with the state of the poorer classes in great towns. This little book is the substance of a speech delivered in the House of Commons by Mr. Robert A. Slaney, a relative of the late Colonel Kenyon-Slaney. If one only had time to read this little book, which was published in 1840, particularly with that part dealing with the consequences and the effects of back-to-back houses, I think we should carry the House with us. We are against back-to-back houses.

Mr. Lupton : That book was written seventy years ago.

Mr. Burns : Yes, but the same rule applies now. The particular town dealt with in this little book now labours under the disability of back-to-back houses.

Mr. Lupton : And that town has the second lowest death-rate in the kingdom.

Mr. Burns : Probably it would have been better if the town had not had back-to-back houses.

Mr. Speaker : I must ask the hon. Member from Sleaford not to carry on a conversation. This is a debate, not a conversazione.

Mr. Burns : I can only say that in one town where back-to-back houses prevail we have this remarkable result: Whereas the average age at death of the gentlemen and the professional classes was 44, amongst the tradesmen it was 27, and amongst operative labourers and their families it was 19 ; that is, 44 as against 19. My medical advisers advise me that the back-to-back houses were responsible in the day of this report for a death-rate of 43 per 1000 over the town as a whole, and an infant mortality of 570 per 1000 of children under five years of age. It is represented to me on the responsibility of Dr. Tatham, Dr. Niven, and Dr. Sykes, and other well-known medical men, that where all causes are responsible for 27 per 1000 of deaths, it is 38, and not 27, in back-to-back houses ; infectious diseases were 4.5 in through-ventilated houses and 8.7 in back-to-back houses ; consumption stood at 2.8 in through-ventilated houses and 5.2 in back-to-back houses. In the ordinary houses occupied by the labouring classes in regard to lung complaints the percentage was 6.6 in through-ventilated houses and 9.2 in back-to-back houses. Where the children die from diarrhœa it is 1.4 in through-ventilated houses and 3.4 in back-to-back houses. In a town that has recently expressed its desire to be allowed to continue these back-to-back houses, I find this very suggestive comment made by one of the best authorities on housing (Mr. Dewsnup) in one of the best books on the subject recently written. He says, speaking of Leeds back-to-back houses : '' Newly built the houses may look attractive, but what will be their condition after years of wear and tear? More than a probability that the conclusion of Manchester will be rejustified."

England is not so destitute of land upon which to house its poor that they should be housed in working-class tenements without a back yard in which to chop the wood and put the coal, and in which the children can play whilst the mother is able to keep a friendly eye on them through the washhouse window, and at the same time continue to carry on her domestic duties. All this is impossible in back-to-back houses, where the children have only a stuffy room for a playground; and in the days of rapid traction you have no right to relegate children to play in a small front garden, or in the road or street, when the community is rich enough to provide the humblest garden, in the majority of cases, and some measure of a back yard in which the youngsters can play whilst the domestic duties in the house are being carried out. This can be done better in through-ventilated houses with a back yard and a garden than is possible in the case of back-to-back houses.

We shall probably be told that there are one or two details with regard to town planning that are more arbitrary than they should be, that they will want amending, and that there are other details we shall have to consider. On all these points I am quite convinced we shall be able to meet hon. Members when this Bill reaches the proper stage. We are extremely anxious that this Bill should go through the second reading before the Easter holidays, and I have contented myself on this occasion with giving a brief outline of the salient features of this Bill, which has been before the House so long, and which has been so favourably received by the country generally. . . .

Before this session is out I hope hon. Members in all parts of the House will be gratified with having contributed in the production of a useful, if a humble, measure affecting the life of the people, the effect of which they will be able to gauge better thirty or forty years hence than at the present moment. . . .

Extract 49

DETAILED EXPLANATION OF THE HOUSING AND TOWN
PLANNING BILL

(*Earl Beauchamp, Lords, September 14, 1909*)

EARL BEAUCHAMP[1]: Your Lordships will see that this Bill is
divided practically into three parts. The fourth part we may dismiss as being supplementary, and, if your Lordships will allow
me, I will take Parts II and III first because they are not likely
to give rise to so much controversy as Part I.

The first clause of Part III — namely, Clause 68 — enjoins the
appointment of a medical officer of health by each county council.
In subsection (5) your Lordships will see the very important provision which affects their appointment. They are to be removable
by the county council with the consent of the Local Government
Board and not otherwise, and they are not to be appointed for a
limited period. Those of your Lordships who have practical experience of the administration of the various sanitary provisions in
different Acts of Parliament must know the difficulty which frequently arises when medical officers of health or sanitary inspectors
are expected to deal with property belonging to the members of
the body which appoints them. It is, I am sure, within the knowledge of everybody who has had anything to do with local government under those circumstances that it is almost unfair to expect
a medical officer of health or a sanitary inspector to report very
adversely upon property, however bad it may be, if it is possible
within the next twelve months that this adverse report will be
succeeded by his dismissal from office. It is an unfair position in
which to put a medical officer of health, and this demand that he
should be irremovable is one that has been made for a long time
by a very large number of people. The next important clause is

1 Parliamentary Debates, Lords, Fifth Series, vol. 2, col. 1141 sqq.

Clause 71, by which every county council is obliged to establish a public health and housing committee to which the council may delegate any of their powers as respects public health and housing as they think fit, with the exception of raising a rate or borrowing money. Your Lordships will see that that will secure throughout the country the appointment of committees charged with the specific duty of looking after public health, and will also secure the appointment of a medical officer particularly well qualified to assist the committee in their work.

Then, may I call your attention to Part II of the Bill, which deals with town planning. Now the idea of town planning, or of dealing with it by Statute, is, I am sorry to say, a comparatively new one in this country, although there have been provisions of a somewhat similar kind very much used in other countries and with very good effect. Your Lordships will see that Clause 54 says, " A town planning scheme may be made in accordance with the provisions of this Part of the Act as respects any land which is in course of development or appears likely to be used for building purposes." The object of a scheme for town planning is to secure " proper sanitary conditions, amenity, and convenience in connexion with the laying out and use of the land, and of any neighbouring lands."

Your Lordships will see that subsection (4) gives the Local Government Board power to approve of a town planning scheme, and without their approval no such scheme will become effective. It is suggested that these are very extensive powers to give to the Local Government Board. Well, my Lords, it is difficult to say in what other way you could deal with this particular point. I think most people who are concerned with local government are anxious to avoid expense as far as possible, and the insertion of a Provisional Order here would not only add greatly to the expense but also considerably delay the putting into force of any of these schemes.[1]

[1] An amendment was subsequently added, embodying such Provisional Orders. Cf. infra, p. 303.

I should like further to call attention to the proviso in Clause 55, by which if the scheme contains provisions suspending any enactment contained in a public general Act, the scheme shall not come into force unless a draft has been laid before each House of Parliament for a period of not less than forty days, so that under this proviso there is a considerable check put upon the Local Government Board, which will not be able to override any public enactment.

If your Lordships will turn to Clause 56 you will see that the Local Government Board are anxious to secure as far as possible the co-operation of the local authority and the landowners and other persons interested in the land in preparing these schemes.

Clause 57 gives the Local Government Board power to enforce a scheme, and I should perhaps remind your Lordships that the idea is not that the Board should do the work unless they are obliged to do it, but that their position should rather be one of supervision and of assistance.

Clause 58 deals with compensation, and here your Lordships will see that, under subsection (3), where the property is increased in value by the operation of any town planning scheme under certain circumstances, the local authority may recover from any person whose property is so increased the amount of that increase. Conversely, if the property is injured by one of these town planning schemes, then by subsection (4) the person will be entitled to recover the amount of the injury which he suffers. Clause 61 deals with compulsion, but I do not think that that is a clause to which any of your Lordships are likely to suggest an amendment.

Now we come to Part I of the Bill, the most important part, dealing with housing. I suppose it is difficult to exaggerate the importance attached by a great many people to this Bill. In the eyes of a great many people housing reform is one of the most important parts of social reform, and, indeed, some think that it lies at the very foundation of that reform. Nobody denies that the problem exists, and this Bill deals with two different departments of the same subject. First of all there is the question of new houses, and there is also the question of insanitary houses and the putting of such houses into proper condition. I think we all admit the difficulty there is in rural districts of building new cottages on an economic basis, and that is why one of the clauses in the Bill provides that the terms on which the loan is to be made to a local authority shall be exceptionally favourable. But the main clause of this Part of the Bill is the first, in which Part III of the Housing of the Working Classes Act of 1890 is adopted throughout the whole of the country. Up till now Part III of that Act has merely been optional, and a rural district council can only adopt it with the consent of the county council, which has to have regard to various considerations before giving consent. In point of fact it has been found that that part of the Act has been made very little use of indeed. It has only been adopted by nine or ten rural district councils. Part III of the Act of 1890 becomes operative at once throughout the whole country.

The clause to which I am afraid there may be some objection in this House is Clause 2, which must be read together with the First Schedule. It is the clause which deals with the acquisition of land. Now I may say at once that in this matter the Local Government Board has followed the precedent of the Small Holdings and Allotments Act. That is a precedent to which your Lordships have already given your approval, and we hope that you will give your assent to the adoption of a similar procedure in this case. The object which His Majesty's Government have in this matter is really two-fold. In the first place we want to simplify procedure, and, in the second place, to reduce expenditure ; and we believe that this method — which I think experience has shown, in connection with the Small Holdings Act, has not worked badly — is one which must really be expected to be of considerable value in regard to this Bill. The necessity of simplifying the machinery is proved by a passage in the Report of the Select Committee, in which they say :

At present one of the chief obstacles in the way of local authorities who desire to put the Housing Acts in operation is the conflicting nature of the machinery by which land can be compulsorily acquired. Not only does this tend to make a local authority reluctant to take any action at all, but in cases where action has been decided upon it almost necessarily increases the expense of their scheme, since local authorities will often be prepared to pay more than the market value of the land required rather than undergo the delay which the resort to compulsory powers now involves.

This particular clause, when read with the First Schedule, simply follows the provisions of the Small Holdings and Allotments Act.

After Clause 3, to which I have already referred, — a clause which deals with the making of loans by the Public Works Loan Commissioners and the terms on which the loans are to be obtained, — there are a number of clauses relating to small matters, such as the expenditure of money for housing purposes in the case of settled land, allowing a local authority to accept a donation of land, and so forth. In Clause 10 we come to the clause which gives powers for enforcing the Housing Acts, and your Lordships will see that here the Local Government Board step in. In Clause 10 the Local Government Board are empowered, if on due complaint, amongst others, from four inhabitants they find that a local authority have failed to exercise their powers, to declare them in default, and to limit the time for carrying out the works required, and in some cases to direct the county council to execute them. Clause 11 provides that if a local authority fail to perform their duty in carrying out an improvement scheme under Part I of · the Act of 1890, or in giving effect to an Order as regards an obstructive building, the Board may make an order requiring the local authority to remedy the default and to do what is requisite. Power is of course necessarily given to the Board to enforce their orders by mandamus.

Then your Lordships will see that in Clauses 12 and 13 provision is made whereby, under certain circumstances, a county council may step in if, in their opinion, a rural district council have failed to exercise their powers. Clause 14 is a clause which increases the implied condition. Your Lordships know that in the case of houses which are of small value there is an implied condition on the landlord to see that they are kept in a proper state of sanitary repair and are fit for human habitation. This clause increases the number of houses to which that implied condition will in future apply. May I say in passing that this clause does no more than carry out what I might almost call a favourite principle of the Liberal party. We all know of good landlords who keep their houses in a state of sanitary repair, and one of the objects of this Bill is to impose upon bad landlords the obligation which good landlords cheerfully and readily admit and already undertake.

It is just the same principle as that which operated in the case of the Old Age Pensions Act. We know that all over the country there were a large number of good landlords who already gave old age pensions. Now, under the Old Age Pensions Act, everybody is given an old age pension who is entitled to one, whatever may be the character of his employer. So it is also with the Employers' Liability Acts. A large number of employers throughout the country did, without doubt, compensate their workmen probably even more liberally than any employer is bound to do now under the Acts, and the object of the Acts was simply to force the bad employer to do that which the good employer was doing already. Here in this clause we have the obligation put upon the bad landlord to keep his houses in that state of sanitary repair in which a good landlord is always pleased to see his own property maintained.

Clause 17 deals with the duty of the local authority as regards the closing of houses which are unfit for human habitation, and here it would, perhaps, be most convenient to deal first of all with the law as it stands at present under the Act of 1890. At the present time it is the duty of the local authority to inspect these houses, but the obligation does not go beyond mere inspection.

Then, if it is considered necessary to close these houses, they are closed by the local authority upon an order made by the magistrates. The alteration proposed by this Bill is that the inspection should in future be made in the same way as before, but that the local authority should also keep such records as may be prescribed by the Board. That will mean that probably the inspection will be done more carefully than it has been in the past. The second point is that the local authority will be able to make the order without referring to the justices for the power to close, as they have to do at the present time before they can act. It is obvious, I am sure, that this must result in a great simplification of the system of making closing orders, and that it will render it easier for the local authorities to shut up insanitary houses, while it will also increase the amount of inspection. This very important clause — Clause 17 — which deals with existing insanitary houses also prohibits underground sleeping rooms. . . .

Clause 18 allows an order for the demolition of a house to be postponed if the owner undertakes to carry out the work necessary to render it fit for human habitation. Then come a number of comparatively unimportant clauses such as those which deal with the vesting of water pipes and the modification of schemes.

The next important clause, which is likely, I am afraid, to meet with some opposition in your Lordships' House, is one which deals with back-to-back houses. That is Clause 44.[1] Your Lordships will see that this Bill deals with Scotland, but not with Ireland, the latter country having been dealt with last year under a special Bill. It is, however, the intention of the Local Government Board, if your Lordships pass this Bill, to introduce next year a General Consolidation Bill dealing with the whole subject, which will, I think, be a matter of considerable convenience to all who are concerned in the work of local administration. I think your Lordships will agree that if the Local Government Board were to use the powers given them under this Bill too drastically, there would be

1 Clause 43 in the measure as finally enacted.

so great a danger of reaction that it would be impossible for the Board to proceed so far as they would wish in this direction. I hope, therefore, your Lordships will think that you may fairly trust the Local Government Board not to go too far, or to use the powers conferred upon them unfairly, but to do your best to make this Bill, if you agree to its passage through this House, a real success. I beg leave to move that the Bill be read a second time.

Extract 50

DANGERS OF BUREAUCRACY

(*Earl of Onslow*, *Lords*, *September 14, 1909*)

THE EARL OF ONSLOW [1]: There is a peculiarity of the Bill which runs through it from one end to the other to which I feel bound to draw attention. That is the proposal to put in the hands of a Government Department a number of duties which hitherto have always been left either to the local authority or to Parliament. This is a practice which I am afraid under His Majesty's Government has been slowly and steadily growing. It is not a practice which I for one can look upon with satisfaction. . . .

I know that the right hon. Gentleman who presides over the Local Government Board is a man of great strength of character. He is a man with great confidence in himself, and I am bound to say he inspires that confidence in other people. I have had the honour of the acquaintance of the right hon. Gentleman for a good many years, first upon the London County Council and afterwards in Parliament, and I have always thought he has been actuated by the highest motives and the greatest desire to discharge the duties of his office with perfect fairness and perfect justness to everybody concerned. But, my Lords, the right hon. Gentleman will not always be at the Local Government Board. We hear talk of an

[1] Parliamentary Debates, Lords, Fifth Series, vol. 2, col. 1150 sqq.

impending General Election, and perhaps the right hon. Gentleman may find that his attention will have to be more closely confined to Battersea than it has been hitherto, or he might be moved to a higher Department of State, and if he is caught up, upon whom is the mantle of Elijah to fall? Whatever good opinion I may have of the present President of the Local Government Board, I for one should shrink from entrusting these powers to any and every possible successor of his in that important office.

We are told that in this repect we ought to take example by what is done on the Continent. We are told that in Germany, Austria, and Holland the local authorities are all required to make town planning schemes. Most of you who have travelled on the Continent would be somewhat loath to see a town laid out even like Vienna or Berlin, with their rings and their rectangular streets. I think travellers visiting some of those cities may look back with affection to the times when we threaded the tortuous labyrinths of Threadneedle Street. Whether that be so or not, at any rate we in this country are not accustomed to be, and do not wish to be, governed by a bureaucracy. Our principles are totally different from those which govern foreign nations. We have our local authorities and our supreme Parliament. I am told there are no fewer than 26,000 local authorities in this country, and I am always filled with amazement and satisfaction when I reflect upon the enormous amount of unpaid labour which citizens of this country are willingly giving in order to look after the affairs of their neighbours. I know it is sometimes said of this House that noble Lords might be more regular in their attendance, and indeed I think I have heard the expression " Wild Peers from the Woods." I do not quite know what it means, but I take it that it refers to those Peers who attend our debates comparatively seldom. Why is that? Is it not because those noble Lords are engaged in the administration of affairs in their own localities? I venture to think that anything which tends to diminish local patriotism will be a very grievous blow to local institutions generally.

Extract 51

FRIENDLY ECCLESIASTICAL ATTITUDE TOWARD TOWN PLANNING

(Bishop of Birmingham, Lords, September 14, 1909)

THE LORD BISHOP OF BIRMINGHAM[1]: My Lords, I will ask you to listen to me for a few moments on this Bill, but what I have to say is entirely with reference to what concerns our great cities, and not to what concerns the rural districts. I suppose there could be no assembly in which there are so many people qualified to speak on the details of rural affairs, so many people versed in the management of rural affairs, but I suppose there are not quite so many who have an intimate knowledge of the concerns of our great and still rapidly growing cities. We are all of us proud of our own city, and certainly I am very proud of the city in which I live. It is one of the very many which have grown up out of a number of villages in which factories were established, which grew together and have grown and become a vast city, altogether without what one might call any guiding mind or plan or scheme.

The noble Earl who has just sat down confessed that he became very easily wearied with the monotony and regularity of a city laid out like Vienna, and that a little experience of a German-planned city made him long for the tortuosity with which we are familiar in London. I venture to think that if any one of your Lordships were to set about the task of learning your way about Birmingham, you would indeed feel that tortuosity and complication and absence of plan had been allowed to run to excess. I do not think it would be possible for anyone to make a survey of many of our great cities, even of that in which I live, without feeling that the condition of things was in the highest degree disastrous to social and public welfare. You may pass vast areas in which there is no open

[1] Parliamentary Debates, Lords, Fifth Series, vol. 2, col. 1157 sqq.

space — for your Lordships must know that London stands in respect to open spaces, as compared to a great many of our provincial towns, in a position of quite infinite superiority — and this is due, no doubt, to the fact that the city grew up totally without planning. There can be no one acquainted at all with the sanitary condition of the poorer parts of our cities who does not know that reform on a very large scale, and of a very drastic character, is necessary. I venture to say also that no one can be acquainted with the conditions in which the suburbs are still being allowed to grow, and the extraordinary rapidity with which the new suburbs of our cities degenerate into slums, without knowing that a very careful, and, indeed, a deep-rooted and far-reaching plan and method of town planning is quite essential.

This Bill is designed, I presume, to meet those two particular evils ; it is designed to meet the evils inherent in our slum dwellings, the small houses in the poorer parts of our cities, and also to limit, as far as can be limited, the evils due to the total absence of plans with which our cities are still being allowed to grow up. I was heartily glad to hear the noble Earl who has just sat down say what he did as to giving a general welcome to this Bill, though I do not exactly feel sure how much of amendment he intends to propose. At any rate, for my own part I heartily welcome the Bill as being on the whole a thoroughly beneficial measure entirely in the right direction. The noble Earl said what indeed is true, that it has not been our manner to encourage centralised government and bureaucracy. Is it not the case that anyone acquainted with our English life must realise that there is a very large opportunity for. us to limit the go-as-you-please policy which Englishmen delight in without by any means speedily or easily arriving at the point of completely centralised bureaucracy. I do not think it would be possible for anyone who knows the history of the efforts made in the last thirty years to remove the appalling evils with regard to housing, who knows the difficulties which those efforts have met with, or has realised how often those efforts have been unsuccessful, to fail to see that we do need a great deal more of what we call central control.

I was glad to hear the noble Earl who introduced the Bill speak of the clause about the appointment of medical officers of health. What the noble Earl said upon this subject touches a point which must be familiar to anyone acquainted with local politics — namely, the extreme need of giving a far greater measure of independence to the medical officer of health. I heartily welcome that particular clause. But there is one other clause with regard to which I should like to say a word. Those who in my neighbourhood are specially interested in this matter are profoundly impressed by the fact that we must rely to a great extent, not only on municipal efforts, but also on the efforts of public-spirited individuals and voluntary societies for the promotion of public utility. Therefore they are very urgent about Clause 61, subsection (*b*), which, I believe, was threatened in the House of Commons and survived with difficulty, and which would give the Local Government Board the power of interference. The clause provides that if the Local Government Board are satisfied on any representation, after holding a local inquiry, that a local authority have failed to adopt a scheme proposed by owners of any land in a case where the scheme ought to be adopted, the Board may order the local authority to prepare and submit for the approval of the Board such a town planning scheme and to adopt the scheme, or to consent to the modifications or conditions so imposed. The persons to whom I refer earnestly hope that His Majesty's Government will adhere to that clause, which gives the Local Government Board power to intervene where it appears that local public bodies have not been sufficiently willing to assist and co-operate with public-spirited individuals.

My Lords, there is one clause which was in the Bill, but which is not in the Bill as it now appears, the absence of which some of us deeply deplore. I would earnestly ask this House whether it is not possible to restore, even at this stage, Clause 30.[1] Clause 30,

1 The clause indicated was not restored.

as it was, instituted a quinquennial survey and register. It made it the duty of every local authority to cause to be made in every parish an inspection survey as regards certain property; and the things which had to be registered included the addresses of the rated occupier and the beneficial owner. Those of us who have been interested in this matter for some time have cause to attach extraordinary importance to such a register. In part there is already an obligation upon the local authority to make a survey of the property within their region, but inquiries made by the National Housing Reform Council led to the recognition that this duty was being very widely neglected. It appears there were only sixteen, I think, out of 112 urban and rural district councils which effectively carried out the requirements of the law. Now I observe that in Clause 11 as it stands in the Bill there is power given to the Local Government Board to intervene to cause the local authority to be more efficient in the fulfilment of what is already their statutory obligation, but that falls very far short of the proposal in Clause 30 as it did stand in the Bill. An important deputation — introduced, I believe, by the most rev. Primate — laid great stress upon the importance of this survey and register, and I think I am right in saying that the late Prime Minister specially recognised the importance of that point. I should very much like to know from His Majesty's Government why it was that that clause was dropped out of the Bill. In part it may be on the plea of expense. It is not for me to estimate what the expense would be; but I venture to say that even considerable expense would be thoroughly justified in order that we might have this register and know who owns, with the different degrees of ownership, the worst kinds of property to be encountered in parts of our cities.

It was once my lot in London to have something to do with a society for the buying up of slum property in order to get it into better hands, and my experience of the extraordinary difficulty of ascertaining the name of the owner rooted in my mind the necessity of all information with regard to occupation ownership being accessible. I very much wondered whether the influences, which I have reason to believe are very strong influences, leading to a desire to conceal the ownership of the worst properties, have not had something to do with the resistance to what was Clause 30. There is no consideration which Parliament ought to entertain which makes it in any way desirable or excusable that the real ownership of the worst properties should be a matter difficult to ascertain, and I very sincerely ask His Majesty's Government whether they will afford facilities for the restoration of Clause 30.

I thank your Lordships for having listened to me, although I know there are very large parts of this Bill with regard to which I have no experience or knowledge to justify me in speaking; but I am quite sure that no one could be acquainted with the actual conditions of our cities without becoming alive to the fact that trenchant and wide reforms are necessarily and primarily required for the welfare of the poorer parts of the population — reforms so trenchant and far-reaching that, human nature being what it is and the interests involved being what they are, no one can hope that they can be carried through without having to encounter resistance and overcome opposition.

Extract 52

HOUSING, TOWN PLANNING, ETC. ACT, 1909

(9 Edw. 7, ch. 44, in part)

An Act to amend the Law relating to the Housing of the Working Classes, to provide for the making of Town Planning schemes, and to make further provision with respect to the appointment and duties of County Medical Officers of Health, and to provide for the establishment of Public Health and Housing Committees of County Councils.   (3rd December 1909)

Be it enacted by the King's most Excellent Majesty, by and with the advice and consent of the Lords Spiritual and Temporal, and Commons, in this present Parliament assembled, and by the authority of the same, as follows:

PART I

HOUSING OF THE WORKING CLASSES

1. Former Act

Part III of the Housing of the Working Classes Act, 1890 [1] (in this Part of this Act referred to as the principal Act), shall, after the commencement of this Act, extend to and take effect in every urban or rural district, or other place for which it has not been adopted, as if it had been so adopted.

2. Acquisition of Lands

(1) A local authority may be authorised to purchase land compulsorily for the purposes of Part III of the principal Act, by means of an order submitted to the Local Government Board and confirmed by the Board in accordance with the First Schedule to this Act. . . .

3. Loans

Where a loan is made by the Public Works Loan Commissioners to a local authority for any purposes of the Housing Acts —

(*a*) The loan shall be made at the minimum rate allowed for the time being for loans out of the Local Loans Fund; and

(*b*) If the Local Government Board make a recommendation to that effect, the period for which the loan is made by the Public Works Loan Commissioners may exceed the period

---

[1] 53 & 54 Vict., ch. 70.

allowed under the principal Act or under any other Act limiting the period for which the loan may be made, but the period shall not exceed the period recommended by the Local Government Board, nor in any case eighty years ; and

(c) As between loans for different periods, the longer duration of the loan shall not be taken as a reason for fixing a higher rate of interest.

[Clauses 4–9 relate to small matters, such as the expenditure of money for housing purposes in the case of settled land, allowing a local authority to accept a donation of land, etc.]

10. Enforcement of Housing Acts

(1) Where a complaint is made to the Local Government Board —

(a) as respects any rural district by the council of the county in which the district is situate, or by the parish council or parish meeting of any parish comprised in the district, or by any four inhabitant householders of the district ; or

(b) as respects any county district, not being a rural district, by the council of the county in which the district is situated, or by four inhabitant householders of the district ; or

(c) as respects the area of any other local authority by four inhabitant householders of the area ;

that the local authority have failed to exercise their powers under Part II or Part III of the principal Act in cases where those powers ought to have been exercised, the Board may cause a public local inquiry to be held, and if, after holding such an inquiry, the Board are satisfied that there has been such a failure on the part of the local authority, the Board may declare the authority to be in default, and may make an order directing that authority, within a time limited by the order, to carry out such works and do such other things as may be mentioned in the order for the purpose of remedying the default. . . .

(5) An order made by the Local Government Board under this section shall be laid before both Houses of Parliament as soon as may be after it is made.

(6) Any order made by the Local Government Board under this section may be enforced by mandamus.

11. Enforcement within a Limited Time

(1) Where it appears to the Local Government Board that a local authority have failed to perform their duty under the Housing Acts of carrying out an improvement scheme under Part I of the principal Act, or have failed to give effect to any order as respects an obstructive building, or to a reconstruction scheme, under Part II of that Act, or have failed to cause to be made the inspection of their district required by this Act, the Board may make an order requiring the local authority to remedy the default and to carry out any works or do any other things which are necessary for the purpose under the Housing Acts within a time fixed by the order.

(2) Any order made by the Local Government Board under this section may be enforced by mandamus.

[In Clauses 12 and 13 provision is made whereby, under certain circumstances, a county council may step in if, in their opinion, a rural district council have failed to exercise their powers.]

14. Contracts by Landlord

In any contract made after the passing of this Act for letting for habitation a house or part of a house at a rent not exceeding —

    (*a*) in the case of a house situate in the administrative county of London, forty pounds;

    (*b*) in the case of a house situate in a borough or urban district with a population according to the last census for the time being of fifty thousand or upwards, twenty-six pounds;

    (*c*) in the case of a house situate elsewhere, sixteen pounds;

there shall be implied a condition that the house is at the commencement of the holding in all respects reasonably fit for human habitation, but the condition aforesaid shall not be implied when a house or part of a house is let for a term of not less than three years upon the terms that it be put by the lessee into a condition reasonably fit for occupation, and the lease is not determinable at the option of either party before the expiration of that term.

15. Obligations of Landlord

(1) The last foregoing section shall, as respects contracts to which that section applies, take effect as if the condition implied by that section included an undertaking that the house shall, during the holding, be kept by the landlord in all respects reasonably fit for human habitation.

(2) The landlord or the local authority, or any person authorised by him or them in writing, may at reasonable times of the day, on giving twenty-four hours' notice in writing to the tenant or occupier, enter any house, premises, or building to which this section applies for the purpose of viewing the state and condition thereof.

(3) If it appears to the local authority within the meaning of Part II of the principal Act that the undertaking implied by virtue of this section is not complied with in the case of any house to which it applies, the authority shall, if a closing order is not made with respect to the house, by written notice require the landlord, within a reasonable time, not being less than twenty-one days, specified in the notice, to execute such works as the authority shall specify in the notice as being necessary to make the house in all respects reasonably fit for human habitation.

(4) Within twenty-one days after the receipt of such notice the landlord may by written notice to the local authority declare his intention of closing the house for human habitation, and thereupon a closing order shall be deemed to have become operative in respect of such house.

(5) If the notice given by the local authority is not complied with, and if the landlord has not given the notice mentioned in the immediately preceding subsection, the authority may, at the expiration of the time specified in the notice given by them to the landlord, do the work required to be done and recover the expenses incurred by them in so doing from the landlord as a civil debt in manner provided by the Summary Jurisdiction Acts, or, if they think fit, the authority may by order declare any such expenses to be payable by annual instalments within a period not exceeding that of the interest of the landlord in the house, nor in any case five years, with interest at a rate not exceeding five pounds per cent. per annum, until the whole amount is paid, and any such instalments or interest or any part thereof may be recovered from the landlord as a civil debt in manner provided by the Summary Jurisdiction Acts.

(6) A landlord may appeal to the Local Government Board against any notice requiring him to execute works under this section, and against any demand for the recovery of expenses from him under this section or order made with respect to those expenses under this section by the authority, by giving notice of appeal to the Board within twenty-one days after the notice is received, or the demand or order is made, as the case may be, and no proceedings shall be taken in respect of such notice requiring works, order, or demand, whilst the appeal is pending.

(7) In this section the expression " landlord " means any person who lets to a tenant for habitation the house under any contract referred to in this section, and includes his successors in title ; and the expression " house " includes part of a house. . . .

[Section 16 amends Acts of 1875 and 1891, extending the power of making byelaws with respect to lodging-houses for the working classes.]

17. Closing of Unfit Dwellings

(1) It shall be the duty of every local authority within the meaning of Part II of the principal Act to cause to be made from time to time inspection of their district, with a view to ascertain whether any dwelling-house therein is in a state so˙ dangerous or injurious to health as to be unfit for human habitation, and for that purpose it shall be the duty of the local authority, and of every officer of the local authority, to comply with such regulations and to keep such records as may be prescribed by the Board.

(2) If, on the representation of the medical officer of health, or of any other officer of the authority, or other information given, any dwelling-house appears to them to be in such a state, it shall be their duty to make an order prohibiting the use of the dwelling-house for human habitation (in this Act referred to as a closing order) until in the judgment of the local authority the dwelling-house is rendered fit for that purpose.

(3) Notice of a closing order shall be forthwith served on every owner of the dwelling-house in respect of which it is made, and any owner aggrieved by the order may appeal to the Local Government Board by giving notice of appeal to the Board within fourteen days after the order is served upon him.

(4) Where a closing order has become operative, the local authority shall serve notice of the order on every occupying tenant of the dwelling-house in respect of which the order is made, and, within such period as is specified in the notice, not being less than fourteen days after the service of the notice, the order shall be obeyed by him, and he and his family shall cease to inhabit the dwelling-house, and in default he shall be liable on summary conviction to be ordered to quit the dwelling-house within such time as may be specified in the order.

(5) Unless the dwelling-house has been made unfit for habitation by the wilful act or default of the tenant or of any person

for whom as between himself and the owner or landlord he is responsible, the local authority may make to every such tenant such reasonable allowance on account of his expense in removing as may be determined by the local authority with the consent of the owner of the dwelling-house, or, if the owner of the dwelling-house fails to consent to the sum determined by the local authority, as may be fixed by a court of summary jurisdiction, and the amount of the said allowance shall be recoverable by the local authority from the owner of the dwelling-house as a civil debt in manner provided by the Summary Jurisdiction Acts.

(6) The local authority shall determine any closing order made by them if they are satisfied that the dwelling-house, in respect of which the order has been made, has been rendered fit for human habitation.

If, on the application of any owner of a dwelling-house, the local authority refuse to determine a closing order, the owner may appeal to the Local Government Board by giving notice of appeal to the Board within fourteen days after the application is refused.

(7) A room habitually used as a sleeping place, the surface of the floor of which is more than three feet below the surface of the part of the street adjoining or nearest to the room, shall for the purposes of this section be deemed to be a dwelling-house so dangerous or injurious to health as to be unfit for human habitation, if the room either —

(*a*) is not on an average at least seven feet in height from floor to ceiling ; or

(*b*) does not comply with such regulations as the local authority with the consent of the Local Government Board may prescribe for securing the proper ventilation and lighting of such rooms, and the protection thereof against dampness, effluvia, or exhalation : Provided that if the local authority, after being required to do so by the Local Government Board, fail to make such regulations, or such regulations as the Board approve, the Board may themselves make them, and the regulations so made shall have effect as if they had been made by the local authority with the consent of the Board:

Provided that a closing order made in respect of a room to which this subsection applies shall not prevent the room being used for purposes other than those of a sleeping place; and that, if the occupier of the room after notice of an order has been served upon him fails to comply with the order, an order to comply therewith may, on summary conviction, be made against him.

This subsection shall not come into operation until the first day of July nineteen hundred and ten, and a closing order made in respect of any room to which this subsection applies shall not be treated as a closing order in respect of a dwelling-house for the purposes of the next succeeding section.

18. Order for Demolition

(1) Where a closing order in respect of any dwelling-house has remained operative for a period of three months, the local authority shall take into consideration the question of the demolition of the dwelling-house, and shall give every owner of the dwelling-house notice of the time (being some time not less than one month after the service of the notice) and place at which the question will be considered, and any owner of the dwelling-house shall be entitled to be heard when the question is so taken into consideration.

(2) If upon any such consideration the local authority are of opinion that the dwelling-house has not been rendered fit for human habitation, and that the necessary steps are not being taken with all due diligence to render it so fit, or that the continuance of any building, being or being part of the dwelling-house, is a nuisance or dangerous or injurious to the health of the public or of the inhabitants of the neighbouring dwelling-houses, they shall order the demolition of the building. . . .

[Clauses 19–35 embody a large number of minor amendments to former laws.]

36. Inspection of Housing

Any person authorised in writing stating the particular purpose or purposes for which the entry is authorised, by the local authority or the Local Government Board, may at all reasonable times, on giving twenty-four hours' notice to the occupier and to the owner, if the owner is known, of his intention, enter any house, premises, or buildings —

(*a*) for the purpose of survey or valuation, in the case of houses, premises, or buildings which the local authority are authorised to purchase compulsorily under the Housing Acts; and

(*b*) for the purpose of survey and examination, in the case of any dwelling-house in respect of which a closing order or an order for demolition has been made ; or

(*c*) for the purpose of survey and examination, where it appears to the authority or Board that survey or examination is necessary in order to determine whether any powers under the Housing Acts should be exercised in respect of any house, premises, or building.

Notice may be given to the occupier for the purposes of this section by leaving a notice addressed to the occupier, without name or further description, at the house, buildings, or premises.

37. Report on Crowded Area

If it appears to the Local Government Board that owing to density of population, or any other reason, it is expedient to inquire into the circumstances of any area with a view to determining whether any powers under the Housing Acts should be put into force in that area or not, the Local Government Board may require the local authority to make a report to them containing such particulars as to the population of the district and other matters as they direct, and the local authority shall comply with the requirement of the Local Government Board. . . .

[Clauses 38–42 are concerned with administrative details.]

43. *Prohibition of Back-to-back Houses*

Notwithstanding anything in any local Act or byelaw in force in any borough or district, it shall not be lawful to erect any back-to-back houses intended to be used as dwellings for the working classes, and any such house commenced to be erected after the passing of this Act shall be deemed to be unfit for human habitation for the purposes of the provisions of the Housing Acts.

Provided that nothing in this section —

(*a*) shall prevent the erection or use of a house containing several tenements in which the tenements are placed back to back, if the medical officer of health for the district certifies that the several tenements are so constructed and arranged as to secure effective ventilation of all habitable rooms in every tenement; or

(*b*) shall apply to houses abutting on any streets the plans whereof have been approved by the local authority before the first day of May nineteen hundred and nine, in any borough or district in which, at the passing of this Act, any local Act or byelaws are in force permitting the erection of back-to-back houses.

[Clause 44 gives power to the Local Government Board to revoke unreasonable byelaws.]

45. *Saving of Sites of Ancient Monuments, etc.*

Nothing in the Housing Acts shall authorise the acquisition for the purposes of those Acts of any land which is the site of an ancient monument or other object of archæological interest, or the compulsory acquisition for the purposes of Part III of the Housing of the Working Classes Act, 1890, of any land which is the property of any local authority or has been acquired by any corporation or company for the purposes of a railway, dock, canal, water, or other public undertaking, or which at the date of the order forms part of any park, garden, or pleasure ground, or is otherwise required for the amenity or convenience of any dwelling-house.

[Clauses 46–53 comprise definitions of technical terms and special provisions as to the application of Part I to Scotland.]

PART II

TOWN PLANNING

54. Preparation and Approval of Town Planning Scheme

(1) A town planning scheme may be made in accordance with the provisions of this Part of this Act as respects any land which is in course of development or appears likely to be used for building purposes, with the general object of securing proper sanitary conditions, amenity, and convenience in connexion with the laying out and use of the land, and of any neighbouring lands.

(2) The Local Government Board may authorise a local authority within the meaning of this Part of this Act to prepare such a town planning scheme with reference to any land within or in the neighbourhood of their area, if the authority satisfy the Board that there is a primâ facie case for making such a scheme, or may authorise a local authority to adopt, with or without any modifications, any such scheme proposed by all or any of the owners of any land with respect to which the local authority might themselves have been authorised to prepare a scheme.

(3) Where it is made to appear to the Local Government Board that a piece of land already built upon, or a piece of land not likely to be used for building purposes, is so situated with respect to any land likely to be used for building purposes that it ought to be included in any town planning scheme made with respect to the last-mentioned land, the Board may authorise the preparation or adoption of a scheme including such piece of land as aforesaid, and providing for the demolition or alteration of any buildings thereon so far as may be necessary for carrying the scheme into effect.

(4) A town planning scheme prepared or adopted by a local authority shall not have effect, unless it is approved by order of the Local Government Board, and the Board may refuse to approve any scheme except with such modifications and subject to such conditions as they think fit to impose :

Provided that, before a town planning scheme is approved by the Local Government Board, notice of their intention to do so shall be published in the London or Edinburgh *Gazette*, as the case may be, and, if within twenty-one days from the date of such publication any person or authority interested objects in the prescribed manner, the draft of the order shall be laid before each House of Parliament for a period of not less than thirty days during the session of Parliament, and, if either of those Houses before the expiration of those thirty days presents an address to His Majesty against the draft, or any part thereof, no further proceedings shall be taken thereon, without prejudice to the making of any new draft scheme.

(5) A town planning scheme, when approved by the Local Government Board, shall have effect as if it were enacted in this Act.

(6) A town planning scheme may be varied or revoked by a subsequent scheme prepared or adopted and approved in accordance with this Part of this Act, and the Local Government Board, on the application of the responsible authority, or of any other person appearing to them to be interested, may by order revoke a town planning scheme if they think that under the special circumstances of the case the scheme should be so revoked.

(7) The expression "land likely to be used for building purposes" shall include any land likely to be used as, or for the purpose of providing, open spaces, roads, streets, parks, pleasure or recreation grounds, or for the purpose of executing any work upon or under the land incidental to a town planning scheme, whether in the nature of a building work or not, and the decision of the Local Government Board, whether land is likely to be used for building purposes or not, shall be final.

55. Contents of Town Planning Schemes

(1) The Local Government Board may prescribe a set of general provisions (or separate sets of general provisions adapted for areas of any special character) for carrying out the general objects of town planning schemes, and in particular for dealing with the matters set out in the Fourth Schedule to this Act, and the general provisions, or set of general provisions appropriate to the area for which a town planning scheme is made, shall take effect as part of every scheme, except so far as provision is made by the scheme as approved by the Board for the variation or exclusion of any of those provisions.

(2) Special provisions shall in addition be inserted in every town planning scheme defining in such manner as may be prescribed by regulations under this Part of this Act the area to which the scheme is to apply, and the authority who are to be responsible for enforcing the observance of the scheme, and for the execution of any works which under the scheme or this Part of this Act are to be executed by a local authority (in this Part of this Act referred to as the responsible authority), and providing for any matters which may be dealt with by general provisions, and otherwise supplementing, excluding, or varying the general provisions, and also for dealing with any special circumstances or contingencies for which adequate provision is not made by the general provisions, and for suspending, so far as necessary for the proper carrying out of the scheme, any statutory enactments, byelaws, regulations, or other provisions, under whatever authority made, which are in operation in the area included in the scheme:

Provided that, where the scheme contains provisions suspending any enactment contained in a public general Act, the scheme shall not come into force unless a draft thereof has been laid before each House of Parliament for a period of not less than forty days during the session of Parliament, and, if either of those Houses before the expiration of those forty days presents an Address to

His Majesty against the proposed suspension no further proceedings shall be taken on the draft, without prejudice to the making of any new scheme.

(3) Where land included in a town planning scheme is in the area of more than one local authority, or is in the area of a local authority by whom the scheme was not prepared, the responsible authority may be one of those local authorities, or for certain purposes of the scheme one local authority and for certain purposes another local authority, or a joint body constituted specially for the purpose by the scheme, and all necessary provisions may be made by the scheme for constituting the joint body and giving them the necessary powers and duties :

Provided that, except with the consent of the London County Council, no other local authority shall, as respects any land in the county of London, · prepare or be responsible for enforcing the observance of a town planning scheme under this Part of this Act, or for the execution of any works which under the scheme or this Part of this Act are to be executed by a local authority.

56. Regulations of the Local Government Board

(1) The Local Government Board may make regulations for regulating generally the procedure to be adopted with respect to applications for authority to prepare or adopt a town planning scheme, the preparation of the scheme, obtaining the approval of the Board to a scheme so prepared or adopted, and any inquiries, reports, notices, or other matters required in connection with the preparation or adoption or the approval of the scheme or preliminary thereto, or in relation to the carrying out of the scheme or enforcing the observance of the provisions thereof.

(2) Provision shall be made by those regulations —

    (a) for securing co-operation on the part of the local authority with the owners and other persons interested in the land proposed to be included in the scheme at every stage of the proceedings, by means of conferences and such other means as may be provided by the regulations ;

(*b*) for securing that notice of the proposal to prepare or adopt the scheme should be given at the earliest stage possible to any council interested in the land ; and

(*c*) for dealing with the other matters mentioned in the Fifth Schedule to this Act.

57. *Power to enforce Scheme*

(1) The responsible authority may at any time, after giving such notice as may be provided by a town planning scheme and in accordance with the provisions of the scheme —

(*a*) remove, pull down, or alter any building or other work in the area included in the scheme which is such as to contravene the scheme, or in the erection or carrying out of which any provision of the scheme has not been complied with ; or

(*b*) execute any work which it is the duty of any person to execute under the scheme in any case where it appears to the authority that delay in the execution of the work would prejudice the efficient operation of the scheme.

(2) Any expenses incurred by a responsible authority under this section may be recovered from the persons in default in such manner and subject to such conditions as may be provided by the scheme.

(3) If any question arises whether any building or work contravenes a town planning scheme, or whether any provision of a town planning scheme is not complied with in the erection or carrying out of any such building or work, that question shall be referred to the Local Government Board, and shall, unless the parties otherwise agree, be determined by the Board as arbitrators, and the decision of the Board shall be final and conclusive and binding on all persons.

58. Compensation in Respect of Property injuriously affected by Scheme, etc.

(1) Any person whose property is injuriously affected by the making of a town planning scheme shall, if he makes a claim for the purpose within the time (if any) limited by the scheme, not being less than three months after the date when notice of the approval of the scheme is published in the manner prescribed by regulations made by the Local Government Board, be entitled to obtain compensation in respect thereof from the responsible authority.

(2) A person shall not be entitled to obtain compensation under this section on account of any building erected on, or contract made or other thing done with respect to, land included in a scheme, after the time at which the application for authority to prepare the scheme was made, or after such other time as the Local Government Board may fix for the purpose:

Provided that this provision shall not apply as respects any work done before the date of the approval of the scheme for the purpose of finishing a building begun or of carrying out a contract entered into before the application was made.

(3) Where, by the making of any town planning scheme, any property is increased in value, the responsible authority, if they make a claim for the purpose within the time (if any) limited by the scheme (not being less than three months after the date when notice of the approval of the scheme is first published in the manner prescribed by regulations made by the Local Government Board), shall be entitled to recover from any person whose property is so increased in value one-half of the amount of that increase.

(4) Any question as to whether any property is injuriously affected or increased in value within the meaning of this section, and as to the amount and manner of payment (whether by instalments or otherwise) of the sum which is to be paid as compensation under this section or which the responsible authority are entitled to

recover from a person whose property is increased in value, shall be determined by the arbitration of a single arbitrator appointed by the Local Government Board, unless the parties agree on some other method of determination.

(5) Any amount due under this section as compensation to a person aggrieved from a responsible authority, or to a responsible authority from a person whose property is increased in value, may be recovered summarily as a civil debt.

(6) Where a town planning scheme is revoked by an order of the Local Government Board under this Act, any person who has incurred expenditure for the purpose of complying with the scheme shall be entitled to compensation in accordance with this section in so far as any such expenditure is rendered abortive by reason of the revocation of the scheme.

59. Limitation of Compensation in Certain Cases

(1) Where property is alleged to be injuriously affected by reason of any provisions contained in a town planning scheme, no compensation shall be paid in respect thereof if or so far as the provisions are such as would have been enforceable if they had been contained in byelaws made by the local authority.

(2) Property shall not be deemed to be injuriously affected by reason of the making of any provisions inserted in a town planning scheme, which, with a view to securing the amenity of the area included in the scheme or any part thereof, prescribe the space about buildings or limit the number of buildings to be erected, or prescribe the height or character of buildings, and which the Local Government Board, having regard to the nature and situation of the land affected by the provisions, consider reasonable for the purpose.

(3) Where a person is entitled to compensation under this Part of this Act in respect of any matter or thing, and he would be entitled to compensation in respect of the same matter or thing under any other enactment, he shall not be entitled to compensation in respect of that matter or thing both under this Act and under

that other enactment, and shall not be entitled to any greater compensation under this Act than he would be entitled to under the other enactment.

60. *Acquisition of Land comprised in a Scheme*

(1) The responsible authority may, for the purpose of a town planning scheme, purchase any land comprised in such scheme by agreement, or be authorised to purchase any such land compulsorily in the same manner and subject to the same provisions (including any provision authorising the Local Government Board to give directions as to the payment and application of any purchase money or compensation) as a local authority may purchase or be authorised to purchase land situate in an urban district for the purposes of Part III of the Housing of the Working Classes Act, 1890, as amended by sections two and forty-five of this Act.

(2) Where land included within the area of a local authority is comprised in a town planning scheme, and the local authority are not the responsible authority, the local authority may purchase or be authorised to purchase that land in the same manner as the responsible authority.

61. *Powers of Local Government Board to make or execute Town Planning Scheme*

(1) If the Local Government Board are satisfied on any representation, after holding a public local inquiry, that a local authority—

(*a*) have failed to take the requisite steps for having a satisfactory town planning scheme prepared and approved in a case where a town planning scheme ought to be made ; or

(*b*) have failed to adopt any scheme proposed by owners of any land in a case where the scheme ought to be adopted ; or

(*c*) have unreasonably refused to consent to any modifications or conditions imposed by the Board ;

the Board may, as the case requires, order the local authority to prepare and submit for the approval of the Board such a town planning scheme, or to adopt the scheme, or to consent to the modifications or conditions so inserted :

Provided that, where the representation is that a local authority have failed to adopt a scheme, the Local Government Board, in lieu of making such an order as aforesaid, may approve the proposed scheme, subject to such modifications or conditions, if any, as the Board think fit, and thereupon the scheme shall have effect as if it had been adopted by the local authority and approved by the Board.

(2) If the Local Government Board are satisfied on any representation, after holding a local inquiry, that a responsible authority have failed to enforce effectively the observance of a scheme which has been confirmed, or any provisions thereof, or to execute any works which under the scheme or this Part of this Act the authority is required to execute, the Board may order that authority to do all things necessary for enforcing the observance of the scheme or any provisions thereof effectively, or for executing any works which under the scheme or this Part of this Act the authority is required to execute.

(3) Any order under this section may be enforced by mandamus.

[Clauses 62–67 deal with administrative details, amendments to former statutes, and application of Part II of this Act to London and to Scotland.]

Part III

County Medical Officers, County Public Health and Housing Committee, etc.

68. County Medical Officers

(1) Every county council shall appoint a medical officer of health under section seventeen of the Local Government Act, 1888.

(2) The duties of a medical officer of health of a county shall be such duties as may be prescribed by general order of the Local

Government Board and such other duties as may be assigned to him by the county council.

(3) The power of county councils and district councils under the said section to make arrangements with respect to medical officers of health shall cease, without prejudice to any arrangement made previously to the date of the passing of this Act.

(4) The medical officer of health of a county shall, for the purposes of his duties, have the same powers of entry on premises as are conferred on a medical officer of health of a district by or under any enactment.

(5) A medical officer of health of a county shall be removable by the county council with the consent of the Local Government Board and not otherwise.

(6) A medical officer of health of a county shall not be appointed for a limited period only:

Provided that the county council may, with the sanction of the Local Government Board, make any temporary arrangement for the performance of all or any of the duties of the medical officer of health of the county, and any person appointed by virtue of any such arrangement to perform those duties or any of them shall, subject to the terms of his appointment, have all the powers, duties, and liabilities of the medical officer of health of the county.

(7) A medical officer of health appointed after the passing of this Act under the said section as amended by this section shall not engage in private practice, and shall not hold any other public appointment without the express written consent of the Local Government Board.

(8) An order under this section prescribing the duties of medical officers of health of a county shall be communicated to the county council and shall be laid before Parliament as soon as may be after it is made, and, if an address is presented to His Majesty by either House of Parliament within the next subsequent twenty-one days on which that House has sat next after the order is laid before it

praying that the order may be annulled, His Majesty in Council may annul the order and it shall thenceforward be void, but without prejudice to the validity of anything previously done thereunder.

[Clause 69 defines special duties of clerk and medical officer of health of district council; and Clause 70 excepts Scotland and London from certain provisions.]

71. Public Health and Housing Committee of County Council

(1) Every county council shall establish a public health and housing committee, and all matters relating to the exercise and performance by the council of their powers and duties as respects public health and the housing of the working classes (except the power of raising a rate or borrowing money) shall stand referred to the public health and housing committee, and the council, before exercising any such powers, shall, unless in their opinion the matter is urgent, receive and consider the report of the public health and housing committee with respect to the matter in question, and the council may also delegate to the public health and housing committee, with or without restrictions or conditions as they think fit, any of their powers as respects public health and the housing of the working classes, except the power of raising a rate or borrowing money and except any power of resolving that the powers of a district council in default should be transferred to the council.

(2) This section shall not apply to Scotland or the London County Council.

[Clause 72 seeks to promote the formation and extension of building societies.]

[Part IV of the Act contains several supplemental provisions (Clauses 73-76). Ireland is excluded from the operation of the Act. An important accompanying Schedule contains detailed provisions as to the compulsory acquisition of land by local authorities.]

FOURTH SCHEDULE[1]

Matters to be dealt with by General Provisions prescribed by the Local Government Board

1. Streets, roads, and other ways, and stopping up, or diversion of existing highways.

2. Buildings, structures, and erections.

3. Open spaces, private and public.

4. The preservation of objects of historical interest or natural beauty.

5. Sewerage, drainage, and sewage disposal.

6. Lighting.

7. Water supply.

8. Ancillary or consequential works.

9. Extinction or variation of private rights of way and other easements.

10. Dealing with or disposal of land acquired by the responsible authority or by a local authority.

11. Power of entry and inspection.

12. Power of the responsible authority to remove, alter, or demolish any obstructive work.

13. Power of the responsible authority to make agreements with owners, and of owners to make agreements with one another.

14. Power of the responsible authority or a local authority to accept any money or property for the furtherance of the object of any town planning scheme, and provision for regulating the administration of any such money or property and for the exemption of any assurance with respect to money or property so accepted from enrolment under the Mortmain and Charitable Uses Act, 1888.[2]

15. Application with the necessary modifications and adaptations of statutory enactments.

[1] Cf. Clause 55.   [2] 51 & 52 Vict., ch. 42.

16. Carrying out and supplementing the provisions of this Act for enforcing schemes.

17. Limitation of time for operation of scheme.

18. Co-operation of the responsible authority with the owners of land included in the scheme or other persons interested by means of conferences, etc.

19. Charging on the inheritance of any land the value of which is increased by the operation of a town planning scheme the sum required to be paid in respect of that increase, and for that purpose applying, with the necessary adaptations, the provisions of any enactments dealing with charges for improvements of land.

Extract 53

CONSERVATIVE OPPOSITION TO THE DEVELOPMENT BILL

(Lord Robert Cecil, Commons, September 6, 1909)

LORD ROBERT CECIL [1]: . . . The Bill consists of two entirely distinct parts. The road part, which occupies by far the larger number of the Clauses, is, in my view, by far the least important part of the measure. With the general principle of the roads in this country no longer being regarded as a purely local interest I find myself in accord. The tendency of all road legislation has been gradually to extend the area over which the upkeep of those roads is spread, and I do not myself dispute that the time has now arrived when the Imperial Exchequer may fairly be asked to bear some portion of the upkeep of the main roads of the country; and if this Bill were consistent in any proposal to make grants in aid of road upkeep to the road authorities who have charge of the roads of this country on some fixed and definite principle which would preclude any possibility of local or political favouritism, I should not certainly be opposing that part of the Bill.

[1] Parliamentary Debates, Commons, Fifth Series, vol. 10, col. 907 sqq.

But the Bill, in fact, embodies a very different scheme. In the first place, it proposes to constitute a new local authority, which is to interfere with, and in some respects to supersede, the existing local authority in the control of the roads. I think that this Bill involves such very important considerations that I do not wish to occupy time unduly in dealing with smaller criticisms, but certainly it does appear to me that the chaos which is likely to be introduced into local administration by adding yet another local authority to deal with strictly local affairs is a matter which deserves in itself the very serious consideration of this House. But, in addition, this part of the Bill is designed exclusively for the benefit of one section of the community. . . .

It is proposed, among other things, to drive through this country great strips of land a quarter of a mile broad for new motor roads on which no speed limit is to be imposed. For that purpose power is to be taken under the Bill to raise a loan, I understand, of no less than £4,000,000, besides the amount that is to be spent annually on the upkeep and improvement of roads for the purpose of motor traffic. And the land — it is important the House should understand this — is to be acquired by those bureaucratic methods which are so dear to the present Government. They have incorporated in the Schedule what are called small holding terms, which means that no inquiry is to be held as to the desirability of improvements to be carried out under the Bill unless the Treasury shall order it, and in any case the land is to be purchased on the greatly modified terms which attend compulsory purchase. I think that, to use a colloquial phrase, is a pretty tall order.

But when you come to the development part of the scheme, all that is really most moderate and infinitesimal by comparison. . . . The proposal is that the Treasury may grant either by way of free grant or by way of loan money not only for the purposes of forestry and developing agriculture — though even in that respect the words are extremely wide, because they include the extension of the principle of the Small Holdings Act and the adoption of any other means which appear calculated to develop agriculture and rural industry — but it is clearly proposed by this Bill that this grant may be made for the reclamation and drainage of land, the general improvement of rural transport, including the making of light railways, the construction and improvement of harbours, the construction and improvement of canals, the developing and improvement of fisheries, and for " any other purpose calculated to promote the economic development of the United Kingdom." It would really puzzle most hon. Members to find a single department of commercial or industrial activity which could not be described by the words " or any other purpose calculated to promote the economic development of the United Kingdom." [Cheers.] I am not at all surprised that hon. Members below the gangway cheer that statement, because it is part of the Socialist programme.

I only stop for a moment at Clause 2 to note the words in paragraph (*c*) of subsection (1) that one of the sources from which the Development Fund is to be replenished and derived is " any profits or proceeds derived from the expenditure of any advance which by the terms on which the advance was made are to be paid to the Treasury," making it abundantly clear that under this Bill not merely unremunerative, unproductive, and unprofitable expenditure for agricultural instruction and the like is contemplated, but works of a profit-bearing nature, like any other works indulged in by a private individual.

SIR G. PARKER: State-trading.

LORD R. CECIL: Of course, it is State-trading; clearly that is what it means.

Clause 3 is almost common form in any Government bill now, and merely provides that the Treasury shall be entitled to direct and draw up regulations to carry out anything they like.

Then we come to the most remarkable clause of the whole Bill, and that is Clause 4, which provides that " the Board of Agriculture and Fisheries" — I thank the President of the Board of Trade for the phrase " Administrative Order" — may without any inquiry or any consideration at all make compulsory acquisition of land throughout the whole of the United Kingdom. I really do not believe — in fact, I am quite sure that such a proposition has *never* been submitted to Parliament. I cannot believe the Government itself realises what that proposition involves. I do not wish to linger over the terms on which the land is to be acquired. They do not seem to me specially unfair. I do not myself see why, for such a purpose, the allowance for compulsory purchase should not be allowed, but I do not really care about that, and the tribunal is fair enough as far as compensation is concerned. The acquisition of any land might mean that any railway might be acquired under the words of this Clause. There is nothing to prevent the complete nationalisation of all the railways and all the land of the country under Clauses 1, 2, and 4. I do not suppose for a moment, and I am not suggesting, that is what the Government intends — of course not — but that is the framework of their Bill. That is what the Bill gives them power to do under these provisions.

What are the safeguards that are suggested? As far as I can see the only two are these: it is suggested that only £500,000 per year for four years is to be allowed for these purposes. That is the suggested provision of Clause 2, but when you look at Clause 2 it does not contain any such limit at all. The words of the Clause are: " . . . the Development Fund into which shall be paid (*a*) such moneys as may from time to time be provided by Parliament for the purposes of this part of this Act." That is quite general. Then in subsection (2) of Clause 2 there is the provision, " There shall be charged on and issued out of the Consolidated Fund in the year ending the thirty-first day of March, nineteen hundred and eleven, and in each of the next succeeding four years, the sum of five hundred thousand pounds." What it comes to is this, that there is an attempt to enact that at least £500,000 should be spent every year on these purposes, and there is no superior limit whatever. Any sum which could be obtained from a docile majority of the House of Commons might be allocated to these purposes, so that the suggested limit of £500,000 is absolutely non-existent. Then there is the provision of an Advisory Committee, and we are seriously asked to regard that as some safeguard. This Advisory Committee is to be appointed by the particular Government that brought in the Bill, but there is nothing to indicate who they are to be. They may be, as the hon. and learned Member for Louth suggests, Lumley. At any rate, we have very good ground for knowing that the Government are not at all moved by the fact that Advisory Committees, or persons that they appoint to make inquiries and report, report in favour or against a particular thing. . . .

That is the scheme of the Bill, and it appears to me it lays itself open to two very serious objections. I think it is likely to produce a great waste of public money, and I think it is almost certain to produce a very grave danger of political corruption. We have not the experience they have in foreign countries of the working of such schemes as this. I believe that a scheme of this kind is in operation in some form or another in almost all our Colonies and in several foreign countries. I see, for instance, that a Mr. Wise has published a work on Australia recently, in which he says that one of the most dangerous classes of politicians in that country are the "roads and bridges men," who are described in this way, "Their value to their constituents is apt to be expressed in terms of the public expenditure in their district."

I do not want to go unnecessarily into that aspect of the question. Everyone who knows anything of political life in many of our Colonies knows that this power of executing public works in the various constituencies is one of the chief political instruments belonging to the Ministry of the day. I was told the other day, and it is common talk in Canada, that the wavering constituency always voted in the same way as the majority of the country appears to be likely to decide, so that they may obtain a share of loaves and fishes when the Government comes into power. A friend of mine described to me how he saw a large army of workmen engaged in repairing a wall of a public building in one of our Colonies. He asked how it was so many men appeared to be engaged in so trivial a work. He was rebuked for his simplicity, and told that a General Election was immediately in prospect. It is not only so in our Colonies. I am sure, and I do not wish to exaggerate, they have had a difficult problem to face in a new country, and no one wishes less than I do to exaggerate failings that may have occurred in connection with that very difficult problem. . . .

With all those examples before us, I do ask the House and hon. Members very seriously to consider how this would work in our own country. Have we any right to suppose that it would work materially better here than in other countries? Let us take it generally. Is it not almost certain that one of the duties of every Member of Parliament who sat at any rate for a country constituency would be to extort from the Government of the day as much as he could in order to develop the various districts which were represented? In addition to the demand for the appointment of magistrates, would it not be one of the favourite employments not only of Radical, but of Tory Members of Parliament, to try and secure for the locality the largest share or slice of the Development Fund? It is a very delicate matter to enlarge upon, but there are constituencies already in this country which benefit largely by expenditure from public sources, and it would be mere affectation to conceal the fact that those who represent them have perpetually pressed upon the Government the expenditure of public money in their localities in order to please their constituents. One can see that that would be the ordinary course of business under which we should live. Just conceive what might happen at a critical bye-election, when, perhaps, a Member of the Government was seeking reëlection on promotion. I can well conceive the telegram that would come from the party managers demanding some great expenditure on a harbour in, say, a division of Yorkshire, in order to secure the return of the newly-appointed Chancellor of the Duchy. It is quite true that now somewhat similar demands take place, but they generally seem to result in abortive projects of legislation. But seriously, does anybody doubt that at a bye-election a great deal of political pressure would be brought to bear upon the Government of the day to spend money out of this Vote ?

That is not the only thing. I have no doubt myself that when a controversial measure was before the Parliament, and it was important to secure in its support the votes of a particular section of this House, the chiefs of that section would demand from the Government of the day some promise of the expenditure of public money out of the Development Fund to benefit the part of the Kingdom from which they came. I have not the slightest doubt of that, because it has already occurred. Everybody knows that considerable negotiations have been going on between the Government and the Irish party in order to obtain from that party support for certain portions of the Finance Bill. The leader of that party, on July 4 last, made a speech at Arklow, reported in the *Times* of July 5, in which, judging from the tone of the speech, he was defending himself against certain critics in Ireland who thought he had been too complacent with the Government in reference to the Finance Bill; and he set out in considerable detail the terms of the changes which the Government had agreed upon in the Finance Bill, and which about two months later they communicated to the House of Commons. In addition to that, this very striking paragraph occurs in the speech :

> Out of the Development Fund it was proposed to create he had reason to know that within the next twelve months money would assuredly be provided for the drainage of the Barrow and the Bann and other rivers which were spreading desolation and ruin by their flooding. Money would also be available which could be used to facilitate the purchase and amalgamation of Irish railways under an Irish local authority.

That has actually been done before the Bill has even been read a second time in the House of Commons. . . .

I say that that is a conclusive example of the way in which this Development Fund may be — and if the present Chancellor of the Exchequer remains in office will be — used, in order to secure political support. We have only to turn to the speech of the President of the Board of Trade on Saturday last to see that this is all part of a gigantic scheme to bribe the electorate.

MR. LLOYD GEORGE: Do I understand the Noble Lord really to suggest that there is any pledge by the Government to give money out of this Development Fund for the draining of the Barrow and the Bann, and the nationalisation of Irish railways? If he or anybody else says so, it is not an accurate statement. Nothing of the kind has been done.

MR. JOHN O'CONNOR: Is the Noble Lord aware that the Leader of the Opposition in the year 1888 promised £10,000 for these drainage works?

MR. SPEAKER: That has no relevancy whatever to the matter under discussion.

LORD R. CECIL: I certainly suggest that these words occur in the report in the *Times* of the speech of the hon. and learned Member for Waterford on July 4 at Arklow: "Out of the Development Fund it was proposed to create he had reason to know that within the next months money would assuredly be provided for the draining of the Barrow and the Bann."

MR. LLOYD GEORGE: I know nothing whatever about the statement. It may, or may not, be an accurate report. All I can say, as Minister in charge of the Bill, is that no such promise has been made to anybody.

LORD R. CECIL: Of course, I fully accept the statement of the right hon. Gentleman that, as far as he is concerned, no such statement has been made; but I do not think he can be quite sure that no such statement has been made on behalf of the Government. There are other Members of the Government besides the right hon. Gentleman.

MR. LLOYD GEORGE: Really I think the Noble Lord is a little unfair. Does he really suggest that any Member of the Government has given a pledge affecting the Treasury to the extent of —

I do not know what it would be; I should say it would be an enormous sum — [AN HON. MEMBER : Millions] — without even intimating it to anybody representing the Treasury?

LORD R. CECIL : I really have not the slightest idea how this Government does its work. All I can say is that this statement was made publicly more than two months ago ; it was reported in the *Times*, and no contradiction whatever has been given.

MR. LLOYD GEORGE : At the first moment it is brought to my notice, which is this moment, I give it an emphatic contradiction.

LORD R. CECIL : It only shows how very unfortunate this legislation is, because apparently the hon. and learned Gentleman the Leader of the Irish party, who is a most accurate man, as I am sure every Member of this House knows, has apparently made that statement in the course of his speech. It set out with great accuracy this offer, which, he says, the Government have made.

However, if the right hon. Gentleman says it is inaccurate, it really makes very little difference to the strength of my argument, because it shows the kind of thing which is expected by this Bill, and the kind of pressure that will be put upon Finance Ministers in the future, whether this particular Finance Minister or not. A Bill of this kind, constructed in this way, is the greatest engine of political corruption which has been attempted to be carried in this House since the days of Fox's India Bill. Hon. Gentlemen opposite make a great accusation against a policy which is favoured by several of my hon. and right hon. Friends that it will lead to great corruption of public life. [AN HON. MEMBER : So it will.] Yes, but I say deliberately that the power of corruption under any scheme of Tariff Reform that has ever been suggested by a responsible statesman is as nothing to the power for corruption in this! This is not confined to municipalities or public authorities. Anybody in the world may receive a grant of public money out of this Development Fund in order to press forward some local industry. In what possible respect does this differ, except in the wording, from the ordinary system of bounties which prevails in protected countries? The thing is absolutely on " all fours." There is no distinction whatever. To my mind this Bill is thoroughly unsound finance. I believe, however carried out, it will result in a colossal waste of public money. I believe myself — and this is the worst part of it — that it will constitute a very serious danger to national political purity.

It is advocated upon the ground of developing national prosperity. I believe that to be a complete misapprehension of the foundation upon which national prosperity rests. I do not believe for a moment you can secure national prosperity in an old country like this by distributing public money in doles to this or that commercial interest. That is not what the prosperity of the country depends upon. The prosperity of the country depends upon national character. I can conceive no greater and more dangerous attack upon national character than holding out this bait of gigantic sums of money which may be granted to this or that industry in different parts of the country. A clause of this Bill provides that in considering how the money is to be distributed regard is to be had to the state of employment in the various districts. What does that amount to? An hon. Member comes and demands from the Finance Minister a grant of public money. The reply is, " You ask for this money, but your scheme is really not worth the assistance of the State." " Oh, but," says the hon. Member, " there is a great deal of unemployment in my district, and you are bound to consider that in making this grant." [AN HON. MEMBER: Why not?] Does anyone doubt how that will end? It means a grant of public money purely directed to the relief of individuals. It will destroy or seriously injure the character of the inhabitants of this country. Apart from its grotesque finance of taking out of one pocket by taxing what you are going to put into the other pocket by doles, it will destroy the very foundation upon which the prosperity of the country rests and its pride of place — at any rate, of its place of predominance — amongst the civilised Powers of the world.

Extract 54

REPLY TO CONSERVATIVE OPPOSITION TO DEVELOP-
MENT BILL

*(Mr. David Lloyd George, Chancellor of the Exchequer, Commons,
September 6, 1909)*

MR. LLOYD GEORGE [1] : This has been a very interesting and a
very significant debate. There is one characteristic of the debate
which I think has considerable significance, and that is that the
attack on the Bill has been confined exclusively to non-agricultural
Members. Up to the present we have not had a single Member for
an agricultural constituency sitting on the other side of the House
attacking the proposals of the Government for the aid of agriculture. The Members who have spoken for agriculture represent
town constituencies. The Noble Lord opposite [Lord R. Cecil]
has spoken for the agricultural community of Marylebone. The
Noble Lord [Viscount Morpeth] has spoken for the market gardeners of Birmingham. The right hon. Gentleman the Member
for Wimbledon [Mr. Chaplin] approves of the Bill —

MR. CHAPLIN : The objects of the first part of the Bill.

MR. LLOYD GEORGE : The right hon. Gentleman said that he
approved of the object of the Bill so long as the Bill was not carried. The Bill is a first-rate one, but if the Government mean to
carry it, it will have his whole-hearted opposition.

MR. CHAPLIN : I am sure the right hon. Gentleman does not
wish to misrepresent me. What I really said was that I approved
in the main of the objects of the first part of the Bill, but that I
disapprove altogether of the machinery by which those objects
were to be carried into effect. I added that the Bill was of such
importance that I did not think it could be properly examined at
this period of the year during a Session like the present, and that

1 Parliamentary Debates, Commons, Fifth Series, vol. 10, col. 961 sqq.

if any attempt was made to force it through the House without due and proper examination, I should oppose its passage to the best of my ability.

MR. LLOYD GEORGE: The right hon. Gentleman will have every opportunity of examining the Bill and of criticising any details to which he may object.

MR. CHAPLIN: When?

MR. LLOYD GEORGE: The Session is not over by any means. We will afford an opportunity. After the speech of the right hon. Gentleman on the second reading of the Budget I really expected something better from him, but I am grievously disappointed. The Noble Lord the Member for Marylebone [Lord R. Cecil] I expected opposition from. The hon. Baronet the Member for the City [Sir F. Banbury] I also expected opposition from.

SIR F. BANBURY: You will get it.

MR. LLOYD GEORGE: They do not agree with anything, not even with each other; therefore, I did not expect any agreement from them. But the right hon. Gentleman [Mr. Chaplin] on the second reading of the Budget devoted nearly the whole of his speech to passionately pleading that he was the man who discovered this idea. He discovered the North Pole; I only got there after him. He explained at great length how he started from, I think, Dublin with the Tariff Reform Commission on a voyage of discovery and had found it; he claimed to be the real discoverer, to whom all the credit of the distinction belonged. He having taken that line, I naturally expected his assistance now that I have tried to develop the idea — his idea, his child. I thought that as a fond parent, at any rate, he would have assisted me in protecting his child against the assassins who sit behind him. Instead of that, he threatens the most virulent opposition under certain conditions, and he does not seem at all anxious that the Bill should be carried. On the contrary, I do not think I should be doing him any injustice if I said that on the whole the right hon. Gentleman would be better pleased if the Bill did not go through the House of Commons during the present Session of Parliament. I really expected better treatment from him at any rate.

The Noble Lord [Lord R. Cecil] started his speech by attacking me for not having made a statement in opening the proceedings on the Bill. He said that it was another insult to the House of Commons. [SIR F. BANBURY: Hear, hear.] I see that his comrade *ad hoc* quite agrees with him. The Noble Lord is rather in the habit of lecturing Ministers in the House of Commons without adequate experience. His experience is confined to this single Parliament, but no one would imagine it, either from his gifts or from the rather superior tone which he adopts. Does he know what happened in the last Parliament ? The Education Bill of 1902 was moved by the lifting of the hat of the Minister. On the Licensing Bill of 1904, a highly controversial measure, no Minister spoke until much later in the evening than the hour at which I have risen to-night. In the present case I had already explained the object of the Bill in my Budget speech,[1] at much too great length I admit — for about twenty minutes. I circulated a full statement on the first reading. I have simply followed the precedent of the Leader of the Opposition, who is certainly a more distinguished authority than the Noble Lord and who would not insult the House of Commons, in simply waiting for two or three hours until I knew the general line of criticism.

The Noble Lord has laid down some very remarkable doctrines. He said that whenever rich motorists were taxed it was the working class who paid. That is a very remarkable doctrine. Why not extend it ? Is it not the simplest plan to tax the rich people, if it is the other classes who pay ? The cost of collection would be so much reduced. You would simply send a demand note to these few thousand people and say : " Would you mind paying us ? Of course, it is not you who will pay ; you are simply the agents. You just sign the cheque. The money will all come back to you." It is so much simpler. The rich man with a motor car of 60 horse-power

1 Cf. infra, p. 361.

simply signs the cheque; it is the poor pedestrian on the road, covered with dust, who pays. When the rich millionaire signs the cheque for £40 or £50 it is the little market gardener along the roadside who pays. It is a very simple method of taxation. You just get these few people to sign the cheque — that is the best method of making the whole community pay. That is the doctrine laid down by the Noble Lord, and it may be worth considering. I can quite conceive that some day or other he will be a member of a Socialist Ministry defending a Socialist Budget, defending the exclusive taxation of the rich, because it is not they who really pay, but somebody else. That is a very remarkable doctrine to come from him. [AN HON. MEMBER: It did not come from him.] I have just quoted his words.

As usual, the Noble Lord discovered Socialism here. All I can say is that some of the least Socialistic States in the world have indulged in experiments of this character. Denmark is certainly not a Socialistic State; on the contrary, it is probably the most individualistic State in Europe. It is a community of peasant proprietors. Yet in Denmark they have already engaged in these experiments, for I forget how long exactly, but twenty or thirty years, and with very great success.

EARL WINTERTON made a remark which was inaudible in the Press Gallery.

MR. LLOYD GEORGE: Yes, but they do not grow turnips in Copenhagen.

EARL WINTERTON: The right hon. Gentleman, I think, is rather unfair to me in his answer to my interruption. He said: "Denmark is the most individualistic country in Europe." I say it is one of the most Socialistic.

MR. LLOYD GEORGE: The Noble Lord is absolutely wrong. It shows really that when the Noble Lord and his colleagues talk about Socialism they have not the most elementary knowledge of what it means. If he would only look at the dictionary before he interrupts, it would be better. Does he really mean to suggest that peasant proprietorship is Socialism? Four-fifths of the land of Denmark belongs to peasant proprietors. That is the very opposite of Socialism! Some hon. Members talk without the slightest knowledge of the phrases they use — phrases which are used wildly in the streets, and, if I may say so, ignorantly. May I just say to the Noble Lord that in Denmark this has been a substitute for Protection. The one community in Denmark that would not have protection for its industry was the farming community. They did ask for this, and it has been a substitute for Protection. They asked for agricultural education, co-operation, the cheapening and the development of the facilities for transport, aid in cattle and horse breeding, and the Government aid in technical education. That is what they asked for. It has been a complete triumph throughout the whole of that country. Not only that, but the communities which demanded and relied upon Protection have not flourished. They have decayed. The farming community who preferred this method of Free Trade prospered year after year, until they have become the most prosperous little farming community in the world. Denmark to-day, a country without any great industries except agriculture — which is Free Trade — a country without any great mineral resources, and a country which not so very long ago was devastated by war, has become the second country in the world so far as wealth is concerned, owing entirely to its intelligent use of Free Trade assistance for agriculture. And this system — [Interruption.] Now, really, hon. Members might give me an opportunity of just stating my case. They have been criticising very freely, and I do not object, but they must allow me to answer. This is the system which has been the making of Denmark. It has not merely made the country prosperous, but it has increased the people's intelligence and made them a stronger and a more self-reliant race.

Look at the Report of the Scottish Commission which went to Denmark. The one thing they dwelt upon was the intelligence and self-reliance which have been promoted as a result of this system which we have embodied in this Bill — this system which, according to the Noble Lord in the rather melodramatic peroration with which he concluded his speech, is going to destroy the national character of this country, and depose us from our pride of place amongst the civilised Powers of the world! This is the language of wild, extravagant denunciation. Does it really become the Noble Lord? He has lost his sense of proportion altogether in examining the Bill. But it is all entirely due to the fact that he is criticising without the slightest knowledge of what has been done in other countries. I am perfectly certain, if he had even spent an half-hour in reading reports, which he could have got from the Library, of responsible Commissioners that examined similar systems in other parts of the world, he would never have given to this House the speech that he has given to it to-day. . . .

Extract 55

LABOUR VIEW OF THE DEVELOPMENT BILL

(Mr. G. N. Barnes, Commons, September 6, 1909)

MR. BARNES [1] : . . . I believe that this is the first real attempt that has been made to deal with unemployment on the lines of what might be called organic change. Hitherto, unemployment has been dealt with by the provision of relief works, and I am afraid that many of them have been costly, uneconomic, and wasteful, while some of them may even be said to have been demoralising. This Bill, however, unlike previous efforts to deal with unemployment, deals with it not only in its effect but its cause. It aims at preventing fluctuations and organising industrial activity in such a way as to prevent those fluctuations taking place. In other words, it does not only propose to deal with sores upon the surface, but it proposes to prevent new sores breaking out, and for

[1] Parliamentary Debates, Commons, Fifth Series, vol. 10, col. 984.

my part I am glad of that, because I am sick and tired of dealing with unemployed workmen as if they were merely pariahs and outcasts, or dealing with them in a mollycoddling sort of way and giving them grants. I am glad that the time will come when we shall deal with the unemployed workmen with the view of absorbing them into the civilised community on terms of equality of citizenship. . . .

Extract 56

EXPLANATION OF THE DEVELOPMENT BILL

(Earl Carrington, President of the Board of Agriculture and Fisheries, Lords, October 14, 1909)

EARL CARRINGTON [1]: My Lords, in rising to move the second reading of the Development and Road Improvement Funds Bill perhaps I may be permitted to say that this Bill marks another step forward in the land policy of the Government outlined by the late Sir H. Campbell-Bannerman at the Albert Hall in 1906. As regards agricultural landlords, we consider that the present method of levying income tax is not altogether fair to agricultural land, imposed as it was by a Chancellor of the Exchequer of the opposite side of politics to ourselves some sixty years ago, and in which there has been no alteration up to the present time; but in a few days I hope that we may be able to submit to your Lordships some proposals for the relief of agricultural landlords, who really have some causes to complain, and also a scheme by which death duties, which are somewhat heavy, may be paid in land as well as in cash.

We have done what we could for the farmers of England by the Land Tenure Bill. We have also tried to help by the Small Holdings Act the agricultural labourer and the landless man, although we have not been so fortunate in your Lordships' House with the

1 Parliamentary Debates, Lords, Fifth Series, vol. 3, col. 1225 sqq.

Housing Bill, in piloting which, if I may be permitted to say so, my noble friend Lord Beauchamp has appeared to so much advantage. Now the Government are proposing to try to follow the example of other nations by bringing in State assistance to the development of our great national industry by the Bill now before the House. Some time ago the Chancellor of the Exchequer consulted me in regard to the agricultural interest and what he said I may, perhaps, be permitted to repeat in the words that he himself used in the House of Commons. He said there is a certain amount of money — not very much — spent in a spasmodic way in the development of national industry, on light railways, on harbours, and indirectly and to a meagre extent for the interest of agriculture, and he said he proposed to gather all these grants into one grant. On the second reading of the Budget my right hon. friend, according to Hansard, vol. 6, p. 340, used some words which I hope your Lordships will allow me to read, as they are very important. He said, " We are proposing a grant for the purpose of doing that class of work which is now very largely done by the great landowners themselves, and this will come to at least a quarter of a million a year, so that we are relieving the great landowners of at least a quarter of a million a year."

This is received, I notice, with a certain amount of amusement by some noble Lords opposite, and perhaps it may seem an extraordinary proposal to come from a Chancellor of the Exchequer who is credited with somewhat Radical ideas. He is supposed by some people to go too far and by others not to go far enough. I may remind the House that it has been publicly thrown in my right hon. friend's teeth that he is a solicitor and a Welshman. I venture, my Lords, to think that perhaps these two facts go some long way to explain the practical sympathy which my right hon. friend has always shown towards the agricultural interest. As a solicitor he has had the opportunity of becoming acquainted with the real difficulties with which agriculturists large and small have to contend, and born and bred among the hard-working farmers of North Wales, he knows from personal experience the passionate attachment to the soil of those among whom he has lived and the courage and industry which not only Welsh farmers but all farmers display in playing their part in the social and industrial life of the country.

Let me now come at once to the Development Bill. It is not a very long Bill and it is not a very complicated one, whilst there is no previous legislation bound up with it. It is composed of twenty clauses and is divided into two parts. The first six clauses relate to development, and the other clauses relate to road improvement. Let me, as briefly as I can, run through our proposals in Part I. The first clause enables the Treasury to make advances by grants or loans to a Government department or through a Government department to public authorities, universities, colleges, associations, or companies not trading for profit. The objects of the Bill are to aid and encourage agriculture, which is put first, and then the promotion of forestry, reclamation and drainage of land, improvement of rural transport — leaving roads to be dealt with in the second part of the Bill — the construction and improvement of inland navigation and harbours, and the development and improvement of fisheries. It will be seen from the second clause that all grants and advances will be made out of a Development Fund which will be fed in three ways — first, by such money as may be voted by Parliament; secondly, by £500,000 charged on the Consolidated Fund for five years; and, thirdly, by the interest on and repayment of advanced and miscellaneous receipts. This, my Lords, will be paid into the Development Fund instead of being paid back automatically into the Treasury as is generally the case.

As regards the Development Fund, I think most of your Lordships will agree that the proposal opens a very wide question and that it might become a source of great danger and almost a national danger. If there is one thing which people in public life on both sides of politics insist on, it is the cautious administration of public money. The standard of public life in this country is very high, and it would be a grievous thing if any Bill was brought in on either side of politics which would affect it. That was at once pointed out by two Members of the House of Commons, one on each side, — Mr. Rufus Isaacs on the Liberal side and Lord Robert Cecil on the Conservative side, — and they plainly showed the danger of putting £500,000 into the absolute control and hands of the Government of the day, whatever that Government might be, as it might end in a scramble for spoils and might be an invitation to almost everybody to press for some share of the grant.

I think those of your Lordships — and here are a great many — who have had the pleasure of visiting Australia will remember that the great difficulty in the old days there was — I do not know if it is so now — that Members of Parliament were known as roads and bridges Members, and their seats entirely depended on the public works which they could induce the Ministry of the day to commence and continue in their constituencies. Speaking in the name of the Government, I ought to express our gratitude to Lord Robert Cecil for the statesmanlike way in which he showed this possible danger and for the machinery which he put forward to avoid it. That machinery was at once adopted by the Chancellor of the Exchequer, and is now part and parcel of the Bill.

To prevent any possible danger of political pressure we propose that the Treasury should appoint five Commissioners, who must be men of independent mind, great capacity, high standing, and high character. They will be appointed by the Treasury for ten years, and two of them will be paid salaries which in the aggregate will not amount to more than £3000 a year — and which will be paid out of the Development Fund. We hope that that money will be sufficient to insure the Government getting the very best and highest class of men for the positions. Three are to form a quorum. With the consent of the Treasury, of course, they can appoint their officers and servants and give certain salaries that they may think fit. The Treasury will refer every application that may be made by a Government department to these Commissioners; but if the applicants are any other body, as mentioned in Clause 1 of the Bill, the Treasury will at once send the application to the Government department which is concerned to report. and then the Government department will refer the scheme to the Development Commissioners. Then, of course, whether the scheme is carried through or not will depend on whether it meets with the sanction or refusal of the Treasury.

The Commissioners — and I hope your Lordships will consider this right — will consider and report at once to the Treasury on every application. They may hold inquiries and appoint advisory committees who may report to them, and they can authorise applicants to obtain land compulsorily, and a single arbitrator will decide the compensation and costs to be paid. I need hardly say that no ten per cent will be given for compulsory purchase of land so that there should be no difficulty or grumbling about who the arbitrator should be. The arbitrator will be appointed in England by the Lord Chief Justice, in Scotland by the Lord President of the Court of Session, and in Ireland by the Lord Chief Justice of Ireland. There is an exemption in regard to compulsory acquisition of land in favour of parks, gardens, home farms, and places of historic interest. . . .

Extract 57

DEVELOPMENT AND ROAD IMPROVEMENT FUNDS ACT, 1909

(9 Edw. 7, ch. 47, in part)

An Act to promote the Economic Development of the United Kingdom and the Improvement of Roads therein.

(3rd December 1909)

Be it enacted by the King's most Excellent Majesty, by and with the advice and consent of the Lords Spiritual and Temporal, and Commons, in this present Parliament assembled, and by the authority of the same, as follows:

Part I

Development

1. Payments

(1) The Treasury may, upon the recommendation of the Development Commissioners appointed under this Act, make advances to a Government department, or through a Government department to a public authority, university, college, school, or institution, or an association of persons or company not trading for profit, either by way of grant or by way of loan, or partly in one way and partly in the other, and upon such terms and subject to such conditions as they may think fit, for any of the following purposes :

(*a*) Aiding and developing agriculture and rural industries by promoting scientific research, instruction and experiments in the science, methods and practice of agriculture (including the provision of farm-institutes), the organisation of co-operation, instruction in marketing produce, and the extension of the provision of small holdings ; and by the adoption of any other means which appear calculated to develop agriculture and rural industries ;

(*b*) Forestry (including (1) the conducting of inquiries, experiments, and research for the purpose of promoting forestry and the teaching of methods of afforestation ; (2) the purchase and planting of land found after inquiry to be suitable for afforestation) ;

(*c*) The reclamation and drainage of land ;

(*d*) The general improvement of rural transport (including the making of light railways but not including the construction or improvement of roads) ;

(*e*) The construction and improvement of harbours ;

(*f*) The construction and improvement of inland navigations ;

(*g*) The development and improvement of fisheries ;

and for any other purpose calculated to promote the economic development of the United Kingdom.

(2) All applications for advances under this Part of this Act shall be made to the Treasury in accordance with regulations made by the Treasury.

(3) No advance shall be made for any purpose which might be carried out under the provisions of the Small Holdings and Allotments Act, 1908,[1] upon any terms or conditions different from those contained in that statute except for some special reason which shall be stated in the annual report of the Development Commissioners.

2. *Establishment of Development Fund*

(1) All advances, whether by way of grant or by way of loan, made under this Part of this Act shall be made out of a fund, called the development fund, into which shall be paid —

(a) Such moneys as may from time to time be provided by Parliament for the purposes of this Part of this Act;

(b) The sums issued out of the Consolidated Fund under this section; and

(c) Any sums received by the Treasury by way of interest on or repayment of any advance made by way of loan under this Part of this Act, and any profits or proceeds derived from the expenditure of any advance which by the terms on which the advance was made are to be paid to the Treasury.

(2) There shall be charged on and issued out of the Consolidated Fund, or the growing produce thereof, in the year ending the thirty-first day of March nineteen hundred and eleven, and in each of the next succeeding four years, the sum of five hundred thousand pounds.

(3) The Treasury may accept any gifts made to them for all or any of the purposes for which advances may be made under this

[1] 8 Edw. 7, ch. 36.

Part of this Act and, subject to the terms of gift, apply them for the purposes of this Part of this Act in accordance with regulations made by the Treasury.

(4) The Treasury shall cause an account to be prepared and transmitted to the Comptroller and Auditor-General for examination, on or before the thirtieth day of September in every year, showing the receipts into and issues out of the development fund in the financial year ended on the thirty-first day of March preceding, and the Comptroller and Auditor-General shall certify and report upon the same, and such account and report shall be laid before Parliament by the Treasury on or before the thirty-first day of January in the following year if Parliament be then sitting, and, if not sitting, then within one week after Parliament shall be next assembled.

(5) Payments out of and into the development fund, and all other matters relating to the fund and the moneys standing to the credit of the fund, shall be made and regulated in such manner as the Treasury may by minute to be laid before Parliament direct.

(6) The Treasury may from time to time invest any moneys standing to the credit of the development fund in any securities in which trustees are by law authorised to invest trust funds.

3. Development Commissioners

(1) For the purposes of this Part of this Act it shall be lawful for His Majesty by warrant under the sign manual to appoint five [1] Commissioners, to be styled the Development Commissioners, of whom one to be appointed by His Majesty shall be chairman.

(2) Subject to the provisions of this section, the term of office of a Commissioner shall be ten years. One Commissioner shall retire every second year,[2] but a retiring Commissioner may be reappointed. The order in which the Commissioners first appointed are to retire shall be determined by His Majesty. On a casual

---

[1] Eight, by amendment of 1910. 10 Edw. 7, ch. 7.

[2] After the first two years, one Commissioner shall retire every year. Ibid.

vacancy occurring by reason of the death, resignation, or incapacity of a Commissioner, or otherwise, the person appointed by His Majesty to fill the vacancy shall continue in office until the Commissioner in whose place he was appointed would have retired, and shall then retire.

(3) There shall be paid to not more than two of the Commissioners such salaries, not exceeding in the aggregate three thousand pounds in each year, as the Treasury may direct.

(4) The Commissioners may act by three [1] of their number and notwithstanding a vacancy in their number, and, subject to the approval of the Treasury, may regulate their own procedure.

(5) The Commissioners may, with the consent of the Treasury, appoint and employ such officers and servants for the purposes of this Part of this Act as they think necessary, and may remove any officer or servant so appointed and employed, and there shall be paid to such officers and servants such salaries or remuneration as the Commissioners, with the consent of the Treasury, may determine.

(6) The salaries of the Commissioners and the salaries or remuneration of their officers and servants, and any expenses incurred by the Commissioners in the execution of their duties under this Part of this Act, to such amount as may be sanctioned by the Treasury, shall be defrayed out of the development fund.

4. Powers and Duties of Commissioners

(1) Every application for an advance under this Part of this Act, whether by way of grant or by way of loan, by any body qualified to receive an advance under this Part of this Act, shall, if the applicant is a Government department, be referred by the Treasury to the Development Commissioners, and, if the applicant is any other body or persons, shall be sent by the Treasury to the Government department concerned, to be by them referred together with their report thereon to the Development Commissioners.

[1] Four. 10 Edw. 7, ch. 7.

(2) The Commissioners shall consider and report to the Treasury on every application so referred to them, and may for that purpose, if necessary, hold inquiries either by themselves, or by any of their officers, or any other person appointed for the purpose.

(3) The Commissioners may also appoint advisory committees, and may submit to any such advisory committee for their advice any application referred to them.

(4) The Commissioners may also frame schemes with respect to any of the matters for which advances may be made under this Part of this Act with a view to their adoption by a Government department or other body or persons to whom an advance may be made.

(5) Before making any recommendation for an advance for the purpose of the improvement of rural transport, the Commissioners shall consult with the Road Board.

(6) The Commissioners shall make to the Treasury an annual report of their proceedings, and such report shall be laid annually before Parliament by the Treasury.

5. *Power to acquire Land*

(1) Where an advance is made under this Part of this Act for any purpose which involves the acquisition of land, the department, body, or persons to whom the advance is made, may acquire and hold land for the purpose, and, where they are unable to acquire by agreement on reasonable terms any land which they consider necessary, they may apply to the Development Commissioners for an order empowering them to acquire the land compulsorily in accordance with the provisions of the Schedule to this Act, and the Commissioners shall have power to make such order.

(2) No land shall be authorised by an order under this section to be acquired compulsorily which, at the date of the order, forms part of any park, garden, or pleasure ground, or forms part of the home farm attached to and usually occupied with a mansion house, or is otherwise required for the amenity or convenience of any dwelling-house, or which at that date is the property of any local

authority, or has been acquired by any corporation or company for the purposes of a railway, dock, canal, water, or other public undertaking, or is the site of an ancient monument or other object of archæological interest.

(3) The Commissioners, in making an order for the compulsory purchase of land, shall have regard to the extent of land held or occupied in the locality by any owner or tenant and to the convenience of other property belonging to or occupied by the same owner or tenant, and shall, so far as practicable, avoid taking an undue or inconvenient quantity of land from any one owner or tenant, and for that purpose where part only of a holding is taken shall take into consideration the size and character of the existing agricultural buildings not proposed to be taken which are used in connexion with the holding and the quantity and nature of the land available for occupation therewith, and shall also so far as practicable avoid displacing any considerable number of agricultural labourers or others employed on or about the land.

6. Definition

For the purposes of this Part of this Act the expression "agriculture and rural industries" includes agriculture, horticulture, dairying, the breeding of horses, cattle, and other live stock and poultry, the cultivation of bees, home and cottage industries, the cultivation and preparation of flax, the cultivation and manufacture of tobacco, and any industries immediately connected with and subservient to any of the said matters.

PART II

ROAD IMPROVEMENT

7. Constitution of Road Board

(1) For the purposes of improving the facilities for road traffic in the United Kingdom and of the administration of the road improvement grant provided under any Act passed in the present

or any future session of Parliament, there shall be constituted in accordance with regulations made by the Treasury a board, to be called the Road Board, consisting of such number of persons appointed by the Treasury as the Treasury may determine.

(2) The Road Board shall be a body corporate with a common seal, with power to hold land without licence in mortmain.

(3) The Road Board may pay the chairman or vice-chairman of the Board such salary as the Board, with the consent of the Treasury, may determine.

(4) The Road Board may appoint such officers and servants for the purposes of their powers and duties under this Part of this Act as the Board may, with the sanction of the Treasury, determine, and there shall be paid to such officers and servants out of the road improvement grant such salaries or remuneration as the Treasury may determine.

8. *Powers of Road Board*

(1) The Road Board shall have power, with the approval of the Treasury —

(*a*) to make advances to county councils and other highway authorities in respect of the construction of new roads or the improvement of existing roads;

(*b*) to construct and maintain any new roads;

which appear to the Board to be required for facilitating road traffic.

(2) Where advances have been made to highway authorities in respect of the construction of new roads, the Road Board may, where they think it desirable, also contribute towards the cost of maintenance of such new roads.

(3) The sums expended by the Road Board out of income on the construction of new roads or the acquisition of land, or in respect of any loan raised for any such purpose, shall not in any year exceed one-third of the estimated receipts of the Road Board for that year.

(4) An advance to a highway authority may be either by way of grant or by way of loan, or partly in one way and partly in the other, and shall be upon such terms and subject to such conditions as the Board think fit.

(5) For the purposes of this Part of this Act the expression "improvement of roads" includes the widening of any road, the cutting off the corners of any road where land is required to be purchased for that purpose, the levelling of roads, the treatment of a road for mitigating the nuisance of dust, and the doing of any other work in respect of roads beyond ordinary repairs essential to placing a road in a proper state of repair; and the expression "roads" includes bridges, viaducts, and subways.

9. Roads constructed by Road Board

(1) Every road constructed by the Road Board under the provisions of this Part of this Act shall be a public highway, and the enactments relating to highways and bridges shall apply to such roads accordingly, except that every such road shall be maintainable by and at the cost of the Road Board, and, for the purpose of the maintenance, repair, improvement, and enlargement of or dealing with any such road, the Board shall have the same powers (except the power of levying a rate) and be subject to the same duties as a county council have and are subject to as respects main roads, and may further exercise any powers vested in a county council for the purposes of the maintenance and repair of bridges, and the Road Board shall have the same powers as a county council for the preventing and removing of obstructions:

Provided that —

(a) Communications between a road or path and a road constructed by the Road Board shall be made in manner to be approved by the Road Board; and

(b) The Road Board and any highway authority in whose district any part of any such road is situate may contract for the undertaking by such authority of the maintenance and repair of the part of such road in their district; and, for the purposes of such undertaking, the highway authority shall have the same powers and be subject to the same duties and liabilities as if the road were a road vested in the highway authority.

(2) Before the Treasury approve of the construction of a new road by the Road Board, they shall consult with the Local Government Board and shall satisfy themselves that notice of the intention to construct the road has been sent by the Road Board to every highway authority in the area of which any part of the proposed road will be situate, and shall consider any objections to the proposed road which they may receive from any such authority.

10. Construction of New Roads by Highway Authorities

(1) Where the Road Board make an advance to a highway authority in respect of the construction of a new road, the Board may authorise the authority to construct the road, and where so authorised the highway authority shall have power to construct the road and to do all such acts as may be necessary for the purpose, and any expenses of the authority, so far as not defrayed out of the advance, shall be defrayed as expenses incurred by the authority in exercise of their powers as highway authority, and the enactments relating to such expenses, including the provisions as to borrowing, shall apply accordingly.

(2) Where the highway authority to whom the advance is made are a county council, the new road, when constructed, shall be a main road and in any other case shall be a highway repairable by the inhabitants at large :

Provided that the maintenance of any such road within the administrative county of London shall devolve upon the local authority responsible for the maintenance of streets and roads in whose district the same is situate.

11. Acquisition of Land

(1) Where the Treasury have approved a proposal by the Road Board to construct a new road under this Part of this Act the Board may acquire land for the purpose, and may, in addition, acquire land on either side of the proposed road within two hundred and twenty yards from the middle of the proposed road.

(2) The Road Board may acquire, erect, and furnish such offices and other buildings as they may require, and may acquire land for the purpose.

(3) Where a highway authority are authorised to construct a new road under this Part of this Act, or an advance is made to such an authority in respect of the improvement of an existing road, the authority may acquire land for the purpose of such construction or improvement.

(4) For the purpose of the purchase of land by agreement under this Part of this Act by the Road Board or a highway authority the Lands Clauses Acts shall be incorporated with this Part of this Act, except the provisions of those Acts with respect to the purchase and taking of land otherwise than by agreement, and section one hundred and seventy-eight of the Public Health Act, 1875, shall apply as if the Road Board and the highway authority were referred to therein.

(5) Where the Road Board or any highway authority are unable to acquire by agreement on reasonable terms any land which they consider necessary, they may apply to the Development Commissioners for an order empowering them to acquire the land compulsorily in accordance with the provisions of the Schedule to this Act, and the Commissioners shall have power to make such an order : Provided that the provisions of Part I of this Act, prohibiting the compulsory acquisition of the classes of land mentioned in subsection (3)[1] of section five of this Act shall apply to the acquisition by the Road Board of land on either side of a road proposed to be constructed by the Board.

[1] Subsection (2) is meant. The mistake was corrected by 10 Edw. 7, ch. 7.

(6) The Road Board shall have full power, with the approval of the Treasury, to sell, lease, and manage any land acquired by them under this Part of this Act and not required for the new road, and any receipts derived from any such land, so far as they are applied for the purposes of the construction of new roads, shall not be treated as part of the expenditure of the Road Board on new roads for the purpose of the provisions of this Act limiting the amount of expenditure of the Road Board on new roads.

12. Expenses and Receipts of Road Board

(1) All expenses of the Road Board under this Part of this Act, including the salary of the chairman or vice-chairman and the salaries and the remuneration of officers and servants, to such amount as may be sanctioned by the Treasury, shall be defrayed out of the road improvement grant.

(2) The Treasury shall cause an account to be prepared and transmitted to the Comptroller and Auditor-General for examination, showing the receipts into and issues out of the road improvement grant in the financial year ending the thirty-first day of March preceding, and the Comptroller and Auditor-General shall certify and report upon the same, and such account and report shall be laid before Parliament by the Treasury.

(3) Any sums received by the Road Board under this Part of this Act shall, subject to regulations made by the Treasury, be carried to the account to which the road improvement grant is required to be carried under the Act under which the grant is provided, and shall be treated as part of that grant.

13. Power to borrow

(1) The Road Board may, with the approval of and subject to regulations made by the Treasury, borrow on the security of the road improvement grant for the purpose of meeting any expenditure which appears to the Treasury to be of such a nature that

it ought to be spread over a term of years, so however that the total amount required for the payment of interest on and the repayment of money so borrowed shall not exceed in any year the sum of two hundred thousand pounds.

(2) If and so far as the road improvement grant is insufficient to meet the amount required for the payment of interest on and the repayment of principal in any year, that amount shall be charged on and payable out of the Consolidated Fund or the growing produce thereof, but any sums so paid out of the Consolidated Fund shall be made good out of the road improvement grant.

14. Annual Report to Parliament

The Road Board shall make to the Treasury an annual report of their proceedings, and such report shall be laid annually before Parliament by the Treasury.

[Clauses 15–20, and an accompanying Schedule, deal with administrative details, definitions, and certain exceptions having force in London, Scotland, and Ireland.]

CHAPTER VIII

THE LLOYD GEORGE BUDGET

[To make proper provision for old age pensions and general elementary education and labour exchanges and town planning and rural development, to say nothing of the new machinery set up by the whole series of social measures enacted since 1905, placed an additional strain upon a treasury already burdened with what seemed to most Englishmen an absolutely necessary, albeit a huge, expenditure for naval construction and maintenance. The Liberal Government, frequently accused of anti-imperialistic leanings and of a " Little England " policy, could not see its way clear to lessening military expenditure, and yet had pronounced in favour of a far-reaching system of national insurance [1] as soon as the requisite funds should be forthcoming.

But whence would the requisite funds come ? The tariff reformers among the Unionists, who had been ably led by Mr. Joseph Chamberlain, had supported an increased militarism and an extended colonialism and had advocated social reform, and had promised to pay for these things by means of the large revenues that would be derived from a high protective tariff. The failure of Mr. Chamberlain's followers was due in large part to their inability to convince their fellow-Conservatives that a revolution in fiscal affairs would be desirable. And now the Liberal Government were committed to a policy of social transformation even more definitely than Mr. Chamberlain, while at the same time they were far more unitedly and certainly opposed to a protective tariff than Mr. Chamberlain's Conservative opponents had been. The Liberal Government could

[1] Cf. supra, pp. 45 sqq., 199 sqq., and infra, ch. x.

347

not add to the financial burdens of the state at the price of abandoning their traditional free-trade principles. Yet they would add to those financial burdens.

It was at this point that Mr. Lloyd George, as Chancellor of the Exchequer, came forward with proposals for a radical application of direct taxation — graduated income tax, super-tax, tax on the unearned increment, and tax on undeveloped property — and for a readjustment of the indirect taxes, such as licensing duties, with a view to equalising the financial burdens among the various classes in the community. The land taxes, intended at once as an attack upon the nobles' monopoly of land and as a means of placing additional funds at the disposal of the government for purposes of social amelioration, would be metaphorically the stone for the killing of two birds at once. It would be the Liberal, Radical, and Labour way out of the dilemma of increasing expenditures and maintaining Great Britain's position as a free-trade country. The enemies of Mr. Lloyd George suggested that it was likewise Socialistic.

On April 29, 1909, Mr. Lloyd George delivered his momentous Budget Speech, which, on account of its clear presentment of the principles underlying the new proposals, its concise statement of the major details, and the obvious connection between its finances and subsequent projects for social legislation, is given below, in part, as *Extract 58.*

It took the Press and the public some time to comprehend the details of the new Budget, but it was eulogised by Liberals as " democratic " and as a triumph of free-trade finance, while it was at once attacked by Unionist organs as Socialistic, as " an electioneering prospectus," as taxing the rich for the benefit of the poor, and as tending to diminish and drive away capital and therefore to create more unemployment than it was likely to relieve. Several special classes assailed it : the financial interests in London were decidedly adverse ; the views of the real estate market were very unfavourable ; the landlords were decidedly opposed ; the tobacco trade and the motor industry resented their new burdens ;

the brewers and distillers were loud in their condemnation; Irish feeling was hostile to the licensing provisions of the Budget.

The general principles of the Budget were debated in the House of Commons, May 3–5; but in view of the vast length of the later discussions, it would be unnecessary, were it practicable, to give a full abstract of the proceedings. Some idea of the progress of the debate and of the arguments advanced *pro* and *con* may be gathered from the "Annual Register." [1]

Mr. Arthur J. Balfour led the Opposition attack with a speech which passed over many features of the Ministerial proposals; its main points were an objection to the abolition of the old Sinking Fund, a criticism of the property taxes as likely to encourage evasion and the sending of capital abroad, and of the taxation of undeveloped land as likely to injure market gardening, an argument that unearned increment arose with other forms of property besides land, and an emphatic denunciation of the proposed taxation of the liquor trade as vindictive. The Budget proposals, he declared, had given a severe shock to confidence and credit. He was answered by the Postmaster-General, and then Mr. John Redmond, the Irish leader, declared that the Budget was admirable and courageous from the British point of view, but, looking at it from an exclusively Irish standpoint, the whisky tax would more than counterbalance the advantage to Ireland of old age pensions, and the tax on tobacco was cruel. What had Ireland to do with *Dreadnoughts*? He condemned, amongst other items, the increased stamp duties on land transfers; but would gladly see issue taken with the Lords on the proposed social reforms which the Nationalists approved. Mr. G. N. Barnes, with some reserves as to details, welcomed the Budget on behalf of the Labour party, and subsequently Mr. Winston Churchill defended the Government programme, declaring incidentally that the Opposition were debarred from criticism by their constant questions tending to indefinite expenditure on national defence and their attempts to expand the old age pension scheme. The

[1] Annual Register, 1909, pp. 101 sqq.

Budget was a vindication of free-trade finance. He was followed by Mr. Pretyman, who was answered by the Attorney-General; and, after other speeches, the Chancellor of the Exchequer made an effective and temperate defence of his plans. Mr. Balfour, he said, had left three-fourths of the Budget uncriticised; Ireland was asked in this Budget for considerably less than her normal contribution to taxation, and should remember her share in old age pensions. The Development Grant would benefit landlords by giving light railways, and next year there might be a relief of local rates. German Conservatives and Protectionists favoured a tax on unearned increment, which had existed for years as a local tax in German towns, and the Housing of the Working Classes Commission had recommended a tax on undeveloped land near towns. He assured the House that the Government was anxious to do what was right and fair. Mr. Chaplin assailed the Budget as the first step in the Socialist war against property; Mr. Philip Snowden, an avowed Socialist, declared that he desired to make the rich poorer in order to make the poor richer; the Budget was the beginning of democratic government; to take only 20 per cent was "compounding a felony." Mr. Asquith remarked that both parties had taken common ground on old age pensions and the navy scheme. The indirect taxes imposed compared favourably with the taxes on coal, sugar, and tea, and he defended the income tax proposals, noting especially that not a word had been said against the super-tax. The tax on unearned increment, due to social causes, dealt with a normal and progressive increase, would only be paid when the value was realised, and might relieve congestion in such places as Glasgow, where 120,000 people were living in one-room tenements. In regard to estate duties, they would listen with an open mind to criticism of the scale. As to the liquor duties, the brewers would make good any losses at the consumers' expense. Whither was capital to fly? Wherever it went it would be confronted by a Finance Minister not less necessitous than the Chancellor of the Exchequer. The Opposition had shown restiveness when asked for their alternative plan, but they might fairly be asked to give some general indication of it. In 1903 there was an alternative adumbrated — taxes on meat, corn, and dairy produce. The *Morning Post* had just suggested a " better way " — import duties on all foreign articles except raw materials. If that was the Opposition proposal, the Government would be happy to meet them. Meantime, they recommended the Budget for acceptance as providing adequately for prospective as well as present needs, without deviation from free trade. Mr. Austen Chamberlain replied that silence as to details did not imply approval, that the Budget was cutting down the resources for war. The taxation was not for revenue only, and was not apportioned according to ability to pay. The liquor taxes were clapped on a declining trade. The death duties would eat into the capital available for the development of the country. He severely criticised the super-tax in its relation to other taxes ; the increased stamp duties on land transfers ; the proposal to tax reversions — which were part of the consideration for the lease ; the tax on unearned increment — since it was difficult to distinguish between " earned " and " unearned " ; the tax on undeveloped land, as promoting speculative building and destroying recreation grounds ; and in conclusion, wondered why the Government kept up the farce of quarrelling with their Socialist allies. Mr. Masterman wound up for the Government, remarking on the absurdity of identifying Socialism with the views of Mr. Henry George. The debate was closured by 308 to 201.

On May 15, 1909, a letter to the Prime Minister was published, signed by leading London financial firms or their representatives, including Messrs. Rothschilds, Barings, Antony Gibbs & Sons, J. S. Morgan & Co., Huth & Co., C. J. Hambro & Sons, Brown, Shipley & Co., Fruehling & Goschen, Lord Avebury, Sir Felix Schuster, Sir Thomas Sutherland, and others. While declaring that they were prepared to bear their full share of increased taxation, which they recognised as necessary, they expressed alarm at the increasing disproportion of the burden placed on a small class.

They held that the increase of the death duties (which, they stated, were usually paid out of capital) and of the income tax, coupled with the super-tax, would injure commerce and industry ; that the prosperity of all classes had been greatly due to the indisputable safety for capital afforded by Great Britain, and that the taxes in question would discourage private enterprise and thrift, thus eventually diminishing employment and reducing wages.

All these arguments and many more were advanced against the Finance Bill, embodying the provisions of the Budget, during the four days' debate which preceded its second reading in the Commons on June 11. An amendment, moved by Mr. Austen Chamberlain, involving its rejection, was negatived by 366 to 209. Sixty-two Nationalists voted in the minority.

Outside Parliament the storm against the Bill had meanwhile been gathering strength. The Earl of Rosebery publicly described [1] the Budget as a social and political revolution to be effected without the participation of the people ; the country, he added, must begin to see that there were vast flaws in the Constitution. The *Times* added a charge — often repeated afterwards — that the Budget, coupled with the Town Planning Bill,[2] was subjecting Great Britain to bureaucratic rule. But the most influential protest was made by a crowded meeting of business men, held at the Cannon Street Hotel on June 23. It was described by Lord Avebury as not political, but financial and economic.

On the same day a " Budget League " was formed by the Liberal members of the House of Commons to conduct a vigorous campaign in its favour in the constituencies, at a meeting held at the House of Commons. Mr. Haldane presided, Mr. Winston Churchill spoke, and it was made clear that no pressure would be put on any Liberal opponents of parts of the Budget. At the same time, it was clearly pointed out that the House of Lords would probably veto the Finance Bill, and that the question of the Budget would therefore be inextricably bound up with the question of the Lords' veto.

[1] The *London Times*, June 22, 1909.   [2] Cf. supra, ch. vii.

As one member expressed it, the inevitably approaching election would raise the question of the Lords, the land, and liquor.

By midsummer, the true import of the Government's proposals was quite thoroughly understood; and agitation was prevalent throughout the country. On July 25, a great Budget demonstration took place in Hyde Park, London; a procession marched thither from the Embankment, and speeches were delivered from twelve platforms. That of the Labour party attracted the largest crowd, and the resolution passed at the other eleven was passed here in a more strongly worded version. Opinions differed as to the significance of the proceedings; the Conservative *Times* said that they were "skilfully engineered"; the Liberal *Westminster Gazette* that an unusually large proportion of the audience was acutely interested; according to some estimates, the numbers reached 250,000. Much had been said of the injury done to building by the Budget; yet the building trades' federation was specially conspicuous in the Park.

Mr. Lloyd George's chief defence of his Budget before a popular audience was made at the Edinburgh Castle, Limehouse, on July 30, before an audience of 4000. The financial interests, he said, had demanded further expenditure on the navy; but while the workmen in Derbyshire, Cleveland and Dumfries had shown themselves willing to pay, there was a howl from Belgravia. The rich said they objected mainly to paying for old age pensions; why then had they promised them? It now appeared they had meant workmen to pay for their own pensions. The Budget was raising money to provide against poverty, unemployment, and sickness; for widows and orphans, and for the development of our own land. The land taxes, especially, were being attacked with ferocity. But land near the London docks, formerly rented at £2 or £3 an acre, had sold at £6000 or £8000 an acre. A piece of land at Golder's Green, near Hampstead, had risen in value from £160 to £2100 through the making of the tube railway. The Duke of Northumberland had asked £900 an acre for a piece of land wanted for a school and rented at 30s. an acre. A bit of land in Scotland wanted for a torpedo range — and affording "an opportunity for patriotism " — was rated at £11 2s. a year and sold to the nation for £27,225. After denouncing as "insolence" a comparison made in the debates of the landlord's increment with that of a doctor in a growing town, he gave the case of Mr. Gorringe, whose lease (in Buckingham Palace Road) had been renewed by the Duke of Westminster, the terms being the increase of the ground rent to £4000 a year, a fine ("a fine, mind you ") of £50,000, and the building of huge and costly premises according to plans submitted to the Duke. Such a case "is not business, it is blackmail." He denounced at some length the owners of mining royalties who would not "spare a copper" for the miners' pensions, and declared that landowning was a stewardship; if landlords ceased to discharge their traditional duties, the conditions of landholding must be reconsidered. The landlords said they were anxious for the small holders, but they had condemned their exemption. As one of the children of the people, he had made up his mind in framing the Budget that no cupboard should be bared, no lot should be harder to bear.

This speech was reprinted and widely circulated ; but its reference to the "Gorringe case" was severely criticised, and what was referred to as its demagogic tone gave widespread offence. Sir Edward Carson declared in the *Times* that it marked "the beginning of the end of the rights of property"; the *Times* said that Mr. Lloyd George and Mr. Churchill were trying to form a new party. Mr. Lloyd George's closing phrases provoked the rejoinder that many "cupboards would be bared " by the reduction of employment on the part of the great landowners, and the Duke of Portland and others laid stress on this point. This, however, served only to bring the landlords into greater disfavour.

Lord Lansdowne, the leader of the Conservatives in the Upper House, denounced the Budget in a public speech on August 9 as a hotch-potch of proposals involving a taxation of capital unprecedented in England, and compared Mr. Lloyd George to the "robber-gull" which lives by stealing fish from other gulls, and intimated that the House of Lords would refer the Finance Bill to the people.

Mr. Winston Churchill, on the other hand, speaking at a Budget League demonstration at Leicester on September 4, made fun of the Dukes' opposition to the Budget and laid stress on the urgency of social reform. On the one side was the gap between rich and poor, the divorce of the people from the land, the lack of discipline and training for the young, boy labour, physical degeneration, the "jumble of an obsolete poor law," the liquor traffic, unemployment, the absence of a minimum standard of life among the workers, and the increase of vulgar, joyless luxury; on the other, the "moral, spiritual, civic, scientific forces" which the Budget would reinforce. The tax-gatherer would now ask, not, what have you got, but how did you get it?[1] The differentiation in treatment of wealth implied a constant relation between acquired wealth and service previously rendered. Where no service had been done, but rather disservice, the State should make a difference in taxation. He welcomed the struggle as likely to "smash" the Lords' veto.

Quite as illuminating as the popular speeches of Mr. Lloyd George, Lord Lansdowne, and Mr. Churchill, was the speech of Lord Rosebery "to business men of Glasgow opposed to many of the principles of the Budget" on September 10. Before delivering it, he resigned the Presidency of the Liberal League; and thenceforth was considered definitely to have broken with the Liberal party. In his opening sentences Lord Rosebery referred to his independent position and then dwelt on the immediate economic dangers set up by the Budget, which he described as "a revolution without a popular mandate." He concentrated his attack on the land taxes and death duties, arguing that the former might be expanded and their principles extended to other forms of property, but he admitted that he should like to see the State settle "a new

---

[1] This phrase, like Mr. Lloyd George's "baring cupboards," was often quoted during the subsequent electoral campaign by opponents of the Budget.

yeomanry " on the land and give towns power to cope with the restriction of their growth due to the high price of land. He dwelt
on the landlord's prospective burdens, which fell not only on dukes,
" a poor but honest class," but on friendly societies and workmen's
insurance companies. The death duties now took " great chunks
of capital " ; " scores of millions " were lying idle in banks owing
to apprehensions of the Ministerial policy ; the Budget was inquisitorial, tyrannical, and Socialistic. He laid great stress on the extension of taxation on gifts *inter vivos*, asked what had become of
retrenchment, and thought " many heedless persons " would prefer
the alternative of tariff reform. He himself declined to offer an
alternative, but suggested retrenchment on the Civil Service and
on expenditure on Ireland. He hoped the House of Lords would
not decide on its action till the Budget was in a final shape ; he
thought that Ministers wished it thrown out, because they dared
the Lords to do so. But its great danger was Socialism ; any form
of Protection was an evil, but Socialism was " the end of all " —
the negation of faith, of family, of property, of monarchy, of the
Empire. He himself must go a different road — that of public economy, of strengthening character, of preserving confidence — the
road by which the English had built up their strength and dominion.

Meanwhile, Committee and Report Stages of the Finance Bill
had been successfully passed in the House of Commons ; and on
November 2, the debate on third reading was opened by another
attempt of Mr. Austen Chamberlain to secure its rejection. A large
number of interesting and important speeches were delivered on this
occasion, the one by Mr. Philip Snowden being given below in
Extract 59 as a clear exposition on the part of an avowed Socialist
of the relations between Socialism and the Budget. At length, on
November 5, Mr. Chamberlain's amendment was rejected by 379
votes to 149, and the Bill was passed up to the House of Lords.

In the House of Lords, the fateful debate began on November 23 before a great crowd, including the King of Portugal. The
Earl of Crewe, in behalf of the Government, moved the second

reading without a speech. The Marquess of Lansdowne replied with a resolution, " that this House is not justified in giving its consent to this Bill until it has been submitted to the judgment of the country." Throughout the ensuing debate, the opponents of the Finance Bill, who constituted a large majority of the House, divided their attention between attacks upon the financial proposals and apologies for their forthcoming veto of a money bill and its reference to the people, whilst the minority — supporters of the Government — undertook to defend the principles of the Budget and to insinuate that such a veto on the part of the Lords would react eventually against the independence of their own House. From a large number of interesting speeches, delivered at this critical time, several extracts have been selected to illustrate various points of view. The Bishop of Bristol expressed an ecclesiastic's opposition to the Bill (*Extract 60*); Lord Sheffield expressed a Liberal lord's opinion of ecclesiastical opposition (*Extract 61*). How bitter was the feeling of many Conservatives against Mr. Churchill, and more particularly against Mr. Lloyd George, appeared in the speech of Lord Willoughby de Broke (*Extract 62*). Lord Revelstoke spoke against the Bill as the representative of the financial traditions of the Barings (*Extract 63*). The Bishop of Birmingham, in remarkable contrast with the Bishop of Bristol, defended the Budget proposals as urgently required for social needs (*Extract 64*). Lord Ribblesdale, though supporting the Bill, could not refrain from attacking Mr. Lloyd George (*Extract 65*). An extreme view of the havoc that might be done to the English Constitution by the adoption of the Budget was offered by the Duke of Marlborough (*Extract 66*). The Earl of Rosebery, always a delightful speaker, bewailed the lamentable Budget, but urged the Lords not to precipitate a constitutional conflict with the Commons, and declared that he could not vote either way (*Extract 67*). The attitude of the Liberal Government toward the Conservative majority in the House of Lords was well stated by Lord Morley of Blackburn on November 29 (*Extract 68*), and by the Earl of Crewe, in closing debate the following day (*Extract 69*). The Bill was defeated by 350 votes to 75, little excitement being manifested. Three bishops and the Archbishop of York supported the Bill; the Bishop of Lincoln voted against it.

The country took the rejection very quietly. But the Ministry was not slow in replying. The day after the rejection of the Budget by the Lords, the Commons reassembled, and Mr. Asquith, who was enthusiastically received by the Liberals and the Labourites, gave notice that he would move on the morrow a resolution " That the action of the House of Lords in refusing to pass into law the financial provision made by the House for the Service of the year is a breach of the Constitution and a usùrpation of the rights of the Commons." The next day, in a House crowded in every part, Mr. Asquith declared that " the House would be unworthy of its past and of those traditions of which it is the custodian and trustee " if it allowed any time to pass without showing that it would not brook this usurpation. In forcible language he dwelt upon the financial disorder created, and laid the whole responsibility on the Peers. He ridiculed the suggestion of a new Budget which the Lords could approve and announced that there would be a dissolution as early as possible, that the new House would assemble at such a time as would make it possible to provide " both retrospectively and prospectively " for the needs of the financial year ; and, should the Government be returned, its first duty would be to reimpose all the taxes and duties of the Finance Bill and to validate all past collections. Meanwhile the duties at the rates sanctioned might be deposited with the proper officials. He then dealt with the constitutional question, insisting that the Constitution was a matter of precedent and declaring that " the power of the purse " which had been used against the usurpation of the Crown would now be used against that of the Lords. He ridiculed the contention that the Bill was not a Finance Bill and declared that the right of the Lords to refer the Commons to the people was " the hollowest political cant." The real question was whether, when the Liberals were in power, the House of Lords should be omnipotent. The Ministry had not provoked the challenge, but welcomed it; they believed that the first principles of representative government were at stake, and would ask the House and the electorate to declare that the organ and voice of the free people of the country was to be found in the elected representatives of the people.

Mr. Balfour, replying for the Conservatives, ridiculed the resolution as an abstract motion, regretted its misrepresentation of constitutional history, and declared that such action by the Lords must be rare. He defended their right, enlarged on the need of a Second Chamber with substantial powers, and maintained that the Lords had not exceeded their functions. They had done their duty, and done it fearlessly.

Mr. A. Henderson, the Labour leader, gave the resolution hearty support on behalf of his party; and, after other remarks, the resolution was carried 349 to 134. The division was taken earlier than members had expected, or the Liberal majority would have been nearer 250.

Parliament was prorogued on December 3, 1909, and subsequently dissolved. And the country was called upon to determine indirectly what should be the fate of the Budget, of the House of Lords, and perhaps of social reform.

The National Liberal Federation denounced the Lords' action, and demanded the veto as its necessary sequel; the Parliamentary Committee of the Trade Union Congress denounced the House of Lords as a menace to political freedom, declared for the Unemployed Workmen Bill, old age pensions at sixty, and the removal of the pauper disqualification, poor law reform on the lines of the Minority Report,[1] free education from the primary school to the university, State payment of members and returning officers' expenses, the holding of general elections on one day, amendment of the Corrupt Practices Act, adult suffrage, redistribution of seats,

[1] Cf. supra, p. 190.

the abolition of plural voting and university representation, and the establishment of an eight hours' day. It urged Trade Unionists and other wage earners to work for the maintenance of the supremacy of the Commons and the abolition of the House of Lords. The Independent Labour Party, while agreeing in these aims, maintained its detachment from Liberalism.

There was little real development in the political situation between the close of the session in December, 1909, and the decision of the electors in the last fortnight of January, 1910. The controversy centred around the future of the House of Lords, the merits of the Budget, Tariff Reform, and social betterment. Mr. Lloyd George on January 1 stated that "the root trouble of our social system was the precariousness of living," and foreshadowed insurance against unemployment. Two days later, Mr. Asquith defended at length what his Government had done on the "outlying territory" of the unemployment problem by old age pensions and labour exchanges, and recommended the Budget as affording a complete and effectual alternative to Tariff Reform. The Unionists, on their side, exalted the Empire, the Navy, and Tariff Reform, condemned the Budget and the attacks on the House of Lords, and declared that any loss of power by the Lords might lead to Irish Home Rule.

The final results of the elections of January, 1910, were : Liberals, 274; Unionists, 272 (of whom 43 were Liberal Unionists); Labour party, 41 ; Nationalists, 71 ; Independent Nationalists, 11. Thus the Liberals could have a majority only by the aid of the Irish Nationalist as well as of the Labour party. The Nationalists, in the main, were hostile to the Budget, but finally agreed to support it in the hope that the Government would fulfil their pledge of abolishing the Lords' veto and so remove the great obstacle to Home Rule.

On February 21, the new Parliament was formally opened. After some time spent in discussing the Veto Resolutions,[1] consideration of the Finance Bill of 1909 was renewed on April 18. The

[1] Cf. infra, ch. ix.

measure was practically unaltered, save a few concessions to Ireland. The debate naturally traversed very familiar ground, so that its review is hardly necessary. It passed a second reading on April 25 and third reading two days later. The Lords accepted the verdict of the country as gracefully as possible, and the much-discussed Lloyd George Budget received the royal assent on April 29, 1910.

A few illustrative provisions of this Finance (1909–10) Act, 1910, constitute *Extract 70*. It should be borne in mind, however, that these provisions are qualified by a vast number of exceptions and explanations too long and too involved to incorporate in this volume.]

Extract 58

THE BUDGET SPEECH OF 1909

(Mr. David Lloyd George, Chancellor of the·Exchequer, Commons, April 29, 1909)

MR. LLOYD GEORGE[1]: . . . I come to the consideration of the social problems which are urgently pressing for solution — problems affecting the lives of the people. The solution of all these questions involves finance. What the Government have to ask themselves is this: Can the whole subject of further social reform be postponed until the increasing demands made upon the National Exchequer by the growth of armaments has ceased? Not merely *can* it be postponed, but ought it to be postponed? Is there the slightest hope that if we deferred consideration of the matter, we are likely within a generation to find any more favourable moment for attending to it? And we have to ask ourselves this further question: If we put off dealing with these social sores, are the evils which arise from them not likely to grow and to fester, until finally the loss which the country sustains will be infinitely greater than

[1] Parliamentary Debates, Commons, Fifth Series, vol. 4, col. 472 sqq.

anything it would have to bear in paying the cost of an immediate remedy. There are hundreds of thousands of men, women, and children in this country now enduring hardships for which the sternest judge would not hold them responsible ; hardships entirely due to circumstances over which they have not the slightest command ; the fluctuations and changes of trade — even of fashions ; ill-health and the premature breakdown or death of the breadwinner. Owing to events of this kind, all of them beyond human control — at least beyond the control of the victims — thousands, and I am not sure I should be wrong if I said millions, are precipitated into a condition of acute distress and poverty. How many people there are of this kind in this wealthy land the figures of old age pensions have thrown a very unpleasant light upon. Is it fair, is it just, is it humane, is it honourable, is it safe to subject such a multitude of our poor fellow-countrymen and countrywomen to continued endurance of these miseries until nations have learnt enough wisdom not to squander their resources on these huge machines for the destruction of human life ?

I have no doubt as to the answer which will be given to that question by a nation as rich in humanity as it is in store. Last year, whilst we were discussing the Old Age Pensions Bill, all parties in this House recognised fully and freely that once we had started on these lines the case for extension was irresistible. The Leader of the Opposition, in what I venture to regard as probably the most notable speeches he has delivered in this Parliament — I refer to his speech on the third reading of the Old Age Pensions Bill and the speech he delivered the other day on the question of unemployment — recognised quite boldly that whichever party was in power provision would have to be made in some shape or other for those who are out of work through no fault of their own and those who are incapacitated for work owing to physical causes for which they are not responsible. And there was at least one extension of the Old Age Pensions Act which received the unanimous assent of the House and which the Government were pressed to give not merely a Parliamentary but a Statutory pledge to execute. I refer to the proposal to extend the pension to the meritorious pauper. . . .

But still, all those who have given any thought and study to this question must realise that the inclusion of the septuagenarian pauper is but a very small part of the problem which awaits solution — a problem of human suffering which does not become any easier of solution by postponement. On the contrary, the longer we defer the task of grappling with it the more tangled and the more desperate it becomes. We are pledged, definitely pledged, by speeches from the Prime Minister given both in the House and outside, to supplementing our old age pensions proposals. . . .

What are the dominating causes of poverty amongst the industrial classes ? For the moment I do not refer to the poverty which is brought about by a man's own fault. I am only alluding to causes over which he has no control. Old age, premature breakdown in health and strength, the death of the breadwinner, and unemployment due either to the decay of industries and seasonable demands, or the fluctuations or depressions in trade. The distress caused by any or either of these causes is much more deserving of immediate attention than the case of a healthy and vigorous man of 65 years of age, who is able to pursue his daily vocation, and to earn without undue strain an income which is quite considerable enough to provide him and his wife with a comfortable subsistence.

When Bismarck was strengthening the foundations of the new German Empire one of the very first tasks he undertook was the organisation of a scheme which insured the German workmen and their families against the worst evils which ensue from these common accidents of life. And a superb scheme it is. It has saved an incalculable amount of human misery to hundreds of thousands and possibly millions of people who never deserved it.

Wherever I went in Germany, north or south, and whomever I met, whether it was an employer or a workman, a Conservative or a Liberal, a Socialist or a Trade Union leader — men of all ranks, sections and creeds of one accord joined in lauding the benefits which have been conferred upon Germany by this beneficent policy. Several wanted extensions, but there was not one who wanted to go back. The employers admitted that at first they did not quite like the new burdens it cast upon them, but they now fully realised the advantages which even they derived from the expenditure, for it had raised the standard of the workman throughout Germany. By removing that element of anxiety and worry from their lives it had improved their efficiency. Benefits which in the aggregate amounted to forty millions a year were being distributed under this plan. When I was there the Government were contemplating an enlargement of its operation which would extend its benefits to clerks and to the widows and orphans of the industrial population. They anticipated that when complete the total cost of the scheme would be fifty-three millions a year. . . .

In this country we have already provided for the aged over seventy. We have made pretty complete provision for accidents. All we have now left to do in order to put ourselves on a level with Germany — I hope our competition with Germany will not be in armaments alone — is to make some further provision for the sick, for the invalided, for widows and orphans. In a well-thought-out scheme, involving contributions from the classes directly concerned, the proportion borne by the State need not, in my judgment, be a very heavy one, and is well within the compass of our financial capacity without undue strain upon the resources of the country.

The Government are also pledged to deal on a comprehensive scale with the problem of unemployment. The pledges given by the Prime Minister on behalf of the Government are specific and repeated. I do not wish to encourage any false hopes. Nothing that a Government can do, at any rate with the present organisation of society, can prevent the fluctuations and the changes in trade and industry which produce unemployment. A trade decays, and the men who are engaged in it are thrown out of work. We have had an illustration within the last few days, to which Lord Rosebery has so opportunely called our attention, in the privation suffered by the horse cabdriver, owing to the substitution of mechanical for horse traction. That is only one case out of many constantly happening in every country. Then there are the fluctuations of business which at one moment fill a workshop with orders which even overtime cannot cope with, and at another moment leave the same workshops with rusting machinery for lack of something to do. Trade has its currents, and its tides, and its storms, and its calms, like the sea, which seem to be almost just as little under human control, or, at any rate, just as little under the control of the victims of these changes, and to say that you can establish by any system an absolute equilibrium in the trade and concerns of the country is to make a promise which no man of intelligence would ever undertake to honour. You might as well promise to flatten out the Atlantic Ocean. But still, it is poor seamanship that puts out to sea without recognising its restlessness, and the changefulness of the weather, and the perils and suffering thus produced. These perils of trade depression come at regular intervals, and every time they arrive they bring with them an enormous amount of distress. It is the business of statesmanship to recognise that fact and to address itself with courage and resolution to provide against it. . . .

Insurance against Unemployment

Any insurance scheme . . . must necessarily require contribu tions from those engaged in the insured trades both as employer and employed; but we recognise the necessity of meeting these contributions by a State grant and guarantee. We cannot, of course, attempt to pass the necessary Bill to establish unemployment insurance during the present Session. But the postponement will not involve any real delay, for the establishment of labour exchanges is a necessary preliminary to the work of insurance, and this will occupy time which may also be advantageously employed in consulting the various interests upon the details of the scheme and in co-ordinating its financial provisions with the machinery of invalidity and other forms of insurance.

Development Scheme

So much for the provision which we hope to be able to make for those who, under the changing conditions which are inevitable in trade and commerce, are temporarily thrown out of employment. We do not put this forward as a complete or an adequate remedy for all the evils of unemployment, and we do not contend that when this insurance scheme has been set up and financed the State has thereby done all in its power to help towards solving the problem. After all, it is infinitely better, in the interests both of the community and of the unemployed themselves, that the latter should be engaged on remunerative work, than that they should be drawing an allowance from the most skilfully-contrived system of insurance. This country is small — I suppose it is the smallest great country in the world — but we have by no means exhausted its possibilities for healthy and productive employment. It is no part of the function of a Government to create work ; but it is an essential part of its business to see that the people are equipped to make the best of their own country, are permitted to make the best of their own country, and, if necessary, are helped to make the best of their own country. [Cheers.] . . . A State can and ought to take a longer view and a wider view of its investments than individuals. The resettlement of deserted and impoverished parts of its own territories may not bring to its coffers a direct return which would reimburse it fully for its expenditure ; but the indirect enrichment of its resources more than compensates it for any apparent and immediate loss. The individual can rarely afford to wait, a State can ; the individual must judge of the success of his enterprise by the testimony given for it by his bank book ; a State keeps many ledgers, not all in ink, and when we wish to judge of the advantage derived by a country from a costly experiment we must examine all those books before we venture to pronounce judgment. . . .

Afforestation

This brings me straight to the question of afforestation. There is a very general agreement that some steps should be taken in the direction, I will not say of afforesting, but of reafforesting the waste lands of this country. Here, again, we are far behind every other civilised country in the world. I have figures here on this point which are very interesting. In Germany, for instance, out of a total area of 133,000,000 acres, 34,000,000, or nearly 26 per cent, are wooded; in France, out of 130,000,000 acres, 17 per cent; even in a small and densely-populated country such as Belgium 1,260,000 acres are wooded, or 17 per cent, out of a total area of 7,280,000 acres. Again, in the Netherlands and Denmark, out of total areas of 8,000,000 and 9,500,000 acres respectively, over 600,000 acres, or between 7 and 8 per cent, are wooded. In the United Kingdom, on the other hand, out of 77,000,000 acres, only 3,000,000, or 4 per cent, are under wood.

Sir Herbert Maxwell, who has made a study of this question for a good many years, and whose moderation of statement is beyond challenge, estimates that, in 1906, "£8,000,000 were paid annually in salaries for the administration, formation and preservation of German Forests, representing the maintenance of about 200,000 families or about 1,000,000 souls," and that, "in working up the raw material yielded by the forests, wages were earned annually to the amount of £30,000,000 sterling, maintaining about 600,000 families, or 3,000,000 souls."

Anyone who will take the trouble to search out the Census Returns will find out that the number of people directly employed in forest work in this country is only 16,000. And yet the soil and the climate of this country are just as well adapted for the growth of marketable trees as that of the States of Germany. . . .

Encouragement of Agriculture

. . . We are not getting out of the land anything like what it is capable of endowing us with. Of the enormous quantity of agricultural and dairy produce and fruit, and of the timber which is imported into this country, a considerable portion could be raised on our own lands. There hon. Members opposite and ourselves will agree. The only difference is as to the remedy. In our opinion, the remedy which they suggest would make food costlier and more inaccessible for the people ; the remedies which we propose, on the other hand, would make food more abundant, better, and cheaper. What is it we propose ? — and, let the Committee observe, I am only dealing with that part of the problem which affects finance.

National Development Grant

I will tell the House therefore, briefly, what I propose doing in regard to this and all kindred matters I have dwelt upon. There is a certain amount of money — not very much — spent in this country in a spasmodic kind of way on what I call the work of national development — in light railways, in harbours, in indirect but very meagre assistance to agriculture. I propose to gather all these grants together into one Development Grant, and to put in this year an additional sum of £200,000. Legislation will have to be introduced, and I will then explain the methods of administration and the objects in greater detail, but the grant will be utilised in the promoting of schemes which have for their purpose the development of the resources of the country. It will include such objects as the institution of schools of forestry, the purchase and preparation of land for afforestation, the setting up of a number of experimental forests on a large scale, expenditure upon scientific research in the interests of agriculture, experimental farms, the improvement of stock — as to which there have been a great many demands from people engaged in agriculture, the equipment of

agencies for disseminating agricultural instruction, the encouragement and promotion of co-operation, the improvement of rural
transport so as to make markets more accessible, the facilitation
of all well-considered schemes and measures for attracting labour
back to the land by small holdings or reclamation of wastes. Every
acre of land brought into cultivation, every acre of cultivated land
brought into a higher state of cultivation, means more labour of a
healthy and productive character. It means more abundant food
— cheaper and better food for the people. . . .

Principles of Taxation

Now what are the principles upon which I intend to proceed in
getting . . . taxes? The first principal on which I base my financial proposals is this — that taxation which I suggest should be imposed, while yielding in the present year not more than sufficient
to meet this year's requirements, should be of such a character
that it will produce enough revenue in the second year to cover
the whole of our estimated liabilities for that year. And, moreover, that it will be of such an expansive character as to grow
with the growing demand of the social programme which I have
sketched without involving the necessity for imposing fresh taxation in addition to what I am asking Parliament to sanction at the
present time. The second principle on which I base my proposals
is that the taxes should be of such a character as not to inflict any
injury on that trade or commerce which constitutes the sources of
our wealth.

My third principle is this, that all classes of the community in
this financial emergency ought to be called upon to contribute.
I have never been able to accept the theory which I have seen
advanced that you ought to draw a hard-and-fast line at definite
incomes and say that no person under a certain figure should be
expected to contribute a penny towards the burden of the good
government of the country. In my judgment all should be called

upon to bear their share. No voluntary association, religious or philanthropic or provident, has ever been run on the principle of exempting any section of its membership from subscription. They all contribute, even to the widow's mite. It is considered not merely the duty, but the privilege and 'pride of all to share in the common burden, and the sacrifice is as widely distributed as is the responsibility and the profit. At the same time, when you come to consider whether the bulk of the taxation is to be raised by direct or indirect means, I must point out at this stage — I shall have a little more to say on this subject later on — that the industrial classes, in my judgment, upon a close examination of their contributions to local and Imperial finance, are paying more in proportion to their incomes than those who are better off. Their proportion to local finances especially is heavier, because, although nominally the rates are not paid by them, as everyone knows, they are really. For that reason the burden at the present moment of new taxation bears much more heavily in proportion to their income on that class than it does upon the wealthier and better-to-do classes.

New Taxation — Motor Cars

I now come — and I trust that the Committee will not think that I have delayed too long — to the most interesting and the most difficult part of my task, the explanation of the various proposals for fresh taxation which I have to lay before them. I think it will be to the convenience of the Committee if I deal first with motor cars. . . .

I propose to substitute . . . a new and increased scale, with graduations, which will come into force next January for the whole of the United Kingdom, and I have decided to base the scale on the power of the cars and not on the weight. The horse-power will be determined in accordance with regulations made by the Treasury, and in the case of petrol cars with reference to the bore of the cylinders. . . .

It will be seen that the tax rises rapidly when we get to cars over 40 horse-power — a provision with which I think the Committee will not quarrel. Doctors' cars I propose to charge at one-half these rates. Motor cycles I would charge at the uniform rate of £1. . . .

One of the chief reasons for imposing additional taxation on motor cars is the fact that the increase in their numbers necessitates a reorganisation of our main-road system, and it will be obvious that, were I to confine taxation to a mere re-adjustment of the scale of licence duties, the burden would be imposed with absolutely no relation to the extent that the car might use the roads. Some cars are out four or five hours a day all the year round, others are used but rarely, and I believe that, were I to obtain anything like adequate contribution from motor cars entirely by direct taxation, I might hinder to some extent the development of the motor industry by discouraging persons from keeping a motor, or an additional motor, should they only want it for occasional use. I, therefore, propose to put a tax of 3d. per gallon on all petrol used for motor vehicles. . . .

Direct Taxation

Now I come to my direct taxation. It must be obvious that in meeting a large deficit of this kind I should be exceedingly unwise if I were to trust to speculative or fancy taxes. I therefore propose, first of all, to raise more money out of the income tax and estate duties. Income tax in this country only begins when the margin of necessity has been crossed and the domain of comfort and even of gentility has been reached. A man who enjoys an income of over £3 a week need not stint himself or his family of reasonable food or of clothes and shelter. There may be an exception in the case of a man with a family, whose gentility is part of his stock in trade or the uniform of his craft. Then, I agree, often things go hard.

Then when you come to estate duties, what a man bequeaths, after all, represents what is left after he has provided for all his own wants in life. Beyond a certain figure it also represents all that is essential to keep his family in the necessaries of life. The figure which the experience of seventy years has sanctified as being that which divides sufficiency from gentility is £150 to £160 a year. A capital sum that would, if invested in safe securities, provide anything over that sum ought to be placed in a different category from any sum which is below that figure.

There is one observation which is common to income tax and the death duties, more especially with the higher scales. What is it that has enabled the fortunate possessors of these incomes and these fortunes to amass the wealth they enjoy or bequeath? The security insured for property by the agency of the State, the guaranteed immunity from the risks and destruction of war, insured by our natural advantages and our defensive forces. This is an essential element even now in the credit of the country; and, in the past, it means that we were accumulating great wealth in this land, when the industrial enterprises of less fortunately situated countries were not merely at a standstill, but their resources were being ravaged and destroyed by the havoc of war. What, more, is accountable for this growth of wealth? The spread of intelligence amongst the masses of the people, the improvements in sanitation and in the general condition of the people. These have all contributed towards the efficiency of the people, even as wealth-producing machines. Take, for instance, such legislation as the Education Acts and the Public Health Acts; they have cost much money, but they have made infinitely more. That is true of all legislation which improves the conditions of life of the people. An educated, well-fed, well-clothed, well-housed people invariably leads to the growth of a numerous well-to-do class. If property were to grudge a substantial contribution towards proposals which insure the security which is one of the essential conditions of its existence, or towards keeping from poverty and privation the old people whose lives of industry and toil have either created that wealth or made it productive, then property would be not only shabby but short-sighted.

Income Tax

. . . Notwithstanding the relief given by the Finance Act of 1907, the burden of the income tax upon earnings is still disproportionately heavy. While, therefore, I propose to raise the general rate at which the tax is calculated, I propose that the rates upon earned income in the case of persons whose total income does not exceed £3000 should remain as at present, namely, 9d. in the pound up to £2000, and 1s. in the pound between £2000 and £3000. In respect of all other incomes now liable to the 1s. rate I propose to raise the rate from 1s. to 1s. 2d.

Abatement on Children

In the case of incomes not exceeding £500, the pressure of the tax, notwithstanding the abatements at present allowed, is sorely felt by taxpayers who have growing families to support, and although a comparatively trifling additional burthen will be imposed upon them by the increased rate, since the aggregate income of this class is to the extent of at least four-fifths exclusively earned income, I think that even upon the present basis they have a strong claim to further relief. . . . And I propose that for all incomes under £500, in addition to the existing abatements, there shall be allowed from the income in respect of which the tax is paid a special abatement of £10 for every child under the age of 16 years. . . .

Income (super) tax

The imposition of a super-tax, however, upon large incomes on the lines suggested by the Select Committee of 1906 is a practicable proposition, and it is upon this basis that I intend to proceed.

Such a super-tax might take the form of . . . a uniform tax not upon the total income, but upon the amount only by which the income exceeded a certain fixed amount which would naturally, but need not necessarily, be the amount of the minimum income which attracts the tax. We might begin, say, at £3000, and levy the new tax upon all income in excess of £3000, or at £5000, and levy the tax upon income in excess of £5000. In the former case some 25,000 assessments would be required, in the latter only 10,000 — from the point of view of administration a very strong argument in favour of the adoption of the higher figure, at any rate in the first instance. . . . Therefore I propose to limit the tax to incomes exceeding £5000, and to levy it upon the amount by which such incomes exceed £3000, and at the rate of 6d. in the pound upon the amount of such excess. An income of £5001 will thus pay in super-tax 6d. in the pound on £2001. . . . Assessments to the new tax will be based upon the Returns of total income from all sources, which will be required from persons assessable. The machinery will be, in the main, independent of the machinery of the existing income tax, but the assessments will be made by the special Commissioners appointed under the Income Tax Acts, and assessable income will be determined according to the rules laid down in the income tax schedules. . . .

My last proposal relating to the income tax is the restriction of the exemptions and abatements to persons resident in the United Kingdom. . . .

Death Duties

The proposals I have to make with regard to the death duties are of a very simple character. The great reconstruction of these duties in 1894, which will always be associated with the name of Sir William Harcourt, has given us a scheme of taxation which is at once logical and self-consistent as a system, and a revenue-producing machine of very high efficiency. Apart, therefore, from one or two minor changes in the law, which experience has shown to be desirable, I intend to confine my attention to adjusting the rates with a view to increasing the yield without altering the basis on which the duties are levied. . . .

Stamp Duties

Under the head of stamp duties I propose to increase the duty upon conveyances on sale from 10s. to 20s. per cent, an exemption from the increased rate being made in favour of conveyances of stock or marketable securities which, by reason of the greater frequency with which they change hands, in comparison with other kinds of property, bear a disproportionate burthen under the present uniform scale. The greater part of the additional revenue under this head will be derived from transfers of real property. . . .

Licences

[A new, and, on the whole, higher, scale of licencing duties advocated.]

Taxation of Land

. . . The first conviction that is borne in upon the Chancellor of the Exchequer who examines land as a subject for taxation is this : that in order to do justice he must draw a broad distinction between land whose value is purely agricultural in its character and composition, and land which has a special value attached to it, owing either to the fact of its covering marketable mineral deposits or because of its proximity to any concentration of people. Agricultural land has not, during the past twenty or thirty years, appreciated in value in this country. In some parts it has probably gone down. I know parts of the country where the value has gone up. But there has been an enormous increase in the value of urban land and of mineral property. And a still more important and relevant consideration in examining the respective merits of these two or three classes of claimants to taxation is this : the growth in the value, more especially of urban sites, is due to no expenditure of capital or thought on the part of the ground owner, but entirely owing to the energy and the enterprise of the community. . . .

Still worse, the urban landowner is freed in practice from the ordinary social obligations which are acknowledged by every agricultural landowner towards those whose labour makes their wealth. . . . The rural landowner has the obligation to provide buildings and keep them in repair. The urban landowner, as a rule, has neither of these two obligations. There is that essential difference between the two. The urban landlord and the mineral royalty owner are invariably rack-renters. They extort the highest and the heaviest ground rent or royalty they can obtain on the sternest commercial principles. They are never restrained by that sense of personal relationship with their tenants which exercises such a beneficent and moderating influence upon the very same landlord in his dealings with his agricultural tenants. And the distinction is not confined merely to the rent. Take the conditions of the tenancy. I am not here to defend many of the terms which are included in many an agricultural agreement for tenancy. I think many of them are oppressive, irritating, and stupid. But compared with the conditions imposed upon either a colliery owner or upon a town lessee they are the very climax of generosity. Take this case — and it is not by any means irrelevant to the proposals which I shall have to submit to the Committee later on. What agricultural landlord in this country would ever think of letting his farm for a term of years on condition, first of all, that the tenant should pay the most extortionate rent that he could possibly secure in the market, three, or four, or even five times the real value of the soil ; that the tenant should then be compelled to build a house of a certain size and at a certain cost, and in a certain way, and that at the end of the term he, or rather his representatives, should hand that house over in good tenantable repair free from encumbrances to the representatives of the ground owner who has not spent a penny upon constructing it, and who has received during the whole term of lease the highest rent which he could possibly screw in respect of the site ? Why, there is not a landlord in Great Britain who would ever dream of imposing such outrageous conditions upon his tenant. And yet these are the conditions which are imposed every day in respect of urban sites ; imposed upon tradesmen who have no choice in the matter ; imposed upon professional men and business men who have got to live somewhere within reasonable distance of their offices ; imposed even on workmen building a house for themselves, paying for it by monthly instalments out of their wages for thirty years purely in order to be within reasonable distance of the factory or mine or workshop at which they are earning a living. . . .

My present proposals are proposals both for taxation and for valuation. Although very moderate in character, they will produce an appreciable revenue in the present year and more in future years. The proposals are three in number.

Unearned Increment

First, it is proposed to levy a tax on the increment of value accruing to land from the enterprise of the community or the landowner's neighbours. . . . The valuations upon the difference between which the tax will be chargeable will be valuations of the land itself — apart from buildings and other improvements — and of this difference, the strictly unearned increment, we propose to take one-fifth, or 20 per cent, for the State. . . .

Duty on Undeveloped Land

The second proposal relating to land is the imposition of a tax on the capital value of all land which is nôt used to the best advantage. The owner of valuable land which is required or likely in the near future to be required for building purposes, who contents himself with an income therefrom wholly incommensurate with the capital value of the land in the hope of recouping himself ultimately in the shape of an increased price, is in a similar position to the investor in securities who re-invests the greater part of his dividends; but while the latter is required to pay income tax both upon the portion of the dividends enjoyed and also upon the portion re-invested, the former escapes taxation upon his accumulating capital altogether, and this, although the latter by his self-denial is increasing the wealth of the community, while the former, by withholding from the market land which is required for housing or industry, is creating a speculative inflation of values which is socially mischievous.

We propose to redress this anomaly by charging an annual duty of ½d. in the pound on the capital value of undeveloped land. The same principle applies to ungotten minerals, which we propose similarly to tax at ½d. in the pound, calculated upon the price which the mining rights might be expected to realise if sold in open market at the date of valuation. The tax on undeveloped land will be charged upon unbuilt-on land only, and . . . all land having a purely agricultural value will be exempt.

Further exemptions will be made in favour of gardens and pleasure grounds not exceeding an acre in extent, and parks, gardens, and open spaces which are open to the public as of right, or to which reasonable access is granted to the public, where that access is recognised by the Commissioners of Inland Revenue as contributing to the amenity of the locality. Where undeveloped land forms part of a settled estate, provision will be made to enable a limited owner who has not the full enjoyment of the land to charge the duty upon the corpus of the property. The valuation upon which the tax will be charged will be the value of land as a cleared site. . . .

Reversion Duty

My third proposal under the head of land is a 10 per cent reversion duty upon any benefit accruing to a lessor from the determination of a lease, the value of the benefit to be taken to be the amount (if any) by which the total value of the land at the time the lease falls in exceeds the value of the consideration for the grant of the lease, due regard being had, however, for the case of the reversioner whose interest is less than a freehold. . . .

Valuation of Real Property

These proposals necessarily involve a complete reconstruction of the method of valuing property. The existing taxes upon real property are levied upon the annual value of such property as a whole without distinguishing between the value which resides in the land itself and that which has been added to it by the enterprise of the owner in erecting buildings or effecting other improvements. . . .

Indirect Taxation

I am not going at this late hour to enter into any discussion of the principles which ought to guide a Finance Minister in the imposition of indirect taxation. But one thing I am sure will be accepted by every Member of this House, and that is that we ought at any rate to avoid taxes on the necessaries of life. I referred some time ago, in the course of a discussion in this House, to the old age pension officers' reports. There was one thing in those reports which struck me very forcibly, and that was that they all reported that the poorer the people they had to deal with, the more was their food confined to bread and tea, and of the price of that tea, which of course was of the poorest quality, half goes to the tax gatherer. That is always the worst of indirect taxation on the people. The poorer they are the more heavily the tax falls upon them. Tea and sugar are necessaries of life, and I think that the rich man who would wish to spare his own pocket at the expense of the bare pockets of the poor is a very shabby rich man indeed, and therefore I am sure that I carry with me the assent of even the classes upon whom I am putting very heavy burdens, that when we come to indirect taxes, at any rate those two essentials of life ought to be exempt.

There are three other possible sources — beer, spirits, and tobacco. . . . [No increase on beer, but an estimated amount of £1,600,000 to be raised by increased taxes on spirits.] . . .

Increase of Tobacco Duty

I have still nearly two millions more to find, and for this I must turn to tobacco — from a fiscal point of view, a much healthier source of revenue. The present rate of duty on unmanufactured tobacco containing 10 per cent or more of moisture is 3s. a pound, with equivalent additions to the rates for cigars, cigarettes, and manufactured tobacco. . . .

Conclusion

I have to thank the House for the very great indulgence which they have extended to me and for the patience with which they have listened to me. My task has been an extraordinarily difficult one. It has been as disagreeable a task as could well have been allotted to any Minister of the Crown. But there is one element of supreme satisfaction in it. That is to be found in contemplating the objects for which these new imposts have been created. The money thus raised is to be expended first of all in insuring the inviolability of our shores. It has also been raised in order not merely to relieve but to prevent unmerited distress within those shores. It is essential that we should make every necessary provision for the defence of our country. But surely it is equally imperative that we should make it a country even better worth defending for all and by all. And it is the fact that this expenditure is for both those purposes that alone could justify the Government. I am told that no Chancellor of the Exchequer has ever been called on to impose such heavy taxes in a time of peace. This, Mr. Emmott, is a War Budget. It is for raising money to wage implacable warfare against poverty and squalidness. I cannot help hoping and believing that before this generation has passed away we shall have advanced a great step towards that good time when poverty and wretchedness and human degradation which always follow in its camp will be as remote to the people of this country as the wolves which once infested its forests.

Extract 59

A SOCIALIST'S VIEW OF THE BUDGET

(Mr. Philip Snowden, Commons, November 2, 1909)

MR. SNOWDEN [1] : . . . I have followed, as far as I have been able, the speeches and arguments advanced in the country in opposition to these proposals, and, so far as I can judge, there have been not many objections but only one objection to this Bill, and that one has been that the Bill is Socialism, or, in the words of Lord Rosebery, it " is the end of all things — religion, property, and family life." . . . Now, I shall confine my remarks to dealing with the objection that this Budget Bill is Socialism. I may begin by attempting to define what we, who profess to be Socialists, mean by Socialism. The Attorney-General was right in saying that Socialism means State action, but that is not exactly the definition of Socialism which was given by the right hon. Gentleman the Leader of the Opposition at Birmingham about twelve months ago. If I may be permitted I will read the right hon. Gentleman's words, because they admirably serve my purpose. The Leader of the Opposition — speaking, I believe, at the opening of that curious anachronism, a Tory labour club, about twelve months ago, a club which I believe has since found its way into the Bankruptcy Court — gave this as his definition of Socialism :

It seems to me there is no difficulty or ambiguity about the subject at all. Socialism has one meaning, and one meaning only. Socialism means, and can mean nothing else, that the community or the State is to take all the means of production into its own hands, that private enterprise and private property are to come to an end, and all that private enterprise and private property carry with them. That is Socialism, and nothing else is Socialism. Social reform —

and I ask here the attention of the House to the distinction which the right hon. Gentleman attempted to draw between Socialism

[1] Parliamentary Debates, Commons, Fifth Series, vol. 12, col 1681 sqq.

and Social Reform — I shall, later on, endeavour to show that there is really no distinction where the right hon. Gentleman attempts to establish it. The right hon. Gentleman goes on to draw a distinction between Socialism and Social Reform, and he says :

Social reform is when the State, based upon private enterprise, recognising that the best productive results can only be obtained by respect of private property and encouraging private enterprise, asks them to contribute towards great national, social, and public objects. That is social reform.

I accepted the statement made by the Attorney-General that Socialism is State action. But it is something more than that. It is State ownership of the means of producing and distributing wealth. There may be State action which is not connected with the ownership, control, and management of industry. We as Socialists recognise that. We recognise, too, the existence of conditions which everybody deplores, and we recognise further that the cause of those conditions is to be found in the monopoly of the means of production and distribution — at any rate in the monopoly of land and capital. Our purpose is to substitute for private ownership of land and capital public ownership and control of both. But that is not a thing which can be accomplished at once. We realise that. Meanwhile we are anxious to do something towards bringing it about. The right hon. Gentleman defines Socialism as the State ownership of the means of producing and distributing wealth. May I say I do not accept that ? The definition by Socialists of Socialism is not the State ownership of land and capital. That is only a condition of Socialism or a means of Socialism. Socialism means that all socially created wealth shall be owned by the community, and that its distribution shall be directed by the community for the good of the community. The national ownership of land and capital is a necessary condition to attaining a state of things like that. We recognise that we cannot reach our goal under the present system and at once, and we are anxious, therefore, in the meantime, to divert as much as we can, and as rapidly as we can, socially created wealth for the purpose of dealing with industrial and social evils which are the result of the private ownership of land and capital. Therefore, although the taxation of socially created wealth may not be Socialism in itself, it is a step towards Socialism, and therefore, in so far as this Budget taxes socially created wealth for social purposes, it is Socialistic. But it is not Socialism.

Now I come to the point whether there is anything new or novel in the proposals of this Budget. The Attorney-General, no doubt, described certain proposals as being novel, but I have not been able to discover any novelty whatever in any one of the proposals of the Finance Bill. To my mind there is nothing new in it. It is too late in the day to begin to talk about the beginning of Socialism ; as a matter of fact we are well on the road to Socialism, and all the legislation of the nineteenth century has been nothing more or less than an effort on the part of this House to deal with the evils resulting from the private ownership of land and capital. Throughout the whole of the nineteenth century we have been moving in our legislation towards Socialism — first of all by constantly increasing legal restrictions in the free and individual use of land and capital. Our public health legislation is an illustration of that. If you require further illustration there is the Factory legislation. There is no difference whatever in the economic effect upon private monopoly of the Workmen's Compensation Act and the factory legislation and public health legislation, and the direct taxation upon the profits on monopoly which has been acted upon by all parties in the State.

The second way in which we are moving towards Socialism has been the gradual supplementing of private voluntary charities by public organisations for dealing with the poorest parts of our population. That is accepted by the party opposite and, indeed, by every party in the House, and the Old Age Pensions Act is an illustration of that. Then we have been trying to raise the condition of the poorest part of the population by such measures as the Education Act. What makes a measure of that kind all the more Socialistic is that to a very great extent it is provided for by taxation on socially created wealth.

The third way in which we have moved towards Socialism is on the lines of the proposals of this Bill by constantly increasing the taxation on rent, interest, and profits for the purpose of dealing with the results of the private ownership of land. Your Income Tax is an illustration of that.

The fourth way, and the most Socialistic of all, is the gradual supplanting of private enterprise and private institutions by public initiative and public organisations. You have that illustrated in our magnificent and highly successful municipal and State undertakings.

Now, one of the four ways in which we have been moving towards Socialism is by increasing taxation upon rent, interest, and profits, which are recognised even by the right hon. Gentleman himself as being Socialistically created. Is there anything novel in any one of these things? What are Land Taxes? Land taxation simply proposes to tax socially created wealth for social purposes. That is nothing new. It is one of the difficulties of attempting to apply a principle partially. If you attempt so to apply a principle, you are certain to create an apparent injustice. I have a certain amount of sympathy with those who urge that it is not fair to discriminate between social increment on land and social increment in other forms. That is an objection which cannot be urged against Socialism. It can be urged only against hon. Gentlemen opposite who do draw a distinct line about land and capital. We do not make any such distinction, and it must be recognised that we are not in a position to put our ideas in a Finance Bill. We have to take what we can get, but if we had the power of saying in what way the revenue of the country is to be raised, I am quite certain no Socialist Chancellor of the Exchequer would distinguish between social increment of land and social increment in regard to the taxes which would ordinarily fall upon the community.

We support the land taxation proposals, not because we think they do everything or go far enough — we support them because they are as much as we can get at present, but when a Chancellor of the Exchequer comes forward to propose and apply taxation of unearned increment to any other form of property, he will find that we shall be quite as hearty in our support as we are in the support which we have given to the Land Taxes in the Budget. In regard to the Income Tax proposals, I remember the right hon. Gentleman himself in Committee when we began to discuss the Income Tax part of the Bill expressed his relief that at last we were coming to legitimate finance. What is Income Tax? It is the taxation of socially created wealth, and the fact that the Government are imposing in this Finance Bill a Super-tax is nothing new. It is only a further graduation of the Income Tax. The graduation below £700 was, of course, adopted in order very roughly to make a man contribute more because of his greater capacity, and the Super-tax is nothing more than an extension of this principle. . . .

There is nothing new or novel in the proposals of this Bill. The Income Tax is not novel, the Land Taxes are not novel, the Estate Duties are certainly not novel. It is Socialistic in part, but it is not Socialistic in other parts. I have already referred to the Tobacco Duty. That is not Socialistic because the Tobacco Tax is indirect taxation, it is not taxation on social wealth, and it is taking from a very needy class of the community a great deal more than they can afford to pay.

We do not expect to have, of course, a measure which is consistently Socialistic from men who are not Socialists. For a long time to come we expect that the legislation which will be introduced even by a Government anxious to promote reform will be of an inconsistent character. It will be Socialistic partly and anti-Socialistic in its other parts. This Budget is neither complete Socialism nor is it revolution. Why, it is such a slight movement of the wheel as to be hardly perceptible, and I will tell hon. Members above the gangway what it is: It is a preventive of revolution. What the right hon. Gentleman calls social reform is only a preventive of revolution. Do hon. Members above the gangway think that such a state of things as exists in this country to-day can be indefinitely prolonged? We have had forty years of elementary education. The masses of the people have been taught to read. Reading has made them think, has made them feel more acutely. They are not going to be content forever to be hewers of wood and drawers of water. The unemployed are not going to continue to walk the streets of our great cities and see their despair and poverty mocked by the evidences before their eyes of ostentatious wealth. Something is going to be done by this Parliament to remove these great inequalities of poverty and wealth, ignorance and culture, want and luxury, and we welcome this Bill because it is a very moderate beginning to deal with questions like that. We welcome the proposals to which I have referred, because they begin to apply, in a small way, proposals which we on these benches have been asserting for many years. We shall support the third reading of this Bill.

I have only one word more to say. I want to refer to the alternative which was put forward by the right hon. Gentleman who moved the rejection of the Bill. I said at the beginning of my remarks that we who are Socialists are opposed to Tariff Reform. We are sometimes told by hon. Members that we are inconsistent in being Trade Unionists for the protection of our trades and in opposing a duty on articles coming from foreign countries. There is nothing inconsistent in that. I will tell why we are opposed to Protection in the way of import duties. So long as you have a monopoly of land and of capital any import duty can only have one result, and that result is to increase the rent of the landlord or to increase the property of the capitalist. It cannot possibly benefit the workman. Where you have competition in employment there is always a tendency for wages to be forced down, and competition will prevent the wages rising, and no system of reform, as long as you have a monopoly of land and capital, can, under such a system, be depended upon to benefit the working classes.

An hon. Member talked of taxing the foreigner. There have been in the last two or three months elections in Germany; those elections have been fought almost exclusively upon the question of taxation. The Socialists to a man in Germany are opposed to taxation on imports. They are Free Traders, and they are opposed to Protection because of their painful experience of it. May I put this question, and possibly some Member who follows me may deal with it? If it is possible to raise a revenue by taxing the foreigner, why did not Germany during this year adopt the practice of taxing the foreigner? It required to raise something like £26,000,000 of taxation, and every penny of it has been raised by internal taxation. No, if I cared to give candid advice and useful information to hon. Members above the gangway in view of the propaganda work which it will be necessary to do during an election campaign, I would say to them, "Do not talk to the workingmen of this country nonsense like that. You are depreciating their intelligence, you are insulting them, you are not playing the game of politics to your own advantage." I know the working people of this country, I belong to them, I have lived with them, and I know their capacity of thinking. I know their capacity of reason, and why I have faith in them is because of it. I think if you appeal to that intelligence it will respond. For these reasons we are going to support the third reading of this Bill, which will leave this House in two or three days backed up by an overwhelming vote. What will happen in another place I do not know, but if the worst comes to the worst, and if it be necessary that we should go to the country on this question, I can assure the Government that those who sit on these benches and the party which we represent outside will not be amongst the least of the earnest and enthusiastic supporters of that part of the Bill which I commend to the House.

Extract 60

ECCLESIASTICAL OPPOSITION TO THE BUDGET

(*Bishop of Bristol, Lords, November 22, 1909*)

THE LORD BISHOP OF BRISTOL [1]: . . . I have been told that a Bishop should not take part in this debate, because the question is one of mere party strife. If it were, I should certainly not think of taking any part in it. But it is very much more than that. We are told that the fortunes of this House, and the fortunes of the nation and of the people depend upon the issue. If that be so, there is no body of men in this House more called upon to take part in a debate of this kind — if the fortunes of the House depend upon the issue of this debate — than the occupants of the Episcopal Benches. For we are the only representatives of the ancient constitutional method of entry into this House, namely, that of careful selection on the part of the Sovereign and of all the people to a certain office involving a seat in the House of Lords. Careful selection by the King goes on still, and by all the people, because the appointed representative of all the people is the Prime Minister. We, therefore, are the only body which keep up the ancient practice. Further than that, we represent a very much older tenure than that of the oldest physical hereditary Peer in this House. The earliest tenure that I can trace of physical heredity is 754 years old, and admirably that Earldom is filled to-day. But there are three persons actually sitting on these Benches now whose tenure is 550 years older than that, and there are no fewer than ten other members on these Benches whose tenure is from 450 to 550 years older than the oldest of the physical hereditary Peers, we having a spiritual heredity. I maintain, therefore, that if there is any question of the honour of this House, from these Benches at least some words should come in support of this House. . . .

[1] Parliamentary Debates, Lords, Fifth Series, vol. 4, col. 767–768.

. . . All of your Lordships know a great deal about the condition of the poorest classes in society, from what you call the lowest to what may be called the highest in the social scale. As a matter of fact it is not the business of any one of your Lordships, except those of us here on these [Episcopal] Benches, to know, and to know intimately, not the conditions only, but the persons of all classes in the social scale in our respective dioceses; and I claim that there are no men sitting in this House who know so completely, from one end of the social scale to the other, the conditions, the needs, the wants, and the demands of every class of the community as we do. We are obliged to know, especially those of us who represent a great city, as I do, the terrible conditions of the very poor. We are obliged to know the great want of employment that affects men who can do excellent work. We are obliged to know the conditions of the artisan, of the shopkeeper, and of the professional classes, and even higher than that. Many of us have to know the condition of the very great capitalists who perhaps farm a little for their own amusement, but who have the whole of their income to spend; and we know, and know intimately, some large landowners who, far from having the whole of their income to spend, have a very narrow margin indeed. All this we have to know intimately as our official business; and although the noble and learned Lord took credit to the Government for having passed certain ameliorating measures, I suppose it was this House that passed them. And it will always be so — when direct measures for the benefit of the very poor are brought forward, this House will give them no niggardly support. . . .

. . . I see the ultimate result of these proposals now brought before us : a dull monotonous level of poverty without any redeeming points at all. We all of us know the familiar joke with regard to persons on a certain island who had to employ one another. They had no money to pay each other, and the old joke was that they could live only by taking in each other's washing. But, my Lords, there is another and a very serious point. Some twenty of us on these Benches have the privilege of reading prayers in your Lordships' House, and the culminating point in the special Prayer for Parliament which so many of your Lordships heard this evening is this : the result of your deliberations is to be " the uniting and knitting together of the hearts of all persons and estates within the realm in true Christian love and charity one towards the other."

That is to be the culminating effect of the deliberations and the legislation of this House. Some of us are accustomed, when we are considering a proposal, to ask ourselves what is the exact argument which the author of the proposal thinks most cognate to it, and thinks best as a means of urging it upon the attention of the people. Now, my Lords, we know who is the official author of this Bill. Not to say a word about his Parliamentary utterances, I only ask your Lordships to consider his speeches out of Parliament, and particularly one delivered near my old charge when I was in Stepney — made in certain language and with evident motive. If the intention of this Bill is to be judged, as I maintain it may fairly be judged, by the expressions of its author in pressing it upon public attention, well, there is nothing in the world for this House to do but to pass the Amendment of the noble Marquess [rejecting the Bill]. . . .

Extract 61

A LIBERAL LORD'S OPINION OF ECCLESIASTICAL OPPOSITION

(*Lord Sheffield, Lords, November 22, 1909*)

LORD SHEFFIELD [1]: My Lords, I was not quite able to follow the argument of the right rev. Prelate, though I followed his conclusion that he meant to vote for throwing out the Budget. The right rev. Prelate not only claimed an antiquated tenure, but said

---

[1] Parliamentary Debates, Lords, Fifth Series, vol. 4, col. 770 sqq.

he descended from a spiritual tenure, and not from an earthly one. He also made the declaration that he and his brother Prelates knew more about the conditions of all classes of the community, cared more about them, and generally had a more earnest desire to benefit them than anyone else. It seems disrespectful to put anything like a note of interrogation to any of his statements. . . .

If I could examine the history of the right rev. Bench and note their attitude towards the innumerable cases of progressive legislation urged upon Parliament during the last one hundred years — if they knew all this, they dissembled their love very successfully. I am glad, however, that there is a desire to act upon the words in the prayer spoken of by the right rev. Prelate, and to work for the whole nation. I only wish the right rev. Prelate would remember some other weighty and valuable words in that prayer — "to put aside all partial affection."

I think if there is one thing we need more than another, it is that we should clear ourselves from association with class, from professions, from all those things that prevent us from having that high light which is so important if we want to deal with intellectual and social problems. And I cannot help thinking that the right rev. Prelate did not seem to bring quite that high light into the matter in considering how he proposed to ameliorate the condition of the poor which he said, from his knowledge of Bristol and Stepney, it was his desire to do. We have had to-night from all three speakers, who have spoken from the Opposition side, a great deal of abuse of the Chancellor of the Exchequer. We know it is a good maxim " when you have no case, abuse the plaintiff's attorney." And it seems to me that that is very much the way this Budget is being treated. I think anyone would be very sorry to have to defend all the speeches of his friends or political associates at any time. We could get plenty of stones to throw at each other, and I expect we shall have an ample supply of these missiles furnished to us from both sides in a very short time.

Extract 62

AN ATTACK UPON THE SPONSOR OF THE BILL

(Lord Willoughby de Broke, Lords, November 22, 1909)

LORD WILLOUGHBY DE BROKE [1]: . . . The Government cannot remain in office except by the consent of the Socialists and the extreme Radicals ; and this proposal about the unearned increment they believe, will, in a very short time, be applied to all forms of property. All this sort of thing is bound eventually to filter down to the working classes of this country. The form of taxation recommended by the Radical party will very soon resolve itself into this sort of thing with regard to unearned increment. When any citizen happens, in vulgar parlance, to "make a hit" by his own energy or thrift or good luck, the Chancellor of the Exchequer will step in, and having labelled him a "blackmailer" or a "swindler," he will not put an end to the transaction, but the Chancellor of the Exchequer will then go shares in the plunder. Yes, but what for? To provide a revenue for Old Age Pensions or something of that sort would be the reply. But I think you will find it will eventually be applied to advancing the schemes of this or that body, whether Socialists or somebody else, probably equally as bad, whom it may be desirable to placate in order to keep the Government in office as long as they possibly can. There is no doubt that the workingmen of this country are beginning to have a very uncomfortable feeling that the rhetoric of Mr. Lloyd George and the vulgarity of the President of the Board of Trade will not fill many empty stomachs or replenish many bare cupboards during the coming winter. And they will not see the advantage of paying a whole horde of officials to pry into the public life of everybody in this country, and who will be paid from money taken from the beer and the spirits and the tobacco consumed by the workingmen. I may mention that the taxation on

[1] Pa.liamentary Debates, Lords, Fifth Series, vol. 4, col. 780–781.

champagne is not increased at all. The luxuries of the rich men contribute hardly anything towards the taxation of this country. . . .

Then we are told that we are violating and overriding the will of the people. All this talk about the voice of the people is cant. It is real cant of the purest description. It is an utterly meaningless phrase, and is merely part of the stock-in-trade of the agitator and of the demagogue. The will of the people is not expressed on this subject at this moment in the House of Commons. Representative government in this country is at an absurd discount, and the talk about representative government and free institutions has now resulted in this sort of thing: that we are the only Government in the whole of the civilised world that is not being dominated and controlled by a small section of Socialists. With regard to the will of the people, I, for one, have not the slightest anxiety about referring this Budget to the people.

What most moderate men are asking us to do is to save them from being jockeyed and bullied and bluffed by the Chancellor of the Exchequer and the President of the Board of Trade into accepting a Budget and a policy for which there was not the slightest mandate at the last General Election. If your Lordships embrace this policy, then I can only say, " Heaven help England." The late Mr. Bromley-Davenport wrote an extremely amusing parody upon " Locksley Hall " which has been described by a ripe critic of literature as one of the finest things in the English language. I hope it will not be considered out of place if I quote something from it. He was endeavouring to foreshadow, with Tennyson, the state of the country at some future date, when he wrote these lines:

> For I looked into its pages, and I read the Book of Fate,
> And saw foxhunting abolished by an order from the State;
> Saw the landlords yield their acres after centuries of wrongs,
> Cotton lords turn country gentlemen in patriotic throngs;
> Queen, religion, State abandoned, and the flags of party furled
> In the Government of Cobden and the dotage of the world.
> Then shall exiled common sense espouse some other country's cause,
> And the rogues shall thrive in England, bonneting the slumbering laws.

Extract 63

A FINANCIER'S VIEW OF THE BUDGET

(Lord Revelstoke, Lords, November 22, 1909)

LORD REVELSTOKE[1]: . . . It has been my lot to have been brought up in the midst of financial and commercial operations, in the conduct and consideration of which I have endeavoured to follow the traditions and to be guided by the experience of many generations of financiers in my own family, whose success in life has been due to their intimate connection with banking and commerce, and whose prosperity, or the reverse, has for many years been bound up with the financial position of the City of London, the home and centre of that great system of " credit " upon which so much depends. . . .

Here is a Budget which, designed to meet expenditure for great social reforms, places an accumulated burden of higher Income Tax, Super-tax, Death Duties, Land Tax, Stamp Duties, all on one particular class. And surely, my Lords, in this matter of heaping taxation upon the few, a double error is committed. Not only is there a penalising of capital, with its consequent ill effects upon the whole community; but the force of public opinion — the greatest, if not the only check upon extravagant expenditure — is weakened, and it is weakened at the moment when it is most urgently required. . . .

It has been said, and said many times within recent months, that capital is leaving this country to a very serious extent, and I have to testify, from my own practical knowledge, that this is true. . . .

This is a new doctrine to be preached by a British Administration. It misrepresents the position of capital as it is understood by all impartial observers removed from the clamour of party politics. It ignores the extent to which the prosperity of this nation has been due to its great capital resources, its heritage of financial supremacy, its unshaken credit. The extreme difficulty of adequately

[1] Parliamentary Debates, Lords, Fifth Series, vol. 4, col. 794 sqq.

conveying to the originators of this Bill a sense of the harm which it has already occasioned, and is likely to still further occasion, lies largely in the very fact that it seems well-nigh impossible to bring home to those responsible a real sense of what is involved in " unshaken credit." As I have read the speeches of the Chancellor of the Exchequer, I can almost hear him ask, like another person better known in history, and, like him, without waiting for an answer, not " What is truth ? " but " What is credit ? " My Lords, I can give him that answer — I can give him the answer he would receive from the sober community among whom I have passed my days. They would tell him — and they are men whose occupations do not lead them to make speeches, but who have read, and read with dismay, the reckless and unconsidered utterances of even the most responsible members of His Majesty's Government. Those of whom I speak, my Lords, are men whose experience and character, whose probity and judgment, have contributed not a little to make this England of ours what she has been — and what she should remain — the Bank and the workshop of the world. They would tell him, my Lords, that they define " credit " as " confidence." Confidence in financial prudence, confidence in ability to pay, confidence in financial equity and stability, confidence in the sanctity of property. Can we say, my Lords, that our confidence in any of these would not be shaken by the passing of the measure which is now before your Lordships' House ?

Extract 64

ECCLESIASTICAL SUPPORT OF THE BUDGET

(Bishop of Birmingham, Lords, November 22, 1909)

THE LORD BISHOP OF BIRMINGHAM [1] : . . . It is impossible to live in our great cities without becoming conscious of the fact that for the great body of the workers our country is not a good

[1] Parliamentary Debates, Lords, Fifth Series, vol. 4, col. 799 sqq.

place to live in at the present moment. As I have shown your Lordships, there is a great, vast, and growing demand for money for public expenditure. How is that money which is required to be obtained? The question is whether in this Budget there is an unjust and oppressive treatment of particular classes, especially of the landed classes and of those who are engaged in the liquor trade. I do not know whether that is the case. With regard to the matter which has been, I suppose, most commented on of all the land taxes — that is, the tax upon the unearned increment on land in and about towns — those of us who have been taught the political economy of John Stuart Mill have been expecting to see this tax in England for a great many years. . . .

. . . It was said in the course of this debate before dinner that the Budget is Socialism. · Of course you can use the terms Conservatism, Liberalism, and Socialism in such a way as to make them apply to almost everything you like. Socialism is a term which I think it is best to employ as a quite distinctive term, representing a quite distinctive view, and a view which no doubt is gaining in its hold especially on the working classes throughout Europe. I do not hold with the Socialistic theory myself, but I know what it means. It means the abolition of private capital, not private property, and the socialisation of the sources and instruments of production and distribution. In the sense in which Collectivists use the word Socialism this Budget is not in any way Socialistic. It does not propose in any kind of way, or point to, the transfer to the community of the sources and instruments of production and distribution, although it might be said that it moves towards it. I venture to think that the most reactionary Budget, the Budget which moves most sharply in the opposite direction, would be the Budget which would be most likely to lead rapidly to Socialism by stirring up the already moving minds of the people to rebellion and revolt against the injustice of our present conditions. . . .

The Budget is only one more instance of the gradual growth towards a more proper distribution of the constantly increasing burdens of public expenditure, broadening out from precedent to precedent, and I cannot but feel that your Lordships will indeed not be acting wisely if you treat this Budget as if it could be accused of containing either revolutionary or unjust principles.

Extract 65

A CONCILIATORY SPEECH ON THE BUDGET

(*Lord Ribblesdale, Lords, November 22, 1909*)

LORD RIBBLESDALE [1] : . . . My Lords, we have all been very much upset — I have myself — by the speeches of the Chancellor of the Exchequer, but I have been able to get over them, and I have no doubt noble Lords opposite have also. But there is one thing I will say for Mr. Lloyd George, and that is that he has stuck to his form throughout. If you take Limehouse as his Ossa, he backed it up with Pelion in the shape of Newcastle. I rather respect him for that, because there is no sort of doubt that, if any speaker starts on a half-pantaloon and. half-highwayman style it is almost too much to ask him, all of a sudden, to turn around and revert to the manner of our classical models, such as the late Mr. Gladstone, the late Lord Goschen, and the present Lord St. Aldwyn. But whatever may have been the infelicity of the style which has recommended the Budget, I am bound to say that the first attacks on it were somewhat infelicitous, too, and it is an infelicity which we have all, somehow or another, learned to connect with the word " Duke." Personally I think Dukes are charming people, but I am bound to say that I have read a good many speeches of Dukes from time to time, and they have stuck to their form too. Their speeches remind me of Tennyson's line, " Tears, Idle Tears," and I cannot help thinking that no one will be very seriously affected by the sobs of quite well-to-do folk. . . .

[1] Parliamentary Debates, Lords, Fifth Series, vol. 4, col. 810.

Extract 66

AN EXTREME CONSERVATIVE VIEW OF THE BUDGET

(The Duke of Marlborough, Lords, November 23, 1909)

THE DUKE OF MARLBOROUGH [1]: . . . The relations of this House with the Lower House, which the Government propose to disturb, are in themselves a monument to the political sagacity of the British people. Their adjustment has been perfected by the genius of great men. That subtle and delicate equipoise has been preserved practically unchanged during centuries by the statecraft of leading men in either House, so that to-day it bears something of that mysterious sanctity which time alone can give. It is as with the Abbey within whose shadow we deliberate. Inspired architects planned its noble outline, its solid walls, its flowing buttresses, and its dominating towers. Zealous masons laboured to transmute the architectual vision into the reality of solid stone. But not all the splendour of the initial conception nor the patient services of its builders could have sufficed to win for the Abbey the place which it holds in our hearts to-day. Time has touched it with his finger, and to his ineffable touch it owes its ultimate consecration. So I say it is with the relations between the two Houses of Parliament in the vital matter of finance. They too have been slowly upreared in the passage of the centuries. They too have been hallowed by tradition. Yet to-day the Government, acting through the Lower House, are prepared to lay rude and irreverent hands upon a political fabric which has won the admiration of the civilised world. This magnificent monument, this unique expression of the temperament of our people, is to be shattered at the bidding of a demagogue from Wales, and may I respectfully add, by the threat of the noble and learned Lord on the Woolsack.

THE LORD CHANCELLOR : I made no threat.

[1] Parliamentary Debates, Lords, Fifth Series, vol. 4, col. 841-2.

THE DUKE OF MARLBOROUGH : Neither the words of the noble
and learned Lord on the Woolsack, nor the silence of the noble
Earl, Lord Crewe,— a self-constituted mute at the obsequies of
the British Constitution,— nor the remarks of the noble Earl on
the Cross Benches have in any way shaken my confidence that
the Amendment moved by the noble Marquess, Lord Lansdowne,
ought to receive our united and unanimous support.

Extract 67

LORD ROSEBERY ON THE BUDGET

(The Earl of Rosebery, Lords, November 24, 1909)

THE EARL OF ROSEBERY [1] : My Lords, I earnestly wish that
the most rev. Primate to whose weighty words we have just listened
with so much attention would throw the ægis of his doctrine of
silence over myself, who am quite as dissociated from Party as any
Prelate that sits upon the Bench behind him, and perhaps more, I
think, than some. I wish it because I never rose to address your
Lordships with more reluctance than on the present occasion —
partly from my sense of the awful gravity of the situation, by far
the greatest that has occurred in my lifetime or the lifetime of any
man who has been born since 1832 ; partly from a sense of the
personal difficulties that I feel in dealing with this question. . . .

My Lords, I am, as I have amply proved, hostile to the Budget.
I cannot, I think, be more hostile to the Budget than I am, but I
am not willing to link the fortunes of the Second Chamber with
opposition to the Budget. I find no fault with the Resolution of
the noble Marquess, if he thought it right to have a Resolution at
all, and I do not suppose that he had much choice in the matter.
No doubt the impetus of his own forces carried him forward
whether he wished it or not, and of course it may be fair to argue,

1 Parliamentary Debates, Lords, Fifth Series, vol. 4, col. 942 sqq.

as has been argued, that it is not a Resolution for the rejection of the Bill, but a method for bringing about an appeal to the people for their assent or negative to the Budget. There is nothing I should rejoice at so much as any reference of that kind if there were any constitutional means of obtaining it without mixing it up with other issues foreign to it, and which may greatly impair the directness and validity of the decision. If, for example, you had the referendum in this country — and I for my part believe that you will never arrive at a final solution of the question of the adjustment of differences between the two Houses without some form of referendum — I would gladly vote that it should be applied on this occasion. . . .

My Lords, I think you are playing for too heavy a stake on this occasion. I think that you are risking in your opposition to what I agree with you in thinking is an iniquitous and dangerous measure, the very existence of a Second Chamber. I do not pretend to be very greatly alarmed at the menaces which have been addressed to us on this and on other occasions. The House of Lords has lived on menaces ever since I can recollect, and yet it seems to be in a tolerably thriving condition still. But I ask you to remember this. The menaces which were addressed to this House in old days were addressed by statesmen who had at heart the balance of the constitutional forces in this country. The menaces addressed to you now come from a wholly different school of opinion, who wish for a single Chamber and who set no value on the controlling and revising forces of a Second Chamber — a school of opinion which, if you like it and do not dread the word, is eminently revolutionary in essence, if not in fact. I ask you to bear in mind that fact when you weigh the consequences of the vote which you are to give to-morrow night. "Hang consequences," said my noble friend Lord Camperdown last night, "let them take care of themselves." That is a noble utterance — a Balaklava utterance. Nothing more intrepid could be said. But the truest courage in these matters weighs the consequences, not to the individual, but to the

State, and thinks not once, but twice or thrice before it gives a vote which may involve such enormous constitutional consequences. . . . Remember, that in hanging up or in rejecting the Budget the House of Lords is doing exactly what its enemies wish it to do. Now, I believe that in life it is a pretty safe maxim to ascertain what it is your enemy wishes you to do, and to do something very much unlike it. I confess I have no doubt when I read the speeches delivered in various parts of the country, speeches unusual and unprecedented in my time as regards speeches by Cabinet Ministers, that they are meant to stir up and incite the House of Lords to do exactly the thing which the House of Lords meditates doing.

I confess that policy does not appeal to me. I should like a less heroic policy, which I think would have answered much better the majority of this House, but which I fear it is too late to ask the House to adopt, although I believe it to be the winning policy for those who are opposed to the Budget. I should have liked to see the House of Lords pass this Finance Bill, not because I have a good opinion of it, but because I have such an excessively bad opinion of it. . . . I believe that if you gave the country an experience of the Budget in operation, you would achieve a victory when you next approach the polls which would surprise yourselves and would give you the power of revising the finance of this country by methods more in consonance with your own principles and your own common-sense. We should then have an anti-Socialist Government, a luxury which I cannot say we possess now. We should have a reformed Second Chamber, not merely in the way of purging it to some extent, and arriving at the choicest part of it by delegation and election, but also by renovating it by means of those external elements that must necessarily give strength to a Second Chamber — all that would have been achieved in the best and, in the non-Party sense, the most conservative interests of this United Kingdom. Unfortunately, that is not the line that the House is going to take. I am sorry — with all my heart I am sorry — that I cannot give a vote against the Budget on this occasion. My interest in this matter is mainly that of the Second Chamber, and I cannot stake all my hopes of its future utility and reform on the precarious and tumultuous chances, involved as they will be with many other irrelevant and scarcely honest issues — the tumultuous hazards of a General Election.

Extract 68

LORD MORLEY ON THE BUDGET

(Viscount Morley of Blackburn, Secretary of State for India, Lords, November 29, 1909)

LORD MORLEY [1]: . . . I particularly, for my part, object to the referendum. Why? Because it weakens what is the most important thing for this country to maintain — the sense of responsibility in the House of Commons. If you tell the House of Commons that they are liable to have a given conclusion of their own submitted to other people — whether they be members of this House or people in the country — you weaken their own personal individual and collective responsibility. . . .

By this Amendment you are subjecting the Budget to what is called, in the jargon to which I have referred, a *plebiscite*. If there is any one matter which cannot be usefully or wisely submitted to a *plebiscite*, it is a Budget. It is one of those things on which you cannot say Yes or No. How can any one say Yes or No to this Budget? Noble Lords here do not like the Budget, but the Budget contains any number of provisions, qualifications, intricacies; it is a complex of things to which you cannot give a plain Yes or No, which is the point of a *plebiscite*. . . .

Now another point. It is argued that you will vote for this Amendment because you want to arrest Socialism. I am, and always have been, a pretty strong individualist. But just let us look at these Socialist allegations and the assumption that by

[1] Parliamentary Debates, Lords, Fifth Series, vol. 4, col. 1137 sqq.

rejecting this Bill and passing your Amendment you are putting a spoke into the wheel of Socialism. The people of this country are either of the predatory species or they are not; they are either in favour of predatory destructive Socialism or they are not. If they are, it is quite certain that the success of this Parliamentary operation of your Lordships will not set up any dam or rampart or barrier against the great destructive flood such as would then arise. Anyone who tells you that by passing this Amendment you are obstructing Socialism is as foolish as were the courtiers of King Canute. But I do not believe, and I am quite sure all your Lordships do not believe, that our countrymen are a predatory species. No Englishman can think so.

If you will forgive a passing personal reference, it was my fortune to be — I only mention it to show that I am not talking of the working people of this country with a Utopian head in the clouds — for twelve years a Member for what was in those days one of the largest constituencies in England. It was an enormous constituency, and my return was always due to the skilled artisans, mainly workers in the famous Elswick factory — skilled and admirable artisans. It is true that at the end of twelve years they turned me out, but I had plenty of time — and I am not entirely without the faculty of observation — to satisfy myself that the skilled artisans of this country, aye, and many more than they, are not men wearing the Phrygian cap. No, they are not " Reds." . . .

There will, no doubt, be foolish proposals made by the pitiful and sympathetic, whether politicians or philanthropists outside politics — there will be proposals made, if you like, full of charlatanry and full of quackery. But, anyhow, it is inevitable to anybody who has followed the course of movements of a Socialistic kind in France and other countries that you should have these experiments tried. My own hope, my own conviction, is that at the end of these experiments there will be left behind a fertile and fertilising residue of good. Mill, whose name has been so often quoted in these debates on fiscal matters, said at the very end of his life he was averse to Socialism, and in a certain production of his, where he described the possible dangers of Socialism, he said, "If Socialism with all its dangers was the only alternative to the horrors of our present system, I would be a Socialist."

The noble Viscount, Lord Milner, said the other day that he would be very sorry to be a member of a dummy House of Lords, and I suppose anyone who sits in an assembly, however new a comer he may be, would be very sorry to sit in a dummy assembly. He would rather absent himself altogether. But there is something worse than a dummy House of Lords, and that is a dummy House of Commons. What else does this operation which you are going to consummate to-morrow night mean than reducing the House of Commons to a dummy? They discussed the Budget for six months. I forget how many hundreds of sittings and how many hundreds of Divisions there were. I understand from those who speak with a certain impartiality that it was discussed with a freedom and a fullness of detail almost, if not entirely, without precedent in our recent Parliamentary annals. . . . There was no guillotine. There were ceaseless interviews with deputations, and yet all this prolonged and careful labour, discussion, thought, contrivance — all that is to go for nothing, and all its results are to be pulverised and brought to naught by a trenchant sweep of the noble Marquess's arm. That is what I call making a dummy House of Commons.

In the Division on the third reading, what were the numbers? They were 379 for the Budget Bill and 149 against it. In this House to-morrow night let us suppose it is 500 against 50. My Lords, the more triumphant your majority, the more huge the disparity between your numbers and ours, the more flagrant the political scandal, and the more blazing in the public eye the Constitutional paradox. Such a contrast as that, 379 against 149 in one House, only a four-year-old House, and 400 or 500 in this House against 40 or 50 — I say it cannot last. . . .

I do not say at all, and have never promised, that this Budget will bring right away the Millennium, but I am quite certain that it will not bring Pandemonium. It will bring neither the Millennium nor Pandemonium, and I think that noble Lords opposite are beginning to feel that perhaps their apprehensions were unduly aroused. Let me make one observation to which I believe the noble Marquess will attach certain weight. When Mr. Gladstone was going through his early financial operations, he was watched by nobody in the world with a more eager interest than by Cavour. I am not speaking quite without the book when I say there are now Ministers in European countries, with their own battles to fight, who are watching with some anxiety and some apprehension the double issue, fiscal and constitutional, in which we are involved by these proceedings. For many glorious generations England has been the stable and far-shining model of reform, and any clouding of her position in either fiscal or constitutional policy will be a gain, and a heavy gain, on the Continent of Europe to the parties of reaction. . . .

Lastly, the noble Marquess must have foreseen that the success of this Amendment and its consequences must lead a pretty straight way to constitutional revision, and I am sure he must know that there is no such battle ground, if you look at our own history in the seventeenth century, at the modern history of the United States, or at that of half of the countries of Continental Europe, for the fiercest and most determined conflicts, as constitutional revision. With regard to the Second Chamber, I venture to call it the *pons asinorum* of democracy. I hope noble Lords will recognise that. The scene in this House during the last ten days must not, I think, be counted one of those brilliant and exciting stage plays, political and party stage plays, of which some of us have seen so many. I think it is much more than a mere stage play. It is the first step on a tremendous journey, and, as we all know, when we troop off home to-morrow night we shall not think that, though the theatre is empty, the curtain has fallen upon a completed drama. We shall all know in our hearts that the note has sounded for a very angry and perhaps prolonged battle.

Extract 69

THE LORDS' REJECTION OF THE BUDGET

(The Earl of Crewe, Lord Privy Seal and Secretary of State for the Colonies, Lords, November 30, 1909)

THE EARL OF CREWE [1] : . . . My Lords, we are now going to vote. In 1860 when the Paper Duty Bill was before this House Mr. Bright said, speaking of the then action of your Lordships' House, " They voted out this Bill by a large majority with a chuckle, thinking that by doing so they were making a violent attack on the Ministry, and particularly upon the Chancellor of the Exchequer." My Lords, that is what you are going to do. Who are going to vote ? The noble Lords who are here. Who are not going to vote ? I cannot help alluding, although it has been mentioned before, to the absence from the noble Marquess's battalions of the noble Viscount, Lord St. Aldwyn — one of the most experienced authorities on political finance in the country, and a Conservative of Conservatives. He is not here. But when the division list is scanned to-morrow, as scanned it will be, by those who desire to weigh as well as to count, many names will be missed from it. There will be the names of many of those who have grown old in the service of the State at home and abroad, particularly of those who have served in distant parts of the Empire ; the names of many of those who do the greater part of the real work of this House — thankless work, and not, I think, often sufficiently rewarded by public appreciation — in the committee room upstairs ; there will be many names of those who possess, if I may venture to say so, the coolest heads and the most amply furnished minds in the House ; many of those who, when it is a question of deciding merits of some great dispute between capital and labour, are called upon to arbitrate in such cases by the common consent of all classes

[1] Parliamentary Debates, Lords, Fifth Series, vol. 4, col. 1324 sqq.

of our fellow-countrymen. My Lords, many of those will not be here. Like the images of the Roman patriots at another kind of funeral some two thousand years ago, when the historian said, *Effulgebant eo ipso quod effigies eorum non videbantur*, they are even more conspicuous by their absence than they would be if they recorded their vote. I know you will not agree with me, but I do say that in tearing up the ancient charters, in removing the venerable landmarks, you are making a most tragic blunder. You are not afraid of the consequences; no one could suppose you would be afraid; if you are afraid of anything in this matter, you are possibly just the least bit afraid of being thought afraid. That is the only scintilla of fear which I think could be recognised on the Benches opposite.

It has been said in debate that there has been a sinister kind of conspiracy, a plot, to lure your Lordships into an impossible position. Perhaps I may be permitted to say that I am in as good a position as anybody to judge whether that is so, and I think I can show you it is not so. I do not think I am breaking any Cabinet confidence when I say that the great majority of my colleagues including — unless I am mistaken — the Chancellor of the Exchequer himself, have been infinitely more sanguine than I have been all through that your Lordships would pass the Finance Bill, and it was only at a very recent date that they recognised the probability of the action your Lordships are taking. That I think is conclusive proof that there has been no conspiracy to put your Lordships into a position where you could not pass it. . . .

If you think that any of us on this side of the House welcome this crisis, you are entirely mistaken. But we are compelled to face it, not only because our political existence as a Party is involved, but because in our view the interests of the country and of the Empire depend upon the maintenance of a reasonable constitutional balance between the governing powers of the State. It may be, my Lords, that when the new Parliament meets we shall be sitting where you sit now. It may be that we shall still be seated on these

Benches here. But, my Lords, whether we sit there or whether we sit here, we must, after the action which your Lordships have thought fit to take to-night, set ourselves to obtain guarantees — not the old guarantees sanctioned by the course of time and enforced by accommodation between the two Houses, but if necessary, if there be no other way, guarantees fenced about and guarded by the force of Statute — guarantees which will prevent that indiscriminate destruction of our legislation of which your work to-night is the climax and the crown.

THE LORD CHANCELLOR: The original Question was " That the Bill be now read a second time," to which an Amendment has been moved to leave out all the words after " That " for the purpose of inserting the following Motion, " This House is not justified in giving its consent to this Bill until it has been submitted to the judgment of the country." The Question I have to put is whether the words proposed to be left out shall stand part of the Motion.

On Question?

Their Lordships divided : Contents, 75 ; Not-Contents, 350.

Extract 70

FINANCE (1909–10) ACT, 1910

(*10 Edw. 7, ch. 8, in part*)

An Act to grant certain Duties of Customs and Inland Revenue (including Excise), to alter other Duties, and to amend the Law relating to Customs and Inland Revenue (including Excise), and to make other financial provisions.

(29th April 1910)

Most Gracious Sovereign,

We, Your Majesty's most dutiful and loyal subjects the Commons of the United Kingdom of Great Britain and Ireland in Parliament assembled, towards raising the necessary supplies to defray Your Majesty's public expenses, and making an addition to the public revenue, have freely and voluntarily resolved to give and grant unto Your Majesty the several duties herein-after mentioned ; and do therefore most humbly beseech Your Majesty that it may be enacted, and be it enacted by the King's most Excellent Majesty, by and with the advice and consent of the Lords Spiritual and Temporal, and Commons, in this present Parliament assembled, and by the authority of the same, as follows :

Part I

Duties on Land Values

1. Duty on Increment Value

Subject to the provisions of this Part of this Act, there shall be charged, levied, and paid on the increment value of any land a duty, called increment value duty, at the rate of one pound for every complete five pounds of that value accruing after the thirtieth day of April nineteen hundred and nine, and —

(*a*) on the occasion of any transfer on sale of the fee simple of the land or of any interest in the land, in pursuance of any contract made after the commencement of this Act, or the grant, in pursuance of any contract made after the commencement of this Act, of any lease (not being a lease for a term of years not exceeding fourteen years) of the land ; and

(*b*) on the occasion of the death of any person dying after the commencement of this Act, where the fee simple of the land or any interest in the land is comprised in the property passing on the death of the deceased within the meaning of sections one and two, subsection (1) (*a*), (*b*), and (*c*), and subsection three, of the Finance Act, 1894, as amended by any subsequent enactment ; and (*c*) where the fee simple of the land or any interest in the land is held by any body corporate or by any body unincorporate as defined by section twelve of the Customs and Inland Revenue Act, 1885, in such a manner or on such permanent trusts that the land or interest is not liable to death duties, on such periodical occasions as are provided in this Act,

the duty, or proportionate part of the duty, so far as it has not been paid on any previous occasion, shall be collected in accordance with the provisions of this Act.

2. *Definition of Increment Value*

(1) For the purposes of this Part of this Act the increment value of any land shall be deemed to be the amount (if any) by which the site value of the land, on the occasion on which increment value duty is to be collected as ascertained in accordance with this section, exceeds the original site value of the land as ascertained in accordance with the general provisions of this Part of this Act as to valuation.

(2) The site value of the land on the occasion on which increment value duty is to be collected shall be taken to be —

(*a*) where the occasion is a transfer on sale of the fee simple of the land, the value of the consideration for the transfer; and

(*b*) where the occasion is the grant of any lease of the land, or the transfer on sale of any interest in the land, the value of the fee simple of the land, calculated on the basis of the value of the consideration for the grant of the lease or the transfer of the interest; and

(*c*) where the occasion is the death of any person, and the fee simple of the land is property passing on that death, the principal value of the land as ascertained for the purposes of Part I of the Finance Act, 1894, and where any interest in the land is property passing on that death the value of the fee simple of the land calculated on the basis of the principal value of the interest as so ascertained; and

(*d*) where the occasion is a periodical occasion on which the duty is to be collected in respect of the fee simple of any land or of any interest in any land held by a body corporate or unincorporate, the total value of the land on that occasion to be estimated in accordance with the general provisions of this Part of this Act as to valuation;

subject in each case to the like deductions as are made, under the general provisions of this Part of this Act as to valuation, for the purpose of arriving at the site value of land from the total value.

(3) Where it is proved to the Commissioners on an application made for the purpose within the time fixed by this section that the site value of any land at the time of any transfer on sale of the fee simple of the land or of any interest in the land, which took place at any time within twenty years before the thirtieth day of April, nineteen hundred and nine, exceeded the original site value of the land as ascertained under this Act, the site value at that time shall be substituted, for the purposes of increment value duty, for the original site value as so ascertained, and the provisions of this Part of this Act shall apply accordingly.

Site value shall be estimated for the purposes of this provision by reference to the consideration given on the transfer in the same manner as it is estimated by reference to the consideration given on a transfer where increment value duty is to be collected on the occasion of such a transfer after the passing of this Act.

This provision shall apply to a mortgage of the fee simple of the land or any interest in land in the same manner as it applies to a transfer, with the substitution of the amount secured by the mortgage for the consideration.

An application for the purpose of this section must be made within three months after the original site value of the land has been finally settled under this Part of this Act. . . .

13. Reversion Duty

(1) On the determination of any lease of land there shall be charged, levied, and paid, subject to the provisions of this Part of this Act, on the value of the benefit accruing to the lessor by reason of the determination of the lease a duty, called reversion duty, at the rate of one pound for every complete ten pounds of that value.

(2) For the purposes of this section the value of the benefit accruing to the lessor shall be deemed to be the amount (if any) by which the total value (as defined for the purpose of the general provisions of this Part of this Act relating to valuation) of the land at the time the lease determines, subject to the deduction of any part of the total value which is attributable to any works executed or expenditure of a capital nature incurred by the lessor during the term of the lease and of all compensation payable by such lessor at the determination of the lease, exceeds the total value of the land at the time of the original grant of the lease, to be ascertained on the basis of the rent reserved and payments made in consideration of the lease (including, in cases where a nominal rent only has been reserved, the value of any covenant or undertaking to erect buildings or to expend any sums upon the property), but, where the lessor is himself entitled only to a leasehold interest, the value of the benefit as so ascertained shall be reduced in proportion to the amount by which the value of his interest is less than the value of the fee simple. . . .

16. Undeveloped Land Duty

(1) Subject to the provisions of this Part of this Act, there shall be charged, levied, and paid for the financial year ending the thirty-first day of March nineteen hundred and ten, and every subsequent financial year in respect of the site value of undeveloped land a duty, called undeveloped land duty, at the rate of one halfpenny for every twenty shillings of that site value.

(2) For the purposes of this Part of this Act, land shall be deemed to be undeveloped land if it has not been developed by the erection of dwelling-houses or of buildings for the purposes of any business, trade, or industry other than agriculture (but including glasshouses or greenhouses), or is not otherwise used bonâ fide for any business, trade, or industry other than agriculture :

Provided that —

(a) Where any land having been so developed or used reverts to the condition of undeveloped land owing to the buildings becoming derelict, or owing to the land ceasing to be used for any business, trade, or industry other than agriculture, it shall, on the expiration of one year after the buildings have so become derelict or the land ceases to be so used, as the case may be, be treated as undeveloped land for the purposes of undeveloped land duty until it is again so developed or used ; and

(b) Where the owner of any land included in any scheme of land development shows that he or his predecessors in title have, with a view to the land being developed or used as aforesaid, incurred expenditure on roads (including paving, curbing, metalling, and other works in connexion with roads) or sewers, that land shall, to the extent of one acre for every complete hundred pounds of that expenditure, for the purposes of this section, be treated as land so developed or used although it is not for the time being actually so developed or used, but, for the purposes of this provision, no expenditure shall be taken into account if ten years have elapsed since the date of the expenditure, or if after the date of the expenditure the land having been developed reverts to the condition of undeveloped land, and in a case where the amount of the expenditure does not cover the whole of the land included in the scheme of land development, the part of the land to be treated as land developed or used as aforesaid shall be determined by the Commissioners as being the land with a view to the development or use of which as aforesaid the expenditure has been in the main incurred.

(3) For the purposes of undeveloped land duty, the site value of undeveloped land shall be taken to be the value adopted as the original site value or, where the site value has been ascertained under any subsequent periodical valuation of undeveloped land for the time being in force, the site value as so ascertained :

Provided that where increment value duty has been paid in respect of the increment value of any undeveloped land, the site value of that land shall, for the purposes of the assessment and collection of undeveloped land duty, be reduced by a sum equal to five times the amount paid as increment value duty.

(4) For the purposes of undeveloped land duty undeveloped land does not include the minerals. . . .

20. *Mineral Rights Duty and Provisions as to Minerals*

(1) There shall be charged, levied, and paid for the financial year ending the thirty-first day of March nineteen hundred and ten and every subsequent financial year on the rental value of all rights to work minerals and of all mineral wayleaves, a duty (in this Act referred to as a mineral rights duty) at the rate in each case of one shilling for every twenty shillings of that rental value.

(2) The rental value shall be taken to be —

(a) Where the right to work the minerals is the subject of a mining lease, the amount of rent paid by the working lessee in the last working year in respect of that right ; and

(b) Where minerals are being worked by the proprietor thereof, the amount which is determined by the Commissioners to be the sum which would have been received as rent by the proprietor in the last working year if the right to work the minerals had been leased to a working lessee for a term and at a rent and on conditions customary in the district, and the minerals had been worked to the same extent and in the same manner as they have been worked by the proprietor in that year :

Provided that the Commissioners shall cause a copy of their valuation of such rent to be served on the proprietor ; and

(c) In the case of a mineral wayleave, the amount of rent paid by the working lessee in the last working year in respect of the wayleave :

Provided that if in any special case it is shown to the Commissioners that the rent paid by a working lessee exceeds the rent customary in the district, and partly represents a return for expenditure on the part of any proprietor of the minerals which would ordinarily have been borne by the lessee, the Commissioners shall substitute as the rental value of the right to work the minerals or the mineral wayleaves, as the case may be, such rent as the Commissioners determine would have been the rent customary in the district if the expenditure had been borne by the lessee. . . .

26. Valuation of Land for Purposes of Act

(1) The Commissioners shall, as soon as may be after the passing of this Act, cause a valuation to be made of all land in the United Kingdom, showing separately the total value and the site value respectively of the land, and in the case of agricultural land the value of the land for agricultural purposes where that value is different from the site value. Each piece of land which is under separate occupation, and, if the owner so requires, any part of any land which is under separate occupation, shall be separately valued, and the value shall be estimated as on the thirtieth day of April nineteen hundred and nine.

(2) Any owner of land and any person receiving rent in respect of any land shall, on being required by notice from the Commissioners, furnish to the Commissioners a return containing such particulars as the Commissioners may require as to the rent received by him, and as to the ownership, tenure, area, character, and use of the land, and the consideration given on any previous sale or lease of the land, and any other matters which may properly be required for the purpose of the valuation of the land, and which it is in his power to give, and, if any owner of land or person receiving any rent in respect of the land is required by the Commissioners to make a return under this section, and fails to make such a return within the time, not being less than thirty days, specified in the notice requiring a return, he shall be liable to a penalty not exceeding fifty pounds to be recoverable in the High Court.

(3) Any owner of land may, if he thinks fit, furnish to the Commissioners his estimate of the total value or site value or both of the land, and the Commissioners, in making their valuation, shall consider any estimate so furnished. . . .

28. Periodical Valuation of Undeveloped Land

For the purpose of obtaining a periodical valuation of undeveloped land the Commissioners shall, in the year nineteen hundred and fourteen and in every subsequent fifth year, cause a valuation to be made of undeveloped land showing the site value of the land as on the thirtieth day of April in that year, and, for the purpose of ascertaining the value at that time, the provisions of this Act as to the ascertainment of value shall apply for the purpose of ascertaining value on any such periodical valuation as they apply for the purpose of ascertaining the original value :

Provided that if on any such periodical valuation the valuation of any undeveloped land which is liable to undeveloped land duty is for any reason begun but not completed in the year of valuation, the Commissioners may complete the valuation after the expiration of the year of valuation, subject to an appeal under this Act. . . .

Part II

Duties on Liquor Licences

[Clauses 43–53.]

Part III

Death Duties

54. Amended Rates

The scale set out in the Second Schedule to this Act[1] shall, in the case of persons dying on or after the thirtieth day of April nineteen hundred and nine, be substituted for the scale set out in the First Schedule to the Finance Act, 1907, as the scale of rates of estate duty, and two per cent shall be substituted for one per cent in section seventeen of the Finance Act, 1894 (in this Part of this Act referred to as the principal Act), as the rate of settlement estate duty. . . .

Part IV

Income Tax

65. Income Tax for 1909–1910

(1) Income tax for the year beginning on the sixth day of April nineteen hundred and nine shall be charged at the rate of one shilling and twopence. . . .

66. Super-tax on incomes over £5,000

(1) In addition to the income tax charged at the rate of one shilling and twopence under this Act, there shall be charged, levied, and paid for the year beginning on the sixth day of April nineteen hundred and nine, in respect of the income of any individual, the

[1] Cf. infra, p. 420.

total of which from all sources exceeds five thousand pounds, an additional duty of income tax (in this Act referred to as a super-tax) at the rate of sixpence for every pound of the amount by which the total income exceeds three thousand pounds.

(2) For the purposes of the super-tax, the total income of any individual from all sources shall be taken to be the total income of that individual from all sources for the previous year, estimated in the same manner as the total income from all sources is estimated for the purposes of exemptions or abatements under the Income Tax Acts; but, in estimating the income of the previous year for the purpose of super-tax, —

(a) there shall be deducted in respect of any land on which income tax is charged upon the annual value estimated otherwise than in relation to profits (in addition to any other deduction) any sum by which the assessment is reduced for the purposes of collection under section thirty-five of the Finance Act, 1894, or on which duty has been repaid under the provisions of this Act relating to the repayment of duty in respect of the cost of maintenance, repairs, insurance, and management; and

(b) there shall be deducted the amount of any premiums in respect of which relief from income tax may be allowed under section fifty-four of the Income Tax Act, 1853 (as extended by any subsequent enactment); and

(c) there shall be deducted in the case of a person in the service of the Crown abroad, any such sum as the Treasury may allow for expenses which in their opinion are necessarily incidental to the discharge of the functions of his office and for which an allowance has not already been made;

(d) Any income which is chargeable with income tax by way of deduction shall be deemed to be income of the year in which it is receivable, and any deductions allowable on account of any annual sums paid out of the property or profits of the individual shall be allowed as deductions in respect of the year in which they are payable, notwithstanding that the income or the annual sums, as the case may be, accrued in whole or in part before that year. . . .

PART V

STAMPS

73. Stamp Duty on Conveyances or Transfers on Sales

The stamp duties chargeable under the heading "CONVEYANCE or TRANSFER on Sale of any Property" in the First Schedule to the Stamp Act, 1891 (in this Part of this Act referred to as the principal Act), shall be double those specified in that Schedule : Provided that this section shall not apply to the conveyance or transfer of any stock or marketable security as defined by section one hundred and twenty-two of that Act, or to a conveyance or transfer where the amount or value of the consideration for the sale does not exceed five hundred pounds and the instrument contains a statement certifying that the transaction thereby effected does not form part of a larger transaction or of a series of transactions in respect of which the amount or value, or the aggregate amount or value, of the consideration exceeds five hundred pounds.

74. Stamp Duty on Gifts Inter Vivos

(1) Any conveyance or transfer operating as a voluntary disposition inter vivos shall be chargeable with the like stamp duty as if it were a conveyance or transfer on sale, with the substitution in each case of the value of the property conveyed or transferred for the amount or value of the consideration for the sale :

Provided that this section shall not apply to a conveyance or transfer operating as a voluntary disposition of property to a body of persons incorporated by a special Act, if that body is by its Act precluded from dividing any profit among its members and the property conveyed is to be held for the purposes of an open space or for the purposes of its preservation for the benefit of the nation. . . .

[Part VI (clauses 80–86) treats of Customs and Excise other than Liquor Licence duties, such as tobacco, motor spirits and special taxes on beer; Part VII (clauses 87–91) provides for payments to local authorities and to the road improvement account; Part VIII (clauses 92–96) is general and supplementary. Six schedules accompany the Act.]

Second Schedule

Scale of Rates of Estate Duty

Where the Principal Value of the Estate						Estate Duty shall be payable at the Rate per Cent of
£					£	
Exceeds	100 and does not exceed				500 . .	1
"	500	"	"	"	"	1,000 . .	2
"	1,000	"	"	"	"	5,000 . .	3
"	5,000	"	"	"	"	10,000 . .	4
"	10,000	"	"	"	"	20,000 . .	5
"	20,000	"	"	"	"	40,000 . .	6
"	40,000	"	"	"	"	70,000 . .	7
"	70,000	"	"	"	"	100,000 . .	8
"	100,000	"	"	"	"	150,000 . .	9
"	150,000	"	"	"	"	200,000 . .	10
"	200,000	"	"	"	"	400,000 . .	11
"	400,000	"	"	"	"	600,000 . .	12
"	600,000	"	"	"	"	800,000 . .	13
"	800,000	"	"	"	"	1,000,000 . .	14
"	1,000,000	. . . .				15

CHAPTER IX

CURBING THE LORDS

[The House of Lords with its overwhelming Conservative majority offered for several years after 1905 a serious check upon the legislative programme of the Liberal Government. In 1906 the Lords rejected important governmental measures dealing with education, licensing, and plural voting, and subsequently displayed no little opposition to various proposals for social reform. The social problem in Great Britain was thus complicated by a political and constitutional question as to the relations between the Houses of Parliament.

This situation the Liberals grasped at once; and as early as June 24, 1907, Sir Henry Campbell-Bannerman, as Premier, presented a resolution in the House of Commons, "That, in order to give effect to the will of the people as expressed by their elected representatives, it is necessary that the power of the other House to alter or reject Bills passed by this House should be so restricted by law as to secure that within the limits of a single Parliament the final decision of the Commons shall prevail." The debate on this resolution, which brought out the most salient features of the constitutional and political issue, is reproduced, in part, below : Sir Henry Campbell-Bannerman's explanation and defence of the proposal (*Extract 71*); Mr. Arthur J. Balfour's opposition in behalf of the Conservatives (*Extract 72*); the attack of Mr. D. Shackleton, a Labour Member, upon the undemocratic character of the House of Lords (*Extract 73*); the scholarly defence of a Second Chamber by Sir William Anson, representing Oxford University and an acknowledged authority on the constitutional history of England (*Extract 74*); a clear exposition of the issue both between the Houses and between the Parties, by Mr. Winston Churchill (*Extract 75*); and Mr. David Lloyd George's scathing arraignment of the Upper House (*Extract 76*). The resolution was carried by 432 votes to 147.

Lord Rosebery and other prominent members of the Upper House had long advocated some kind of reform in the constitution of their House; and in 1907 they succeeded in securing the appointment of a Select Committee. This Committee, in a lengthy report published on December 3, 1908, proposed to distinguish between Peers and " Lords of Parliament" or Members of the House of Lords ; and recommended that, except in case of a Peer of the Blood Royal, a peerage should not entitle one to a seat in that House. The hereditary Peers, including those of Scotland and Ireland, should be entitled to elect 200 representatives to sit in that House for each Parliament, this election being conducted by a form of cumulative voting. The Archbishops should hold seats as of right, the Bishops should elect eight representatives. The Committee would gladly see representatives of the other great Churches in the House, but could formulate no recommendation. Official representatives of the great self-governing Colonies might be introduced into the House without the danger of involving the Colonies in British party politics ; as to the representation of India, they could formulate no specific recommendation, but thought its interest would be secured by the presence of ex-Viceroys and other qualified persons in the House. Besides the elective Peers, any Peer should be entitled to sit in the House who had been Cabinet Minister, Viceroy of India, Governor-General of Canada or Australia, High Commissioner for South Africa, or Lord-Lieutenant of Ireland, or who had held any of certain Colonial Governorships or high offices or had been Lieutenant-General or Vice-Admiral on the active list, or had sat for a certain period in the Commons. This recommendation would add about 130 Peers to the House. The Crown should be empowered to summon four life Peers annually, the total not to exceed forty. This would give a House of somewhat less than 400, as against the existing number of considerably over 600. Among many other interesting items the Report stated that proposals had been discussed to admit elected representatives from County Councils and Municipal Corporations, whether Peers or not, but that the Committee, being almost equally divided, made no recommendation.

On the report of the Select Committee on the reform of their own House, the Lords took no action during the year 1909. But as the year advanced, it became increasingly clear to the Liberal Government that they themselves must endeavour to solve the difficulties between the Houses of Parliament by drastic legislative application of the Campbell-Bannerman Resolution of 1907. To have one political party dominant in the House of Commons, and another in the House of Lords, was not only an anomaly, but a serious impediment to constructive legislation. In 1909, it will be remembered, the Upper House weakened the Housing, Town Planning, and Development Acts and rejected altogether the Lloyd George Budget.[1] That rejection of the financial measure for the year — usurpation, the Liberals called it — was the immediate occasion for the break between the two Houses.

What would be the outcome? Lord Rosebery, supporting the Select Committee of the House of Lords, had one solution to suggest; Mr. Asquith's Government had another. The majority of the Upper House naturally hoped that the elections of January, 1910, which so closely followed the rejection of the Budget, would restore their Conservative friends to power in the Lower House, in which case any radical parliamentary reform would be quite unnecessary. But their hopes were doomed to disappointment[2]; and when Mr. Asquith met his new Parliament in 1910 he declared that not only would the passage of the 'Budget now be insisted upon, but also a definite settlement of the constitutional question along the lines laid down in the Commons Resolution of 1907.

[1] Cf. supra, chs. vii, viii.   [2] Cf. supra, p. 360.

Lord Rosebery determined to anticipate the Government's action. On February 24, 1910, he gave notice that on March 14 he would move that the House of Lords resolve itself into committee to consider the best means for so reforming its organisation as to constitute it a strong and efficient Second Chamber. On March 12 a report was published of the numbers and services of temporal Peers. Eighteen had held high judicial office ; forty-three had been Cabinet Ministers or Parliamentary heads of Government departments, or Speakers of the Commons ; twenty had been Lords-Lieutenant of Ireland, Viceroys of India, or Governors-General of Canada, Australia, or the South African Union ; twenty-four had been Governors of Dominions, Colonies, Indian Presidencies or Provinces, or High Commissioners of South Africa ; fifty-one had held minor Ministerial offices ; two had been Ministers or Ambassadors to foreign Powers ; 148 had sat in the Commons, and seven had attained the rank of Vice-Admiral or Lieutenant-General. The number of Peers on the roll at the beginning of the session in 1765 was 202 ; in 1835, 423 ; in 1865, 454 ; in 1885, 524 ; in 1900, 593 ; in 1906, 613 ; and at the time of issuing the return it was 622, of whom four were Royal, twenty-six Episcopal, and five life Peers. In 1909 eighty-one out of a total of ·589 temporal Peers (including minors and Peers kept away by their official duties or by ill-health) did not attend, and 168 attended less than ten times.

The debate on Lord Rosebery's Resolutions extended from March 14 to March 21, when they were carried by substantial majorities, and served to bring out the chief arguments on both sides. The Earl of Rosebery, in introducing the subject, stated that since his reform proposals of 1888 he had expected real reform in the House of Lords to come from outside ; but it was now thought better that it should be proposed from some neutral source within the House in which there had long been a consciousness of its imperfections — its excessive numbers, its exclusive representation of a class, and its basis in heredity. It had splendid traditions and,

according to Freeman, was the lineal descendant of the Witenage-
mot; even Mr. Redmond had eulogised it in 1894. Of the various
efforts at reform from within, Lord Newton's Committee alone had
reached a definite conclusion and the general election had returned
a hostile majority of 125. The Irish and Labour parties respectively
were hostile for the sake of Home Rule and of nationalisation
schemes, but Scotland and the North of England had an insuper-
able objection to the hereditary principle. The Government plan
would first disable the House and then reconstitute it, but the
reconstitution would never be agreed to by the more advanced elements; the plan was like hamstringing a horse and then starting
him for the Derby. After citing Cromwell's famous condemnation
of single-chamber Government, he asked what self-respecting person would care to sit in the House which the Government would
some day propose to re-establish? There would be a violent reaction and a demand for a House of Lords stronger than the present
one; but meanwhile a Home Rule Bill might be passed, and the
country might be at the mercy of a momentary ebullition of feeling.
The Second Chamber would secure that the voice of the people
should be deliberate. Revolutions in history had been carried by
small and determined minorities. The Greater Britains, who had
been provided with strong Second Chambers, would lose faith in
England if single-chamber Government were established; strong
Senates had been deliberately established in France and the United
States; the only two Single-Chamber States were Greece and Costa
Rica. It was felt better to proceed by resolutions, as a basis for a
Bill to be framed by some future Government. The Peers might
now do the country a service greater than any since that of the
Barons at Runnymede, or they might cling to obsolete privileges
and await in decrepitude their doom. But he had confidence in
their action.

Lord Morley of Blackburn, replying to Lord Rosebery, distrusted
historical and colonial analogies; in Canada and Australia the Second Chamber was nominated. Lord Rosebery had not come even

to the fringe of the existing emergency. It would have been better to await the proposals of the Government. In November, 1909, the Lords rejected the Budget, and were held up as a model of political virtue; now, having killed the Budget, they were committing suicide by declaring their unfitness. The Government thought it inexpedient to discuss proposals for reform until an effective method had been provided for settling disputes between the Houses. The question had been raised by a practical emergency; the gulf between the Houses had widened and deepened since 1894, and great changes had become inevitable. To make a "strong and efficient" Second Chamber would be to take back part of the electoral power established by the Liberals and to intensify friction; reform would not remove the grievance that that House did not receive Bills in time to debate them; the changes proposed would not free the House from the imputation of class prejudice, and there was no provision for removing or diminishing deadlocks. He applied to Lord Rosebery his own description of "the riddle that perplexed Cromwell"—"Like smaller reformers since, he had never decided to begin with, whether to make his Lords strong or weak; strong enough to curb the Commons, and yet weak enough for the Commons to curb them."

The Earl of Onslow, speaking next, desired a Second Chamber based on the House of Lords, with some representation of the Dominions overseas; this latter proposal was unfavourably criticised by Lord Northcote. Of subsequent speakers some favoured reform; among them Earl Cawder, who desired the retention of a large hereditary element and maintained that on Home Rule, the Education Bill, the Licensing Bill, and the Budget, the Lords represented the minds of the people better than the Commons. Earl Carrington laid stress on the deadlock between the Houses, which Lord Rosebery's proposal did nothing to diminish. On this question he declared that the Government were ready to lead the whole progressive party, and on its decision to stand or fall.

On behalf of his Government, Mr. H. H. Asquith introduced

the main features of the proposed Parliament Bill under the form of Resolutions in the House of Commons on March 29, 1910. He began by noting the advance of the question since June 24, 1907, as marked by the rejection of the Finance Bill; the general election, at which the relations of the two Houses constituted at least a leading issue; and the spontaneous movement of the House of Lords towards its own reform. His motion assumed that two Chambers were necessary; but Great Britain did not possess a truly bi-cameral system. The Commons must predominate; but a Second Chamber might usefully discharge the functions of consultation, of revision, and, subject to proper safeguards, of delay. Such a Chamber should be relatively small; its basis should be democratic, not hereditary; it must not be "governed by partisanship tempered by panic," and should be representative of and dependent on the will of the nation. The Government resolutions, therefore, were not put forward as a final or adequate solution. Meanwhile, however, they had to deal with the House of Lords as it was. The resolutions to be moved in Committee [1] were not to be treated as clauses in a Bill, but as basis for a Bill. The first he justified by citations from Pitt, Lord Rosebery, Lord Salisbury, and Mr. Balfour, and explained that tacking, a purely speculative possibility, was guarded against by entrusting to the Speaker the decision as to what was or was not a Money Bill. He should strongly deprecate leaving the decision to the Law Courts. The second resolution provided a new remedy for a deadlock between the two Houses. But for the right of the Crown to create new Peers — which he defended, amid some Opposition protests, by citations from Erskine May, Dicey, and Bagehot — there was now no way out of such a deadlock; and the resolution passed in the Lords that a Peer should not necessarily have the right to sit and vote in the Upper House would deal a fatal blow at the Royal Prerogative. Apart from this power, which should be exercised only in extreme cases, but then without fear, there were only two possible checks on the Upper House:

[1] Cf. the provisions of the Act, infra, p. 474.

(1) The referendum, which he had formerly been inclined to favour, would be unsuited for cases where the two Houses agreed unless it were accompanied by some power of initiative; it would tend to undermine the responsibility and dependence of the Commons and would not really be confined to a single issue. (2) A joint sitting of the two Houses would not be applicable with the existing House of Lords. The Government proposal as to the Lords' Veto had been recommended in a more drastic form by John Bright in a speech at Birmingham on August 4, 1884. Sir Henry Campbell-Bannerman had modified it; the Government had carried the modification farther and coupled with it the limitation of the term of Parliament to five years. After replying at length to the argument that its adoption would mean single-chamber government, Mr. Asquith eloquently described how the forms of the Constitution had been adapted to modern needs. Queen Elizabeth in one session vetoed forty-eight Bills out of ninety-one; but the Veto of the Sovereign was dead, yet the Monarchy was far more secure than under the Tudors. But one sterilising factor in the Constitution still remained: the absolute Veto of the House of Lords; it must go, as the Veto of the Crown had gone.

Mr. Arthur J. Balfour, replying in behalf of the Opposition, bantered the Government on the divergence of views among their supporters. The Prime Minister had settled down to a moderate approval of the functions of a Second Chamber, provided it had no real power; Sir Edward Grey and the Home Secretary each took a different view; some Ministerialists desired to abolish it altogether; and, probably owing to its divergence, the Government had brought forward proposals which would neither mend the evils of the Second Chamber nor end them. If the House of Lords were unfit for its functions, reform it; but the Government could not agree on a reform. That it delayed the legislation of a revolutionary Government was not surprising, but there was no deadlock. Since Mr. Bright's speech of 1884 it had been shown that the House of Lords alone stood between the country and great constitutional changes of which the country profoundly disapproved. Alone among the great countries of the world, we had no written Constitution and no safeguards against violent changes. It was absurd to put dissolution and the creation of Peers on a par. The proposal was an absurd experiment in Constitution making; the House of Lords had, and ought to have, the power to reject Money Bills. To make the Speaker the judge of tacking would make him in a sense the author of legislation, and there was a kind of virtual tacking, by bringing in Money Bills for other than money objects, on which his opinion would not be asked. In all great free self-governing communities there were safeguards, insuring that measures could be referred to the electors. Moreover, if the Finance Bill were voted on simply upon its merits, everyone knew it would be rejected. It was therefore absurd to say that the House of Lords had misused its admittedly very delicate function as to Money Bills. The Government scheme under the second resolution would divide the life of a Parliament into a single-chamber period — " like Costa Rica " — and a two-chamber period. It would be a piebald, harlequin Constitution ; it was really the coming election — not the past one — that influenced a House of Commons. The Government under this scheme would bring in all their great measures early and would never be able to improve them. The scheme could not survive, and would initiate a Constitutional controversy which would be fatal to all plans of social reform.

Mr. John Redmond, the leader of the Irish Nationalists, on whom, as well as upon the Labour Members, the Government must now rely for support, described Mr. Balfour's speech as amusing, but not serious. He enumerated a number of Irish Bills, from Catholic emancipation onwards, which the House of Lords had treated in a way prejudicial to Ireland, and assured the Government of his hearty support of the resolutions. He could not support a reform of the House of Lords, as it would tend to strengthen it. A settlement of a deadlock by a Referendum Bill would bring them back to the Royal prerogative. After commenting on Lord Rosebery's denunciation of the action of the House of Lords and of the idea of reforming it in 1894, he expressed regret that the resolutions had not been before the country at the election and urged the Government to press on with them. If the Lords rejected them, let the Prime Minister ask for an assurance from the Crown that Peers would be created, and, if the request were refused, let him go to the country at once.

Mr. Asquith's resolution was agreed to on April 4, 1910. The majority was composed of 256 Liberals, 34 Labour Members, and 67 Nationalists. None but Unionists were in the minority.

The Bill founded on the resolutions was introduced by Mr. Asquith on April 14, 1910. Subsequently he explained that if the Lords rejected or declined to consider the Government policy, the Ministers would either resign or recommend a dissolution, and would not recommend a dissolution except under such conditions as to insure that in the new Parliament the judgment of the people as expressed at the election would be carried into law.

The progress of the Parliament Bill was temporarily delayed on account of the death of King Edward VII on May 6, 1910, and the accession of King George V. It was generally felt that it would be unfair to lay the burden of deciding whether or not to override the resistance of the Peers on the new King at the outset of his reign, and that in any case the controversy, though it could not be dropped, would have to be approached with an increasing readiness for a settlement. On June 8, the day fixed for the reassembling of Parliament, it was announced that the Ministry were ready to propose a small private conference between themselves and the Unionist leaders. Though not favourably received by the extremists on either side, the proposal was welcomed by the moderates of both parties.

On June 16 the Conference was formally decided upon by the leaders on both sides, and next day it held its first meeting in the Prime Minister's room, behind the Speaker's Chair in the House of Commons. It numbered eight members — Mr. H. H. Asquith, Mr. David Lloyd George, the Earl of Crewe, and Mr. Augustine

Birrell, representing the Government, and Mr. Arthur J. Balfour, the Marquess of Lansdowne, Earl Cawder, and Mr. Austen Chamberlain, the Opposition. An official statement was issued that the negotiations were entirely untrammelled and the proceedings would throughout be strictly confidential. Advanced Liberal and Labour opinions continued unfavourable, however; so was the main body of the Nationalists. Twenty-one meetings of the Constitutional Conference were held during the summer and autumn. At length, on November 10, the Prime Minister announced its complete failure and stated that, so far as the Government were concerned, another general election would be necessary in December.

The centre of interest then shifted to the House of Lords. On November 21, 1910, the Earl of Crewe, in behalf of the Government, moved the second reading of the Parliament Bill, setting forth in outline the controversy between the two Houses opened by the Education Bill of 1906 and presenting an analysis of its provisions (*Extract 77*). The Marquess of Lansdowne expressed strong opposition to the Bill in principle and in detail (*Extract 78*). In the subsequent debate, the Earl of Rosebery complained (*Extract 79*) that the House was regarded simply as a condemned criminal without the usual indulgences. The Lord Chancellor asked why Lord Rosebery or some other Peer had not brought forward some definite plan earlier (*Extract 80*).

The Peers would hardly feel inclined to go to the country on the question of the Veto without an alternative proposal to the Government's Parliament Bill. Therefore, on November 23, the Marquess of Lansdowne presented to the House of Lords the Opposition Scheme in the form of resolutions (*Extract 81*). Among the supporters of these resolutions was Lord Ribblesdale (*Extract 82*). They were at once passed, the Ministers holding aloof, and communicated to the House of Commons. The deadlock between the Houses and between the Parties was complete.

The Parliamentary session of 1910 was now virtually over, and the interest lay in the constituencies. The Ministerial case was effectively restated by the Prime Minister at Hull on November 25, before an audience of 3000, after the annual meeting of the National Liberal Federation, which had concentrated its attention on the Veto. Mr. Asquith first replied at length to the charge that the election was being rushed in order to set up single-chamber government. The Veto had been the dominant issue at the January election; the Peers had then no alternative policy; the King's death had prevented the fulfilment of his own promise; the failure of the Conference had necessitated a dissolution. It was said that the Government were hurrying on a dissolution to prevent the Lords from presenting their case and to avoid submitting the Budget to the Commons, and Lord Lansdowne's call for the Parliament Bill was supposed to have defeated the manœuvre. But before Parliament reassembled the Government had decided to present the essential features of the Budget to it, and to give the Peers full opportunity to criticise the Government's proposals on the Veto, or to present their own. The dissolution was undertaken to settle the question before proceeding with Liberal legislation. An adverse vote would bring Protection disguised as Tariff Reform; but he preferred to concentrate his criticism on Lord Lansdowne's "crude and complex" scheme. He did not believe the "backwoods Peers" or a Tory majority in the House of Commons would accept it, and he insisted especially on the obscurity of its details, the sacrifice of the Royal power to create Peers, the uncertainty as to the numbers of the new House, and the indefiniteness of the term "questions of great gravity." He objected to the referendum on three grounds: it would enable the House of Lords to enforce what would virtually be a general election — and, if the Ministry were beaten, there would be a general election besides; it would destroy the Parliamentary sense of responsibility, and therefore representative government. The Ministerial scheme was not a scheme for single-chamber government and was not final; it was the minimum necessary to get on with the Liberal programme, which he had stated at the Albert Hall in 1909. He saw no cause for shame in the givers or takers of American dollars ; and, in securing self-government for Ireland and afterwards lightening the work of Parliament, the Government should have the sympathy of the Dominions, who had learned how easy it was to combine local autonomy and Imperial loyalty. But the immediate task was to secure fair play for Liberal legislation and popular government.

The Unionist case was put on the same evening by Lord Lansdowne at a demonstration held at Glasgow after the annual meeting of the Liberal Unionist Council. After regretting that the Conference had not made for a reasonable settlement, he ridiculed the contention that the conflict was " Peers against People." The last four Liberal Ministries had created 136 Peers ; the Liberal Peers now numbered only 120. Of about 230 Ministerial measures introduced since January, 1906, the House of Lords had rejected only six. He mentioned nine of first-class importance that had become law and referred to Lord Carrington's eulogy of Liberal achievement. After defending at length the Lords' action on the Education, Licensing, and Finance Bills, he asked, Why was their interference regarded with jealousy ? Many people held that the hereditary principle was anomalous ; but moderate men would say that in Great Britain, especially at present, a real Second Chamber was needed. Ministers began at the wrong end ; they abused the House of Lords, but would not touch its reform. He outlined and upheld the alternative policy of his resolutions, and thought the outline might be filled up satisfactorily, but the Government refused to discuss it. The issue was between reform and revolution. He reaffirmed Tariff Reform and the Unionist land policy.

Parliament was prorogued, preparatory to its dissolution, on November 28 ; and the candidates for the House issued their customary appeals to constituents. Mr. Balfour's declared that " behind the single-chamber conspiracy lurk Socialism and Home Rule." Mr. Asquith's said that the appeal to the country was almost narrowed to a single issue, and on its determination hung the whole future of democratic government.

The general election which extended over the period from December 2 to December 20 returned 272 Liberals, 42 Labour Members, 76 Nationalists, 8 Independent Nationalists, — 398 Ministerials, — and 271 Unionists. On the whole, the result was much the same as in January. In London the Liberals had gained a little; in Scotland the Unionists had slightly strengthened their position. Speaking broadly, industrial England returned Ministerialists, except the Birmingham area, while the chief ports, except London, Liverpool, and Plymouth, and also the pleasure and residential towns and districts were Unionist. Class cleavage had increased.

The motion for leave to introduce the Parliament Bill in the new House of Commons was made by the Prime Minister on February 21, 1911, and the next day it passed first reading by 351 votes to 227. Second reading was passed amid noisy demonstrations on March 2 by 366 to 243. Some nine hundred amendments, most of which had been offered by Unionists, were considered during Committee and Report stages from April 3 to May 10. On May 15 the final effort of the Unionists in the House of Commons to reject the Bill was frustrated by a vote of 363 to 243, and the third reading carried by 362 to 241.

The Bill had been somewhat modified in its passage through the Commons. It had been made clear that it did not apply to private Bills; the wording of the clause relating to Money Bills had been made more precise, and the Bills relating to the raising of money by local authorities for local purposes had been expressly excluded; the certificate of the Speaker was required to be endorsed on all Money Bills when sent up to the Lords and presented for the royal assent, but the prohibition was struck out prohibiting any amendment which, in the opinion of the Speaker, would prevent the Bill from remaining a Money Bill. The two years' period was to run from the second reading in the first session to the passing the Commons in the third session, and amendments certified by the Speaker to have been made by the House of Lords in the third session and approved by the Commons were to form part of the Bill in question when presented for the royal assent.

In the House of Lords, the Parliament Bill now speedily passed first and second reading, the real struggle being deferred by the Conservative Peers until after the coronation. But in July the struggle became acute between the majority in the Upper House and the Government. On July 20, 1911, the Bill passed third reading, accompanied by several important amendments, which, had they been finally agreed to, would have defeated the purpose of the measure.

It was under these circumstances that the Prime Minister addressed the following letter to the leader of the Opposition:

10, Downing Street, July 20
Dear Mr. Balfour,
I think it is courteous and right, before any public decisions are announced, to let you know how we regard the political situation.

When the Parliament Bill in the form which it has now assumed returns to the House of Commons we shall be compelled to ask that House to disagree with the Lords' amendments.

In the circumstances, should the necessity arise, the Government will advise the King to exercise his prerogative to secure the passing into law of the Bill in substantially the same form in which it left the House of Commons, and His Majesty has been pleased to signify that he will consider it his duty to accept and act on that advice.
Yours sincerely,
H. H. Asquith

At a meeting of the Unionist Peers on July 21, Lord Lansdowne read a copy of the foregoing letter and pointed out that the Parliament Bill was to be passed, either with or without the creation of Peers. If the creation took place, the passage of the Parliament Bill and such measures as the Home Rule Bill would not be prevented, while the King's prerogative would have been brought into the political arena and a step taken which must be deplored. He therefore held that the Opposition Peers were no longer "free agents." The Earl of Halsbury strongly opposed surrender, and was supported, according to various accounts, by the Earl of Selborne, the Duke of Bedford, the Marquess of Salisbury, and Lord Willoughby de Broke; but Viscount St. Aldwyn, Lord Curzon of Kedleston, and the Duke of Devonshire strongly supported Lord Lansdowne in advocating submission. It was said by the *Times* that the minority against surrender numbered about fifty. The Irish Unionist members, according to a statement by their chairman, Sir Edward Carson, informed Lord Lansdowne that "the disgrace and ignominy of surrender on the question far outweighed any temporary advantage" derived from the fact that Home Rule would be subject to the delay of two years imposed by the Parliament Bill; and a dinner to the Earl of Halsbury as the leading advocate of resistance was given on July 26. Against "surrender" the chief arguments were that the country would be roused against the Liberals by the creation of new Peers, and that the latter would soon cease to be Radical.

The House of Commons met to deal with the Lords' amendments on Monday, July 24, 1911. It was thronged in every part, and the situation favoured an explosion. Mr. Asquith, on entering, was received with Liberal and Nationalist acclamations, and murmurs and cries of "Traitor" from the Opposition, who loudly cheered Mr. Balfour. After questions and the introduction of five new members, Mr. Asquith rose, but was again received with uproar and cries of "Traitor." The Speaker intervened without avail; several members on both sides rose to points of order, Lord Hugh Cecil taking a prominent part in the disturbance. There were shouts to the Prime Minister of "Consult your masters!" and "Let Redmond speak!" Sir Edward Carson, after further interruptions, moved the adjournment of the debate, but the Speaker pointed out that as yet there was no debate, and urged a little later that the right of free discussion was far more important for the Opposition than for the Government. Mr. Asquith was then able to begin his speech and sketch the history of the Parliament

Bill. There were, however, constant derisive interruptions, among the cries being "Leave the King out!" and "Who killed the King?" At last he declined "to degrade himself further" by pressing his arguments on the Opposition; he merely stated that unless the House of Lords would consent to restore the Bill with reasonable amendments Ministers would be compelled to invoke the exercise of the Royal prerogative. One thing was certain — the determination of the Government and the vast majority of the people that without further delay the Bill should become law.

The motion for disagreeing with the Lords' amendments was at length carried in the House of Commons on August 8, 1911, by 321 votes to 215.

The momentous debate on the question of acquiescence by the House of Lords in the treatment given to their amendments by the Commons took place on August 9 and 10, 1911. Lord Willoughby de Broke, a leader among the resisters, declared in the course of a vigorous speech that the Government might win a dozen general elections without altering his opposition to the Bill; he warned the bishops that the Established Church could be retained only through the agency of the Tory party. The Earl of Halsbury, the Dukes of Norfolk, Bedford, and Marlborough, and others, supported resistance. Lord Newton, in an answering speech, described the attitude of the resisters as that of the Chinese who killed themselves on the doorstep of the person who had ill-treated them, and said that, so far from ridicule killing the creation, "they would have the ridicule, and the Government, the Peers." The Marquess of Lansdowne likewise urged surrender, as did Lord Ribblesdale, Viscount St. Aldwyn, the Earl of Camperdown, and others.

At last, the Archbishop of Canterbury said briefly that he had intended to abstain from voting, but he had been influenced by the callousness and levity with which some noble Lords contemplated the creation of 500 Peers, which would make the House and the country a laughing-stock in the Dominions and in foreign countries.

Lord Curzon of Kedleston most earnestly advocated submission, because the Bill would pass in any case; it might be rejected — owing to the actions of a small minority of the Unionists — and then there would certainly be a creation of Peers large enough to upset the Constitution. "You will have to start fresh. God knows how we shall do it." The Marquess of Bristol interjected, "It is because 400 Peers are going to run away to-night." Lord Curzon replied, "I would sooner run away with the Duke of Wellington than stand with the noble Lord." The Earl of Halsbury vigorously contested Earl Curzon's argument; the Earl of Rosebery, in extremity, announced his intention of supporting the Government; and the Earl of Selborne, in an impassioned speech, asked, Should they perish in the dark by their own hand, or in the light, killed by their enemies?

In intense excitement, the division took place, and the result was for some time uncertain. But the motion "that the House do not insist on the amendment" was carried by 131 to 114, thirty-seven Unionist Peers voting with the Government.

The Parliament Act of 1911, in its final form, is given as *Extract 83.*]

Extract 71

PROPOSALS FOR RESTRICTING THE POWER OF THE HOUSE OF LORDS

(Sir Henry Campbell-Bannerman, Prime Minister and First Lord of the Treasury, Commons, June 24, 1907)

SIR H. CAMPBELL-BANNERMAN [1]: I rise to move, "That, in order to give effect to the will of the people as expressed by their elected representatives, it is necessary that the power of the other House to alter or reject Bills passed by this House should be so restricted by law as to secure that within the limits of a single

[1] Parliamentary Debates, Fourth Series, vol. 176, col. 909 sqq.

Parliament the final decision of the Commons shall prevail." In moving this Resolution we are following the notable precedent of the famous Resolutions of 1678 and 1860; and I hope our method of procedure will commend itself to the House. . . .

My Motion affirms the predominance of the House of Commons as the representative House of Parliament, and I submit that in spirit and in fact that is a strictly true constitutional proposition. I may claim for it, up to a point, the adhesion of the Party opposite and of the House of Lords itself. The supremacy of the people is admitted in theory even by the House of Lords. It is admitted that the will of the people — that will upon which the poet tells us our Constitution is broad-based — is in the long run entitled to prevail. It is admitted even by those whose natural leanings and proclivities would lead them to a very restricted order of representative institutions. To that extent, therefore, we are seemingly at one. How, then, is that will of the people to be got at and ascertained unless you take the view of the elective House as expressing it? The supremacy of the people in legislation implies, in this country at any rate, the authority of the Commons. The party for which I speak has never swerved from that position, and unless you are going to fall back upon some foreign method, such as the referendum or the mandate or the plebiscite, or some other way of getting behind the backs of the elected to the electors themselves, such as was advised by both the first and third Napoleon — unless that is the example you are going to follow, then there is no course open but to recognise ungrudgingly the authority which resides in this House and to accept the views of the Nation as represented in its great interests within these walls. The Resolution embodies, therefore, a principle the logic of which at any rate is accepted by both Parties and both Houses — the principle of the predominance of the House of Commons.

But let us be quite clear as to what we mean by predominance, and especially what we mean by 'the ultimate prevalence of the House of Commons. We do not on this side of the House mean

an abstract, a deferred supremacy; that is not what we mean by
the supremacy of the House of Commons. We do not mean a
supremacy that comes into play after one or two or more appeals
to the country, before which a determined resistance of the other
House will give way. That is not what we mean by the supremacy
of the House of Commons. That arrangement does not in the
least fulfil the requirements of the Constitution. Where we differ,
therefore, is as to the point at which the authority of this House
becomes effective. . . .

What meaning does the supremacy of the House of Commons
convey to the minds of the House of Lords? In the first place, it is
matter of common knowledge that its working varies according to
circumstances. When their own Party are in power — that is the
Party to which the vast majority of the Members of the House of
Lords belong — they recognise without reservation, they even make
what I would almost call indecent haste, to recognise this supremacy.
There is never a suggestion that the checks and balances of the
Constitution are to be brought into play; there is never a hint that
this House is anything but a clear and faithful mirror of the settled
opinions and desires of the country, or that the arm of the executive falls short of being the instrument of the national will. No,
Sir; the other House, in these circumstances, may be said to adopt
and act upon the view of the inherent authority of this House, which
was expressed by Edmund Burke in these words, "The virtue, spirit,
and essence of the House of Commons consists in its being the
express image of the nation." I know of no instance under a con-
genial régime, that is to say, not in recent times, when the House
of Lords seriously challenged the decisions of this House except
— it is rather comical — in the solitary case of the Deceased Wife's
Sister Bill; on two separate occasions this House has passed this
Bill when the Conservatives were in power — a private Bill it was
— and on both occasions the other House rejected it. It is almost
refreshing to come upon this marked action in the revising House.
But certainly the supposed characteristic of a single-chamber system

of Government which prevails in Unionist times has never been broken by any hint or suggestion that the Government and the House of Commons should go to the country and ascertain what the people were thinking. That is a novel innovation. . . .

. . . Witness the transition that takes place the moment a Liberal House of Commons comes into being. A complete change comes over this constitutional doctrine of the supremacy of this Chamber. They rested and reposed on its supremacy during the period that I have been dealing with. Now they challenge it; and it becomes a deferred supremacy — a supremacy which is to arrive, it may be, at the next election, or the election after that, or may be never at all. Suppose a difference to arise between the two Houses, not the existing House of Commons but some future one is to prevail. What is the good of electing us to the House of Commons? [Ironical Opposition cheers.] What is the good of electing Members of either side to the House of Commons, if the opinion of the House of Commons is to be of no account? If the House of Lords knows better than the House of Commons, what is the good of the House of Commons? I do not know, I never have known, and I have never been able to discover, by what process the House of Lords professes to ascertain whether or not our decisions correspond with the sentiments of the electors; but what I do know is that this House has to submit to carry on its existence in a state of suspense, knowing that our measures are liable to be amended, altered, rejected, and delayed in accordance with the mysterious intuition, almost divination, which enables the Lords to keep in immediate touch with the electors during a Liberal administration. It is a singular thing, when you come to reflect upon it, that the representative system should only hold good when one Party is in office, and should break down to such an extent as that the non-elective House must be called in to express the mind of the country whenever the country lapses into Liberalism. . . .

Now I come to another question which we have to ask ourselves, and that is: What is the nature of the authority under which the other House, during its intermittent period of activity claims to override and suspend the decisions of this House and to afford it a merely nominal and deferred predominance? What are the grounds on which the Lords intervene? There is no occasion to go back very far. Before the Reform Act there was really no question of this kind before the country, for this reason: Both Houses were in the habit of working together in the interests of the existing state of society, which was very far from being a democratic state, and any tendency to independence on the part of the House of Commons was held in check by the fact that there were some 300 votes in this House under control of the Members of the other House. There was, therefore, in these circumstances, no particular occasion for a veto. Nor do I propose to go over subsequent history — a dismal history in this respect, in which beneficent measures were flouted or rejected or mutilated and violent hands laid upon them by the other House. Their actions are all of a piece, and I think we may be quite content to take the most recent instances as a pattern and example of what has been happening ever since the Reform Bill was passed. We take them because we have them fresh in our minds. They happened under our eyes in the present Parliament, which has not had a long life yet. These events, marking as they do, in my opinion, the climax of this long series of rebuffs put upon this House, and through this House upon the electors, embody in themselves in a sufficiently striking manner the claims that are really put forward to stultify the action of the Commons. When you find a general election like the last treated as mere irrelevance, and a House of Commons which returned with an unexampled majority regarded elsewhere as a body devoid of real vitality and vital authority, I say we then have to look upon its claims with a stronger feeling, because they are put forward with a degree of violent aggressiveness which compels us to challenge them. If we are concerned at all with the authority of the House of Commons — and I trust that everyone within these walls is concerned — it is impossible for us to let this pass. I therefore take the actual cases within our own immediate experience as the touchstone of the claims of the other House. The first thing I would point out is that the merits and demerits of the Bills that we deal with are not in question at all. The Education Bill and the Plural Voting Bill may be thoroughly bad Bills in the estimation of hon. Members opposite and of the right hon. Gentleman at the winding of whose horn the portcullis over the way comes rattling down. If the country shares the view of the right hon. Gentleman, it is not there [The Front Opposition Bench] he would be, but here. But let hon. Gentlemen observe that the other House, when it proceeded, within twelve months of the election, summarily to dispose of these measures of ours, did so, according to its own account, not on their merits, but because it claimed to know the mind of the country. That was the plea that was urged. "Your Education Bill," they said, "does not square with the professions of the people or the desires of the people, and as for your Electoral Reform Bill, it ought to be part of a larger scheme of reform such as the country desires." Of course, they dwelt on the vicious qualities of our poor Bills. So they did in the case of the Trade Disputes Bill, which was an even blacker and more iniquitous Bill than the others. But they passed this Bill, and they rejected the less infamous Bills; and they were strictly logical in so doing. By that I mean that the reason they gave was an intelligible reason. They professed to be satisfied that a powerful section of opinion demanded the one Bill and they professed to be unsatisfied that the others were so demanded. They acted on their own judgment. Their whole case rests upon that. And I may add as a subsidiary reason that in the case of the infamous and iniquitous Bill it was considered desirable to exercise some circumspection. We all remember the words of Lord Lansdowne that they were passing through a period when it was necessary for the House of Lords to move with great caution. Conflicts and controversies might be inevitable. Let their Lordships, as far as they were able, be sure that if they were to join issue they did so on ground which was as favourable as possible to themselves — not to the country — in the interests of good and sound legislation. In this case he believed the ground would be unfavourable to the House. So they passed that most iniquitous and dangerous and disastrous Bill. They made friends with the mammon of unrighteousness with a view to maintaining themselves in their own habitation. Therefore, in addition to this intermittent action we have to take note of this further singular fact that the powers of that House are avowedly exercised without reference to the merits of what is sent up to it, and on the ground that we, who are the representatives of the people as the result of all our elaborate electoral machinery, are incapable of speaking and acting on their behalf.

Such a claim will not stand a moment's investigation. The Constitution knows nothing of this doctrine of the special mandate, nothing whatever. It is an invention apparently of the Lords, designed to afford them some kind of shelter behind which they may get rid of the Bills they dislike. Now, I am anxious to make this matter clear, because it is important to my proposition — namely, that the relations of the Houses call for definition ; and if the action of the House of Lords is based on assumptions which are fatal to a true representative system, then the question of how far they are entitled to push such action surely requires serious consideration. If this House was elected on a mandate for this or a mandate for that, or a mandate for the other, I could understand, even if I did not approve of, the process of sifting and trying our decisions in order to see whether they corresponded with what passed at the elections. In its absence such a claim becomes grotesque. Yet how seriously is it urged. We are invited to go to the country *ad hoc* to test whether the other House or this House is 'right whenever we come to a deadlock. We have not been elected on any such system as that. We were elected to carry out certain broad principles, and yet, forsooth, we are to go back, and be re-elected on Bills and on sections of Bills and subsections of Bills if we are to convince the other House. I shall have a

word to say directly on this demand for a dissolution, but I want
first to say how glad I am to be able to claim the right hon. Gentleman opposite as a sworn foe of the doctrine of the mandate.
He has described it as fundamentally essentially a vicious theory.
" You could not work Parliamentary institutions," he says, " on
that principle at all." [Opposition cheers.] Yes, but it is on that
very principle that the House of Lords are working. Why has the
right hon. Gentleman not warned the House of Lords that they
are pursuing a course under which, as he says, Parliamentary
institutions cannot be worked at all, and that they are seeking
to inveigle us into an unconstitutional and vicious system ? It is
strange that when they challenge us because we have not got a
mandate for this, or that we have misread a mandate for that, or
that we must go to the country for a mandate for the other thing,
the right hon. Gentleman sits quietly and allows them to flounder
in the morass. . . .

Now I come to the outline of the plan which the Government
propose. It is proposed that, if a Bill is sent up to the other
House, and in the result the two Houses find agreement impossible, a Conference shall be held between Members appointed in
equal numbers by the two Houses. The conference will be of
small dimensions. Its proceedings will be private, and its objects
will be to enable each Party to negotiate and to seek for a common measure of agreement which the Government might find
itself able to adopt. There is nothing novel in this proposal, because the two Houses formerly did meet in conference ; but there
were certain inconveniences in the procedure, and, whether it was
due to the fact that the Commons were expected to go into the
other House bareheaded and to remain standing, or whether it was
due to the obvious practical difficulties of arriving at any decision
at a joint meeting carried on by a large number of persons in this
singular manner, no Conference has been held since 1836. Informal conferences between members of the Government and Opposition in the two Houses have, of course, not infrequently been

held since that date, and sometimes good results have followed. But what the Government proposes is that statutory provision should be made for such meetings in the event of disagreement, and that the Conference should occupy a definite place in the transactions between the two Houses. Supposing, then, the Conference to be unproductive. The Bill — either the same Bill, with or without modifications, or a similar Bill with the same object — might at the discretion of the Government be reintroduced after a substantial interval; and by a substantial interval I have in my mind a minimum of perhaps six months, unless in cases of great urgency. This Bill would be passed through its various stages in the House of Commons under limitations of time — limitations of time adapted to the requirements of the case — discussion being restricted, so far as possible, to the new matter, if any, introduced. The Bill would then be sent up again, so that the other House would have a second and ample opportunity of considering it. If there was still a difference between the two Houses, a Conference might again be summoned. Supposing this time an arrangement again failed, this second Bill would be reintroduced and passed swiftly through all its stages in this House in the form last agreed to and sent to the other House with an intimation that unless passed in that form it would be passed over their heads. Yet again there would be a Conference, and a further effort to agree. Now the House will see that the plan which I have sketched gives ample — some will think too ample — opportunities for discussion and reflection, and that it provides full room in the intervals for consideration by the country. And we are convinced that it leaves no opening for hasty or arbitrary action. . . .

Here is a most important point. It may be said that it will be in the power of an effete Government in the last years of an effete Parliament, when the sentiment of the country may have become cold, or, at least, uncertain, to carry things with a high hand, and in such circumstances any amount of deliberation and consultation would fail to prevent rash and arbitrary measures being taken. It is quite true, Sir, that we have known cases where an effete Government, trading on the initial strength it had lost, has dragged out an undesirable existence amid the flickering activity which we associate with the exhausted candle. But no one can say that that is a favourable moment for legislation. Therefore, I have to state that we are strongly of opinion that the way to guard against such an evil is the very simple way of shortening the duration of Parliament.

This reform can be justified on other and broader grounds. But I am here speaking of it only in face of this particular matter with which my Resolution deals; and we consider that the undoubted danger that the House of Commons, with the increased power which we claim for it, might for some years of its life have its genuine representative character impaired, can be best guarded against by a more frequent reference to the electorate. This is, as is known, no new proposal. Most of us on this Bench have voted for quinquennial Parliaments, and we believe that the reduction of the period of Parliamentary existence to five years will add vigour, freshness, and life to our Parliamentary system.

There are, indeed, very vague, and, I think, not very well-informed proposals for a foreign institution, called a referendum, whereby a particular Bill can be submitted to a special vote on the part of the electors of the country. I see the strongest objections to any such proposal. The necessary isolation of the subject from the whole range of political feeling is well-nigh impossible; it is inconsistent with, and, in my opinion, destructive of, Parliamentary government as we understand it; and it has the peculiarity that you would be introducing a new element into our Constitution which would never come into play while one order of things was represented in the Government, but when Liberals were in a majority would be employed for the purpose of flouting and defeating the Government of the day, the majority in the House of Commons, and the electorate itself.

Let me point out that the plan which I have sketched to the House does not in the least preclude or prejudice any proposals which may be made for the reform of the House of Lords itself. The constitution and composition of the House of Lords is a question entirely independent of my subject. My Resolution has nothing to do with the relations of the two Houses to the Crown, but only with the relations of the two Houses one to the other. At present we are face to face, as I have shown, with the ultimate supremacy of the House of Lords. I see that this is the theory almost nakedly put forward by some of those gentlemen in the Press who are good enough to tell us what we ought to do. They evidently have in their minds as a model some of those Continental States whose system is essentially and fundamentally autocratic, but in which the autocracy ornaments and supplements itself with a representative body, useful for occupying public attention and for hammering out the details of legislation, but bearing much the same relation that the kitchenmaid bears to the cook. The House of Lords, according to this theory, is to be the cook. Sir, the House of Commons is spoken of by these instructors of the public in language of formal, guarded, traditional respect, but is treated as a wayward, impulsive body allowed to do useful work and on occasion to have its fling, but to be pulled up by the House of Lords as soon as it ventures upon the pet prejudices and interests of that which used to be the ruling class in this kingdom. Sir, we have not so learned our existing Constitution. We have perfect confidence in the good feeling, the good sense, the wisdom, the righteousness, and the patriotism of our country. We need no shelter against them ; and, therefore, we would invert the rôles thus assigned to the two Houses. Let the country have the fullest use on all matters of the experience, wisdom, and patriotic industry of the House of Lords in revising and amending and securing full consideration for legislative measures ; but, and these words sum up our whole policy, the Commons shall prevail.

Extract 72

DEFENCE OF THE HOUSE OF LORDS

(Mr. Arthur J. Balfour, Commons, June 24, 1907)

MR. BALFOUR [1] : The very last words that fell from the mouth of the right hon. Gentleman indicate sufficiently the difference which lies between us. His contention, expressed with considerable reiteration in the course of his speech, is that any House of Commons, elected at any particular date, is competent within the term of its own existence to deal with the whole interests of the State and modify them completely, without further reference to the people who gave it birth. He lays it down categorically in the last sentence he uttered that it is the House of Commons alone whose rights and privileges we have to consider. I venture to consider that we might occasionally think of the people. The real and only problem which ought to be before the minds of those who are engaged in dealing with the Constitution of a free country is how the continuous will of the people — the interests of the existing generation and the interests of generations to come — can be best considered. And it is to that problem alone that I shall endeavour to direct the attention of the House to-day in the few observations I have to make upon the right hon. Gentleman's proposals. . . .

I do not at all deny that this House is the predominant partner. By the practice of the Constitution it undoubtedly is so. But just see how great are the powers that this House possesses which the other House neither possesses nor makes any claim to. We must always remember that the most important decision the country makes at the election is who shall control the administrative machinery and the general policy of the country. That decision the House of Lords neither claims to touch, nor can touch. The Government of the day, the House of Commons of the day, would treat with

---

[1] Parliamentary Debates, Fourth Series, vol. 176, col. 926 sqq.

derision any vote passed by the House of Lords condemning a particular Ministry or a particular member of a Ministry. They would not suggest for a moment that such a vote carried with it either the resignation of the Government or the Minister, or a dissolution, or any consequence whatever except a mere statement of opinion on the part of their Lordships that they disapproved of a Ministry to whom this House gave its confidence. That, after all, is the greatest of the powers which this House possesses. We can put an end to a Government; we can bring a Government into being; we can destroy the career of a Minister; and we can pass a vote of censure which carries with it an immediate resignation. We have our hand upon the administrative machine to this extent at all events — that we cannot prevent a Government doing that of which we disapprove; we can afterwards punish it for having done so.

It is true that the Administration is in many particulars far out of the reach of the House of Commons, and ought to be. The House of Commons cannot make a treaty; it cannot prevent the Government making a treaty; if it could, would the New Hebrides Convention ever have been made? It cannot prevent the Government making war; it cannot prevent the Government making peace or exercising any one of these great administrative responsibilities. All it can do is afterwards to pass some condemnation upon the Government. In passing that condemnation it takes into account not merely the particular executive transaction, but whether upon the whole it desires to see the Government retained in office or not; and the House of Commons will constantly condone actions of which it disapproves simply because it does not wish to dispossess the Government of office. In that sense the Government always possesses the confidence of the House of Commons. . . .

We all being agreed that the House of Lords under our existing system occupies a very subordinate position, the question is whether that position, subordinate as it is now, shall be made yet more subordinate by the House of Lords being deprived altogether of the power of preventing a particular House of Commons, elected at some particular conjuncture, from doing everything it wishes, not merely in the sphere of administration, where you must leave it to the Government of the day for good or for ill, but doing whatever it likes in the sphere of legislation, where you may in one day, or at all events in a few weeks, upset institutions which have taken centuries to rear and which once destroyed can never be replaced. . . .

I gather from the right hon. Gentleman that he thinks this is a very undemocratic way of looking at the matter. What is a democratic way of looking at it? I understand the democratic theory of Government to be that those who are concerned with the decision should be the people who make it; and as far as that can be attained, I, at all events, desire to see it attained. But who is concerned with the decision which we make when a great constitutional issue is involved? Is it the particular Parliament? Are the particular male adults in a given year who have got the given qualifications the only people whose interests are concerned? Those adult males are, in the first place, the heirs, and, in the second place, trustees of many centuries; and it is preposterous to say that we should so frame our Constitution that the holders of power for the moment should be regarded as in every respect the irresponsible managers, not only of their own affairs for the moment, but of the affairs of their country for all time. Because, remember, there are many things which can be done which are irreversible when you are dealing with great growths in the region of politics; just as when you are dealing with them in the region of nature you cannot replace that which you destroy. You may pull down a building and erect another exactly like it; you cannot cut down a tree and say, " To-morrow I will have another tree in its place." So it is with an institution. You are absolutely bound to see that no hasty decision shall upset in one reckless hour interests which have been slowly and painfully built up by our predecessors, and which our successors never can replace.

Therefore, I say, you must in this country do what every other country has done, what some other countries have done with

over-caution and over-care, — see that there is some permanence
and continuity in your institutions. I am no favourer of perpetual
entails, I do not wish to see the institutions of this country in any
particular stereotyped and perpetuated for all time, made absolutely
petrified and immovable, as, for instance, the institutions of the
American Commonwealth are, or almost are, under the peculiar
regulations of their Constitution. But while I do not wish to imitate
the immovable conservatism of the republican institutions of America, I think we should be perfectly insane — setting aside not only
the lessons of our own history, but of every other history — if we
did not so arrange our Constitution that when the people decide
upon a change it shall be after the most mature consideration, after
the thing has been weighed and looked at from all sides, and after
it has been considered in isolation from all those perturbing considerations which operate at a moment. It is folly to call that
anti-democratic ; on the contrary, it is democracy properly understood. It is government of the people by the people — [AN HON.
MEMBER : For the people ?] — and for the people. Not by the
people for the people living under one Parliament, be it of seven
or five years' duration, but by the people for the people for generations. If the interests we had to deal with were the interests of a
particular set of electors at a particular time, let them manage or
mismanage their own affairs as they please ; but let us take care
that as interests far beyond their own immediate and personal interests are confided to them, they should exercise the great duties
thrown on them with full responsibility and full knowledge after
mature reflection. Let us not hand over, as the right hon. Gentleman proposes to hand over, to a House of Commons elected, it may
be in some moment of passion, like 1900 — [Ministerial cheers] —
like 1906, the eternal and perpetual interests of the country. . . .

I wish the right hon. Gentleman had given us more details in
regard to the disasters which have followed from the present state
of things. He skipped lightly from the beginning of time to the
first Reform Bill, and still more lightly from the first Reform Bill

to last year; but in this agile procedure he never made any reference to the greatest attempt at constitutional change which has been made in our time. That, of course, was Mr. Gladstone's attempt to establish Home Rule in 1886 and 1893. Home Rule may be right or wrong. I am not going to argue that question. But it would be a very great constitutional change. It would fundamentally alter the relations between Great Britain and Ireland; and even those who believe in it most firmly, and who look forward to it with the most sanguine confidence, must admit that it would carry in its train a whole series of consequences, which it is quite impossible for any prophet, however endowed, adequately to foresee. Caution, therefore, is eminently required in making such a change as this. Our existing institutions have not prevented Home Rule. Home Rule may come. But they have insured that Home Rule shall not, at all events, be carried in the way which the right hon. Gentleman wants to carry everything in future. If ever there was a decision of the country upon Home Rule, surely that decision was taken, first in 1886, and secondly in 1895. The decision may have been wrong, but that decision in 1895 absolutely reversed the decision which the House of Commons had come to in 1886 and 1893 respectively.

MR. LLOYD GEORGE : The Home Rule Bill of 1886 did not pass the Commons.

MR. BALFOUR : It was adopted by the Government of the day dependent upon the House of Commons. That is quite as good for the purpose of my argument. But if you quarrel with the instance of 1886, let us confine our attention to 1893. The election which followed in 1895 showed that the people, perhaps mistakenly, — I am not arguing that, — were not in favour of Home Rule. Now, let us examine how Home Rule would have worked under the right hon. Gentleman's plan. He says he is going to introduce quinquennial Parliaments, and thinks by that means the House of Commons will never be out of touch with the people. But the House of Commons which was dissolved in 1895 only lasted for three years. It therefore fell far short of the quinquennial term, upon which the right hon. Gentleman relies for this perpetual co-ordination between the views of the House of Commons and the views of the people. And yet the people stated as decisively as they could that the House of Lords had properly exercised in the greatest of all cases the functions entrusted to it by the Constitution. Had the right hon. Gentleman's so-called reform been in existence in 1893, Home Rule, I presume, would now be law — perhaps to the benefit of the community, but certainly against the will of the people. Is it possible, with that instance fresh in our memories, to say that this change, whatever its other merits may be, is intended, in the words of the Resolution, to " give effect to the will of the people ? " If those who framed this Resolution had in their minds recent history in which they themselves were personally engaged, this Resolution is hypocritical on the face of it. It is intended not to carry out the will of the people, but the will of the House of Commons of the moment. Am I not, then, justified in repeating the words with which I began my speech, that the right hon. Gentleman when he talks about the people is think-ing rather of the House of Commons, and that it is our business to think rather of the people than the House of Commons?

But this does not exhaust my criticism of the right hon. Gentle-man's motives. He has no claim, or even the pretence of a claim, to be carrying out the will of the people by this Resolution. It is his own will that he wants to carry out. I think the facts go fur-ther than that. The right hon. Gentleman belongs to the school of Radicalism, which holds as inveterate superstition and prejudice that the one object you should always be driving at is not to bring in good legislation, but to alter the legislative machinery. Social legislation appears in their speeches, but it never appears anywhere else. . . . They have not desired to bring in Bills which were so good that nobody could quarrel with them, but Bills so bad that no Assembly left to free discussion could reconcile itself to passing them unamended. That makes legislation extremely easy ; and it makes quarrelling with the House of Lords still more easy. But easy as that policy seems, much as it saves any undue waste of brain tissue on the part of the Ministers, I see no signs that it is carrying great favour in the country. I think the people see through this transparency. Many of them, I dare say, voted for right hon. Gentlemen opposite in the mistaken view that it was in the power of this Government or, indeed, of any Government, to carry certain schemes, or at all events to attain to certain objects which they had much at heart. Right hon. Gentlemen opposite gave them to understand that they had panaceas for all those evils if they came to office; but when they had to turn those panaceas from perorations into Bills they found it extremely difficult, if not in some cases impossible. Under these circumstances, it was far easier for the Government to try to quarrel with the House of Lords, to say to the people, "Oh, if you only knew what wonderful schemes we have in our heads, what admirable measures we have in our pigeon-holes! But there is the House of Lords, which will certainly reject them if we send them up." Great is their disappointment, almost unaffected, when the House of Lords passes a measure — not, indeed, the result of the brains of the Government, but the result of the Labour representatives — when the House of Lords, instead of doing what they were intended to do, does the opposite, then the right hon. Gentleman cannot control himself. Their flagitious, unscrupulous opportunism moves his wrath and arouses his indignation, and for the simple reason that the right hon. Gentleman's Bills, as I have said, were never brought in to pass, but to be rejected. ["Oh, oh."] And I think they were so drafted that there was great difficulty in some cases in not rejecting the Bills. I venture to suggest to the House that that is not the way to prepare a road for a great constitutional change. You ought not, if you find yourself impotent in constructive legislation, to turn round and try to curry favour with what you call the democracy by pulling down a portion of the Constitution. . . . Sir, the whole thing is insincere from beginning to end.

The right hon. Gentleman is treating the Constitution of which he ought to be the guardian as a plaything of the moment, as a mere political expedient, as a means for electrifying and revivifying, if he can, the waning popularity of himself and his colleagues. It will serve no useful end; and even that relatively contemptible object which the right hon. Gentleman has in view will not, in my judgment, be fulfilled, as time will show when next he goes to that people in whose name he affects to speak in this Resolution, and whose confidence, if not already lost, he is losing every day.

Extract 73

THE UNDEMOCRATIC CHARACTER OF THE HOUSE OF LORDS

(*Mr. D. Shackleton, Commons, June 24, 1907*)

MR. SHACKLETON [1]: . . . We have been told that we are wasting our time to-day. Some of us on these Benches have thought that for a long time. We feel that so far as the country is concerned the sooner it does devote a little time to attempting to remove this terrible obstacle to all improvement in the condition of the people the better. It may have the effect of putting off other legislation for the time being, but it may make legislation quicker in the future. We are not now considering the question of a Single Chamber as against two Chambers, but whether we are to go on forever with an hereditary Chamber.

Even the Leader of the Opposition has not attempted to defend the hereditary principle. I listened most carefully to all his references to the House of Lords, and he did not utter one single sentence in favour of that principle. The question is whether an hereditary and non-representative House shall be perpetual in this country. That is the situation we have got to face. I take no other

[1] Parliamentary Debates, Fourth Series, vol. 176, col. 941 sqq.

text for my remarks than the words of the Leader of the Opposition, who said on November 28, " I do not for one moment believe that the Lords, in the exercise of the high functions entrusted to them by the Constitution, will waver in their duty. Their duty is not to thwart the will of the nation, but to see that its will is really and truly carried out." The House of Lords has no right to decide what is the will of the people. Can it be said that a non-representative body, composed entirely of gentlemen drawn from one class, is a proper body to decide what is the will of the people of this country? What are we here for? If we do not represent the will of the people, it is time we came to some understanding as to what we do represent. But a mere assertion of that kind is not sufficient. That argument has gone forever, and a determined House and a determined people will refuse to allow a non-representative body drawn entirely from one class to decide what is the will of the people.

In the early days there were struggles between this House and the other; I read the other day that in 1648 a debate took place as to whether Black Rod should be the supreme person. Black Rod had ordered certain people to be arrested, and in the end King Charles dissolved Parliament and took away from the House of Commons the right to have anybody put into prison. And what did the House of Commons decide? That " The House of Peers is useless and dangerous, and ought to be abolished." That is the view to-day of the hon. Members who are sitting beside me, and they believe that the Government would have done better if they had proceeded on those lines.

During the last hundred years the pages of our history are full of their actions against the people. In 1807 they started by throwing out a Bill appointing a Committee of Council for Education. During the last century Bills for the benefit of the people were stopped and delayed. Question after question, such as Parliamentary Reform, land reform, the Roman Catholic position, religious equality, municipal and educational reform, and legal, social, and industrial measures might be quoted in which the House of Lords prevented the will of the people being carried into effect. Surely it is time that those who represent the people should challenge the right of the House of Lords to force the people to the verge of a revolution before giving way. . . .

Hasty legislation has been referred to. Is there ever any hasty legislation of a progressive character? There may be some of a retrograde character. What reform have we to-day that has not been talked about for years and generations before it has been embodied in an Act of Parliament? There is no chance in this country of hasty legislation, for all proposed reforms are subjected to long discussion in public before we hear of them in the shape of legislative measures. Illustrations could be given of cases in which the other House has delayed the changes in the law which the people desired. No better illustration could be given than that which took place between 1833 and 1857 in regard to Jewish emancipation. Majorities in this House on seven occasions were in favour of that reform, but the House of Lords refused to pass it. In the end, in 1858, the other House passed the Bill which conferred political freedom and equality on that class of our countrymen. . . .

The hereditary principle is indefensible from every point of view of public policy. The fact that it is not defended is its best and greatest condemnation. If it is good, why not apply it to other governing bodies and the various forms of business? Why should Parliament be the only place where the hereditary principle is applied? How often have we heard business men whom we have known refer in sorrow to the inclinations of their sons? The big businesses set up by the fathers have been lost under the management of the sons. Is that not so in regard to Parliamentary affairs as well as anything else? Surely the time has come when the right to govern by birth should be abolished in this country. A caustic writer puts it in this way, " We allow babies to be earmarked in their cradles as future law-makers, utterly regardless as to whether they turn out to be statesmen, or fools, or rogues." That is exactly the situation put in blunt language. . . .

I am old enough to remember that on a previous occasion I had the honour, along with my hon. friend the Member for Sowerby Bridge, to carry a banner in 1884 in a campaign against the House of Lords. We were in earnest then, and we are doubly in earnest now, and I trust that whatever else may be said the taunt of the right hon. Gentleman will not hold true that His Majesty's present advisers are simply using this as a red herring. I trust that they mean serious business. The recollections of 1884 are not very pleasant to some of us. There was a great opportunity then, and the country was ripe for legislation in regard to the House of Lords. I believe that in 1893 the mistake that was made was that there was too much made of " mending " and too little about " ending " the House of Lords. I know the opinion of workingmen fairly well, and I am confident that they are not in favour of any truckling or mending. What they are in favour of is an ending process, judging from the expressions of opinion given at conferences and other congregations of men. They are not in favour of any mending because they believe that would mean that the Lords would have greater power to interfere with measures sent to them from this House. If there is to be a revising Chamber, let it be on different principles altogether from the present House of Lords. I hope, therefore, we in this House shall determine to put our shoulders to the wheel in this matter. . . .

But in regard to the propositions which have been put before the House by the Prime Minister, let me say this — I think them far too generous. It appears to me that once a measure is rejected, if it goes a second time that ought to be sufficient. Why take up the time of the House in sending it back to the Lords a third time when you have the people behind you, and when you are certain that your decisions are those of the country? That is the only criticism I make at the present time. I think if the House of Lords gets two opportunities of considering a Bill that should be enough.

Extract 74

DEFENCE OF TWO-CHAMBER GOVERNMENT

(Sir William Anson, Oxford University, Commons, June 24, 1907)

SIR WILLIAM ANSON [1]: . . . You are practically proposing to make this a Single-Chamber Constitution. Are we in accord with the general experience in accepting a Constitution of that kind? I will venture to say that there is no civilised government which has not secured itself in some way or other from rash or hasty legislation by the popular Assembly, either by a written Constitution, or by a referendum, or by a Second Chamber — by one of these three methods which are universally employed for protection against this undoubted risk. The object of a Second Chamber, as stated by an eminent Colonial authority is, to delay great changes until the will of the people has been permanently and conclusively ascertained. We are not singular in retaining this precaution; we are rather singular in having so little precaution against violent and revolutionary changes.

May I refer to other democracies and republics? Turn to the United States, and note the precaution taken against legislation which runs counter to the will of the people. The Federal Government is based on a written constitution and on two legislative Chambers, whose powers of law-making are defined and expressly limited by the constitution, and a change in the constitution can only be effected by something in the nature of a referendum. Not only that, but every State has a written constitution, and although the legislative powers of those States are unlimited, except in so far as the federal constitution prescribes, I may say that the tendency of the constitution is to add to the number of subjects which are excluded from the general legislative powers of the State, and in which the constitution requires that there should be a referendum

[1] Parliamentary Debates, Fourth Series, vol. 176, col. 998 sqq.

CURBING THE LORDS 461

to the people of the country. And not only that, but every State has two Chambers. Mr. Bryce, one of the chief authorities on this subject, says, " The need of two Chambers has become an axiom of political science, based on the belief that the innate tendency of an Assembly to become hasty, tyrannical, or corrupt, can only be checked by the co-existence of another House of equal authority." He further states that " the only States that have ever tried to do with one House are Pennsylvania, Georgia, and Vermont, each of which gave up the system, one after four years, the other after twelve years, and the third after fifty years."

Turn to the constitution of the French Republic. There you have a Senate and a Chamber of Representatives co-ordinate in respect of legislative power, except that the Senate has no initiative in matters of finance. The power of demanding a dissolution of the Chamber does not rest with the Prime Minister, but with the President acting with the consent of the Senate. And the Senate, according to a recent authority, does very valuable work in correcting the over-hasty legislation of the Chamber, and, in case of disagreement, often has its own way, or effects a compromise.

Lastly, I take the Australian Commonwealth. I think that the democratic character of the Australian Colonies can hardly be called in question. But there is a difference in the two Chambers of the Australian Commonwealth. The procedure is as follows : The House of Representatives passes a proposed law, and if the Senate rejects or amends it in any way to which the House of Representatives cannot agree, the Bill drops for the time. It comes up again after three months, and if the Senate still disagrees, the Governor may dissolve both Houses. If afterwards the same difference arises, and the disagreement still goes on, then the two Houses sit together and the opinion of the majority of the whole number prevails.

There you have three great modern democracies, each of which guards itself against such legislation as might well be effected by this House of Commons, if it received the unlimited powers which are proposed to be given to it by the Prime Minister. I venture to think that there is nothing pedantic in looking at the actions, the law, and the practice of other constitutions as democratic as our own. If these safeguards are necessary for them, they are necessary for us. If they cannot trust a single Chamber, we may learn from them how to guard against the possibilities of a House of Commons whose powers were limitless.

But setting aside those examples, if we look simply at the proposals of the Prime Minister, these two questions arise. What are the faults of the House of Lords that they should be superseded and set aside in this way, and what is the claim of the House of Commons to arrogate to itself this unbounded legislative power? Now, I am perfectly ready to admit that the House of Lords has its faults as a Second Chamber; but it was never constructed to discharge the purposes of a Second Chamber in the modern sense; it is, historically, the estate of the baronage, a co-ordinate estate of the realm with the House of Commons. It has become a Second Chamber, I admit, and to my mind discharges extremely well many of the duties of a Second Chamber. I admit that it is too large, that it contains too many men who take no active part in politics, and that, like every Second Chamber that can be devised, it is conservative in its tendencies, because the very object of the existence of a Second Chamber is to preserve the nation from the over-hasty legislation of the other House. But I will undertake to say that the House of Lords has never crossed the will of the people where that will has been clearly expressed. Take any instance since the Reform Act of 1832, which you may say is the beginning of our modern constitution. Take cases in which it was extremely possible that a majority of the House of Lords were not wholly in accord with the legislation that was passed. Take the disestablishment of the Irish Church, the Irish land legislation of Mr. Gladstone, the changes in the franchise of 1884–1885, or the Trade Disputes Bill of last year. On every one of these measures the country had clearly expressed its opinion. . . .

Why do you not take the measures which are open to you to ascertain the will of the people? The Under-Secretary for the Colonies [Mr. Winston Churchill] wrote an article in the *Nation* in which he expressed his view as to the constitution of a Second Chamber, and his view is not the view of the Prime Minister. The Under-Secretary thinks that the Ministry should constitute a Second Chamber to suit their own purposes at the commencement of every Parliament, for he wrote:

Since the political supremacy of the House of Commons must be the vital characteristic of any Liberal scheme, we must reject with regret, but with decision, all proposals for enabling the House of Lords to force every Liberal measure to the test of a referendum. Such a provision would be contrary to the whole spirit of the British Constitution.

The Under-Secretary for the Colonies maintains that the referendum is contrary to the spirit of the British Constitution. There is a curiously undemocratic ring about that. I thought the Party opposite were going to breathe a new spirit into the Constitution, but it seems that while we may abolish the House of Lords without reference to the people, yet that to consult the people on any great legislative measure on which their opinion is not ascertained is contrary to the spirit of the Constitution. I urge hon. Members opposite not to disguise the full effect of what is being proposed. The proposition is this — that when the House of Commons is once elected it shall do as it likes and that the people shall be powerless. You say to the people, " When you have once elected us the virtue is gone out of you; for five years we are your masters; at the end of that time you may enjoy a brief opportunity of expressing a will of your own."

I doubt whether the country desires this great change, and I feel sure that when the matter is clearly placed before them they will express a very decided opinion upon it. If the Lords have traversed the will of the people, and resisted reasonable suggestions for a reform of that Chamber, then you may appeal to the country on those grounds. But what you are asking us to do is to forego the

safeguards which all the democracies in the world have found to
be necessary; and to have nothing between the will of the House
of Commons and the veto of the Crown. Put this question plainly
to the country; you will get a clear answer, and I have no doubt
as to what the answer will be.

Extract 75

THE ISSUE BETWEEN THE HOUSES AND THE PARTIES

*(Mr. Winston Churchill, Under-Secretary of State for the Colonies,
Commons, June 25, 1907)*

MR. CHURCHILL [1]: . . . We are only at the beginning of this
struggle. We are not necessarily committed to every detail of
the proposal; we are opening the first lines for a great siege, we
have to sap up to the advanced parallels, to establish our batteries,
and at no distant date open our bombardment. It may be many
months before we shall be able to discern where there is a practicable breach, but the assault will come in due time.

The right hon. Gentleman opposite said he welcomed this con-
test with great confidence. I wonder if hon. Members opposite
realise, to use an expressive vulgarism, what they are "letting
themselves in for" when this question comes to be fought out on
every platform in every constituency in the country. They will
not have to defend an ideal Second Chamber; they will not be
able to confine themselves to airy generalities about a bi-cameral
system and its advantages; they will have to defend this Second
Chamber as it is — one-sided, hereditary, unpurged, unrepresenta-
tive, irresponsible, absentee. They will have to defend it with all
its anomalies, all its absurdities, and all its personal bias; they will
have to defend it with all its achievements that have darkened the
pages of the history of England. And let me say that considerable

---

[1] Parliamentary Debates, Fourth Series, vol. 176, col. 1243 sqq.

constitutional authorities have not considered that the policy on which we have embarked in moving this Resolution is unreasonable. Mr. Bagehot says of the House of Lords: "It may lose its veto as the Crown has lost its veto. If most of its members neglect their duties, if all its members continue to be of one class, and that not quite the best; if its doors are shut against genius that cannot found a family, and ability which has not £5000 a year, its power will be less year by year, and at last be gone, as so much kingly power is gone — no one knows how." . . .

Has the House of Lords ever been right?

MAJOR ANSTRUTHER-GRAY: What about Home Rule?

MR. CHURCHILL: Has it ever been right in any of the great settled controversies which are now beyond the reach of Party argument? Was it right in delaying Catholic emancipation and the removal of Jewish disabilities? Was it right in driving this country to the verge of revolution in the effort to secure the passage of reform? Was it right in resisting the Ballot Bill? Was it right in the almost innumerable efforts it made to prevent this House dealing with the purity of its own electoral machinery? Was it right in endeavouring to prevent the abolition of purchase in the Army? Was it right in 1880, when it rejected the Compensation for Disturbance Bill? I defy the Party opposite to produce a single instance of a settled controversy in which the House of Lords was right.

MAJOR ANSTRUTHER-GRAY: What about Home Rule?

MR. CHURCHILL: I expected that interruption. That is not a settled controversy. It is a matter which lies in the future. The cases I have mentioned are cases where we have carried the law into effect and have seen the results and found that they have been good. . . .

But there is one other feature in the House of Lords which the Conservative party will have to exercise their ingenuity in defending in the next few years — I allude to the presence in that body of those interesting Lords Spiritual. By what violation of all ideas of religious equality the leaders of one denomination only should be represented I do not pause to inquire; but no doubt when such very delicate and ticklish questions as Chinese labour and the prevalence of intemperance, and great questions of war and the treatment of native races beyond the seas come up, it is a very convenient thing to have the Bishops in the House of Lords in order to make quite sure that official Christianity shall be on the side of the upper classes.

I proceed to inquire on what principle the House of Lords deals with Liberal measures. The right hon. Member for Dover says they occupy the position of the umpire. Are they even a sieve, a strainer, to stop legislation if it should reveal an undue or undesirable degree of radicalism or Socialism? Are they the complementary critic — the critic who sees all the things which the ordinary man does not see? I say that the attitude which the House of Lords adopts towards Liberal measures is purely tactical. When they returned to their " gilded Chamber " after the general election they found on the Woolsack and on the Treasury Bench a Lord Chancellor and a Government with which they were not familiar. When their eyes fell upon those objects there was a light in them which meant one thing — murder; murder tempered, no doubt, by those prudential considerations which always restrain persons from acts which are contrary to the general feeling of the society in which they live. But their attitude towards the present Government has from the beginning been to select the best and most convenient opportunity of humiliating and discrediting them, and finally of banishing them from power. . . .

The House of Lords as it at present exists and acts is not a national institution, but a Party dodge, an apparatus and instrument at the disposal of one political faction; and it is used in the most unscrupulous manner to injure and humiliate the opposite faction. When hon. Gentlemen opposite go about the country defending a Second Chamber, let them remember that this is the kind of Second Chamber they have to defend, and when they defend the veto let them remember that it is a veto used, not for national purposes, but for the grossest and basest purposes of unscrupulous political partisanship.

I have dealt with the issues between Houses, and I come to that between Parties. . . . Constitutional writers have much to say about the estates of the realm, and a great deal to say about their relation to each other and to the Sovereign. All that is found to be treated at length. But they say very little about the Party system. And, after all, the Party system is the dominant fact in our experience. . . . There are two great characteristics about the Party institutions of this country: the equipoise between them, and their almost incredible durability. We have only to look at the general elections of 1900 and 1906. I do not suppose any circumstances could be more depressing for a political Party than the circumstances in which the Liberal party fought the election in 1900, except the circumstances in which the Conservative party fought the election of 1906. At those two elections, what was the salient fact? The great mass of the voters of each political Party stood firm by the standard of their Party, and although there was an immense movement of public opinion, that movement was actually effected by a comparatively small number of votes. . . . When Parties are thus evenly balanced, to place such a weapon as the House of Lords in the hands of one of the Parties is to doom the other to destruction. I do not speak only from the Party point of view, although it explains the earnestness with which we approach this question. It is a matter of life and death to Liberalism and Radicalism. It is a question of our life or the abolition of the veto of the House of Lords. But look at it from a national point of view. Think of its injury to the smooth working of a Liberal Government. At the present time a Liberal Government, however powerful, cannot look far ahead, cannot impart design into its operations, because it knows that if at any moment its vigour falls below a certain point, another body, over which it has no control, is ready to strike it a blow to its most serious injury. It comes to this, that no matter how great the majority by which a Liberal Government is supported, it is unable to pass any legislation unless it can procure the agreement of its political opponents. . . .

Much might be said for and against the two-Party system. But no one can doubt that it adds to the stability and cohesion of the State. The alternation of Parties in power, like the rotation of crops, has beneficial results. Each of the two Parties has something to give and services to render in the development of the national life, and the succession of new and different points of view is a great and real benefit to the country. The advantage of such a system cannot be denied. Would not the ending of such a system involve a much greater disturbance than to amend the functions of the House of Lords? Is there not a much greater cataclysm involved in the breakdown of the constitutional organisation of democracy, for that is the issue which is placed before us, than would be involved in the mere curtailment of the legislative veto which has been given to another place? I ask the House, What does such a safeguard as the House of Lords mean? Is it a safeguard at all? . . .

Great powers are already possessed by the House of Commons. It has finance under its control; it has the Executive Government; the control of foreign affairs and the great patronage of the State are all in the power of the House of Commons at the present time. And let me say that if you are to proceed on the basis that the people of this country will elect a mad House of Commons, and that the mad House of Commons will be represented by a mad executive, the House of Lords is no guarantee against any excesses which such a House of Commons or such an Executive might have in contemplation. Whatever you may wish or desire, you will be forced to trust the people in all those vital and fundamental elements of government which in every State have always been held to involve the social stability of the community.

Is the House of Lords even a security for property? Why, the greatest weapon which a democracy possesses against property is the power of taxation, and the power of taxation is wholly under the control of this House. If this House chooses, for instance, to suspend payment to the Sinking Fund and to utilise the money for any public purpose or for any social purpose, the House of Lords could not interfere. If the House of Commons chooses to double taxation on the wealthy classes, the House of Lords could not interfere in any respect. Understand, I am not necessarily advocating these measures; what I am endeavouring to show to the House is that there is no real safeguard in the House of Lords even in regard to a movement against property.

But surely there are other securities upon which the stability of society depends. In the ever-increasing complexities of social problems, in the restrictions which are imposed from day to day with increasing force on the action of individuals, above all in the dissemination of property among many classes of the population, are the real elements of stability on which our modern society depends. There are to-day, unlike in former ages, actually millions of people who possess not merely inert property, but who possess rent-earning, profit-bearing property; and the danger with which we are confronted now is not at all whether we shall go too fast; no, the danger is that about three-fourths of the people of this country should move on in a comfortable manner into an easy life, which, with all its ups and downs, is not uncheered by fortune, while the remainder of the people shall be left to rot and fester in the slums of our cities, or in the deserted and abandoned hamlets of our rural districts. That is the danger with which we are confronted at the present moment, and it invests with a deep and real significance the issue which is drawn between the two Parties to-night. It is quite true that there are rich Members of the Liberal party, and there are poor men who are Members of the Conservative party, but in the main the lines of difference between the two Parties are social and economic — in the main the lines of difference are increasingly becoming the lines of cleavage between the rich and the poor. Let that animate and inspire us in the great struggle which we are now undertaking, and in which we shall without rest press forward, confident of this, that, if we persevere we shall wrest from the hands of privilege and wealth the evil and ugly and sinister weapon of the Peers' veto, which they have used so ill so long.

Extract 76

AN ARRAIGNMENT OF THE HOUSE OF LORDS

(Mr. David Lloyd George, President of the Board of Trade, Commons, June 26, 1907)

MR. LLOYD GEORGE[1]: . . . Then there is property. You must defend property! The only Bill that I can recall which deprived anybody of property without compensation was passed by the Leader of the Opposition. It was valuable public property, the reversion to the public of the licences, recognised by law as a vested interest. True, it was only a vested interest for the benefit of the public, not of a class. That property the right hon. Gentleman wiped out, nay, he handed it over as a political bribe to a powerful section of the community. It was the greatest act of plunder and confiscation since the days of Henry VIII. The House of Lords consented. This is the defender of property! This is the leal and trusty mastiff which is to watch over our interests, but which runs away at the first snarl of the trade unions.

VISCOUNT TURNOUR: What about your Party?

MR. LLOYD GEORGE: We did what we promised at the last election. A mastiff? It is the right hon. Gentleman's poodle. It fetches and carries for him. It barks for him. It bites anybody that he sets it on to. And we are told that this is a great revising Chamber, the safeguard of liberty in the country. Talk about mockeries and shams. Was there ever such a sham as that? No wonder

[1] Parliamentary Debates, Fourth Series, vol. 176, col. 1429 sqq.

the right hon. Gentleman scolds the naughty boys who throw stones at it. The House of Lords, it seems, defends capital. Of a kind, yes. But generally against whom does it defend capital? Against the House of Commons? Why should this House destroy capital?

VISCOUNT TURNOUR interposed an observation which did not reach the gallery.

MR. LLOYD GEORGE: The noble Lord represents land, but it is not the only form of capital, though it is the only form you cannot scare away. The noble Lord finds some comfort in that. We are told, too, that the House of Lords defends capital. Why should the House of Commons be supposed to be in a conspiracy against capital? The *Times* the other day talked about the danger to property of an absolute House of Commons.

Has it ever occurred to the *Times* that practically every profession, every great trade, every great industry, no matter what Party is in power, sends its very best men to the House of Commons? I can say without hesitation about the House of Commons that this is true. All the great industries, the land, shipping, mining, textile trades, the iron trade and every great industry and interest in this country, are represented by men who have devoted their lives to those particular industries before they were elected to the House of Commons. The other Chamber represents substantially only one form of capital. Yet it claims that it has to watch in the interest of property the House of Commons, which is composed of men engaged in every form of industry and commerce, to which they devote their services, and out of which they make their livelihoods. That being so, is it not folly and nonsense to talk of the House of Lords being necessary to protect property?

I know of only one Bill passed in the last few years which represents a great inroad upon the profits of capital. That is the Workmen's Compensation Act. I do not say it is unjust, save in one particular; but the exception is important. Suppose there is an accident in a colliery. The man who has put his capital into its development may lose every penny. But the man who derives his income out of royalties from the same colliery has not to risk a farthing. Is not that unfair? Yet it is that injustice — the absence of a provision to make royalties pay their fair contribution towards these accidents — which enabled the Bill to pass through the Assembly which is supposed to be the special protection of capital.

It is also well known that the House of Lords has plundered the railways to a huge extent. Railways have cost twice more in this country than in any other country in the world. Why? Because the House of Lords has piled the cost onto the railways when they came to acquire land; and now the trade and industry and capital of the country have to pay heavily on account of the action of this Chamber which is supposed to be our appointed guardian. . . .

The argument which the right hon. Gentleman has used in regard to administration is doubly important when it comes to legislation. The right hon. Gentleman knows perfectly well what the object is — no revision, no check, when a Tory Government is in power, but every check when there is a Liberal Government in power. He is afraid of a revolution. If there is a revolution, it is not the House of Lords that will arrest it. It will be the first institution that will vanish without a struggle. In the English revolution it was the House of Commons that made the last fight. The House of Lords was abolished by a Resolution. The House of Commons made the fight, and when the time for a revolution comes — if it ever does come — the only share which the House of Lords will have in the revolution will be in creating it.

The right hon. Gentleman the Member for West Birmingham [Mr. Joseph Chamberlain] has pointed this out in one of his most powerful passages — and this is the answer to his followers who now ask when the House of Lords have done any harm — " We know for our part that in the course of the last hundred years they have more than once brought the country to the verge of revolution ; and that they have again and again mutilated, delayed, or rejected Bills of the first importance which are now universally accepted to be salutary and expedient." But the people are slow to embark on revolutions, and the fact that it has taken fifty or sixty years to curtail the powers of the House of Lords is the best proof of that. They are tolerant of long-standing grievances. No one can doubt their wrongs. But I know the people; I was brought up amongst them. It is only when they are driven by a long course of injustice and of denial of justice that they are ever exasperated into a revolution, and the surest and greatest security against that is not the House of Lords, but some machinery which will deal effectively, promptly, and justly with their requirements.

It is very remarkable that every great Liberal statesman who has ruled this Empire for fifty years has always come to the same conclusion about the House of Lords. I have quoted the right hon. Gentleman the Member for West Birmingham. Lord Rosebery, in language no less strong, came to the same conclusion, and the two greatest names of all — John Bright and Mr. Gladstone — who had given long service to the State and who were no revolutionaries, were of the same opinion. John Bright, although he has been denounced in language stronger than even the present Prime Minister, was a prudent, cautious, and temperate man in action, and always essentially anti-revolutionary. Mr. Gladstone had an almost exaggerated reverence for existing institutions, especially hereditary institutions. He was the last man to lift his powerful arm against them, and yet after the longest and most distinguished public career that this country probably has known, when he had no further personal interest in the matter, and when he had no responsibility for the leadership of the Party, he said that practically progress was impossible until you had dealt with this barrier. The present Prime Minister, who after all has had a longer experience of Parliamentary life than any man here, comes and deliberately asks the House of Commons, and from the Commons appeals to the country, to accept the counsel given at the end of a great career by a statesman who stands to-day not merely in the British Empire but throughout the world as the man who embodies the noblest and the most exalted traditions of British statesmanship.

Extract 77

EXPOSITION OF THE PARLIAMENT BILL

*(Earl of Crewe, Lord Privy Seal and Secretary of State for India,
Lords, November 21, 1910)*

THE EARL OF CREWE[1]: . . . In regard to the Parliament Bill,
the origin of this particular controversy goes back four years. It
goes back to the winter of 1906 when the first Education Bill of
Sir Henry Campbell-Bannerman's Government failed to pass into
law. The Bill failed to pass into law after strenuous attempts to
arrive at a compromise, but compromise was found impossible and
the Bill was lost. It was lost owing to the unwillingness of your
Lordships' House to include in its provisions principles upon which,
as we believed, the mind of the country had been most clearly expressed at the General Election of the preceding winter, and, as
your Lordships will all remember, its loss was received not merely
with regret but with no little indignation on the part of those who
had its success at heart. On December 20, 1906, Sir Henry
Campbell-Bannerman, speaking in another place, said, " A way
must be found and a way will be found by which the will of the
people, as expressed through their elected representatives in this
House, will be made to prevail." Then in the King's Speech,
when Parliament met on February 12 in the following year, that
thesis was developed by the then Prime Minister in words which
will be found in the pages of " Hansard." The almost immediate sequel to that challenge, for I think I may so call it, was the
Resolution which the House of Commons passed on June 26 of
the same year. That Resolution read:

That in order to give effect to the will of the people as expressed by
their elected representatives, it is necessary that the power of the other

1 Parliamentary Debates, Fifth Series, Lords, vol. 6, col. 777 sqq.

House to alter or reject Bills passed by this House should be so restricted by law as to secure that within the limits of a single Parliament the final decisions of the Commons shall prevail.

That Resolution was carried on a Division by 434 against 149.

Perhaps I may be permitted very briefly to remind your Lordships of what the terms of the plan at that time were. Speaking generally they were these. When a disagreement occurred between the two Houses a private Conference was to take place; and if agreement was not arrived at through that Conference, the Bill was lost for the time. It could be reintroduced either with or without amendment after a period of six months, and if the two Houses again failed to agree, a second Conference was to be called. If agreement was then not reached, the Bill was to be reintroduced and passed by some rapid process, and a third Conference might be held, but if agreement was then not reached, the Bill was to become law over the heads of your Lordships' House. The remainder of the plan consisted in a provision for quinquennial Parliaments — that is to say, Parliaments of which the ordinary duration would be four years, for reasons with which your Lordships are all familiar.

Well, my Lords, as the controversy proceeded, the relations as between the two Houses I fear did not improve. The Plural Voting Bill had already been rejected by your Lordships' House very summarily, and not less summarily the Licensing Bill of 1908 received its short shrift at your Lordships' hands. In 1908, also, fresh attempts were made at a settlement of the education question, but those attempts proved to be again a failure. Then came the unprecedented rejection in 1909 of the whole financial arrangements for the year. The General Election followed, but the Government, although returned to power, found itself in no degree nearer the capacity of carrying controversial Bills than it had been all through the Parliament preceding. That, my Lords, is in brief the reason and the justification for the introduction of this measure.

Now, it is desirable to explain in what essentials this Bill differs from the earlier proposals which I have described. I will do so by going rapidly through its operative provisions. The first clause deals with finance. It gives to the other House complete control over Money Bills, but it contains the important provision and makes the important admission on which your Lordships laid stress in your famous Standing Order of 1702 — namely, that it was not proper to annex to a Money Bill matter foreign to or different from matters of aid or supply. The force of that Standing Order is admitted in Clause 1, and the decision as to whether a Bill is a Money Bill or not is left by Clause 1 to the Speaker of the House of Commons — an impartial authority, at any rate an impartial authority so far as the memory of any man now alive goes back, and to whom in the opinion of His Majesty's Government that immensely important duty may be fitly entrusted. But I may perhaps venture to say that if some other tribunal within Parliament could be found which could be expected to carry out these duties with equal authority and equal impartiality, that is not a matter which we should regard as vital to the Bill.

The second part of the Bill deals with general legislation, and the effect of its provisions is that if a measure passes in another place during three successive sessions spreading over two years it will become law. In the earlier proposals much was said about conferring between the two Houses, and it is a matter upon which the late Prime Minister dwelt at length when he introduced his proposals. The Bill which is before us does not explicitly provide for the holding of Conferences, but in the opinion of the framers of the Bill the holding of Conferences is a cardinal matter in relation to the whole question. Nothing, I think, is more curious to any one who takes the trouble to look at the history of the relations between the two Houses than the gradual decline and final disuse of the practice of Conferences between the Lords and the Commons. The causes may be numerous, but one cause undoubtedly was that the later Conferences which were held — I am speaking for the moment of formal Conferences — seem to have become so rigid and so un-natural in their character that it was felt that the practice carried with it little of value. But I do not hesitate to say that in my opinion one of the reasons why the relations between the two Houses have hardened and crystallised into their present condition — a condition, that is to say, of something like perpetual conflict when one Party is in power and of perpetual acquiescence when the other Party is in power — may be traced to the complete abandonment of this habit of conferring. Conferences between the two Houses are of old date. They go back, I believe, to the reign of Edward III ; and from the time when the Commons' Journals were regularly kept, I am told that within the one hundred fifty years from 1547 to 1702 anyone who searches the Index to these Journals will find that upwards of twenty pages of the Index are given up to reports of the Conferences that were held between the two Houses on every variety of subject and covering the widest possible field. I therefore do not hesitate to say that the revival of the custom of frequent Conferences between the two Houses is of the very essence of the proposals which we are placing before your Lordships to-day.

Then, my Lords, I would call your attention to an important change from the former proposals, and it is that relating to the identity of the Bill to be sent up on a later occasion — identity except so far as may be agreed — as compared with the proposal originally made that the Bill might be amended in another place and sent up as the same Bill. It seems to me that the real issue as between the two Parties — and this I gather from what has been said in this House and on many platforms — the real issue as between the two Parties with regard to these proposals is, " What is the real value of delay and of opportunities for consideration for the purpose of amending Bills ? " That is to say, Are you more likely to get a Bill into final shape that sensible men, its principle having been approved, will agree is the best shape — are you more likely to get it into such a shape by delay, consultation, and consideration than by a process of summary rejection, followed, perhaps, by a General Election, and if not by a General Election by a referendum, as I understand is proposed in a Motion on the Paper by my noble friend Lord Balfour of Burleigh ?

It is useful in discussing the question of delay and consideration on the one side, and a more immediate appeal to the country on the other, for the purpose of improving a Bill or of deciding its fate, to consider one or two concrete instances. I believe it is to the benefit of both Parties, and, what is more important, to the benefit of the whole country, to get out of the region of abstract Constitution-making, because what the country is most interested in is, " What is likely to be the effect of these proposals or of any other alternative proposals in their practical import and in relation to the fate of Bills before Parliament ? " Now Parliament is not an end in itself ; it is a means, a machine for doing certain things for the nation. It is a machine for doing three things. It exists for the purpose of keeping a check on the Executive ; it exists for the purpose of raising money for the public service ; and it exists also, although it is not its primary object of existence, for the purpose of passing legislation. I ask your Lordships to consider what would have been the probable fate of one or two well-known measures either under our proposals, or under the proposals which I understand to be generally those of the other side.

I will take the first Home Rule Bill of 1893, a favourite battle-horse, I need not say, of noble Lords opposite, because it is a measure which above all others is supposed to have vindicated the judgment of your Lordships' House. I say without hesitation that the Home Rule Bill of 1893, looking back at it from this distance of time, would not have passed either test — it would not have passed the test of a General Election or of a referendum, which I understand would be the proposal, according to Mr. Balfour's speech at Nottingham, for dealing with the question. Neither would it have stood the test of the proposals under the Parliament Bill. The Home Rule Bill of 1893, supported by the majority with which it was supported, would not have stood the test in the then temper of the country of three sessions of discussions. Therefore, I think that we may regard ourselves as quits as to the merits of the two systems on that particular question. Then I will take a Bill of noble Lords opposite — the Education Act of 1902. I presume that the Education Act of 1902 would have passed this House very much in the form in which it did pass for the simple reason that even if the House of Lords had been reformed according to the ideas of noble Lords, it would not have become the subject of discussion between the two Houses; but if Lord Balfour's plan had been in force, and if the Act of 1902 had had to be submitted to a referendum, it certainly would not have been the law of the land at this moment. Therefore from that point of view our proposals, I think, are kinder to the legislation of noble Lords opposite than the proposals of a distinguished member of their Party, supported, as I understand, by many other distinguished members.

Next I come to the Education Bill of 1906. I say without hesitation that if the Education Bill of 1906 had had to go through the processes enjoined by this Parliament Bill, it would have come out, as I believe, a satisfactory measure, and a measure which would have given us a settlement of our elementary education question for many years to come. But here again I am making a present to noble Lords opposite, because if that Education Bill had been made the subject of a General Election or of a referendum, the Bill which would have been put to the country would have been the Bill in its House of Commons form. That, I think, is quite evident. If you differ you can only put one measure to the country, and the measure which you put to the country, is, I assume, the measure as it passed the House of Commons. That would have undoubtedly involved the carrying of the Education Bill of 1906 in a form which would have been very much more satisfactory to many of those who support us on this side of the House, and very much less satisfactory to those who hold the views of the noble Lords opposite. I venture to think that the Parliament Bill does not come very badly out of a comparison of those three cases ; and I believe that noble Lords opposite have not attempted to realise the immense effect upon a measure of delay and discussion — long delay and repeated discussion — both in another place and here. I believe that in this country, as far as we are able to know the mind of the country, the danger of anything like cataclysmic legislation is an absolute minimum. Hurried and violent legislation is in my view thoroughly foreign to our national temperament. And if noble Lords agree with me, it is hard to see what danger they find in our proposals. But, of course, noble Lords take some wild speech made by some quite insignificant person and point to it as indicating the probability that revolutionary changes — changes of the kind desired by the Social Democratic Party — are likely to be the result of passing into law this moderate and harmless piece of legislation. Well, my Lords, I think I have shown that to describe this measure as in any sense a measure for the establishment of a Single Chamber is an absolute misnomer. If there is anything in what I have said — and I shall be interested to see if noble Lords opposite attempt to deny it — as to the power and force of delay and discussion, this is not a measure for the establishment of a Single Chamber.

To this policy of delay and discussion various alternatives are suggested, alternatives which may themselves involve some delay and discussion, but which cannot be taken as if they would necessarily involve the same amount of delay and discussion as we have provided for in this Bill. One of these alternative methods of proceeding was alluded to by Mr. Balfour at Nottingham. It is what is known as a joint sitting — that is, that the two Houses on the event of disagreement may meet and the combined vote of both Houses together decides the question. The idea of holding a joint session is not a new one, and I am very far from saying that it is a bad one. I ought to be the last person to say it is a bad one, because, as is well known to your Lordships, the plan of a Joint Session forms part of the South Africa Act, for which I had the honour of being responsible last year. Section 63 of that Act provides for the holding of a Joint Session in case of difference. But I am bound to point out this : that when you talk of a Joint Session between the House of Commons and the House of Lords, however constituted, the problem which you have to face is not quite the same as that which presents itself in South Africa. The two Houses in South Africa are respectively 121 and 40 in number. For them to meet and discuss is a comparatively simple affair. But when you come to joining to a House of 670 members another House which, so far as I am able to gather, may be at least 400 in number, you collect together an enormous public meeting ; and your difficulty is not merely the physical difficulty of getting them together, but the intellectual difficulty of carrying on a discussion between the members of a body so enormous. Therefore in a country like this, where both Houses are large, where the Party system prevails to the extent that it does, and where both Houses are not elected Houses, the system of Joint Sessions — although, as I say, I do not decry it — offers difficulties which I think your Lordships ought very carefully to consider before you plunge into it as a definite policy. Your Lordships must also remember that when you speak of a Joint Session much depends upon the numbers of the Upper and more Conservative House. I say more Conservative House because, without entering into the question of number or degree, it will, I am sure, be admitted by noble Lords opposite that they mean the Upper House to be Conservative in its complexion. Your Joint Session, in that case, if the relative numbers of the Upper House are very small, may come much nearer to Single-Chamber Government than the proposals which we are now putting before your Lordships. On the other hand, if the proportionate numbers of the Conservative House are going to be very large, then there would not seem to be very much difference between the future position and that of which we complain to-day.

I do not propose on this occasion — I do not know whether we may have the opportunity of doing so before the House rises — to enter into the question of the referendum. It is a question which, as everybody knows who has attempted to study it, bristles with difficulties. But here again I would just ask your Lordships to consider this: Are you quite sure that the clean-cut operation of the referendum, with the possibility, in fact, almost the probability, that the question which is asked of the country for that purpose will be couched in a somewhat extreme form — are you quite sure that the establishment of the referendum in this country would make for moderate legislation — if that is what you desire — to so great an extent as the proposal which we have included in the Parliament Bill?

I have not said anything yet about the Preamble of the Bill. Your Lordships are very familiar with the phrase so often spoken in Committee by my noble friend the Lord Chairman, "that the Preamble be postponed." That is what I have done in these few observations. We have always admitted "that the Preamble be postponed" is also our policy. But the postponement of the question of the reform of the House of Lords, either in a speech or as a matter of policy, does not mean, and cannot mean, that we are unmindful of that aspect of the subject. There are more reasons than one why we cannot — speaking of ourselves as a Party — neglect this question of the reform of the House of Lords. When the noble Earl, Lord Selborne, was speaking last Thursday he stated — though whether he was speaking for the whole of the Party opposite, or even for the Front Bench I am not certain — that the Party opposite would not accept this measure, and that if it became a law, and they came into power later, they would take the first opportunity of reversing it. That is to say, that if the Bill passed through this House in its present state, any scheme of reform which noble Lords opposite might initiate would be taken, as I understand, as an excuse for adding to the powers of the House something which had been taken away from it by this Bill. If that is so, it is from our point of view a good reason for our attempting to assist in the work of reforming the House while we have some voice in the matter, because in the other event I am quite sure we should have no such voice. Then again, the Bill as it stands provides a further reason for making a reform of your Lordships' House desirable. We do not want to rush legislation through Parliament. We know very well that any attempt so to use the provisions of this Bill — even if they could be so used, which I greatly doubt — would only recoil upon those who so attempted to use them.

As I have said, we desire to substitute delay and revision for hurried Party rejection. Delay and the function of revision mean that you desire the best minds that you can find to be applied to that revision. The theory of this Bill is that the delay and the process of revision will, if the country does not like some particular points in a measure, cause such pressure to be put upon the House of Commons that at its next consideration the measure will have to be modified ; and it is quite evident that if such pressure is to be brought to bear, and if it is to be useful pressure, the higher the character, the more brilliant tl.e ability, and the larger the experience of those who sit in the Upper House, the stronger that pressure will be, because the power of ultimate and final rejection does not exist if this Bill becomes law. It would be as wrong to say that the character of the Upper House in these circumstances was no longer of importance, as it would be to say that because a Constitutional Sovereign is not an absolute despot, therefore his character and capacity are a matter of no importance.

There is another point. Some little time ago Mr. F. E. Smith — one of the most brilliant, though, I think, at times inconvenient supporters of noble Lords opposite — stated that in his opinion the measures of both Parties should be given an equal chance of becoming law. We do not attempt anything so ambitious. Our Bill falls far short of Mr. Smith's ideal. Under it our measures will have to go through this dragging process described in our Bill, while yours, I imagine, will go through on the india-rubber tires on which they have always passed through this House. I quite admit I do not think that is very fair, and if the House of Lords can be so reformed as to afford some check, I do not say as complete a check as this, but at any rate some check, to the possible extreme and wild legislation which may be proposed by noble Lords opposite and their friends, and if that can be brought about by some reformation of the constitution of the House, that supplies a third reason why this matter of reform ought not to escape our notice. We still maintain the proposal for quinquennial Parliaments — that is to say, it is practically only during the first two years of a Parliament, when it may be reasonably supposed, I think, to possess the confidence of the country, that the process by which measures can be made law during the lifetime of a single Parliament will be in practical operation.

These are the proposals in the Bill. They have been, as we say, and as we honestly believe, forced upon us by the repeated action of your Lordships' House. It seems to us as if your Lordships had of late years learned what I cannot help thinking is the fatal lesson — that it is worth your while to reject our measures on Party grounds in the hope that before they can come up again something may have turned up. It may be a forced election — perhaps not altogether a very popular thing in itself. It may be a cycle of bad trade — that is all to the good. It may be a wave of unemployment — also all to the good. Those things, as we all know, make any Government unpopular. It may be some heavy national expenditure involving new taxation. That again may be expected to make for the unpopularity of the Government. If you can reject our measures, some of these things or all of them may turn up and may give you a chance that our Bills should not become law. As I say, I venture to think that that is a disastrous game to play. It is a game that cannot be played forever. And, admitting as you do the essential unfairness of the present condition — because it has been admitted in varying degree by members of the Party opposite — I cannot think that this House desires to go on playing it indefinitely. But I am bound to say that among the reform proposals which have been brought forward from the other side of the House I have not seen an indication of any which, so far as we are able to judge, would materially alter or amend this state of things. Therefore, in asking the country to support us in passing this measure we have to ask — I frankly admit it — that the matter should be taken out of your hands and that the power to deal with it may be given to us. I only beg the House to believe that we ask this in no factious spirit and we ask it with no desire to lay our ancient institutions in the dust. What we do ask the country to do is to restore a reasonable measure of freedom to the chosen representatives of a free nation.

Extract 78

OPPOSITION TO THE PARLIAMENT BILL

(The Marquess of Lansdowne, Lords, November 21, 1910)

THE MARQUESS OF LANSDOWNE[1]: . . . I wish to thank the noble Earl for having made a speech at all this evening. I carry in my mind a memorable occasion on which he moved the second reading of a very important measure by a slight and graceful gesture of hand and hat. To-night he has been more indulgent to us and has given us a speech which I think must have seemed to most of your Lordships a very temperate and persuasive speech. I except, perhaps, one or two sentences in his peroration. I venture to say that if we were now commencing a long discussion, or a long series of Parliamentary discussions, upon this Bill, the speech of the noble Earl would have formed an invaluable introduction or preface to the debate. But the noble Earl forgot that he has warned us off anything like full discussion of this measure. He has forgotten that terse phrase in which he told us that the Bill would be here for us " to take or to leave." He has forgotten the intimation that any alternative schemes or proposals were not to be

[1] Parliamentary Debates, Fifth Series, Lords, vol. 6, col. 788 sqq.

regarded as in order for the purposes of this discussion. Well, if
that is so, if those are the conditions under which we are to discuss
the Parliament Bill, are we greatly assisted by the noble Earl's
dissertations upon such subjects as the value of Conferences, the
possible use to which Joint Sittings might be put, or the desirability of having recourse to the referendum? All these are full
of interest to us, but when are we going to be allowed to talk
about them?

We are face to face not only with the announcements of the
noble Earl himself but with an even more striking and memorable
announcement which was made to the country on Saturday last by
no less a personage than the Prime Minister, who told his audience
that negotiations were at an end, and that war had begun. How
then are we to deal with this Bill? It is, in the view of most of us
on this side, highly open to criticism, but it contains, nevertheless,
the admission of two or three principles which might very well have
formed the basis of discussion, if discussion had been permitted
— I mean the admission that it is necessary to find some machinery
for dealing with what we commonly speak of as deadlocks between
the two Houses ; the admission, which is to be found in the Preamble, that the ultimate settlement of these great Constitutional
questions implies that there shall be a reform in the House of Lords;
and again, the claim which, within reasonable limits, many of us are
inclined to admit, that the other House of Parliament is entitled to
a preponderance in the region of what I may call pure finance.
There is a certain amount of common ground at these points ;
and that being so, I am under the impression that if a full and
free discussion of this Bill had really been open to us, if we had
been promised an opportunity of amending the Bill and sending
our Amendments down to the House of Commons, a considerable
number of your Lordships would have been in favour of giving
the measure a second reading. I should, I say frankly, have taken
upon myself to advise those who might care to know what my
opinion was to take that course. The Bill would, in that case, have

been thoroughly debated, the House of Commons would have had its opportunity of commenting upon the changes which we recommended, and an attempt would then, no doubt, have been made to arrive at an understanding. The noble Earl very likely will tell me that the kind of course which I had in mind is altogether too dilatory for himself and his friends. I must say that if that rejoinder is made, I am bound to ask your Lordships whether there has ever been in the history of Parliament a case of a Bill of the kind of importance which this Bill possesses being hurried through either House of Parliament within the space of seven days. Our debate, therefore, must, to a certain extent, be an unreal debate, and our criticisms, if we attempt any, must be in a sense perfunctory criticisms, and all that we can do within the time at our disposal is to indicate in general terms the points to which we attach the most importance.

I will accordingly venture in a very few sentences to tell the House how some of us are struck by the main provisions of the Bill. I take, in the first place, the clauses dealing with the question of finance. Now, I think it is perfectly obvious, whatever one's feelings may be on this point, that the scheme of the Bill is an entirely incomplete and badly thought-out scheme. We may go far in the direction of admitting the preponderance of the House of Commons, where the legislation is purely financial legislation, but we are all of us quite aware that there are many Bills which, although nominally financial measures, in reality are directed to purposes quite other than financial purposes. I am speaking, of course, not only of that which is known in the text-books as "tacking" — that is what I take it the clause in the Bill is aimed at; but we all of us must have in our minds the case of other Bills in which it cannot be said that the matter complained of is, strictly speaking, foreign to the purpose of the Bill, but of which it can be said with perfect truth that the consequences other than mere financial consequences of the Bill entirely outweigh and overtop the purely financial results.

I find in this Bill in the first place what seems to me to be a very inadequate attempt to guard against tacking in the stricter sense of the word. If your Lordships will look at the end of the first clause, you will find a definition of a Money Bill which ends with these words, " Or matters incidental to those subjects or any of them." That is a loophole through which any provision, however mischievous and dangerous, could easily find a way. Then to come to the other kind of abuse which many of us desire to guard against. There is no attempt, so far as I can see, in this Bill to deal at all with the more insidious plan of presenting, under the cloak of finance, measures so framed as, for instance, to discriminate unjustly between one set of persons and another — to penalise a certain trade, a certain profession, or to bring about great social or political changes. The only safeguard I find against tacking of any kind is the reference of the point to the Speaker of the House of Commons. I desire to express my concurrence in all that was said by the noble Earl as to the respect due to that high official. No one feels that respect more than I do, but what I think we have to remember is that the Speaker of the House of Commons is an official of the House of Commons. He is not in a judicial position as one who might hold the balance or whose business it was to hold the balance between the two Houses of Parliament. His business is to watch over the privilege of the House of Commons and whenever he sees what seems to him an invasion of that privilege to stand up for his own House. If it had been possible to insert in this Bill a provision which would really effectually safeguard us, not only against tacking of the more technical kind, which I attempted to describe, but against tacking in the broader sense, I for one would have been ready to suggest that your Lordships might well forego the Constitutional right which you at present possess to deal with Money Bills of a purely financial character. The concession would obviously be a considerable one, and it is one which could not be for a moment entertained unless the kind of abuses to which I have referred were effectually guarded against.

Then may I say one word as to the clauses dealing not with financial but with ordinary legislation? They seem to me to fall very far short indeed of anything that is due to a self-respecting Second Chamber in a properly-balanced Constitution. All that Clause 2 would leave to the House of Lords is an opportunity of interposing comparatively brief delay when it regarded a measure as inexpedient in the public interest. It is true that this House would be given the right of three rejections in two years, but those rejections would take place with the knowledge that there was hanging over us, whatever happened in the third year, the inexorable right of the House of Commons to end all further discussion and to pass the Bill into law over our heads. I noticed in a remarkable speech delivered by the Prime Minister on Saturday last that he apparently attached what I conceive to be a very exaggerated importance to this opportunity of delay which would be accorded to us. He said, "Where the two Houses differ we provide for such opportunities of Conference and such an interposition of delay as would effectually frustrate any attempt by a scratch majority to rush unpopular legislation out of touch with public opinion." I confess that when I read that statement I referred to my copy of the Bill, and I searched it in vain for any mention of the word Conference. But I have no doubt the Prime Minister had in his mind what was said by the noble Earl in his speech just now. The noble Earl evidently contemplates, and I think rightly contemplates, that there would be more frequent and more regularised resort to procedure by Conference, and if that is his view, I entirely agree with him, and agree that such procedure should be made as little rigid and difficult as possible.

But, my Lords, just let us consider for a moment on what sort of terms of equality should we confer with the other House of Parliament if it were a part of the Constitution that supposing our Conferences came to nought the Bill was nevertheless to become an act over our heads. The noble Earl was eloquent upon the value of delay. He said that nothing was more alien to the intentions of his colleagues than that a Bill should be rushed through Parliament, — if we are to talk of rushing, what are we to say of this Bill being rushed through before Monday next? — but under the Bill a measure of any magnitude might be sprung upon the country and, let us say, in the second or third year of a Parliament might be passed into law by the sole consent of the House of Commons. I wonder whether the noble Earl can point to any precedent for a Second Chamber constituted upon these lines — I mean a Second Chamber which discharges its functions upon the understanding that not only the Second Chamber itself but the constituencies are to be of no account and that the sole power is to devolve upon the popular House of Parliament. I believe that you may search precedents in vain for any arrangement which would thus put the entire control over public affairs in the hands of one House. But if a scheme of this kind is, as I believe it to be, full of danger when you are dealing with ordinary legislation, what are we to think and what are we to say when we become aware that the same procedure is to apply even to what I should call capital legislation — I mean legislation dealing with the Constitution of the country, dealing with such questions as the disestablishment of the Church and the breaking up of the Union between these islands? Do not let us lose sight of the fact that this danger is not by any means an imaginary one. We know perfectly well, and the noble Earl knows perfectly well, how we stand at this moment with regard to the question of Home Rule for Ireland. The Prime Minister spoke of scratch majorities. He has done so more than once during the last few months, and perhaps not unnaturally, as he lives and has his being under a sense of the inconvenience which may be experienced from a scratch majority.

Let me read another sentence spoken by Mr. Asquith early in the present year. He said, "There were conceivable cases where you have a scratch majority combining under the coercion of Party exigencies for a particular and transient purpose." Have we not just seen an announcement by the head of one of the groups upon which His Majesty's Government depends that he has arrived here from America with a large sum of money in his pocket in order to take advantage of Party exigencies and the difficulties of the Government of the day? I ask the noble Earl, How would the plan of this Bill do what Mr. Asquith apparently expects it to do, namely, frustrate the operation of a combination of groups, a scratch majority, bent upon taking advantage of the necessities of the Government of the day for a transient purpose? One other word with regard to this portion of the Bill. The whole scheme of the Bill is, on the face of it, an interim arrangement. The Preamble looks forward to the time when this House shall be differently constituted, and evidently to a different arrangement in regard to deadlocks when that time shall come. I find in this Bill no indication of the manner in which we are eventually to pass from that interim arrangement to an arrangement of a more permanent and thoroughly thought-out character. That seems to me to be a defect to which attention should be called.

I come now to the question which must be present to all our thoughts. Why is it that these violent things are to be done? The noble Earl gave us at the beginning of his speech a recapitulation of what he regarded as the facts of the case. He went back four years to what I will not call the rejection of the Education Bill, but to our inability to come to terms over the Education Bill, and he said that upon that occasion the House of Lords was going against the principles which had been clearly expressed by the country at the General Election. Was that quite the case? What happened when His Majesty's Government returned to the charge and resumed their attempt to legislate on the subject of Education? Why, the whole of the principles which were supposed to have been affirmed by the country at the General Election were thrown overboard by His Majesty's Government. You had a Bill connected with the name of Mr. McKenna; you had another Bill connected with the name of Mr. Runciman. I think there was a fourth Bill which was under informal discussion but which did not see the light, or, at any rate, did not come to this House. When the noble Earl cites these subsequent attempts as illustrations of the difficulties interposed by the House of Lords in the way of useful legislation, he forgets that neither the McKenna Bill nor the Runciman Bill ever came near this House. All that those two Bills prove is that His Majesty's Government on consideration thought it desirable to mend their own hand very considerably. Then I come to the Licensing Bill, which I need not discuss at this moment. Assuming that we threw out the Licensing Bill and the Education Bill, does that justify the statement made on Saturday by the Prime Minister that in almost every attempt which the House of Commons made to give effect to the wishes of those who elected it, it was systematically thwarted, baffled, and defeated by the House of Lords? I should like to ask the noble Earl how many Bills which the people have really shown any desire to get have the House of Lords thrown out, and how many Liberal measures promoted by His Majesty's Government, some of them very far-reaching measures indeed, have passed into law, not only without opposition by this House, but with all the assistance we could give to make them into good and practicable measures?

The Prime Minister is usually conspicuous for the sobriety of his language. On this occasion it seems to me that he went rather beyond his usual tether, and it is perhaps fortunate that upon the particular occasion on which his speech was delivered the noble Earl opposite, the Minister for Agriculture, was also present in the chair. If I may put it this way, I would say that if the Prime Minister supplied the poison, the noble Earl immediately supplied the necessary antidote. I have read the Prime Minister's words. Now I will read the noble Earl's words. The noble Earl explained that the policy of His Majesty's Government was what he called "a policy of results," and he added that during their five years they had had peace with all its attendant blessings, loyalty and contentment in South Africa, India wisely governed, the maintenance of a magnificent Navy, the creation of an Army — he did not say a magnificent Army; I have no doubt he had the fear of the noble and gallant Field-Marshal, Lord Roberts, in his mind. And then the noble Earl went on to say they had also had land reform, labour legislation, old age pensions, and a temperance and people's Budget. And now pray let me invite the attention of the House particularly to the climax: "Two questions remained to be solved, Home Rule for Ireland and the Education problem. Those until quite lately were in the lap of the Lords." So that this famous indictment of habitual obstruction is whittled down by the noble Earl to two measures — two measures in five years. I would venture to ask him whether he is quite sure that these matters are in the lap of the House of Lords. I do not quite know whose lap the Education Bill is in — it has been in a good many different laps — but I am quite sure the noble Earl knows, or, if he does not, he will very soon find out, whose lap the Home Rule measure lies in.

I return reluctantly to the question which I put to the House a few moments ago, What is it our duty to do with this Bill? and I come to this conclusion, that all we can do is to avail ourselves of the few remaining days, I might almost say the few remaining hours, which are left to us in order to endeavour to put on record, if we can, in a simple form and in an intelligible shape, the proposals which we ourselves would be inclined to lay before the country for the settlement of this part of the question. I say this part of the question because I regard the Resolutions of the noble Earl on the Cross Benches as having taken us as far as we can go at present in regard to the question of the constitution of the House of Lords. I thought the Prime Minister, in the same speech, was perhaps unduly severe upon my noble friend. He said my noble friend's scheme was to all intents and purposes a "ghost," and then, by a rather splendid confusion of metaphors, he said, "the parricidal pick-axes" were already at work on the fabric of this House. I do not know how one could operate upon a ghost with parricidal pick-axes. In the leading ghost case, which is to be found in Shakespeare's " Hamlet," the officer in command of the guard proposed to attack the ghost with a partisan, whatever a partisan is, but I suppose it must be something different from a parricidal pick-axe. But the Prime Minister was not content to leave the matter there. He charged my noble friend and your Lordships' House with doing what he called applying a thin coat of democratic varnish to the " ghost." I must say that any attempt to varnish a ghost would require a considerable amount of ingenuity.

The Resolutions which, before our proceedings terminate this evening, I shall venture to lay before the House will, then, have reference not to the question of the constitution of this House, but to the manner in which deadlocks between the two Houses, persistent differences of opinion, might be dealt with. And let me add this observation. We on this side have always been in favour of making some change in our procedure for the purpose of meeting that particular difficulty. I say that because the noble Earl opposite told us the other evening that he had never heard, that he had not the faintest idea, that that was a part of the case we were interested in. I looked up the speech which I delivered in this House, I think, in March of this year, and I find I then stated as clearly as I possibly could that in our view both questions demanded attention — on the one hand, the constitution of this House ; on the other, the procedure to be resorted to in case of differences between the two Houses. . . .

Extract 79

GOVERNMENT HASTE AGAINST THE HOUSE OF LORDS

(The Earl of Rosebery, Lords, November 21, 1910)

THE EARL OF ROSEBERY [1]: . . . You do not seem to realise what you are doing. You bring in a Bill of this kind with the trivial elegance with which you might introduce a turnpike Act or the mysterious local government measures which are moved by the

[1] Parliamentary Debates, Lords, Fifth Series, vol. 6, col. 800 sqq.

dozen by some lower official of the Government. What you are attempting to do is none of these things. You are attempting to do away with one estate of the realm without substituting anything in its place. You have the face to tell us that we are acting in an unprecedented manner when in the last four, five, or six dying days of the session you bring forward this Motion without any option to us but to say Yes or No to any of the provisions of the Bill.

The noble Marquess behind me quoted a phrase from the remarkable, I might almost say extraordinary, speech delivered by my right hon. friend the Prime Minister at the National Liberal Club on Saturday. I make every allowance for the exuberance of a speech made under the hospitable auspices of the National Liberal Club, where I have so often enjoyed myself in past days. But I am a little shocked that the noble Marquess did not mark the most significant part of that speech, which was accentuated by my noble friend who spoke last. The Prime Minister quoted Dr. Johnson as saying that nothing concentrates a man's mind so much as the knowledge that he is going to be hanged, and he applied the remark to your Lordships' House. My noble friend opposite spoke of a deathbed repentance. This is the spirit apparently in which this great Government approaches this vast Constitutional question. They regard the House of Lords as simply a culprit to be hanged without shrift and without repentance, and only with the rather trite consolations of my noble friend opposite to cheer its last hour. I have always understood that when a man is going to be hanged he has, besides the opportunity of concentration of mind, some little mercy shown to him in the disposal of his last moments. He is admitted to certain indulgences. My noble friends opposite, having put on the black cap, are not inclined to any such leniency. We claim that we shall employ the few hours which we have to live to the best purpose that, in our judgment, we can, and we will not allow any other necessities to override that which dictates to this ancient Assembly the right to present its own case to the country without being gagged by an ultra-Liberal Government.

Extract 80

FUTILITY OF REFORMING THE HOUSE OF LORDS FROM WITHIN

(*Lord Loreburn, Lord Chancellor, Lords, November 21, 1910*)

LORD LOREBURN [1]: My Lords, the question before your Lordships' House at this moment is that this debate be now adjourned. I will only say a very few words on what I call the fringe which the noble Lord added to the point under discussion. He has spoken of our precipitancy and desire to avoid discussion. Let me remind your Lordships what is the history of the question of the reform of the House of Lords and the adjustment of the relations between the two Houses.

The noble Earl has been, I admit, a pioneer, a protagonist in this business all his life. He dropped it, I suppose, as an impossible task during the period of twenty years of Conservative ascendancy preceding 1905. In 1905 when a Liberal Government came in the noble Earl took no step. The year 1906 passed. In 1907 Lord Newton brought the matter forward and the Committee which was appointed reported in December, 1908. Why was nothing said about all these proposals for reform during the year 1909? Lord Newton put down a motion relating to the subject, but only to one side of it, — namely, the constitution of the House, — and it constantly disappeared from the Paper. It seemed always to vanish. If I were not aware of his want of reverence for the Whips, I should have supposed that the Whips had exercised some influence upon him not to bring the matter forward in the year 1909. Your Lordships will remember that at that time a raid was contemplated upon the Budget, and that might not be a convenient time to draw attention to the supposed shortcomings of your Lordships' House ; you do not go to confessional just at the time when you are about to stop a mail-coach. . . .

[1] Parliamentary Debates, Lords, Fifth Series, vol. 6, col. 801 sqq.

Extract 81

CONSERVATIVE SUBSTITUTE FOR THE PARLIAMENT BILL

(The Marquess of Lansdowne, Lords, November 23, 1910)

THE MARQUESS OF LANSDOWNE [1] rose to move —

That this House do resolve itself into Committee in order to consider the following resolutions upon the relations between the two Houses of Parliament:

That in the opinion of this House it is desirable that provision should be made for settling differences which may arise between the House of Commons and this House, reconstituted and reduced in numbers in accordance with the recent Resolutions of this House.

That as to Bills other than Money Bills, such provision should be upon the following lines:

If a difference arises between the two Houses with regard to any Bill other than a Money Bill in two successive Sessions, and with an interval of not less than one year, and such difference cannot be adjusted by any other means, it shall be settled in a Joint Sitting composed of members of the two Houses.

Provided that if the difference relates to a matter which is of great gravity, and has not been adequately submitted for the judgment of the people, it shall not be referred to the Joint Sitting, but shall be submitted for decision to the electors by Referendum.

That as to Money Bills, such provision should be upon the following lines:

The Lords are prepared to forego their constitutional right to reject or amend Money Bills which are purely financial in character.

Provided that effectual provision is made against tacking; and

Provided that, if any question arises as to whether a Bill or any provisions thereof are purely financial in character, that question be referred to a Joint Committee of both Houses, with the Speaker of the House of Commons as Chairman, who shall have a casting vote only.

If the Committee hold that the Bill or provisions in question are not purely financial in character, they shall be dealt with forthwith in a Joint Sitting of the two Houses.

1 Parliamentary Debates, Lords, Fifth Series, vol. 6, col. 838.

Extract 82

SUPPORT OF THE LANSDOWNE RESOLUTIONS

(Lord Ribblesdale, Lords, November 23, 1910)

LORD RIBBLESDALE[1]: My Lords, I think I shall follow the advice of my noble friend below me and not make a dash into the referendum, which the noble Lord [Ellenborough] who has just sat down explained to us much more clearly than I have ever heard it explained before. Neither do I propose to follow the noble Lord into Lough Swilly or the deeply indented coast of Ireland in a gunboat or in any other way. What he said about our being surrounded by Jacobins and Girondists would have made me feel thoroughly uncomfortable were it not for the extremely pleasant smile with which he accompanied this disagreeable piece of news.

I was very sorry that the noble Viscount, Lord Ridley, towards the end of his interesting speech, when he got to closer quarters with the Resolutions before us to-night, complained of suffering from a feeling of want of reality. To my mind these Resolutions of the noble Marquess and their full discussion by this House at the present moment are as real a thing on as real an issue for us all in this country as we have had before us since the Home Rule Bill of 1892 or 1893.

Whatever may be the measure of consent, or quasi consent, or qualified consent on the two sides of the House, I think we may all agree that we are getting on wonderfully pleasantly with this debate. It is evidently possible, as Mr. Carlyle once said, to agree very tolerably except in opinion. I do not suppose that the two sides of the House to-night are agreed in opinion, but even if noble Lords below me are right in saying that it is quite impossible that this great Constitutional difficulty in which we now find ourselves can be settled by consent, it is quite clear that in this House,

[1] Parliamentary Debates, Lords, Fifth Series, vol. 6, col. 895 sqq.

at all events, the matter can be agreed in a cordial and generous and fair spirit. Now on Monday night I thought we were on the verge of getting a little cross. I know that I suffered myself — and my noble friend below me, Earl Beauchamp, will perhaps corroborate it — from two or three spasms of noble irritation. But to-night an intelligent foreigner with Virgil at his fingers' ends and with two or three selected tributes of the noble Lord, Lord Curzon, to your Lordships' House in his mind as well, could not possibly say *Tantaene animis caelestibus irae?* as he might have done on Monday night.

Now I proceed to the Resolutions, and let me say at once that not only do I welcome them and thank the noble Marquess for putting them on the Paper and bringing them forward, but, speaking for myself, I am prepared to swallow them whole. That, no doubt, sounds a hardy and indigestible proceeding, but, after all, I am taking this course on Lord Crewe's advice to us to do the same thing with the Parliament Bill, which, as Lord St. Aldwyn and Lord Weardale pointed out with great force, has not even been discussed in the House of Commons except in a rudimentary way, and has only just flitted as it were into this House, but the clauses and Preamble of which are the Party ticket and the grounds for the General Election upon which the country is to be fought. When I say that I am prepared to swallow the Resolutions whole, I think it is also right to say that as regards the Government Bill I must admit myself to have become rather a waverer. Whatever the Conference did, it gave us considerable time for reflection, and I became so convinced that we should have to find some sort of constitutional adjustment of the relations of the two Houses that, speaking for myself, I was prepared to go a very long way for the sake of a settlement by consent towards the Government Bill. But I am bound to say that holding those views, I greatly prefer the Resolutions which the noble Marquess has put upon the Paper, and I prefer them for this reason : I feel that these Resolutions are altogether a more decorous and proper approach towards the solution of this great Constitutional question, and I prefer them very much to the Parliament Bill for the further reason that they are not stamped with the hall-mark, as that Bill is, of a particular majority in this particular Parliament and in particular relation to the Irish vote and the Irish demand.

I feel now that I should like to put myself right with the noble Earl who sits on the Cross Benches [Lord Rosebery] and perhaps with the House for the line I took the other night when Lord Rosebery's Resolutions were discussed and when he said that I had not made it clear to him what I meant. I should be sorry to think that I had in any way taken a wayward or an ungracious line that evening — wayward in the sense of being out of harmony with the self-denying ordinance which we have all affirmed by passing these Reform Resolutions. My mind has been much concentrated upon the present difficulties in which we find ourselves, and I have felt all along that the immediate *crux* of the situation did not lie in domestic reform from within, but in presenting to the electorate alternative proposals which would bring about a Constitutional readjustment. It seemed to me that in the very short time at our disposal, owing to what I can only call this electioneering General Election, this could only be done by giving a second reading to the Parliament Bill and going into Committee. But now that these Resolutions have been put forward I quite admit I was wrong. I did not know at the time that the Resolutions were coming forward, and I was nervous lest in our passion for self-reform from within we should do anything which should jeopardise our time and our chance of getting alternative proposals, by way of arriving at some agreement by consent, put fully before the constituencies before the 28th, when the Dissolution has been fixed. . . .

Speaking for myself, I am not, I am afraid, a very ardent reformer. I have no desire to strike any doleful note, or to sing any sort of Swan Song. I hope we are a long way off from that yet. The Resolutions which were passed the other night must inevitably have very great effect. Here again I make my *amende* to the noble Earl, Lord Rosebery, for if he had not gone on with them, those Resolutions could not have been grafted on to the Resolutions which the noble Marquess has now moved, thus providing for a reformed Second Chamber. It is quite clear that under these Resolutions, as Lord Newton said the other night, a large number of us will have to go, and personally I shall miss a great many things which I associate with the House of Lords and of which I have become fond. I do not want to be sentimental, but I shall miss the stationery, the quill pens, and even the superlative coal fires and draughts of your Lordships' House. I have been here all my life, but whether or not it is due to some inherited aptitude, I have intuitions about the House of Commons which make me put all these personal feelings on one side and desire above all things to secure a settlement of this question. I do not know that the Resolutions can effect that, but I believe, as one or two speakers have said this evening and as even the noble Earl, Lord Crewe, said, they do provide a basis for settlement by consent which I do not believe any Government or any constituency will altogether put aside.

The Resolutions of the noble Marquess seem to me to have this very considerable advantage over the Parliament Bill, even the Parliament Bill taken at its very best, that they do not lay us open now, — thanks, as I have just said, to Lord Rosebery for having stuck to his Resolutions, — they do not lay us open to the charge or to the actuality of a Single-Chamber Government, whereas, whatever the result may be in practice, there is no sort of doubt that the Government proposals are logically open to the charge not of adjusting Constitutional relations but of substituting till such good time as in the Government view may best suit them a Single-Chamber for a Double-Chamber Government. Under these circumstances the noble Marquess and his friends will have my hearty support in these Resolutions.

Extract 83

PARLIAMENT ACT, 1911

(1 & 2 Geo. 5, ch. 13)

An Act to make provision with respect to the powers of the House of Lords in relation to those of the House of Commons, and to limit the duration of Parliament.   (18th August 1911)

Whereas it is expedient that provision should be made for regulating the relations between the two Houses of Parliament :

And whereas it is intended to substitute for the House of Lords as it at present exists a Second Chamber constituted on a popular instead of hereditary basis, but such substitution cannot be immediately brought into operation :

And whereas provision will require hereafter to be made by Parliament in a measure effecting such substitution for limiting and defining the powers of the new Second Chamber, but it is expedient to make such provision as in this Act appears for restricting the existing powers of the House of Lords :

Be it therefore enacted by the King's most Excellent Majesty, by and with the advice and consent of the Lords Spiritual and Temporal, and Commons, in this present Parliament assembled, and by the authority of the same, as follows :

1. Power of House of Lords as to Money Bills

(1) If a Money Bill, having been passed by the House of Commons, and sent up to the House of Lords at least one month before the end of the session, is not passed by the House of Lords without amendment within one month after it is so sent up to that House, the Bill shall, unless the House of Commons direct to the contrary, be presented to His Majesty and become an Act of Parliament on the Royal Assent being signified, notwithstanding that the House of Lords have not consented to the Bill.

(2) A Money Bill means a Public Bill which in the opinion of the Speaker of the House of Commons contains only provisions dealing with all or any of the following subjects, namely, the imposition, repeal, remission, alteration, or regulation of taxation; the imposition for the payment of debt or other financial purposes of charges on the Consolidated Fund, or on money provided by Parliament, or the variation or repeal of any such charges; supply; the appropriation, receipt, custody, issue or audit of accounts of public money; the raising or guarantee of any loan or the repayment thereof; or subordinate matters incidental to those subjects or any of them. In this subsection the expressions "taxation," "public money," and "loan" respectively do not include any taxation, money, or loan raised by local authorities or bodies for local purposes.

(3) There shall be endorsed on every Money Bill when it is sent up to the House of Lords and when it is presented to His Majesty for assent the certificate of the Speaker of the House of Commons signed by him that it is a Money Bill. Before giving his certificate, the Speaker shall consult, if practicable, two members to be appointed from the Chairmen's Panel at the beginning of each Session by the Committee of Selection.

2. *Restriction of Powers of House of Lords as to Bills other than Money Bills*

(1) If any Public Bill (other than a Money Bill or a Bill containing any provision to extend the maximum duration of Parliament beyond five years) is passed by the House of Commons in three successive sessions (whether of the same Parliament or not), and, having been sent up to the House of Lords at least one month before the end of the session, is rejected by the House of Lords in each of those sessions, that Bill shall, on its rejection for the third time by the House of Lords, unless the House of Commons direct to the contrary, be presented to His Majesty and become an Act of Parliament on the Royal Assent being signified thereto, notwithstanding that the House of Lords have not consented to the Bill:

Provided that this provision shall not take effect unless two years have elapsed between the date of the second reading in the first of those sessions of the Bill in the House of Commons and the date on which it passes the House of Commons in the third of those sessions.

(2) When a Bill is presented to His Majesty for assent in pursuance of the provisions of this section, there shall be endorsed on the Bill the certificate of the Speaker of the House of Commons signed by him that the provisions of this section have been duly complied with.

(3) A Bill shall be deemed to be rejected by the House of Lords if it is not passed by the House of Lords either without amendment or with such amendments only as may be agreed to by both Houses.

(4) A Bill shall be deemed to be the same Bill as a former Bill sent up to the House of Lords in the preceding session if, when it is sent up to the House of Lords, it is identical with the former Bill or contains only such alterations as are certified by the Speaker of the House of Commons to be necessary owing to the time which has elapsed since the date of the former Bill, or to represent any amendments which have been made by the House of Lords in the former Bill in the preceding session, and any amendments which are certified by the Speaker to have been made by the House of Lords in the third session and agreed to by the House of Commons shall be inserted in the Bill as presented for Royal Assent in pursuance of this section :

Provided that the House of Commons may, if they think fit, on the passage of such a Bill through the House in the second or third session, suggest any further amendments without inserting the amendments in the Bill, and any such suggested amendments shall be considered by the House of Lords, and, if agreed to by that House, shall be treated as amendments made by the House of Lords and agreed to by the House of Commons ; but the exercise of this power by the House of Commons shall not affect the operation of this section in the event of the Bill being rejected by the House of Lords.

3. *Certificate of Speaker*

Any certificate of the Speaker of the House of Commons given under this Act shall be conclusive for all purposes, and shall not be questioned in any court of law.

4. *Enacting Words*

(1) In every Bill presented to His Majesty under the preceding provisions of this Act, the words of enactment shall be as follows, that is to say :

Be it enacted by the King's most Excellent Majesty, by and with the advice and consent of the Commons in this present Parliament assembled, in accordance with the provisions of the Parliament Act, 1911, and by authority of the same, as follows.

(2) Any alteration of a Bill necessary to give effect to this section shall not be deemed to be an amendment of the Bill.

5. *Provisional Order Bills Excluded*

In this Act the expression " Public Bill " does not include any Bill for confirming a Provisional Order.

6. *Saving Clause*

Nothing in this Act shall diminish or qualify the existing rights and privileges of the House of Commons.

7. *Duration of Parliament*

Five years shall be substituted for seven years as the time fixed for the maximum duration of Parliament under the Septennial Act, 1715.[1]

8. *Title*

This Act may be cited as the Parliament Act, 1911.

[1] 1 Geo. 1, stat. 2, ch. 38.

CHAPTER X

NATIONAL INSURANCE

[Since the Liberal Government came into power in 1906, they had promoted, as has been seen, a large number of social reforms, such as the protection of the legal rights of labourers and trade unions, assurance of child welfare, regulation of sweated labour, establishment of labour exchanges, old age pensions, housing and town planning schemes and almost revolutionary tax arrangements. Their efforts, interrupted and possibly imperilled for a while in 1910 on account of the two General Elections and the accompanying struggle to reduce the political power of the House of Lords, were put forth again in 1911 to secure the passage of what is perhaps the most important measure of social betterment ever introduced in the British Parliament — "an Act to provide for insurance against loss of life and for the prevention and cure of sickness and for insurance against unemployment."

In the German Empire, a system of national compulsory insurance of workingmen against sickness and unemployment had been in successful operation for many years, but despite considerable agitation and many promises, similar action in Great Britain had been long delayed. However, in the course of the debate in 1906 on the Workmen's Compensation Bill, several speakers, notably Sir Charles Dilke,[1] urged the fundamental character of such an insurance. Again, the discussion on old age pensions served in the main to support the contention that insurance was a natural corollary to pensions.[2] And in outlining the Government's plans for the establishment of labour exchanges, Mr. Winston Churchill

[1] Cf. supra, p. 38. [2] Cf. supra, p. 142.

declared [1] that that would constitute a beginning in the preparation and perfecting of a program for general state insurance.

From 1908 to 1911 various officials and committees of Government departments worked on the problem, which proved most knotty and intricate. At length, on May 4, 1911, Mr. David Lloyd George, as Chancellor of the Exchequer, brought in the Bill, containing eighty-seven clauses and nine schedules; and, in a remarkably clear speech (*Extract 84*), sketched its purpose and explained its chief provisions. The Chancellor's appeal was well received by the leaders of the other parties. Mr. Austen Chamberlain, of the Opposition, would have preferred to deal separately with insurance against sickness and that against unemployment, but expressed general sympathy with the objects. Mr. John Redmond, leader of the Irish Nationalists, assured the Government of his support (*Extract 85*); and the Labour Members, while expressing some fear as to the details of the measure, were naturally favourable.

The Bill came up for second reading in the Commons on May 24. It had been much discussed in the interval, and the Chancellor of the Exchequer had invited and encouraged criticisms. Though the general public reception appeared favourable, misgivings were expressed by some employers and some representatives of the friendly, or benefit, societies. The most active criticism came from the medical profession and its organisation. They held that they would lose practice among the lower middle and artisan classes, and that the fees fixed by the Bill for medical attendance upon the insured were altogether too low. Mr. Sydney Buxton, President of the Board of Trade, in moving second reading, explained the general principles of the Bill and answered several criticisms (*Extract 86*). Speaking for the official Opposition, Mr. H. W. Forster complained about the coupling of sickness and unemployment in one measure, the creation of a debt of £63,000,000 to start the scheme, the increased contribution from employers where wages

[1] Cf. supra, p. 200.

were low, and the possible effect upon the doctors and friendly societies; the Opposition hoped, however, that the second reading would be passed without a single dissentient vote. The Nationalists and the Labour party again welcomed the Bill, though with considerable reserve as to certain points. After a number of other speeches, Mr. Rufus Isaacs, the Attorney-General, cited several important lessons that might be drawn from German experience along similar lines (*Extract 87*).

In the course of the debate on second reading, Mr. Ramsay Macdonald, the leader of the Labour party, pointed out that the Insurance Bill marked a fundamental change in public opinion, both larger parties now accepting the principle that social welfare was the care of the state — social affairs the main business of politics (*Extract 88*). His criticisms suggested the desire of his party for alternative provisions to certain ones in the Government Bill.

Committee stage was begun on July 5 and continued intermittently into November. Several hundreds of amendments were adopted, the chief of which may be roughly outlined as follows:[1] Sick pay (10s. per week for men, 7s. 6d. for women) was to continue for twenty-six weeks instead of thirteen. Maternity benefit was extended to the wife of an insured person even if she herself was an insured person. Sanatorium for consumption might be extended to the dependants of the insured consumptive. Married women might now come in during their husband's lifetime as voluntary contributors with reduced payments, receiving sickness and disablement benefit. Soldiers, sailors and other naval men, and mercantile seamen, might come in under special provisions; so might fishermen co-partners under regulations to be made by the Commissioners according to varying local customs. Where it was the custom for the employer to pay full wages during sickness the contributions of both employers and employed might be reduced

---

[1] Cf. The Annual Register, 1911, p. 281. The same volume gives, in various places, details of the debate, whose incorporation in this work space precludes.

and the sickness benefit likewise if the employer would agree to pay wages for six weeks of illness. Persons earning less than 9s. a week paid no contribution, those between 9s. and 12s., 1d. per week less than under the original Bill. The local Health Committees were to be called Insurance Committees, and their numbers and powers had been considerably increased. The " Post Office " part of the Bill was made distinctly provisional. There were to be separate Commissioners for Ireland, Scotland, and Wales. The provisions for Ireland were considerably altered; *inter alia* the employer's contribution was reduced to 2½d. a week; migratory labourers and outworkers whose work was done in leisure time were exempted, medical benefit was withdrawn in view of the existence of the dispensary system and the constitution of Health Committees adapted to Irish conditions. Part II (Unemployment) was but little altered in the Standing Committee. The weekly benefits in the building trades were raised to 7s., the minimum age reduced from eighteen to sixteen, with reduced contributions and benefits below eighteen; apprentices were exempted; an employer giving regular employment would be rewarded by rebates, not by a reduction of contributions; and employers were prohibited from deducting their own contribution from wages.

On December 6 the Bill reached third reading in the House of Commons. In the meanwhile, protests against it had been multiplying from the medical profession, representatives of hospitals, and clerks; the General Federation of Trade Unions had protested against the severance of the four kingdoms; and many domestic servants had been organised by their employers to resist the provisions which affected their relations. It was rumoured that the Conservatives would utilise this agitation in order to oppose a measure which at heart very few of them really favoured, despite the support that they had promised on first and second readings.

At any rate, the Opposition met the motion for the third reading with an amendment to the effect that, under the part dealing with health insurance, public and individual contributions would not be used to the best advantage, that the discussion and explanation of the Bill had been defective, and that its operation would be unequal, and that it should therefore be again considered in 1912, draft regulations for its operation being published meanwhile. This was moved by Mr. H. W. Forster, who disclaimed any intention of wrecking the measure. His speech (*Extract 89*) explained the changed attitude of the Conservatives.

Mr. Ramsay Macdonald, re-entering the debate, said that misgivings were certainly widespread, but that the choice was between partly satisfactory legislation and none at all. Mr. Lloyd George bitterly assailed the Conservative position. Postponement, he stated, would upset the business of the friendly societies and insurance companies and reopen unfortunate controversies; and he especially assailed Lord Robert Cecil, who replied with his usual plea in behalf of individualism (*Extract 90*).

Mr. Bonar Law, the new Leader of the Opposition, closed the debate for his party, insisting that the amendment did not necessarily mean the rejection of the Bill and reviewing the main Conservative objections (*Extract 91*). Mr. Asquith replied in an eloquent speech (*Extract 92*). The amendment was defeated by 320 to 223, and the third reading carried by 324 to 21. In the first division two Unionists voted with the Government, seven Independent Nationalists with the Opposition; the minority in the second division comprised three Labour members, the seven Independent Nationalists, and eleven Unionists.

The progress of the Bill through the House of Lords was uneventful, and it received the royal assent on December 16, 1911. The extraordinary length of the National Insurance Act (1 & 2 Geo. 5, ch. 55) — it covers one hundred and fifteen pages of the Statute Book — prevents its inclusion in this volume.[1]]

---

[1] An excellent edition of the full act, together with explanatory notes, tables, and examples, is that of Orme Clark, with an introduction by Sir John Simon, Solicitor-General (1912). For analyses and explanations, cf. L. G. Chiozza Money, A Nation Insured (1912); Carr and Taylor, National Insurance (1912); and E. Porritt, "The British National Insurance Act," in *Political Science Quarterly*, June, 1912.

Extract 84

EXPOSITION OF THE NATIONAL INSURANCE BILL

*(Mr. David Lloyd George, Chancellor of the Exchequer
Commons, May 4, 1911)*

MR. LLOYD GEORGE[1]: . . . I think it must be a relief to the
Members of the House of Commons to turn from controversial
questions for a moment to a question which, at any rate, has never
been the subject of controversy between the parties in the State.
I believe there is a general agreement as to the evil which has to
be remedied. There is a general agreement as to its urgency, and
I think I can go beyond that and say there is a general agreement as to the main proposals upon which the remedy ought to
be based.

In this country . . . 30 per cent of the pauperism is attributable
to sickness. A considerable percentage would probably have to be
added to that for unemployment. The administration of the Old
Age Pensions Act has revealed the fact that there is a mass of
poverty and destitution in this country which is too proud to wear
the badge of pauperism and which declines to pin that badge to
its children. They would rather suffer from deprivation than do
so. I am perfectly certain if this is the fact with regard to persons
of seventy years of age, there must be a multitude of people of
that kind before they reach that age.

The efforts made by the working classes to insure against the
troubles of life indicate they are fully alive to the need of some
provision being made. There are three contingencies against which
they insure — death, sickness, and unemployment. Taking them in
the order of urgency which the working classes attach to them,
death would come first. There are 42,000,000 industrial policies
of insurance against death issued in this country of small amounts

1 Parliamentary Debates, Commons, Fifth Series, vol. 25, col. 609 sqq.

where the payments are either weekly, monthly, or occasionally quarterly. The friendly societies, without exception, have funeral benefits, and that accounts for about 6,000,000. The collecting societies are about 7,000,000, and those are also death benefits. Then the great industrial insurance companies have something like 30,000,000 policies. There is hardly a household in this country where there is not a policy of insurance against death. I will not stop to account for it. After all, the oldest friendly societies in the world are burial societies. All I would say here is we do not propose to deal with insurance against death. It is no part of our scheme at all, partly because the ground has been very thoroughly covered, although not very satisfactorily covered, and also because this, at any rate, is the easiest part of the problem and is a part of the problem which is not beset with the difficulties of vested interests. Fortunately, all the vested interests which deal with sickness and unemployment are of a thoroughly unselfish and beneficent character, and we shall be able, I think, to assist them, not merely without interfering with their rights and privileges, but by encouraging them to do the excellent work they have commenced and which they are doing so well.

Sickness comes in the next order of urgency in the working-class mind. There are over 6,000,000 policies — that is hardly the word, perhaps, for friendly societies, but there is provision made by 6,000,000 people against sickness. Most of it includes a provision for medical aid. There are, I think, about 300,000 or 400,000 members who have insured for medical aid alone, but I think almost without exception the friendly societies include medical relief in the provisions which they make. That is not, I think, the case with the trade unions. There are 700,000 members in the trade unions insured for sick benefits, but I do not think that includes medical relief. In addition to those, there are a good many unregistered assurances at works, where a man leaves a shilling a month at the office for the purpose of paying the works' doctor. I should say, therefore, that between 6,000,000 and 7,000,000 people in this country have made some provision against sickness, not all of it adequate, and a good deal of it defective.

Then comes the third class, the insurance against unemployment. Here not a tenth of the working classes have made any provision at all. You have got only 1,400,000 workmen who have insured against unemployment. It is true that perhaps about half of the employment of this country is not affected by the fluctuations of trade. I do not think agricultural labourers or railway servants are affected quite to the same extent. Then there is provision for short time in some of the trades. Taking the precarious trades affected by unemployment, I do not believe more than one-third or one-quarter of the people engaged in them are insured against unemployment. That is the provision which is made at the present moment by the working classes: 42,000,000 policies against death, about 6,100,000 who have made some kind of provision against sickness, and 1,400,000 who have made some provision against unemployment.

Now comes the question which leads up to the decision of the Government to take action. What is the explanation that only a portion of the working classes have made provision against sickness and unemployment? Is it that they consider it not necessary? Quite the reverse, as I shall prove by figures. In fact, those who stand most in need of it make up the bulk of the uninsured. Why? . . . The first explanation is that their wages are too low. I am talking now about the uninsured portion. Their wages are too low to enable them to insure without some assistance. The second difficulty, and it is the greatest of all, is that during a period of sickness or unemployment, when they are earning nothing, they cannot keep up the premiums. They may be able to do it for a fortnight or three weeks, but when times of very bad trade come, when a man is out of work for weeks and weeks at a time, arrears run up with the friendly societies, and when a man gets work, it may be at the end of two or three months, those are not the first arrears which have to be met. There are arrears of rent, arrears of the grocery bill, and arrears for the necessaries of life. At any rate he cannot consider his friendly society only. The result is that a very considerable number of workmen find themselves quite unable to keep up the premiums when they have a family to look after.

Undoubtedly there is another reason. It is no use shirking the fact that a proportion of workmen with good wages spend them in other ways and therefore have nothing to spare with which to pay premiums to friendly societies. It has come to my notice, in many of these cases, that the women of the family make most heroic efforts to keep up the premiums to the friendly societies, and the officers of the friendly societies whom I have seen, have amazed me by telling the proportion of premiums of this kind paid by women out of the very wretched allowance given them to keep the household together.

I think it is well we should look all the facts in the face before we come to consider the remedy. What does it mean in the way of lapses? I have inquired of friendly societies, and, as far as I could get at it, there are 250,000 lapses in a year. That is a very considerable proportion of the 6,000,000 policies. The expectation of life at twenty is, I think, a little over forty years, and it means that in twenty years' time there are 5,000,000 lapses; that is, people who supported and joined friendly societies, and who have gone on paying the premiums for weeks, months, and even years, struggling along at last, when a very bad time of unemployment comes, drop out and the premium lapses. It runs to millions in the course of a generation. What does that mean? It means that the vast majority of the workingmen of this country at one time or other have been members of friendly societies, have felt the need for provision of this kind, and it is only because they have been driven — sometimes by their own habits, but in the majority of cases by circumstances over which they have no control — to abandon their policies. That is the reason why, at the present moment, not one-half the workmen of this country have made any provision for sickness and not one-tenth for unemployment. I think it necessary to state these facts in order to show that there is a real need for some system which would aid the workmen over these difficulties. I do not think there is any better method, or one more practical at the present moment, than a system of national insurance which would invoke the aid of the State and the aid of the employer to enable the workman to get over all these difficulties and make provision for himself for sickness, and as far as the most precarious trades are concerned, against unemployment.

I come at once to the plan of the Government. The measure of the Government is divided into two parts: the first will deal with sickness and the second with unemployment. The sickness branch of the Bill will also be in two sections: one will be compulsory, and the other voluntary. The compulsory part of the Bill involves a compulsory deduction from the wages of all the employed classes who earn weekly wages, or whose earnings are under the Income Tax limit. There will be a contribution from the employer and a further contribution from the State.

There are exceptions from the compulsory clause. The first will be in the Army and Navy. We are making special provision for soldiers and sailors. It is a crying scandal, I think, that at the present moment there are so many soldiers and sailors who have placed their lives at the disposal of the country and are quite ready to sacrifice them, as we know from past experience — not merely that they should be liable to, but that, as a matter of fact, hundreds and thousands do actually leave the Army and Navy broken through ill-health. I am talking now of ill-health not due to misconduct. These men leave the Army without any provision from either public or private charity, and they are broken men for the rest of their lives. I think it is a crying scandal that that should occur in a country like this, and I hope this scheme will put an end to it. There will be special provision made for that. But these men will not be regarded as in the employed class for the purposes I am about to explain. The same thing applies to the teachers, and I hope to be able, with the assistance of my right hon. Friend the President of the Board of Education [Mr. Walter Runciman], to largely strengthen their present position. I think their provision is very inadequate, and, compared with the provisions made in other countries, I think a very paltry allowance is made for their superannuation.

MR. JOHN REDMOND : Does that apply to Ireland ?

MR. LLOYD GEORGE : Certainly, I think the Irish case a very bad case. I have had a number of Irish teachers before me, and some of them told me that they were getting about £1 a week. There are about 300 of them in the workhouses. They are doing their work for the Empire under very trying conditions, and I shall certainly consider it the duty of the Government in any scheme of superannuation to include the Irish teachers as well.

MR. JOHN REDMOND : When ?

MR. LLOYD GEORGE : I hope it will be possible this year. We propose excepting all people employed under the Crown or under municipalities where, at the present moment, there is no deduction from their wages when they are ill, and where there is some superannuation allowance. There is no need to make provision for them because provision is already made. The same thing will apply to commission agents employed by more than one person. There is also an exception in the case of casual labour employed otherwise than for the purpose of the employer's trade or business. We think it is vital that casual labour should be included. Otherwise the same thing may happen here as I am told happens in Germany, where the exclusion of casual labour is rather encouraging its growth. That is a very bad thing in itself, and there is really no class which it is more important to include than casual labour.

SIR C. KINLOCH-COOKE : Does that include casual labour in dockyards ?

MR. LLOYD GEORGE : Casual labour at dockyards and in warehouses will be included. I think, too, that casual labour such as that of golf caddies should be brought in. I am making special provision for labour of that kind. Hotel waiters will be another difficulty. They are not paid salaries. I am told that they very often pay for the privilege of waiting, and we have to make special provision for them. Cab drivers are another class we propose to include. All casual labour of this kind will be included, as well as casual labour of the kind referred to by the hon. Member opposite. The man who offers to carry your bag for sixpence you can never draw in, but it is our intention to attract all casual labour possible within the ambit of our Bill.

MR. AUSTEN CHAMBERLAIN : Are we to understand that all the classes which the right hon. Gentleman has enumerated are exceptions to the compulsory provisions which he is about to describe ?

MR. LLOYD GEORGE : Certainly they can come in the voluntary part if they like, so long as they answer to the definition which I have given. I think that is rather anticipating, but the right hon. Gentleman will later on find what class of persons will come in. I come to the amount of contribution. The workman now pays to his friendly society 6d. or 1s. The usual contribution to a friendly society is something between 6d. and 9d. as far as I have been able to discover, and anything under that produces benefits which are benefits I do not think it would be worth our while to include in an Act of Parliament. The House will be interested to know what German workmen have to pay, because that was the first great scientific experiment in insurance on a national scale. It has been enormously successful. That is the testimony borne by all classes of Germans. I have taken some trouble to inquire, and the German Government have been exceedingly kind and helpful in placing information at our disposal. They have shown every disposition to be helpful throughout, and their testimony is that all classes of the community are very much benefited by it. In Germany the payment is in proportion to wages, and the benefits are also in proportion to wages, so that the higher class of workman, who pays a very high contribution, gets a very substantial benefit. There are in Germany, I think, five classes of individual contributors, and for sickness every man pays according to his income. They divide their insurance into two separate branches of sickness and invalidity. There are two separate branches, but we propose to include them in one branch. In Germany a man who earns 30s. pays 10¾d. weekly for sickness and invalidity. There are not many of these. The man who is paid 24s. a week, which I think is about the average wage in this country, if you were to strike an average, which is a difficult thing to do — the man who is paid 24s. a week pays 9d. a week. For that 9d. the benefits he gets will not be equal to the benefits we shall be able to give under our Bill twenty years hence. The 20s. a week man pays 7¼d., the 18s. man 6¾d., the 15s. man 5¾d., the 12s. man 4¾d., and the 9s. man 3¾d.

That is what the workman pays in Germany, and when you come down to these lower classes, the benefits are so small that the workmen in Germany say they prefer to resort to parish relief, as the benefits are much too inadequate. For that reason we have decided in favour of one class, because if you have a scale which is proportionate, it would be very difficult to give benefits to the lower class except by making special conditions which it would not be worth our while to make. It would certainly not give them a minimum allowance to keep their families from want. So we have decided to have one scale for all classes, with a provision for the lowest wages. Therefore, we have decided to propose a deduction of 4d. for men and 3d. for women. That is about a halfpenny a day and a penny on Saturday, or, as somebody told me, about the price of two pints of the cheapest beer per week, or the price of an ounce of tobacco. Now comes the difficulty of the man who is earning 15s. a week and under, and who finds it rather difficult to pay 4d. a week. We meet that case by saying that a man or a woman who earns 2s. 6d. a day or less shall pay 3d., 2s. or less, 2d., and 1s. 6d. a day or less, 1d. a week. Let me make a very important exception. That would not include the cases where there is board and lodging in addition to the wage. These cases are excluded altogether. This is purely the case where the wage represents the whole payment.

Who will pay the difference? If you make the State pay the difference, then it means that the employers who pay high wages to their workmen will be taxed for the purpose of making up the diminished charge for the workmen of other employers who are paying less, and I do not think that would be fair. We have come to the conclusion that the difference ought to be made up by the employer who profits by cheap labour, and therefore in the lowest case (in the case of 15s. a week and downwards) the employer will pay more. I hope I have made it clear that our scale of deduction for the workmen is a uniform one, with the exception of that descending scale when you come to the very lowest wages and where you cannot really expect a man to pay 4d. a week.

There is another difficulty. Are we going to include in the benefits of the scheme men of all ages at the present moment? If we are, on what scale? Are we going to charge the man of fifty more than the man of twenty-five? That is a question which of course presents itself the moment you begin to consider the actuarial position, because, after all, sickness doubles, trebles, and quadruples as you get along in life, until when you get between sixty-five and seventy the average sickness in five years is fifty-two weeks. It begins with three or four days, then on to a week, then to a fortnight, and a man as he gets on in life becomes a heavier charge upon his friendly society, and no society can possibly take a man at fifty or fifty-five on the same terms as if he were only sixteen or twenty unless they make special provision. Of course, we are now starting a new scheme, and the Government have decided to do this — to charge a perfectly uniform rate throughout. . . . The only difference we make is with regard to men over fifty. We then propose to pay them reduced benefits. Men who are over sixty-five at the present moment we do not propose should join the scheme at all, because that is an impossible undertaking ; the burden would be much too heavy, and, after all, we must be fair to the man who comes in young with his money. He must be encouraged, he must get his reward for it, and if we take over too heavy a burden in

the way of those who are at present very old, the young people
will suffer. I am told that is the criticism in Germany — that the
young people do not get full value for their own money and the
money of their employers. We propose to admit everyone up to
sixty-five to insurance so long as it is done within twelve months
after the passing of the Act. We are going to give twelve months'
grace. If they come in after twelve months, they will come in on
the terms either of paying a rate appropriate to their age or of
taking reduced benefits, which comes to practically the same thing.

So much for the contribution by the employee. Now we come to
the contribution of the employer. What interest has the employer
in the matter? His interest is the efficiency of his workmen, and
there is no doubt at all that a great insurance scheme of this kind
removes a strain of pressing burden and anxiety from the shoulders
of the working classes and increases the efficiency of the workmen
enormously. The workingmen whom I met during the trades-union
movement told me that many a time they used to go on working
at their business because they dared not give it up, as they could
not afford to, and it would have been better for them to have been
in the doctor's hands. This procedure generally brings about a very
bad breakdown, and not only that, when a man is below par neither
the quantity nor the quality of his work is very good. I have taken
the trouble to make some inquiry from the German employers as
to their experience of insurance from this point of view, and I have
got a number of answers which, perhaps, later on the House would
be interested in having circulated. Here is one instance I had out
of many. It is the opinion of an employer engaged in the steel
industry. He said, "There can be no doubt that the Insurance
Laws, together with the increase of wages, have exercised an enormously beneficial influence upon the health, standard of living, and
the efficiency of workers." Another great employer of labour says
that "from the employers' standpoint these laws pay, since the
efficiency of the workman is increased." And now there is this
very curious position in Germany that the employers, and the

largest employers, are voluntarily offering to increase their contributions to national insurance for increased benefits. That is the view taken by the employer in Germany. What does he pay for sickness and invalidity insurance? He pays for a 30s. a week man 7¼d. For a 24s. a week man the employer would pay 5¾d. and for an 18s. a week man he pays 4¼d.; then when it goes down below that the contribution is very much lower, and the benefits are very poor. We propose that the employer should pay 3d. a week; the workman will pay 4d., or 3d. for a woman, and the employer will pay 3d. for man and woman alike. That is our proposal.

I come to the contribution of the State. The advantage of the scheme to the State is, of course, in happy, contented, and prosperous people. The German contribution is not a very large one. I believe it is about £2,500,000, and that includes Old Age Pensions. We have already got a burden of £13,000,000 a year for Old Age Pensions. But let me point this out to the House — that payment is equivalent to something like 5d. a week for employer and labourer under this scheme — and it makes matters very much easier. We certainly could not have offered the benefits which we are offering in this measure — 4d. for a workman and 3d. for an employer — had it not been that the whole burden of pensions over seventy years of age had been taken over by the State. That is the first actuarial fact which was borne in upon me the moment I came in contact with the actualities — what an enormous difference that made in the scheme, and how it eased matters. Had it not been for that I should have proposed very much dearer and sterner terms both for the employer and the employed. We do not propose that the State contribution should end with that £13,000,000. We propose that the State contribution shall be the equivalent of 2d. a member — 4d. from a workman, 3d. from an employer, and 2d. from the State. . . .

What is the workman to do when he is out of work? How is he to pay his contributions? We propose allowing a 6 per cent margin for unemployed; that means three weeks a year. As long as a man is employed you deduct 4d., but we allow a margin of three weeks a year for unemployment. That means in a cycle, say, of four years — bad times may come once every four years let us say — a margin of twelve weeks of unemployment. We propose to do more than that. After he has exhausted his twelve weeks, if he still is unemployed, then up to 25 per cent — that means thirteen weeks a year — we still allow him, but at reduced benefits. . . .

I now come to the voluntary contributors. There are two classes of voluntary contributors. There are persons who, whilst not working for an employer, are engaged in some regular occupation and are mainly dependent on their earnings for their livelihood. Take the village blacksmith who is not working for any employer, but is depending on his earnings for his livelihood. The same thing will apply to the small tradesman. I find looking through the lists of the friendly societies, in some of them there is a very high percentage of men who do not belong to the employed class in the ordinary sense of the term. For instance, in rural districts you will find that all the publicans, all the tradesmen, the schoolmaster, the village blacksmith, and the man who is joinering on his own, who is not anybody's man, are members of the friendly societies. We propose that they should be allowed to be members of this insurance scheme. They are really a great source of strength to the friendly societies. They help them in the management, and their business knowledge is of infinite value. It would be a great accession of strength to any scheme of this kind that we should still retain in it men of that type.

Then there is the other class of men — those who have been employed working for others and have ceased to do so, and are working on their own account. So long as they have been contributors for five years, we allow them still to join. With regard to this class, there is a difficulty in allowing them to come in at any age. . . . We propose that all those of that class who wish to join within six months, and who are forty-five years of age and under, can join at a rate which covers the 4d. or 3d., as the case may be, whether they are men or women, they themselves paying the employers' contribution. That would mean that they would pay 7d. for men and 6d. for women, and they, of course, get the benefit of the State contribution. Those over forty-five join at rates appropriate to their ages, but they also get the benefit of the State contribution for what it is worth to them, and, of course, it is worth a good deal.

Another exception we are bound to make to this class of voluntary contributors. I do not think it would be advisable to allow married women who are not workers to join. . . . You have, I think, about 700,000 married women who are workers and come into the compulsory scheme as workers, but I do not think we can possibly agree to married women unless they are workers. . . .

As to employed contributors, we anticipate that 9,200,000 men will be in the compulsory class, and there will be 3,900,000 women, making a total of 13,100,000 in that class. Then the voluntary contributors will number 600,000 men and 200,000 women, making a total of 800,000. . . . With the 800,000 voluntary contributors, the total will be 9,800,000 men, 4,100,000 women, making 13,900,000 altogether. But to that has got to be added 800,000 persons under sixteen years of age, consisting of 500,000 boys and 300,000 girls. That makes a grand total of 14,700,000 persons who shall, we hope, enjoy the insurance scheme.

Now I come to benefits. These will be distributed under three or four different heads. There will be medical relief. There will be the curing side of the benefit, and there will also be allowance for the maintenance of a man and his family during the time of his sickness. . . . If one of the 14,700,000 persons, who practically include all the industrial population of this country, falls ill, he can command the service of a competent doctor, and command it with the knowledge that he can pay. But not only that, the doctor whose service he commands will know also that he will be paid. That is going to make a very great difference in the doctoring of these people. . . .

The second branch of medical attention will be in cases of maternity. There are only one or two friendly societies at the present moment which allow any maternity benefit, but they are all alive to the necessity of it, and they are gradually going to establish branches for maternity benefit. Undoubtedly there is no more urgent need. Women of the working classes in critical cases are neglected sadly, sometimes through carelessness but oftener through poverty, and that is an injury not only to the woman herself, but to the children who are born. A good deal of infant mortality and a good deal of anæmic and rickety disease among the poorer class of children is very often due to the neglect in motherhood. . . . We propose that there should be a 30s. benefit in those cases which would cover the doctoring and the nursing, but only conditional upon those who are women workers not returning to work for four weeks, for I am told that in the mills you have very often cases where the women work up to the last moment and the maternity is over in a comparatively few days. . . .

I have now to refer to another branch of medical benefit. We propose to do something to deal with the terrible scourge of consumption. There are, I believe, in this country about four or five hundred thousand persons suffering from tubercular disease. . . . There are 75,000 deaths every year in Great Britain and Ireland from tuberculosis and, a much more serious matter, if you take the ages between fourteen and fifty-five among males, one out of three dies of tuberculosis between those ages in what should be the very period of greatest strength and vigour and service. It is a very sinister fact that at the very period which is responsible for the continued life of the race one out of three between those ages is stricken down by tuberculosis. It kills as many in the kingdom in a single year as all the zymotic diseases put together, and a very terrible fact in connection with it is that the moment a man is attacked and compromised he becomes a recruit in the destructive army and proceeds to injure mortally even those to whom he is most attached and to scatter infection and death in his own household. . . . The proposal of the Government is that we should first of all assist local charities and local authorities to build sanatoria throughout the country. We propose to set aside £1,500,000 of a capital sum for the purpose . . . and a fund of a million a year for the purpose of maintaining these institutions. . . .

I come next to the sick allowance for the purpose of maintaining the families of the sick persons who are insured. In the friendly societies I think the allowance is six months, then it is dropped again to half. In some societies it is still further dropped, generally at twelve months. I propose that the first stage should be a three months' grant, because the real reason why six months' allowance is given is because of tubercular patients. They are the people who take over three months on the fund. Outside of them a man is generally cured or off the funds before that period. I propose that in the first three months there should be an allowance of 10s. per week. Power will be given to the society to extend that to twenty-six weeks if they think it necessary. I point out later on that there are funds for that purpose, but, perhaps, at any rate, a start should be made with three months at 10s. Afterwards the allowance will be reduced to 5s. for another three months. After that, at the end of six months, if a man is broken down altogether, there is a permanent disablement allowance of 5s. as long as he is unable to earn his living in any way. That is for men. For women the contribution is lower, and, as we are keeping the accounts separate, the actuaries say we would not be justified in giving more than 7s. 6d. per week for the first three months, and then 5s. We do not propose to make the allowance less in that case.

There will be a waiting period of six months in the case of sickness. No man will be allowed to get his sickness allowance within six months after he has joined the society. No man is entitled to claim for a disablement allowance unless he has paid for two years. In Germany that has been extended to five years. The allowance is conditional in every case on the patient obeying the doctor's orders — a very difficult thing to do. But at any rate you cannot allow a man artificially to perpetuate his sickness at the expense of the community by defying every rule that is laid down for his cure by the professional gentleman who is in charge of him. In Germany they have this power. They give instructions as to what a man is to do, and if he does not obey them, his allowance is docked, and I think it is a very salutary rule. I have no doubt that it will be very liberally interpreted, but still it is a very necessary rule. There is another rule. The friendly societies do not admit sick allowance to any man whose illness is due to his own misconduct. What we have done in that case is this. If a man's illness is due to his own misconduct, we do not allow him sick pay, but he is entitled to a doctor, not merely for his own sake, but for the sake of the community, and because eventually he will come back again, and he will fall on the sick fund, and the burden will be much heavier. Now I come to the exceptions. In the case of persons fifty years of age at the date of insurance the men will only be entitled to 7s. a week and the women to 6s. a week, unless they have paid 500 contributions. Men and women over sixty years of age will only be entitled to 5s. Persons under twenty-one years of age, if unmarried, will be entitled to 5s., if males, and to 4s., if females. There is another very important exception from the point of view of checking malingering. When you come to the lower rate of wages you must not give a sick allowance which would make it more profitable for a man to be sick than to be working. Therefore, we propose that where the sick benefit is more than two-thirds of the wages the amount shall be reduced. . . .

After paying for the doctor, after paying for the sanatorium, after paying maternity benefit, after paying 10s. a week and 5s. sick allowance, and 7s. 6d. for women, there will be left a balance of £1,750,000 in the hands of those who administer the funds. That is the actuarial calculation. We do not now propose to distribute those benefits, because we want to give an interest to those who are administering the funds, to administer them economically and to declare alternative benefits, if they save the amounts which we anticipate they can save. We propose, therefore, to have a list of alternative benefits, optional benefits, and additional benefits. The first benefits, as I have indicated, will be the compulsory minimum benefits. They will be in every scheme. I now come to the additional benefits from which the society may choose, with this surplus at their disposal. This surplus will be £1,750,000 immediately the scheme begins to work, but at the end of fifteen years and a half, when the loss on the older persons has been wiped out, you will then have an addition of something like £5,500,000 to the fund, and, of course, that will involve a further contribution from the State of £1,500,000 per annum. That means £7,000,000. . . . I have a long list of additional benefits which they can choose, but I think the most interesting of all would be that when the fifteen and a half years had elapsed, when the loss has been paid off, and when you have released a fund of £7,000,000 between the State and the contributors, we shall then be within sight of declaring either a pension at sixty-five, or, what I think would be better still — and I propose this as an alternative — if a man does not choose to take his pension at sixty-five, but prefers to go on working, he shall increase his pension at a later stage in proportion to each additional year he goes on working. So much for the benefits.

I now come to the machinery of the Bill we have got to work. Collection is the first thing. We shall collect our funds by means of stamps. That is purely the German system. A card is given to a workman ; he takes it to his employer at the end of the week ; the employer puts on the workman's 4d. stamp and his own 3d. stamp ; he deducts the 4d. out of the wages of the man, and he pays the 3d. himself ; the card is in the possession of the man, who takes it to the post office, whence it is transmitted to the central office. The employer does not necessarily know — there is nothing on the face of the card to say — what society the man belongs to. It is entirely a matter for himself. The card is sent along to the central office, and the whole of the money is paid to the central office.

Then comes the question, Who is to dispense the benefits? In this country we have fortunately a number of well-organised, well-managed, well-conducted benefit societies who have a great tradition behind them and an accumulation of experience which is very valuable when you come to deal with questions like malingering. We propose, as far as we possibly can, to work through those societies. We propose that all the benefits shall be dispensed through what the Bill would call " approved societies."

What are the conditions attaching to an approved society? It must be a society with at least 10,000 members; otherwise, it becomes a matter of very great complication, which is much more difficult to manage from the actuarial and financial point of view. It must be precluded by its constitution from distributing any of its funds otherwise than by the way of benefits, whether benefits under this Act or not, amongst its members. It must not be a dividing society; it must be a benefit society which provides for sickness and for old age. Therefore it cannot be a society that divides its profits at the end of each year. It cannot be a society that allows anybody to make a profit out of this branch of its business, and it must be mutual so far as this branch of its business is concerned. Its affairs must be subject to the absolute control of its own members; it must be self-governing, and its constitution must provide for the election of its committees, representatives, and officers. There are other conditions. It must provide a reasonable security that the funds will be dispensed in the way the Act provides. It must have local committees. There are several societies, as hon. Members know very well, which have branches. There are other societies which are purely central. Both are very excellent societies in their way. The Hearts of Oak, I believe, is a centralised society. The Foresters, I believe, is a society with branches, and the Odd Fellows the same. But the societies which have central control and no branches must have some sort of local committees and management; otherwise it will be quite impossible to distribute the benefits, and it will be very difficult to arrange about doctoring and other matters. There are other things about keeping books and so forth. . . .

You may find men who say, "We will not join any society." You cannot compel a man to join a society. If he chooses to remain outside, he can do so, but he does it at his own cost. Every inducement is offered to a man in this scheme to join a society, and I will show how that works. We propose that all the men in a county who have not joined a society should be collected together in a body called Post Office Contributors. You will form a fund of those people. Most of the people who remain outside will be uninsurable lives, men who would be rejected by all sorts of societies, because really they are ill at the time or display symptoms of illness and therefore are quite uninsurable, or they may be drunkards. Those are the sort of reasons for which a society now excludes them. That must necessarily make it impossible for us to pay the same benefits to the Post Office Contributors as would be paid to the men who are in the friendly societies, because they contain pretty much all the bad lives. It will be largely a temporary difficulty and a dwindling one, for the simple reason that in future men will be taken on at the age of sixteen, and at that age the vast majority of people have not developed any kind of disease. Therefore it will dwindle almost to nothing in the future, and this difficulty is purely temporary. It will be a body of people who are not a very good insurable proposition. . . .

I now come to the finance of the scheme. In the first year the sums paid by all classes of contributors will amount to nearly £20,000,000, of which employers will contribute nearly £9,000,000, and the employees, £11,000,000. The expenditure on benefits and administration will, in consequence of the waiting periods, be only £7,000,000 in 1912–13, but will have risen to £20,000,000 in 1915–16, when the additional benefits begin to be granted. By 1922–23 the State contribution will also have risen. In the first year there will be no charge, because the Act does not come into operation until May 1 next year. There must be time to make arrangements. There will be only a charge for the necessary expenses of making preparation. But in 1912–13 the charge on the State will be £1,742,000; in 1913–14, £3,359,000; and in 1915–16 — a full year — £4,563,000. That is the expense, as far as the State and the contributors are concerned, of that part of the scheme.

I will now briefly outline the unemployment insurance. My explanation will be considerably curtailed, owing to the fact that the Home Secretary [Mr. Winston Churchill] very fully explained[1] to the House year before last the principles upon which the Government intended to proceed. The scheme only applies to one-sixth of the industrial population. We propose to apply it only to the precarious trades, which are liable to very considerable fluctuations. The benefit will be of a very simple character; it is purely a weekly allowance. The machinery is already set up; therefore it will not be necessary to explain that. The machinery will be the Labour Exchanges and the existing unions which deal with unemployment. I will not say anything about the suffering caused by unemployment. All I will say is that, whoever is to blame for these great fluctuations in trade, the workman is the least to blame. He does not guide or gear the machine of commerce and industry; the direction and speed is left almost entirely to others. Therefore, he is not responsible, although he bears almost all the real privation. I think it is about time we did something in this matter, because it is not something which has happened once or twice, but something that comes regularly every so many years. We know it will come, and know that distress will come with it; therefore, we ought to take some means to alleviate the misery caused by phenomena which we can reckon on almost with certainty within a year or two of its advent.

No real effort has been made except by the trades unions. That, of course, is a purely voluntary matter, and the burden is a very heavy one. It only applies, in their case, to very few trades,

---

[1] Cf. supra, p. 199.

and I think to only about 14,000,000 workmen altogether. The others cannot afford it. Other trades have attempted it, but have laid it down because they could not afford the expense. On the Continent many efforts have been made, mostly failures, because they all were on the voluntary principle. In Cologne there was a great effort. It ended in about 1800 people being insured out of a population of 200,000 or 300,000. There it meant people who knew they would be out of work, and who insured against almost certain unemployment in the winter. That is very little good. I came back, after examining some of these schemes, with the conviction that you must have, at any rate, three or four conditions. You must have a trade basis, to begin with. A municipal basis will not do ; it must be a trade basis, because the fluctuations are according to trades. You must start with the more precarious trades. The scheme must be compulsory. I also came to the conclusion that the workmen's unsupported efforts are quite useless. These are the principles we have incorporated in our Bill. We have started, first of all, by taking two groups of trades, and we propose to organise them individually — the engineering group and the building group. They include building, construction of works, shipbuilding, mechanical engineering, and the construction of vehicles. These are the trades in which you have the most serious fluctuations — I think for a very good reason. The depression seems to fall more heavily on these trades ; it seems to concentrate upon them, because they produce the permanent instruments of industry. We propose that in these trades a fund shall be raised for the purpose of paying an unemployment distress allowance.

I ought to say here that you have not the same basis for actuarial calculation that you have in reference to sickness. It is very necessary to warn, not merely the House, but rather more especially the workmen upon this point. You cannot say with the almost certainty that you can in sickness that a certain fund will produce such and such benefits. In the case of sickness you have nearly one hundred years' experience behind you, and you have the facts with regard to sickness and death. You have not got the facts with regard to unemployment, and the question is very difficult. All we know is that in certain branches of trade unemployment is prevalent and appalling. Some trades meet it by short time, but in other trades you cannot do that. As a matter of fact, in the building trade you may get men working overtime in one place at the very time 20 per cent of the workmen are out of work in another.

We propose that the workmen should pay 2½d. per week and the employer 2½d., and that the State should take upon itself one-fourth of the total income. We propose that there should be an abatement to those employers who choose to pay for their work by the year. I will show the extent of that abatement; it is very considerable. If you take the two contributions of employers and workmen at 2½d., they come to 21s. 8d. per annum; we propose that the employer who will undertake to insure a workman for the whole of a year can do so for 15d. He will get the whole benefit of the reduction. It is proposed that the workman shall pay the full 2½d., but that the employer should get the whole benefit of the abatement. It seems a very serious abatement. It is practically telling him that he can take one-half if he undertakes to insure the workman for a year at a time. It is an inducement to him to give regular employment; it is a discouragement of casual labour; it is a reward to the employer who keeps his workmen for a whole year. It is a very heavy one, but I think it is worth while. That is the only exception made by the employer.

We propose, by way of benefits, to give in the engineering trade 7s. per week unemployed pay, and in the building trade 6s., for a maximum of fifteen weeks. The number of weeks is limited to fifteen, because, I again say here, there is no basis of actuarial calculation, and you will have to watch the thing. Now you will have a huge distress fund, to which the employers will contribute very nearly £1,000,000 and the State, £700,000 or £800,000 for the purpose of relieving the distress, and to enable the workmen to insure where otherwise they could not do it. But you cannot guarantee that it will work out at these figures. All we can say, having consulted the best actuaries at our disposal, is that we are firmly convinced that the fund will work out in this way. What will happen ? The workman who is out of work will go to the Labour Exchange. We want someone there to check him, so that you will not have a man who is not genuinely unemployed getting unemployed pay. Therefore you have to do this through the Labour Exchanges. The man will take his card and they will offer him a job. If he refuses a job, then comes the question, Who will decide whether he is unemployed or not? We have appointed an impartial court of referees to decide this ; we cannot leave it to the Labour Exchanges entirely, or to the workmen, to decide whether the man is to take a job or the 7s. unemployed benefit. There will be no payment for a workman dismissed through his own misconduct. There will be no payment under this scheme where there is unemployment by reason of strikes or lockouts, because this scheme has absolutely nothing to do with them. It is purely a relief scheme for unemployment which is due to fluctuations of trade.

I now take the trade unions which insure themselves against unemployment. We propose in that case that they should reap the benefit, but we cannot possibly hand over State funds — certainly not employers' funds — to an organisation, the object of which, in the main, is to fight out questions of wages and conditions of labour with the employers. What we propose is this, that the trade union shall pay its unemployed benefit to the men and claim from the fund repayment in respect to the amount which the men would have been entitled to draw had they gone direct to the Labour Exchanges. The State in effect allows trade unions to spend this money, and at the same time it protects against the unfairness of subsidising what, after all, is a war-chest, — as the trade unions admit. . . .

If any other trade wishes to come in, they are to have, what I think they call in the Court of Chancery, " liberty to apply." If they make out their case and are prepared to make their contribution, it will be possible to include them in our scheme. But for the moment we propose to begin the experiment with these trades, which are the very worst trades from the point of view of unemployment. This scheme will apply to over 2,400,000 workmen. The contributions of the workmen will be £1,100,000. The contributions of the employers will be £900,000. The cost to the State —

MR. AUSTEN CHAMBERLAIN: But you said the contributions from the workmen and the employers are to be the same.

MR. LLOYD GEORGE: I thought I had made it quite clear that there is a very considerable abatement to the employer. It is equivalent to £200,000 on the whole scheme to the employers if they undertake the responsibility of insuring the whole of their workmen by the year. The cost to the State will be approximately £750,000 a year. The expenditure will undoubtedly fluctuate with the state of trade, and a fund will therefore have to be created for the purpose of dealing with times of very great distress. That is the position as far as both of these branches are concerned. The total sum to be raised in the first year is £24,500,000, of which the State will contribute £2,500,000. By the fourth year the State's contribution will have risen to nearly £5,500,000. That is the finance of the scheme.

I have explained to the House as best I could this great matter, and I thank Members for the courtesy with which they have listened to me. I have explained as best I could the details of our scheme — the system of contributions and of benefits and the machinery whereby something like 15,000,000 people will be insured, at any rate against the acute distress which now darkens the homes of the workmen wherever there is sickness and unemployment. I do not pretend that this is a complete remedy. Before you get a complete remedy for these evils you will have to cut in deeper. But I think it is partly a remedy. I think it does more. It lays bare a good many of those social evils, and forces the State, as a State, to pay attention to them.

Meantime till the advent of complete remedy, this scheme does alleviate an immense mass of human suffering, and I am going to appeal, not merely to those who support the Government in this House, but to the House as a whole, to the men of all parties, to assist us. I can honestly say that I have endeavoured to eliminate from the scheme any matter which would cause legitimate offence to the reasonable susceptibilities of any party in the House. I feel that otherwise I would have no right to appeal, not only for support, but for co-operation. I appeal to the House of Commons to help the Government not merely to carry this Bill through, but to fashion it; to strengthen it where it is weak, to improve it where it is faulty. I am sure if this is done we shall have achieved something which will be worthy of our labours.

Here we are in the year of the crowning of the King. We have men from all parts of this great Empire coming not merely to celebrate the present splendour of the Empire, but also to take counsel together as to the best means of promoting its future welfare. I think that now would be a very opportune moment for us in the Homeland to carry through a measure that will relieve untold misery in myriads of homes — misery that is undeserved; that will help to prevent a good deal of wretchedness, and which will arm the nation to fight until it conquers " the pestilence that walketh in darkness, and the destruction that wasteth at noonday."

Extract 85

IRISH SUPPORT OF THE NATIONAL INSURANCE BILL

(Mr. John Redmond, Commons, May 4, 1911)

MR. REDMOND [1]: . . I would like to say that there are no men in this House who for the last thirty years have more consistently supported every effort which has been made by any party in this

[1] Parliamentary Debates, Commons, Fifth Series, vol. 25, col. 652.

House to redress the balance which has for so long been against the poor in our modern civilisation. No hon. Members have more consistently supported all measures of that kind than the Irish Members. I entirely agree with the opening words of the right hon. Gentleman the Member for East Worcestershire [Mr. Austen Chamberlain]. I think it would be impossible, and, indeed, it would be a bad compliment to the Chancellor of the Exchequer for any one to attempt to deliver anything like a considered opinion with reference to this measure at the present moment. All one can do is to take a view of the general aspect of it. It is on the face of it 'a great and comprehensive measure; it must be judged very largely after an examination of its details. With the objects the right hon. Gentleman has in view every portion of the House must sympathise. So far as we in Ireland are concerned, we have special reason to sympathise with objects of this kind. Ireland is a poor country. In Ireland there are more of the poor and of the very poor than in any other portion of the United Kingdom. Therefore Ireland stands in a special degree to benefit by measures of this kind, if only they are so constructed and adapted as to suit the peculiar circumstances and conditions of Ireland. . . .

Extract 86

DEFENCE OF THE NATIONAL INSURANCE BILL

(Mr. Sydney Buxton, President of the Board of Trade, Commons, May 24, 1911)

MR. BUXTON [1]: . . . The Bill, apparently, is a somewhat complex Bill; but, as a matter of fact, the principles involved are simple. The idea on which it is based is that under existing conditions the whole burden of sickness, invalidity, and unemployment over which the workingman has no control, falls directly with crushing force

[1] Parliamentary Debates, Commons, Fifth Series, vol. 26, col. 270 sqq.

on the individual, whether he be provident or improvident, and I think the House is generally agreed that it is time that the employer and the State should enter into partnership with the workingman in order as far as possible to mitigate the severity of the burden which falls upon him. The principle on which these two schemes is based is that the burden of insurance against sickness and unemployment should be shared by workmen, employers, and the State. The system must be contributory and compulsory, and it should not, as far as can be avoided, interfere with existing voluntary machinery. It should also aid as far as it can towards the diminution and prevention of sickness and unemployment as well as towards their alleviation. It is important also that both sections of the Bill should bring into touch and into partnership the various interests concerned, so that they may have a direct interest in the efficient carrying out of this scheme.

The question is whether a scheme of insurance against invalidity and unemployment is a feasible one. The principle of the insurance of late years has enormously increased. You can insure practically against anything. I believe there were insurances given against the effects of the Budget of my right hon. Friend [1] a year or two ago. I believe you can now get an insurance against the House of Lords throwing out the Veto Bill, though what premium is charged at the present moment I have been unable to ascertain. The two parts of the scheme — the invalidity part and the unemployment part — are practically interdependent, though in some respects they are naturally worked differently. The scheme is a large one, and, with the permission of the House, I shall desire to confine myself largely to the consideration of the second part of the Bill.

I make this personal observation. I do not desire, in moving the second reading of the Bill, especially in regard to Part II, to claim its parentage. The first idea was that of my right hon. Friend the Chancellor of the Exchequer [Mr. David Lloyd George]. The

1 The Lloyd George Budget. Cf. supra, ch. viii.

details were carefully worked out by my right hon. Friend the Home Secretary [Mr. Winston Churchill], assisted, as I am sure he will be the first to agree, by the very able staff which the country fortunately possesses at the Board of Trade, and I know that one of his principal regrets when he was leaving the Board of Trade was that he had to leave it before he had been able to bring this particular proposal to fruition. I took it over at the Board of Trade, and with the assistance of my advisers I hope I have done something to improve the Bill. It is now presented to the House, as we believe, as a workable and water-tight proposal. I can say for myself that, although I am only the foster-parent, I have a profound interest in this question, and a profound belief that the proposals we are making will do something towards the solution of the question.

The point is, Will this scheme actually carry out the object we have in view? We believe it will. We believe, further, that it will not only prove a palliative, but, by the various provisions of the Bill, especially in connection with our Labour Exchanges,[1] which are, after all, the corollary of the Unemployed Bill, we shall be able to do something, by organising in various ways, towards the steadying of labour and the regularity of employment.

Let me deal with some of the criticisms which have been directed against the Bill since it came before the country. There are two points of great importance — one is a criticism, the other a suggestion. Both are of serious moment to the life of the Bill. The criticism is this — that the unemployment part of the Bill is a hazardous experiment. The suggestion is that it is premature, and that it ought to be divided from the other part of the Bill and taken at a later stage. . . .

It was assumed on the first reading, I think, that we had no substantial available data on which we could found our proposals; but the very able report of the very able actuary, Mr. Ackland, to whom the matter was referred, has, I think, dispelled the illusion,

1 Cf. supra, p. 213.

and shows that we have sufficient information and that the safeguards which we present in the Bill are sufficient to enable us to offer the proposal as an acceptable one to the House of Commons. May I point out this, that the postponement of the proposals would give us no further information than we have at the present time. Such data as we have, such bases for calculation as we have at the present moment, will speedily increase ; and we hope if the Bill is passed, and these insurance proposals are introduced and applied to certain trades, before long we shall have better experience in order, if necessary, to extend the system still further. I would point out, and I think it is an important point, that the data on which we are acting — the data of our actuary on which he proceeded — are based on the actual experience for many years past of the great trade unions, including in insured trades something like 300,000 persons, and the data seem to me to be very sound, direct data, founded entirely on the payment of unemployed benefits. . . .

Then there is a further argument, perhaps of a rather more specious character, which has been raised on the first reading and since. It is that we should not carry out the compulsory part of this scheme, but make a beginning with voluntary insurance alone. That also, I hope, will be strenuously resisted by the House, because without the compulsory part we cannot make a real effort — we cannot carry out a comprehensive system of National Insurance against unemployment. All the experience abroad goes to show that a purely voluntary scheme will not really be of an effective character. It naturally includes bad risks, and almost from the beginning it is bound to be more or less financially unsound. The only scheme — a scheme which has some supporters, and which no doubt in itself has had some success — is what is called the Ghent system. That scheme we have already adopted in our Bill as regards the voluntary part of it, but, as the sole contribution of this great question, it is totally and wholly ineffective. The Ghent system is this : it is a simple and direct contribution of recognised associations, which in these cases means trade unions alone, and of a State contribution to such unemployment benefits as they give. We desire to encourage not only those who are at present able to insure for themselves, but we are even more desirous by compulsion to secure the provision of unemployed benefits for those who for any reason at present are unable or unwilling to insure themselves. . . .

The scheme is obviously confined to certain classes of the population, and it would certainly be fatal to any scheme of insurance to say that it must not be applied to limited cases. That has never deterred us from attempting any social reform or any social legislation which, in the first instance, applied to a limited class. I contend, on the other hand, that we are entitled — and we are doing it every day — to utilise the resources of the community for the purpose of instituting such reforms, even though of a limited character, and applying them only to limited classes. I think we can say that, although in a sense this contribution is to a limited class and a limited number, it is really a contribution benefiting all trades and all classes of the community. . . .

Allegations have been made in many quarters that the scheme of the Bill as a whole is going to throw great additional burdens on workmen, employers, and the State. That I deny altogether. Insurance against sickness and unemployment will involve no new burden. The burden exists at present, but in future it will be better distributed and more easily and equitably borne, and more people will be benefited by this system of insurance. Take the case of unemployment. At present the burden appears in the national ledger as pauperising Poor Law expenditure, as systems of State or municipal doles, and as sudden emergency works which very often are a waste of money. So far as the provident workman is concerned, it is met by the contribution to the trade union, and where he is improvident, it is met by the neighborly assistance he receives, and which is so freely and ungrudgingly given among the working classes, and by the costly realisation of his belongings, costly credit, and costly arrears. In connection with these operations, the man is subjected both mentally and physically to the suffering which the unemployment brings in its train. I think it will stand to reason that it must be infinitely better to have permanent machinery to anticipate the " rainy day " and to distribute the money more equitably over various interests and more uniformly over the period. I think one can safely assert that the burden, far from being greater, would really be less than before.

There is one other objection to the scheme upon which the House will allow me to say a word. We are told that we ought to differentiate — this is an important point — our contributions and benefits according to the risks of a trade as a whole, and that we ought to distinguish more between trade and trade, and even distinguish between various sections of a trade. I do not think that will receive the support of my hon. Friends below the gangway. Trade unionism has always preached the solidarity of labour, and that, so far as it goes, the regular man and the irregular man should be put together. We are providing in this Bill for certain differentiation, and as our experience extends we may be able to provide that still further, but I think, at all events, in the first instance, it is very important that we should, as far as possible, take what is called the flat rate and apply it to engineering and shipbuilding and to the other trades in the building construction group, and see how it will work out, and with what justice, to. the various interests concerned. . . .

I wish to refer to another point upon which I think there has been on the part of my hon. Friends below the gangway considerable apprehension, and that is in regard to the effect this Bill may have upon trade unions — whether the provisions are drafted sufficiently wide to enable a trade union to become and remain an approved society without necessitating any effective alteration in its practice, or in its ordinary functions as a trade union. I can well understand the anxiety that all trade union men have if they feel that the real effect of this Bill is going to undermine or destroy trade unions. These great organisations, built up during many years in

the past, and whose position has become so strong, might very well
feel that any proposal whereby their general position was in any
way weakened or undermined would be indefensible, and that no
such Bill ought to be put on the Statute Book. I am one of those
— I have always said so publicly — who believe, and I believe it
is the opinion of the House now, that it is not only in the interest
of labour itself, but in the interest of employers as well, that these
trade unions should be strong, representative, and independent, and
I can assure my hon. Friends and the House generally that nothing
is further from the object and desire of the framers of the Bill than
that when it becomes an Act it should be used as a disruptive force
against any trade union. . . .

I have endeavoured to deal with the chief criticism, most of
which has been directed against Part II, and some of which has
been directed against Part I of the Bill. There is just one other
point which I may refer to incidentally. I have seen the scheme
criticised with reference to its being too bureaucratic. We are,
after all, going to deal with it through the Labour Exchanges, and
the voluntary associations through the combination, and we hope
co-operation, by means of joint committees of representative employers and workmen. If it can be shown in any way that those
panels of referees can be made more representative than those
proposed by this Bill, we shall very much welcome any suggestions
that can be made ; but I can assure the House that our sole desire
is to put the system, as far as we can, on a representative basis. . . .

This is our proposal, and this is our contribution to social reform.
I am sure that my right hon. Friend, and certainly I, would be the
last to claim that in any sense this is a final solution of the problem
of sickness or unemployment, but I think it has this great merit,
that while it is a considerable step forward in the direction which
we all desire to follow, it is not only no obstacle to, but I think it is
an avenue towards, the extension of various other systems, also in
the same direction. We have founded it, as we believe, on a business basis and on sound actuarial calculations, and we offer it to

the House as a great and beneficent step forward, which, if the House accepts it, will do much to achieve that which we all desire — the improvement of the social condition of the working classes.

Extract 87

LESSONS FROM GERMAN EXPERIENCE

(Sir Rufus Isaacs, Attorney-General, Commons, May 24, 1911)

SIR RUFUS ISAACS [1]: . . . In the framing of this measure the Chancellor of the Exchequer and those who have been privileged to take part at all in the discussion of the details of this measure have had the incalculable advantage of the experience of the German Empire in relation to this compulsory insurance. Germany has gradually built up a system which by common consent is of a most beneficent character and is working to the advantage not only of the employer, but also of the employed. The White Paper which has been circulated quite recently contains the opinions of a number of German employers which really are most valuable in considering what we can anticipate as the probable result of this measure, certainly upon employers. I am not going to attempt to read them or quote them to this House, but I will summarise them in two or three sentences, and I believe fairly, having regard to the opinions therein expressed. The general opinion in Germany is that by freeing the working classes from anxiety by reason of sickness, infirmity, and accidents, their conditions of life have been materially bettered, and, from the employers' standpoint, the contributions they make have proved an excellent investment. The insurance law has tended to improve the relations between the employer and the employed, without impairing the independence of the workers.

Indeed, if you study the history of the last twenty-five years, the period covered by the insurance legislation in Germany, it will be

[1] Parliamentary Debates, Fifth Series, Commons, vol. 26, col. 368 sqq.

discovered that trade unions have flourished and multiplied exceedingly in the German Empire, concurrently with the progress and
development of this industrial legislation. On the other hand, so
satisfied are the employers with the result of this legislation that it
is roundly asserted by one prominent employer, speaking, as he
believes, on behalf of the employers, or the majority of the employers in Germany, that they do not desire, and indeed would
oppose, the repeal of these insurance laws, which, nevertheless,
necessitate their making a contribution to certain funds according
to the legislation of the country.

At one time, as was naturally to be expected, when this scheme
was launched or mooted in 1881 by Prince Bismarck, there was
the greatest anxiety among German employers as to what was to
be expected as a result of this proposal. It was said, at first, that
it would fine employers, that it would tend to cripple industry, and
that the cost of production would be increased without any correl-
ative advantage. It was explained, according to their views, that
these new contributions to be made by the German employer would
act injuriously upon the employers' interests, and that it would consequently react to the disadvantage of the employed. But all
these apprehensions have long since disappeared, and Germany
has continued to develop under this insurance legislation, and at
the present moment — it is a curious coincidence worthy of observation that during this very week, in the German Reichstag, there
has taken place a debate on the second reading of a measure for
the consolidation and codification of the German insurance laws,
running, I believe, to something like 1517 paragraphs. That is the
position at the present moment.

Mr. Booth : It has been in Committee for twelve months.

Sir Rufus Isaacs : Of course, if there are from 1500 to 1700
clauses, I am not at all surprised that it has been in Committee for
twelve months. But we, during these twenty-five years, have not
progressed along the same line as Germany. But, nevertheless, we
have made great strides. We have ourselves instituted workmen's

compensation. We have instituted — it was originally introduced by the present Opposition and developed and extended by the Liberal Government since 1906 — old age pensions, which in this country are on a non-contributory basis. In Germany, as no doubt the House is aware, it is on a contributory basis. The difference is that at the present moment, for the year 1911–12, the Government requirement for old age pensions is £12,840,000, whereas in Germany there will be required of the State as its contribution to old age pensions, £2,575,000, which is a contribution to the £7,500,000, which is the total amount provided under old age pensions for the working classes in Germany. The average old age pension under the scheme in Germany works out at 3s. 1d. per head. It is not surprising, therefore, to know that, notwithstanding that there is this scheme of old age pensions, very often the working classes who are in receipt of old age pensions have to have recourse to the Poor Law.

One of the striking features of the system in Germany to which I desire to call attention is this, that the compulsory provisions for sickness and disablement insurance have proved a stimulus to thrift in other directions. This is confirmatory to the views which we hold. It shows that the habit of saving increases as you make provision, and as you help by contributions either from the employer or the State, so you induce the worker to make further insurance for his own benefit. He comes to realise what is the true advantage of insurance. He would, further, appreciate that, in the case of sickness or temporary destitution, when he has either to withdraw or to exhaust the fund which he has managed to accumulate with great difficulty and great trouble because of the receipt of sick benefit or disablement in insurance benefit, the money which he has managed to save for himself is still there in the savings bank, still accumulating from day to day, increasing in amount, and to which he can add his little store from week to week, and month to month. The desire to save becomes greater and the appetite for it increases daily, and consequently, as we believe, if we can only manage in this country, by reason of these contributions, to instil into our people the desire to save, not only by those contributions that they have to make under the Insurance Law, but to save in order that they may be able to make their own provision, to create their own independence altogether apart from this scheme, I do believe that we shall have taken a most notable step along the path of progress, the self-respect and the independence of the workpeople of this country.

One further point which we learn from Germany is that the curative and preventive effect of the treatment of disease by means of sanatoria and other institutions, such as convalescent homes and kindred establishments, in Germany, have not only succeeded in arresting the ravages of the disease of consumption, but have helped to prevent it. . . .

I think that it is a great satisfaction to us to find that Germany, which has been the pioneer in this movement, and which has hitherto held the leading place in the world for social legislation of this kind, is itself much impressed with the measure which has been introduced by my right hon. Friend.   I notice in reading the German newspaper dealing with the inductory speech of my right hon. Friend that the German criticism of the measure is that, owing to its directness, its simplicity, and its comprehensiveness, it will excel what one German newspaper, the *Tageblatt*, calls the " bureaucratic hotchpotch of the German insurance system." Let us note, as we pass, the compliment that is paid to my right hon. Friend the Chancellor of the Exchequer. In German press articles German experts are advised to study the measure which has been introduced by my right hon. Friend, lest they should be left behind, and, indeed, one German newspaper I happened to read, said that the introduction of this measure had earned for my right hon. Friend a statue in Westminster Abbey. I hope the time is long distant before we shall have to consider whether it will be desirable to erect a statue for him in Westminster Abbey. . . .

Extract 88

ATTITUDE OF THE LABOUR PARTY TOWARD NATIONAL INSURANCE

(Mr. Ramsay Macdonald, Commons, May 29, 1911)

MR. MACDONALD [1] : By the consent of everybody in this House, I think I may say that the Bill, the second reading of which we are now discussing, is a very unique Bill. More than that, the debate which has taken place upon it has been a very unique debate. If this Bill had been introduced ten years ago, it would not have found, I think, a single supporter from either of the Front Benches. The point of view which the Chancellor and the Government have taken is one which is quite new, and which marks a fundamental change of public opinion, and the most extraordinary thing for those who are sitting on these Benches is to find that that point of view is not challenged by any section of this House.

The old assumption upon which we used to approach questions of legislation, by which State aid and State organisations were regarded as something which ought to be suspected by every wise man, has been thrown over, thrown over not only by those who sit in this quarter of the House, but thrown over by everybody. That is a very substantial advance, one of those advances which one finds in public opinion happening periodically about once every century, and I think it is an indication that to-day in the times that have come upon us the old political parties are largely losing their significance ; and the combination which has taken place, during the last week or two, on both sides of the House, to praise this Bill and facilitate its passage is one that is welcomed, at any rate, very heartily and most sincerely by those who sit with me here.

The purpose of this Bill is twofold. First of all, it proposes to fill up the gaps in the life of the industrial classes that have been

1 Parliamentary Debates, Fifth Series, Commons, vol. 26, col. 718 sqq.

only too frequent. What has happened has been something like this : Very often when going along long roads in mountainous districts, the wayfarer finds that a heavy fall or an avalanche of snow has completely broken the road which, up to that point, had been smooth and easy walking. Every now and again the wage-earner has come to points like that on his way ; sickness, unemployment, or misfortune of some kind seems completely to have smashed the road right away in front of him, and he has been left behind struggling for existence, severely handicapped, and without any chance of using the opportunities which otherwise would be at his disposal. For the first time in a clear, unmistakable, sympathetic way a Government has come before the country and has said that the repair of these breaches in the way of life is a responsibility imposed upon the Government, and an Opposition has also offered to say to the Government, " We support you in your efforts and agree with your general position."

The second point of the Bill is one which is equally of importance. Its idea is so to improve the general public health that those gaps will be less frequent than they have been. The intention of the Bill is not only to repair gaps that have been effected, but to repair the road against those avalanches that fall from time to time.

I wish to ask the indulgence of the House to examine the Bill in a more or less general way from those two points of view. I shall take the public health point of view first. When one sits down and thinks of it seriously, and apart from one's own experience, it really is the most extraordinary thing that up to now our doctors have been paid for attending disease. The more diseases, the better it has been for the medical faculty of this country. That is absurd, absolutely absurd.

The whole medical service had been so disorganised that, in so far as it has been prompted by economic considerations only, the interest of every doctor was to get as many diseases, as much illness, as he could possibly create amongst the people. A doctor attending a sick person only drew fees when the persons were sick. My name might be on my doctor's list of possible patients, but so long as I am well, my doctor is making nothing out of me. The moment I become ill, then my doctor begins to regard me in the light of an income. I understand the protest was raised from the other side. I know perfectly well that of no profession in the whole country is it truer to say that their economic interests have never regulated their conduct. It has been one of the most encouraging and remarkable manifestations, that, on account of humanitarian considerations, and on account of the intellectual interest they have taken in their profession, our doctors have never allowed their economic interests to dictate their relationship to the general public. But there the facts remain, and until this Bill has been brought before the House there has not been any attempt to establish a system of social organisation which used the doctor not merely for the purpose of attending disease but for the purpose of eliminating disease altogether.

With that general point of view before us, it becomes very necessary that medical men under this Bill should have the very fairest treatment. I am not quite sure how far the claims made by medical men up to now are well founded. It is a remarkable fact that the medical faculty, speaking of them as a whole, feel themselves injured, or possibly injured, by this Bill. I think they are very wise to take the gloomiest view of their prospects under the Bill. We ought not to object to their taking that point of view, because they know enough of life to come to the conclusion that if they do not take that view, nobody else will. Therefore I, for one, do not regard the doctors as being hostile to the Bill because they are putting in claims that the scale of fees and the financial provision made for them are not at all adequate. I hope the Chancellor of the Exchequer will very seriously consider that matter. . . .

Let me take the second point, which I mentioned first of all, and which is the main purpose of the Bill — the purpose of filling up the gaps in life and making them less frequent. In that connection I. think the House should be very careful not to use two very erroneous expressions that have been employed frequently by the previous speakers. The Bill proposes, they say, to make deductions from wages and give free medical attendance. Both those expressions are absolutely wrong, and if the public once gets it into its mind that these expressions adequately and accurately represent what the Bill proposes, enormous difficulties will be raised in consequence. As a matter of fact there is no deduction from wages at all. In the proper sense of the term " deduction " there is no deduction from wages, because sooner or later the chances are that everyone of us will have to pay a doctor's bill, and what is done by this Bill is simply, instead of paying the doctor's bill in the lump we are asked to pay it in instalments. But that is not a deduction from wages. Accurate words, I think, would conduce to accurate thinking in this respect, and would enable the public to appreciate much more than I am afraid it now appreciates what is precisely the effect of this Bill. Again, free medical attendance is not given under this Bill. Why, one might as well say that if one insures one's life, and one's heirs put in a claim against the insurance society to which one belonged, that this insurance society is making a free gift to one's heirs. As a matter of fact that is not the case at all. There is no free medical attendance proposed under this Bill. It is simply the application of the method and principle of insurance against certain events which overtake most of us during our life.

The Bill, if I may say so without being misunderstood, is, after all, superficial; it deals with the problem of poverty when that poverty has arisen. If we all had £200 per year, and if the average income of the working classes was something like £250 per year, this Bill would be unnecessary. It would be necessary to organise public health, it would still be necessary to consider the conditions under which the individual lives, but so far as insurance is concerned of the individual in respect to his doctor's bill this Bill would not be at all necessary.

That being so, the Chancellor of the Exchequer must expect that every step he takes to meet special hardships will have grave danger of only creating hardships. Take, for instance, the cases of those with from 9s. to 15s. per week. It is perfectly evident, and I do not think anybody will dispute this proposition, that a man or woman with 9s. a week as an income has not a sufficiently big income to enable him or her to live a decent life, and certainly not a sufficiently big income to justify the State taking 4d. per week. We all agree that that is not a disputable proposition at all, but I am not at all sure that the Chancellor of the Exchequer is able to devise any exemption or any system of gradation that will not to a certain extent have the effect of stereotyping the present bad conditions. We must do our very best by careful consideration of the economic circumstances to make these too low-paid forms of labour, such a very striking and rather common feature of modern society — we must do our level best not to stereotype them by anything of a humanitarian character and in the character of a concession which this Bill may give. . . .

It is unfair to ask the man whose strength is below the average, to bear his own burdens. I do not think anybody will dispute that. If we proceed upon the insurance method and apply the insurance principle, we must strike an average, and that average ought not to be struck merely on the workmen themselves, but ought to be an average in which other responsibilities and other interests than those of the workman can find adequate place. Moreover, the State is going to organise health, and health must not be organised at the charge of the individual workman. Therefore the workman's contribution ought to be supplemented by other contributions, and there we will leave it for the moment.

What about the employers? I am bound to say, from my point of view, and I am trying to argue the thing down from general principles, it is more difficult to impose, and to discover justification for imposing, responsibility upon the employer than either upon the workman or the State in this respect. What is the responsibility of the employer? It is, first of all, to provide good conditions for his workmen, but that is secured by legislation. Then there are employers working especially dangerous trades, and yet that again is secured by special legislation. . . . The employer has got a third responsibility, and that is to pay proper wages. If the employer pays proper wages, or, in other words, if the workers' share of the national income is adequate, then we do not want charity and we do not want assistance at all. Therefore the employers' main responsibilities are to obey the law and pay good wages. Still he does come in in one way. If the Bill operates and produces the results which we expect it will produce, then it will undoubtedly mean that it will give to the employer a more and more efficient body of workers than he has got now, and it will enable him to run his machinery more efficiently than machinery is now being run. It will enable him to use his capital more economically than his capital is being used now. . . .

The third partner is the State. The State is going to receive enormous benefits from this Bill; rates are going to be lowered, taxes are going to be made less, all sorts of public charges, necessary on account of the low state of vitality and bad state of health of a large section of the people, are going to be eased if this Bill is going to do what it is expected it will do.

When you come to apportionment it is quite impossible to translate into mathematical relationship and ratio the various benefits to the workman, the employer, and the State respectively. But I am perfectly certain of this — that if 9d. is required, then 4d. for the workman, 3d. from the employer, and 3d. from the State is not a fair apportionment. I am perfectly certain of that, and that cannot be justified, but we are quite willing to accept, during the experimental stages at any rate, an equal apportionment of 3d., 3d., and 3d. That is fair play, and at all events, on the face of it, substantially it is a nearer approach to fair play than 4d., 3d., and 2d. I think that we shall have in Committee to move Amendments which will effect that redistribution of premiums.

Those of us who sit here must also scrutinise the Bill very carefully, very systematically I hope, but still very carefully, as to what the effect on wages is going to be. The prime consideration of everybody who is concerned in raising the status of the working classes is the amount of wages the working class get. You cannot get out of that. We do not want charity and we do not want doles, and we do not want Grants-in-Aid, and we do not want relief, and this is necessary at the present moment, simply because things are as they are, and in order to cure our present evils. I do not believe that the trade-union movement, the members of the trade unions, and the wage-earners, as a whole, will look twice at any proposal that will make it more difficult for them than it is now to increase the general wages of the general group of wage-earners of the country. . . .

We must be very careful about our economic facts. We cannot carry out high and dry economics. That is absurd. We are not in a vacuum. We are living under conditions which compel us to modify and change those broader abstract dogmas which in the abstract are perfectly true, but which in everyday life cannot quite be applied. I hope the House when it gets into Committee, in making a departure from sound economics will make that departure as little as the circumstances will allow. I feel perfectly certain that the great mass of trade unionists in the country will agree with me in that statement. It is so important that there should be no shadow of doubt about it that I repeat it. We are not here for aids for wages, but we are here for better wages. We are here to raise the wages, and not to make it easier for low-paid labour to exist at all.

With this in mind I should like to draw the Chancellor of the Exchequer's attention to the effect of one of its beneficent provisions. We all understand why he has provided in the Bill that every worker under twenty-one years of age shall pay the full premium, but that when the age of twenty-one is reached, the graded scale is to come into operation. Nobody will quarrel with this intention. But what will happen? There are scores of thousands of women in the country employed at mechanical labour. One has simply to go to Birmingham and see women working in front of big punching presses. The only thing they do is to feed them; sometimes they do not even do that; they only watch certain long carefully prepared strips of brass or iron going through the presses. They simply pull away baskets when they are filled and put empty baskets in their place. What will happen with regard to these women? Up to the age of twenty-one they will have to pay 3d., but when they reach the age of twenty-one and their 3d. becomes 2d. or 1d., and the contribution of the employer becomes 4d. or 5d., they will be discharged. There is no doubt about that. I think that must be taken into account because that, again, would be an exceedingly unfortunate result of this Bill. . . .

With reference to the unemployment section of the Bill I need say very little. We all admit that the Chancellor of the Exchequer has gone upon ground which has not been statistically explored. The very interesting actuarial report is admirable proof of that. The experiment is going to be carried out for five years in accordance with the provisions of the Bill. During that time readjustments are to be made, and observations made in regard to the various risks, and so on. I think the House and the Committee will be very well advised not to try to make this Bill verbally perfect. You cannot do it. We have not got the experience to do it. It will be far better to let it go through with the certain admitted defects and shortcomings so that we may not establish too elaborate a system now. It is much easier to change a simple system and make it more perfect after we have had the requisite experience than to begin with a very elaborate system and then to change it five years from now. . . .

I believe that we all can foresee that the tightness of time may endanger this Bill, but I think we can candidly confess to ourselves that fact and approach this question with the assumption that this Bill cannot be made perfect because we have not got the material which will make it perfect, that every anomaly cannot be eliminated from the Bill, and that it must contain some injustice to some section or the other. If we will begin with the assumption and supplement that by the other assumption that we are producing something that is going to enable us to construct tables from experience which in a few years to come will permit the House of Commons to construct a measure of insurance against sickness, invalidity, and unemployment that will be fair, and will, of course, be constructed from top to bottom, we will not allow this Bill to be stifled, strangled, or dropped because the time is rather short. With the consent, good-will, and co-operation of all sections of the House, I hope, I believe, that this Bill can be put upon the Statute Book this year, and this beneficent provision be brought into operation about twelve months from now.

Extract 89

ATTITUDE OF THE UNIONIST PARTY TOWARD NATIONAL INSURANCE

(Mr. H. W. Forster, Commons, December 6, 1911)

MR. FORSTER [1]: I beg to move to leave out all the words after the word " That," and to insert instead thereof the words, " while approving the objects of national insurance, this House is of opinion that under Part I of the Bill public funds and individual contributions will not be used to the best advantage of those most closely affected, and that, as the Bill has been neither adequately discussed in this House nor fully explained to the country and would in its present form be unequal in its operation, steps should be taken to enable further consideration of Part I to be resumed next Session, and in the meanwhile to have the draft regulations published." . . .

[1] Parliamentary Debates, Fifth Series, Commons, vol. 32, col. 1419 sqq.

What is the meaning of the Amendment? The meaning is patent on the face of it, and any man who reads the Amendment can see precisely what it means. This is the object of it, that the detailed discussion of this Bill should not now be closed. I ask that further opportunity should be given, both to the House and to the country, for further consideration of the measure before it is passed into law. The part of the Bill to which I refer especially is Part I, which, in my view, stands in a totally different category from Part II, and I am bound to say that the House has always treated it almost as if it were a different Bill. . . . This is not a wrecking Amendment. I want the Government and the House to understand that this is not a wrecking Amendment, and it is not intended to be a wrecking Amendment. It is a demand for further time; it is a demand that the Government might accede to without loss of prestige to themselves; it is a demand which, if they grant it, will carry great benefit to the Bill upon which we are engaged.

If I may turn from justification for my Amendment to its terms, I would like to say a few words with reference to some questions which are specifically raised by the Amendment itself. We begin by declaring that we approve of the objects of National Insurance. That is a perfectly genuine and a perfectly honest statement, and a statement that I need not labour. Indeed, right hon. Gentlemen and the House generally know enough of us to believe what we say in this regard is perfectly sincere and perfectly genuine, and I do not think this requires further elaboration.

In the second place, we say that, in our opinion at any rate, the public funds and individual contributions are not used to the best advantage. In the course of the debates in Committee attempts have been made to suggest alternative schemes. Those attempts have not met with a very large measure of success. We were met with difficulties whenever we endeavoured to move them. The rules of the House, the rules of our debates, the rules under which we conduct our debates, the strict and narrow terms of the Financial Resolution, all combined to make it impossible for us to develop, as we should have wished to develop, alternative proposals. . . .

This matter is a matter which, of course, very largely affects the taxpayers, and there is one particular class of taxpayers who, I think, are very closely affected by the proposals, and that is the class of persons drawn from the same stratum as the employed contributors will be drawn from, the persons who, because they are working on their own account, will have to contribute towards the provision of benefits for their neighbors, benefits that they do not receive themselves. And I could show, if opportunity offered, that it would be quite possible to have given to those people reduced benefits in return for a reduced voluntary contribution, so that they would not have been left out in the cold altogether, and they would have been brought within the beneficent sphere of the proposals of this Bill. The class of persons I have in mind are persons like the smaller trader, the costermonger, the waterman plying for hire in his own boat, the small tailor, the bootmaker, the window cleaner, and the jobbing gardener, who are sections of the population that may not be very large in themselves, but which, added together, form a not inconsiderable portion of the population. . . .

I pass from that part of my Amendment to consider the suggestion that is made in another part, that this Bill is unequal in its operation. Surely, I think it will be admitted in all quarters of the House that it is desirable where you are creating a national scheme that the scheme should affect all classes of contributors equally. All employed persons in this country are brought within the sphere of this Bill. Are they all treated equally ? I think they are not, and I think there is one class of person the inequality of whose treatment is so patent that it requires no argument from me, and that is the class of deposit contributors. What the deposit contributor is doing in an Insurance Bill I have never been able to discover, and I should have thought that while the Bill was still in Committee, or at any rate before we reached the present stage, the Chancellor of the Exchequer might have changed the wholly fictitious name, the wholly fictitious title, which stands at the head of that section of the Bill, and that he would no longer have continued to describe this as deposit insurance, for insurance it undoubtedly is not.

I am not at all satisfied that women under the Bill are going to be treated on the same terms as men; I will say very briefly why. It depends very largely on what effect the separation of the women's from the men's funds is going to have upon the security of the women's insurance. I am rather inclined to doubt whether the divisions of the funds will not make the position of women far less secure under the Bill than it would have been if the fund had remained united. . . .

There is another way in which, I think, the various contributors will be unequally dealt with. . . . I hold, in common with many other people, that the effect of this Bill, giving, as you are bound to do, to the societies the free choice of their members, will be to throw into the ranks of the strongest societies the most valuable risks from the societies' point of view. You will gradually find the second-class risk going into the second-class societies, and so forth, until you come to what the Chancellor of the Exchequer calls the uninsurable risk of the deposit contributor. The effect of that will be that the less desirable the life the more unstable will be the insurance. That is a prospect which we cannot face without considerable misgiving.

One further aspect of the question that I should like to touch upon is the creation of the so-called National fund. When the Bill was introduced it was intended to be a great national scheme, embracing all parts of the United Kingdom, carrying " the rare and refreshing fruit to the parched lips " of the employed contributors in whatever part of the country they lived, under precisely the same conditions and administered by precisely the same authorities. Since then we have seen this great national scheme split up into four sections, to my mind to great disadvantage to the insured people, and with greatly increased cost for administration. One further result is that there is no sort of guarantee that we shall have the same kind of scheme in operation in any one of these sub-divisions of our nationalities that we have in another. Under the new provisions of the Bill the Insurance Commissioners in Ireland will be given a practically free hand to create almost a different system of insurance altogether from that which obtains in this country. . . .

I come now to the assertion in the Amendment that the Bill has been neither adequately discussed in this House nor fully explained to the country. I have only to enumerate the Clauses which were passed without discussion to show how ruthlessly our debates have been curtailed and how incomplete our work is as it stands at present. . . . In Part I thirty-two Clauses have been passed without a word of detailed discussion. Eighteen were passed in one night under the guillotine in Committee. As evidence of the haste with which these new Clauses were drawn, we may point to the fact that two of them were struck out of the Bill by the Chancellor of the Exchequer himself as soon as we came to the Report stage. . . .

It is not only in Committee that we have been denied the opportunity to discuss the Clauses of the Bill. What happened on Report? When we came to the Report stage the Bill was practically recast, but we have never had any hand in the discussion of it. Out of the first seventy-seven Clauses as passed through Committee the two Clauses to which I have already referred were struck out, and sixty-eight were amended, though not one of them was discussed. The Report stage of the Bill which suffered this treatment came to an end on Monday last, and we are now invited to read it a third time, after only one day's interval. I think it is absolutely impossible for anyone who has not — it is difficult enough for those who have — followed the debates on this Bill hour by hour, almost minute by minute, to say how closely this Bill resembles the Bill which was first introduced, or how widely it differs from it! . . .

I have referred to the question of the division of the Irish, Scottish, and Welsh funds from the English funds. I have pointed out that that formed no part of the original scheme. It weakens the stability of the fund; it leads to administrative difficulties, as the trade unions will find. This alteration has found no favour with those who have looked at this Bill as a method of insurance and not as an indirect method of initiating a policy of Home Rule all round. . . .

People have spoken on the Committee stage, and people still speak in the country, as if the Bill we are discussing contained the whole scheme. It does not. The great mass of regulations are just as important. I am not sure they are not even more far-reaching than the provisions of the Bill itself, and we cannot judge fairly of the scheme as a whole until we see in print the regulations as well as the Bill itself.

In the earlier part of what I said I invited the House to consider the whole meaning of the Amendment I am moving. We ask in that Amendment that the door should be kept open for further discussion, believing that further discussion would lead to further improvements — to improvements that would be the outcome of matured thought, of sober reflection, and of quiet and considered judgment. . . .

On the night of the introduction of the scheme, when the whole House lay under the spell of the magic eloquence of the Chancellor of the Exchequer — I very well remember the effect it produced — I ventured to make a very short speech. I do not think it lasted five minutes, and I think its brevity was, perhaps, its chief merit, but in the course of what I said I laid down for my own guidance a distinct line of policy, which I, at any rate, intend to follow in regard to this Bill, and perhaps the House will allow me to quote a few words from what I said:

This is not a scheme of charity; the right hon. Gentleman advanced it as a business proposition. If you advance it as a business proposition, and such proposition it undoubtedly is, it lies with you to justify the claim you make upon each constituent party in the tripartite partnership — the workman, the employer, and the State. As you are able to justify the contribution that you invoke, so shall you receive the support of all classes of the community. Speaking, if I may, on behalf of my hon. Friends on this side of the House, I will say that believing as we do that you are animated by the sole desire to confer a lasting benefit upon all classes of the community, so we will aid you in the perfection of the details of the scheme with all the zeal and all the energy and all the good will we can give it.

To the line of policy indicated in these few sentences we have adhered strictly and constantly. Discussion has not always been easy. The temptation to wander into the field of controversy and to enter into the joy of fight has not always been so easy to escape, and I am bound to say that the Chancellor of the Exchequer has occasionally strewn temptations in our path. On the whole, our action from the first has been clearly consistent. We have sought by all the means in our power to improve this Bill. . . .

I believe, with full and free discussion, with full and fair Amendments, this Bill could be made into a most potent instrument of good, touching as it does at every point the lives and the fortunes of the poorer members of our community, the men and women who have the least opportunity of striking a fair balance between its merits and defects which cry aloud for further consideration and further amendment, and it is in part that spirit and with that object that I beg to move the Amendment standing in my name.

Extract 90

NATIONAL INSURANCE AND SELF-RELIANCE

(Lord Robert Cecil, Commons, December 6, 1911)

Lord R. Cecil[1]: . . . If you once make the State a partner in private enterprise, it means the absorption of that private enterprise by the State. I believe that to be a principle which scarcely requires to be defended. If you want to see it in full operation, you

1 Parliamentary Debates, Fifth Series, Commons, vol. 32, col. 1476–1477.

have merely got to look at the history of the voluntary schools of this country. A partnership was created between the State and the voluntary schools in the matter of elementary education, and that principle was advanced in 1870. What has been its history since then? Every decade has seen a further advance of the State and a further retirement of the voluntary principle, until at the present time the State schools are all compulsory, all free, and practically they are absolutely under the control and management of the State. The voluntary principle has practically expired, and if the right hon. Gentlemen and their Friends had their way, they would give it its death blow. Therefore, anyone who considers the history of the voluntary schools under the legislation which began in 1870 will see what will inevitably happen to the friendly societies under the legislation which has now begun. More than that, the voluntary schools have been — rightly or wrongly — kept alive by a strong religious sentiment. You have no such sentiment — at all events not of that strength — to keep alive friendly societies. Depend upon it, this Bill when it passes is the death warrant of the friendly societies of this country.

For those reasons I am strongly opposed to a compulsory scheme. Finally — and this is the one reason which moves me most of all — I regard it as a very dangerous precedent to liberty and independence in this country, and that, undoubtedly, however the Chancellor of the Exchequer may sneer at domestic servants, is the backbone of the agitation against this Bill. This is not a question of particular figures, or of particular discussions, or of argumentative leaflets, or whether this or that person pays. The backbone of the agitation against this Bill is that the people bitterly resent in this country being made to apply their own money for the benefits in a way they do not approve. It is defended by the German example; but that example is wholly irrelevant. The whole history of Germany is the history of the control of the individual by the State. Frederick William established an elaborate system of State control over the whole lives of everyone of his subjects. That has been the history of Germany, and that cannot be transplanted to this country without great injury to the institutions of this country.

I have a fanatical belief in individual freedom. I believe it is a vital thing for this country, and I believe it is the cornerstone upon which our prosperity and our existence is built, and, for my part, I believe that the civic qualities of self-control, self-reliance, and self-respect depend upon individual liberty and the freedom and independence of the people of this country. We all remember a great phrase of a great prelate, who said he would sooner see England free than England sober. It has been greatly misrepresented, but properly understood I agree with that proposition. I think it could be put more thoroughly by saying that you cannot have sobriety without freedom. The essence of the virtue of sobriety and all civic virtues is self-control and self-reliance, and you cannot have these without freedom. And it is because I believe that in its present form this Bill is a great danger to liberty, and was so regarded by the electors I had the honour of addressing during the three or four weeks of my election campaign, that I think it is vital it should be further considered, and that the country should have a further opportunity of expressing its opinion upon it and of saying whether it desires to have these German shackles put upon it, or whether it would not prefer to have a scheme founded upon the principle of liberty and independence.

Extract 91

DEFECTS IN THE GOVERNMENT BILL

(Mr. Bonar Law, Commons, December 6, 1911)

MR. BONAR LAW[1]: . . . Whatever may be the opinion of the House of Commons, I am perfectly certain of this, that three-fourths, and I believe nine-tenths, of the people of this country

1 Parliamentary Debates, Commons, Fifth Series, vol. 32, col. 1504 sqq.

take our view to-day. They are not hostile to the proposals of the Bill, neither are we; but they are convinced that it has not been either properly considered by this House or properly understood in the country, and that further time should be given for both purposes. That is our Amendment, and when we have voted for it, so far as I am concerned, I shall take no further part in any further Amendment. I shall leave to the Government the responsibility, and it is a very big responsibility, of forcing an immense scheme like this upon the country, when there is not a man in this House who does not know that it has not been properly considered and is not a measure which, in its present form, can be otherwise than disadvantageous to the people of this country. . . .

I hardly venture to mention the trade unions, because I remember the Chancellor of the Exchequer was very sarcastic about my hon. Friend who was leading the Opposition [Mr. Arthur J. Balfour], because he took an interest in these bodies. I venture, with all humility, to say that I also am interested in them. Is there any member of a trade union who doubts that, judging by the pounds, shillings, and pence interest, it will be to the advantage of members of trade unions to leave their societies (for they cannot give the same benefits), and join societies which will give higher benefits? It must be so. I do not mean to say that trade unionists may not be actuated by other motives. I am the first to acknowledge that the working-class have always shown a readiness to sacrifice themselves for the interests of their class as a whole. I admit that, and I do not say that actuated by these unselfish motives they may not still continue to be members of trade unions. But if they do, it will be against their interests, and the temptation will be very great for the best lives to leave the trade unions and join societies where they will get better benefits.

If that is true, even within the limits of approved societies, what is it when you come down to the wretched outcasts who are deposit contributors? We have been accused a great deal this afternoon of a change of front, more or less, on this Bill. I am not going to say anything stronger on this subject than I said on the second reading. I pointed out, as every Member of the House recognised, that the condition of these deposit contributors is an utterly unjustifiable one. The right hon. Gentleman, I remember, interrupted me while I was speaking and asked me what we would propose. I said that it was not my business to propose, but that if I were on that bench I would be glad to do so. . . .

I do not think the House in the least realises what this Bill means from the financial side. The right hon. Gentleman always states the matter in connection with the old age pensions. When these two schemes are in full operation, the amount of money which will be deposited in this way will be, — I have not made a calculation of what then will be the amount of the National Debt, — I think, two or three times the annual charge on our National Debt. I am sure it will amount to a larger sum of money than the whole of the revenue of any country in the world except the first six or seven great countries. I speak of the whole of the money dealt with. It is a prodigious sum and surely worth while spending a little time on to be assured that it is dealt with in the best manner. There is something else to be said. The right hon. Gentleman has always spoken of the charge of those two burdens on the State as something like £18,000,000. It is nothing like that, and he knows it.

Take old age pensions alone. They began under the present Prime Minister at £6,000,000. That amount has now doubled. [An Hon. Member: More than doubled.] More than doubled, but that is only the beginning. Thirty years hence that charge will be more than double what it is now. That is not an estimate. [An Hon. Member: Oh!] Hon. Members below the gangway misunderstand my argument. I do not say the money is not well spent. All I say is that we should realise what the amount of it is. This is not an estimate. It does not depend upon the growth of the population. Our population thirty years hence may be precisely as to-day, yet the charge for old age pensions will be doubled. [An Hon. Member: How?] I think that ought to be pretty obvious. It is obvious to those who have followed the subject. It depends upon the number of people born at the time which will bring them under the Pension Act, and it will depend upon the mortality rate. The number of people born forty years ago who will become old age pensioners thirty years hence, coupled with the steady decrease in the rate of mortality, means that there will be double the charge whatever happens.

The Old Age Pension Act is a fact. I do not suggest that any change should be made about it. The country has got to face the burden. But surely, as men of common sense, anyone responsible for this new scheme would say, inasmuch as the old age pensions are rolling up a debt for posterity, it is our duty in this scheme to see that we pay our full share to-day ; and if there is any shifting of the scale, it should be in favour of coming generations and against ourselves. Is that not common sense ? That is naturally what would have been done if the Chancellor of the Exchequer had given his honest 2d. a week from the beginning in the same way as the employer and the employed have given theirs. He does not do it. I can conceive no earthly reason why, except that by his present method he is able to say that the State is giving 2d. when it is giving nothing of the kind. Had this Bill been introduced by any other Minister except the Chancellor of the Exchequer, and if the Chancellor of the Exchequer had thought it his duty to do so, — and we have all thought it was the duty of the Chancellor of the Exchequer to look after the stability of the national finances, — whatever else might have been done, this Bill would not have been financed in the way it has been financed. In private business the method which the right hon. Gentleman has adopted is everywhere recognised as the most rotten method that anyone could conceive. It is the method adopted by directors of companies who pay big dividends without looking at the liabilities which they know are confronting them. It is the method which brings such companies into the Bankruptcy Court, and very often brings the directors to the prison cell. . . .

The Chancellor of the Exchequer has squared hon. Gentlemen below the gangway. That is not a very difficult thing to do. The right hon. Gentleman the Patronage Secretary for the Treasury is one of the most astute politicians we have got, and he made some remarks at the annual meeting of the Liberal party which I think were very instructive. They were to this effect. I have got his actual words if necessary. " I think it is to our interest as a party that the Labour party should be quite independent of us in the constituencies, but their co-operation in the House has been most useful and most fruitful." In other words, let them appear to be independent outside, but let them be in our pockets inside. That is an ideal arrangement, but I do not think it will last long. He squared these Gentlemen, and surely they are easily squared. . . .

At the Hull election in June the following leaflet was sent by the Liberal headquarters to that election, and I have made inquiries about it. Until after that no leaflet of any kind against the Insurance Bill was sent from our central office. What is this leaflet? It is the picture of a workingman ill in bed and the Chancellor of the Exchequer with a copy of the Insurance Bill. If you look only at the picture we have no reason to take offence, but I think the right hon. Gentleman could bring a successful action against the artist, because looking at the picture alone one would be more inclined to think he had come to pick his pocket. That was not, of course, the intention of the picture, and this is what it said, " The Dawn of Hope." And this is the moral of it, " Support the Liberal Government." . . .

That is the Gentleman who accuses us of using the Insurance Bill for electioneering purposes. Obviously that was not the reason for the second nature coming into play. We all know it is one of the penalties the country has to pay for having a Government in office and not in power. They have signed their bond. For two years they have been allowed to swagger about like free agents, but next year the bond has to be redeemed and for that reason, whatever the effect of the Bill on the millions of people in this country, it must be shoved aside so that the bond may be paid. Now the right hon. Gentleman is coming to prophesy about the future. He gave a hint of it to-night at the end of his speech. He put it more clearly in his sermon at the Tabernacle. He says that we who are refusing to shut our eyes and open our mouths and swallow whatever he gives us — I am not giving his exact words — will be praying soon for the cloud of oblivion to come down and cover our heads. That is the prophecy. Carlyle once said, "You cannot argue with a prophet. You can only refuse to believe him." I do refuse to believe him. I have never, certainly in my time in this House, given any vote with more absolute certainty that I was consulting the best interests of the country than I shall give to-night, and if a cloud of oblivion is required, it will not be for those who have decided in, as near as I can recall, the words of the Amendment that this Bill is unequal in its operation and should be further considered by this House.

Extract 92

FINAL PLEA FOR NATIONAL INSURANCE

(Mr. H. H. Asquith, Prime Minister and First Lord of the Treasury, Commons, December 6, 1911)

MR. ASQUITH [1]: . . . Here is a great party on a great occasion dealing with a great Bill, and they are going to follow their leader and say neither "Yes" nor "No." That is the new programme of the Tory party. I wish them joy of it. The right hon. Gentleman must give me leave to say to him that peoples' intentions are to be judged not by the motives which in the more or less nebular background operate upon their minds. They must be judged by the consequences of their conduct. All this lip service and zeal for insurance against sickness and unemployment, all this loud-mouthed

[1] Parliamentary Debates, Fifth Series, Commons, vol. 32, col. 1518 sqq.

profession of a desire to attain the ends of this Bill, and to accept its principle, will be construed, and construed rightly, by the electorate of this country by action which you are taking to-night. Let us assume, — and we are bound to assume it for the purposes of argument, although it is not likely to happen in fact, — let us assume that the Amendment is carried. What becomes of the Insurance Bill? Everybody knows that it is dead. [HON. MEMBERS: Why?] For the very sufficient Parliamentary reason [HON. MEMBERS: No, no.] that whenever an Amendment on the third reading is carried, a Bill ceases to exist. I say quite plainly to this House, and I shall say it to the country, that the persons responsible for the framing of this Amendment and those who go into the Lobby in support of it are people who have killed the greatest scheme for the social benefit of the people of this country that has ever yet been conceived. They will not understand your fine distinctions between Yes and No, seeing that the adoption of this Amendment would be fatal to the carrying of any insurance scheme for an indefinite time.

Let me examine the reasons which have been alleged for this delay. I have heard the Committee criticisms of this Bill. No one has attacked its central principle. Its central principle is this — that as regards both sickness, invalidity, and unemployment there shall be a compulsory contribution to which the employer, the workman, and the State shall be party. When we brought forward our proposals for old age pensions three years ago, that principle was very strongly advocated, and by no one more strongly than the Leader of the Opposition. I think we were perfectly right not to adopt the principle of contribution in regard to old age pensions, because I am satisfied — as I was then — that a system of old age pension based upon contribution would have been futile and a failure. But three years ago we laid the ground without which this Bill would not have been possible.

As regards the principle of compulsory contribution for the purposes which are contemplated under this Bill, I am not the least ashamed to confess — my words have been quoted — that I was a somewhat reluctant, although I am now a completely convinced, convert. I do not think that there is any other way in which we can provide for the risks and hazards of industrial life.

The real and only ground, apart from the criticisms, alleged in support of this Amendment, is the insufficiency of the time which has been given to the consideration of it. Let me just look into that. On the question of time, when the Bill was first introduced, what was the demand? It was that the unemployment part — Part II — should be dropped on the ground that it was experimental in its character. It was never suggested that there would not be time for the discussion of the sickness and invalidity insurance. As a matter of fact, the twenty-five Clauses which compose Part II were passed upstairs after a very full and very friendly discussion practically without opposition, and they were only briefly dealt with on Report. I do not think that in any quarter of the House there is any doubt as to the desirability of Part II passing into law. If this Amendment is carried, that will not be carried out; it will be indefinitely postponed.

In regard to Part I let us see how the case stands. I cannot follow the right hon. Gentleman in some of the points taken. But there were four important points with regard to this vital and most important part of the Bill. The points were who was to be insured, what contributions were to be paid, what benefits were to be given, and what provision ought to be made for those who are called Post Office contributors and who are left outside the general scheme of insurance. I have gone most carefully — and if time permitted I could demonstrate to the House by evidence what I am going to say — into the amount of time which has actually been spent on each one of these four points, and I will venture to say that if there had been no guillotine at all, if there had been no allocation of time, and no curtailment of debate, there is not one of them which could, under reasonable conditions, have been more fully and more amply discussed than they have been.

Looking forward to the future, let me ask the House, and ask the right hon. Gentleman himself, what would be the effect of carrying an Amendment for the postponement of the further consideration of this Bill? In the first place, if you accept the principle of compulsory contributions and the desirability of the scheme as a whole, it is of the utmost importance that the machinery — the Commissioners and so forth — should at once be set into operation, and that they should be able to bring about what I believe to be the essential condition for the successful working of a scheme like this, namely, co-operation between the Commissioners, the Joint Committee, the friendly societies, the trade unions, the doctors, and all the other interests concerned, in order that when misunderstandings have been removed, they should all combine together, as I believe they will in the course of a very few months, to make this not only a workable, but a successful scheme. All that is to be thrown away and to be postponed to the remote future if this Amendment is carried.

Further, I cannot, in view of what the right hon. Gentleman has said, ignore, and nobody can ignore, what would be the results of leaving this matter open as a subject of public controversy for months or even years. I am not going into the recriminations which have been legitimately and naturally interchanged [Laughter.] — I hope that is a remark free from offence — both upon the one side and the other, or what has been said at bye-elections in regard to this particular Bill, but, without going into the rights or wrongs of that matter, is there a single man, in whatever quarter of the House he sits, who is really anxious for a settlement of this great social problem, at any rate upon the general lines of the Bill, who would not lament if at bye-elections for the next twelve or twenty-four months it should be cast into the forefront of political controversy and become the subject of the more envenomed interchange of amenities such as we have heard read out? Is there anyone who has really the interests of society at heart who thinks it is likely to contribute to a permanent and considered settlement? I will say nothing as to the campaign of misrepresentation which has been carried on in certain quarters and which is certain to be carried on with increased intensity and virulence so long as the question remains open and which happily will be brought to an end if the question is settled. I would like to make, in an entirely — if I may say so for the moment — non-party spirit, before the House comes to a decision, one final appeal.

We are nearing the close of an exceptionally arduous Session. I think it ought to be to Members an adequate and even an ample reward for their long and assiduous labours that the same Parliamentary year which has already witnessed the close of a great constitutional struggle [HON. MEMBERS: No, no; the beginning.] — well, the close of one stage of the great constitutional struggle, fought upon purely political ground — when this Bill has passed into law, as I believe it will, witnesses also the statutory enactment of a second and a larger instalment of that policy of social reform of which old age pensions was the first chapter.

I have said before, and certainly history proves, while it is possible, while it is even easy to put down the mighty from their seats without exalting the humble and the meek, the most ardent spirit among us in the cause of political equality, still far short of complete achievement, will be the first to recognise that political machinery is only valuable and is only worth having if it is adapted to and used for worthy social ends.

I brush aside, and I hope the House will brush aside, this Amendment — this halting, faltering, paltering Amendment — and I say the House, in reading this Bill a third time, are conferring upon millions of our fellow countrymen by the joint operation of self-help and of State help, the greatest alleviation of the risks and sufferings of life that Parliament has ever conferred upon any people.

APPENDIX

THE BRITISH CABINET, 1905–1912

PRIME MINISTER AND FIRST LORD OF THE TREASURY: Arthur J. Balfour (U), 1902; Sir Henry Campbell-Bannerman (L), 1905; Herbert H. Asquith (L), 1908.

LORD PRESIDENT OF THE COUNCIL: Marquess of Londonderry (U), 1903; Earl of Crewe (L), 1905; Viscount Wolverhampton (L), 1908; Viscount Morley of Blackburn (L), 1908.

LORD HIGH CHANCELLOR: Earl of Halsbury (U), 1895; Lord Loreburn (L), 1905; Viscount Haldane (L), 1912.

LORD PRIVY SEAL: Marquess of Salisbury (U), 1903; Marquess of Ripon (L), 1905; Earl of Crewe (L), 1908; Earl Carrington (L), 1911; Marquess of Crewe (L), 1912.

CHANCELLOR OF THE EXCHEQUER: J. Austen Chamberlain (U), 1902; Herbert H. Asquith (L), 1905; David Lloyd George (L), 1908.

SECRETARY OF STATE FOR FOREIGN AFFAIRS: Marquess of Lansdowne (U), 1900; Sir Edward Grey (L), 1905.

SECRETARY OF STATE FOR THE HOME DEPARTMENT: A. Akers-Douglas (U), 1902; Herbert J. Gladstone (L), 1905; Winston S. Churchill (L), 1910; Reginald McKenna (L), 1911.

SECRETARY OF STATE FOR INDIA: St. John Brodrick, Viscount Midleton (U), 1903; John Morley (L), 1905; Earl of Crewe (L), 1910.

SECRETARY OF STATE FOR THE COLONIES: Alfred Lyttelton (U), 1903; Earl of Elgin (L), 1905; Earl of Crewe (L), 1908; Lewis Harcourt (L), 1910.

SECRETARY OF STATE FOR WAR: H. O. Arnold-Forster (U), 1903; Viscount Haldane (L), 1905; Col. J. E. B. Seely (L), 1912.

FIRST LORD OF THE ADMIRALTY: Earl of Selborne (U), 1900; Lord Tweedmouth (L), 1905; Reginald McKenna (L), 1908; Winston S. Churchill (L), 1911.

CHIEF SECRETARY TO THE LORD-LIEUTENANT OF IRELAND: George Wyndham (U), 1900; Walter H. Long (U), 1905; James Bryce (L), 1905; Augustine Birrell (L), 1907.

PRESIDENT OF THE BOARD OF TRADE: Gerald W. Balfour (U), 1900; Marquess of Salisbury (U), 1905; David Lloyd George (L), 1905; Winston S. Churchill (L), 1908; Sydney Buxton (L), 1910.

PRESIDENT OF THE LOCAL GOVERNMENT BOARD: Walter H. Long (U), 1900; Gerald W. Balfour (U), 1905; John Burns (L), 1905.

PRESIDENT OF THE BOARD OF EDUCATION: Marquess of Londonderry (U), 1902; Augustine Birrell (L), 1905; Reginald McKenna (L), 1907; Walter Runciman (L), 1908; Joseph Albert Pease (L), 1911.

PRESIDENT OF THE BOARD OF AGRICULTURE AND FISHERIES: Earl of Onslow (U), 1903; Earl Carrington (L), 1905; Walter Runciman (L), 1911.

SECRETARY FOR SCOTLAND: Marquess of Linlithgow (U), 1895; Lord Pentland (L), 1905; T. McKinnon Wood (L), 1912.

POSTMASTER-GENERAL: Earl of Derby (U), 1903; Sydney Buxton (L), 1905; Herbert Samuel (L), 1910.

CHANCELLOR OF THE DUCHY OF LANCASTER: Sir Henry Fowler (L), 1905; Lord Fitzmaurice (L), 1908; Herbert Samuel (L), 1909; Joseph Albert Pease (L), 1910; C. E. Hobhouse (L), 1911.

FIRST COMMISSIONER OF WORKS: Lewis Harcourt (L), 1907; Earl Beauchamp (L), 1910.

ATTORNEY-GENERAL: Sir R. B. Finlay (U), 1900; J. Lawson Walton (L), 1905; William S. Robson (L), 1908; Sir Rufus Isaacs (L), 1910.

INDEX

Afforestation, 315, 335, 367
Agriculture, 315 sqq., 335 sqq., 368
sq.
Akers-Douglas, A., on workmen's
compensation, 20, 32 sqq.
Alden, Percy, 3, 19, 185
Anglican Church, in House of Lords,
5, 7, 388 sq., 390 sq.
Anglo-French Convention on workingmen's insurance, 72 sqq.
Anson, Sir William, on the Lords'
veto, 421, 460 sqq.
Asquith, H. H., 14; on child welfare,
107; on old age pensions, 131, 134
sqq., 138 sqq.; on the budget, 350
sq.; on the Lords' veto of the budget, 358 sq.; on the Lords, 423;
on parliament bill, 426 sqq., 430,
432 sq., 436 sq; and the parliamentary conference, 430 sq.; on
national insurance, 510, 568 sqq.
Australia, social politics in, 3; Second Chamber in, 461
Austria, sweated labour in, 233; town
planning in, 286 sq.

Babœuf, 2
Back-to-back houses, 275 sqq., 284
sq.
Balfour, A. J., 11; on old age pensions, 133, 151 sqq.; on minimum
wage for sweated industries, 219,
236 sq.; on the budget, 349; on
the Lords' veto of the budget,
359; on powers of the House of
Lords, 421, 449 sqq.; on parliament bill, 428 sq., 433; and the
parliamentary conference, 431
Banbury, Sir Frederick, on labour
exchanges, 186; on minimum
wage, 218, 225 sq., 230; on development bill, 325 sq.

Bankers, protest against the budget,
351 sq., 394 sq.
Barnes, G. N., on workmen's com-
pensation, 20, 34 sqq.; on land
development, 268, 329 sq.; on the
budget, 349
Beauchamp, Earl, on housing, 266,
278 sqq.
Birmingham, Bishop of. See Gore,
Charles
Birrell, Augustine, 14; on meals for
school children, 109, 116 sqq.;
and the parliamentary conference,
431
Bismarck, 3, 363, 544
Bonar Law, A. See Law, A. Bonar
Boyd-Carpenter, William, on old age
pensions, 133, 165 sqq.
Bristol, Bishop of. See Browne,
G. F.
Browne, G. F., on the budget, 357,
388 sqq.
Bryce, James, 14
Budget of 1909, introduction of, 361
sqq.; adopted provisions of, 408
sqq.; public demonstrations on,
352 sqq.; and land monopoly, 265
sqq.; and the Lords' veto, 423
Bureaucracy, dangers of, 285 sq.,
288, 562 sq.
Burns, John, 14; on old age pensions, 131; on housing and town
planning, 265, 269 sqq.
Buxton, Sydney, 14; on old age
pensions, 132; on national insurance, 507, 536 sqq.

Campbell-Bannerman, Sir Henry,
14, 18, 131; on trade unions, 78;
on land development, 330; on
powers of House of Lords, 421,
438 sqq.

575

LIBRARY OF DAVIDSON COLLEGE

Books on regular loan may be checked out for **two weeks**. Books must be presented at the Circulation Desk in order to be renewed.

A fine is charged after date due.

Special books are subject to special regulations at the discretion of the library staff.